Go, Flight!

Outward Odyssey
A People's History of Spaceflight

Series editor:
Colin Burgess

Go, Flight!

The Unsung Heroes of Mission Control, 1965–1992

Rick Houston and Milt Heflin

Foreword by John Aaron

UNIVERSITY OF NEBRASKA PRESS • LINCOLN & LONDON

Library of Congress Cataloging-in-
Publication Data
Houston, Rick, 1967–
Go, flight!: the unsung heroes of Mission
Control, 1965–1992 / Rick Houston and
Milt Heflin; foreword by John Aaron.
pages   cm.—(Outward odyssey:
a people's history of spaceflight)
Includes bibliographical references and index.
ISBN 978-0-8032-6937-8 (cloth: alk. paper)
ISBN 978-0-8032-8494-4 (epub)
ISBN 978-0-8032-8495-1 (mobi)
ISBN 978-0-8032-8496-8 (pdf)
1. Project Apollo (U.S.)—Biography.
2. Lyndon B. Johnson Space Center—
Officials and employees—Texas—
Houston. I. Heflin, Milt. II. Title.
TL789.8.U6A5H68 2015
629.4500973'09045—dc23
2015008522

Set in Adobe Garamond Pro by M. Scheer.

Foundations of Mission Control

To instill within ourselves these qualities essential
for professional excellence:

Discipline: Being able to follow as well as lead,
knowing we must master ourselves before
we can master our task.

Competence: There being no substitute for total
preparation and complete dedication, for space will
not tolerate the careless or indifferent.

Confidence: Believing in ourselves as well as others,
knowing we must master fear and hesitation
before we can succeed.

Responsibility: Realizing that it cannot be shifted
to others, for it belongs to each of us; we must
answer for what we do, or fail to do.

Toughness: Taking a stand when we must;
to try again, and again, even if it means
following a more difficult path.

Teamwork: Respecting and utilizing the ability of
others, realizing that we work toward a common goal,
for success depends on the efforts of all.

To always be aware that suddenly and unexpectedly
we may find ourselves in a role where our performance
has ultimate consequences.

To recognize that the greatest error is not to
have tried and failed, but that in trying, we did
not give it our best effort.

Contents

Illustrations

Foreword

20 July 1969—The *Eagle* had landed, and *Apollo 11* commander Neil Armstrong and Lunar Module pilot Buzz Aldrin were now preparing for man's first walk on the moon. In contrast to the intense drama that played out earlier in the day, activities in mission control had settled down, and my fellow mission controllers were starting to relax, at least a little.

What a day!

What a day indeed!

Around 9 p.m., I realized I was drained. The day's excitement and cliff-hanging moments had taken their toll on me. My relief, Charlie Dumis, had arrived earlier to take over the console duties, so I decided to unplug from my console and take a break before Neil and Buzz were scheduled to make their way out of the lander for the historic moonwalk. There was no way I was going to go home. Not yet. Not today.

I headed for the exit of the Mission Control Center building not realizing what I was about to experience. As I stepped out of the front door of the building, there it was, maybe thirty or forty degrees above the western horizon. A beautiful crescent moon appeared through the haze of that July Houston evening. That was the moment it hit me like a ton of bricks.

Neil and Buzz are on the moon. They are really *there.*

I was completely awestruck by the view. As a boy growing up in rural Texas and Oklahoma, I spent many evenings outdoors and had watched and wondered about our moon countless times over, but suddenly things changed. The impact was immediate, and in a way that I have never looked at the moon the same way since.

I reported for work that morning feeling a bit anxious about the day's challenge, even though I felt prepared for the task at hand. During previous Gemini and Apollo missions and for countless numbers of mission

1. Although John Aaron very nearly left the agency early in his career, he went on to become one of the most capable flight controllers ever to sit a MOCR console. Courtesy NASA.

simulations, my days had been spent preparing, monitoring, and managing spacecraft systems using my console's racks of status lights, data displays, and voice communications circuits.

However, today was to be no simulation. This was the real deal. Two months earlier, Tom Stafford and Gene Cernan performed a powered descent to within nine miles of the lunar surface. Neil Armstrong and Buzz Aldrin were going to try to go the rest of the way and settle the *Eagle* spacecraft down on the dusty plains of the Sea of Tranquility. And sure enough, following a nail-biting, drama-saturated, should-we-keep-going powered descent to the surface, it actually happened at just past 3:17 p.m. Houston time.

As EECOM, my attention was focused on the Command and Service Module (CSM) *Columbia*. I closely monitored the CSM to ensure all systems were ready for supporting the undocking and solo flight phase of the *Eagle*. After undocking, and with Command Module pilot Michael Collins still on board and orbiting sixty miles above the surface, the mother ship was performing well and all systems were in good shape. The focus in the room was now on the *Eagle*'s powered descent and attempt at a landing. In addition to keeping an eye on *Columbia*, I could now sit back and take in the bigger picture of everything that was taking place.

I had the best seat in the house. Just across the aisle to my left was capcom Charlie Duke, relaying messages back and forth to the crew, and Gene Kranz was right behind me at the flight director's console, polling for go/no go calls each step of the way. Guidance officer Steve Bales was down in the front row to my right, sweating out multiple unexpected computer overload alarms. Steve was assisted by Staff Support Room controller Jack Garman, while Lunar Module control officer Bob Carlton sat three consoles down from me on the second row, keeping a careful eye on *Eagle*'s descent braking engine's fuel supply that was depleting quickly. As the LM began approaching near the lunar surface, I listened in as Neil took over the controls, skirting *Eagle* across the surface, looking for a safe place to set down. I was watching and listening to an incredibly proficient and well-honed team. I sat quietly holding my breath, wondering whether Neil could set *Eagle* down before the depletion of fuel resulted in a descent abort and powered climb back to orbit. Then, suddenly it happened. Neil announced, "Houston, Tranquility Base here, the *Eagle* has landed."

Although I was temporarily stunned, somehow the moment had the same look and feel it had during all those many, many training sessions and prior spaceflights. In a very real sense, I had gotten used to such drama.

So, how could this happen? How was it that in such a short period of time, a fresh team of a mostly young, talented, yet inexperienced collection of individuals could be assembled and trained to pull off such a feat?

Like most of my team members, I arrived at NASA straight out of college with no experience in spaceflight. I found that although our team's objective had been clearly defined, the necessary techniques were very much in their infancy. In addition to developing the necessary mission control techniques, we quickly became aware that being a flight controller required that we prepare ourselves to handle the unexpected, no matter how unlikely the event. Preparing for those kinds of situations demanded that we know everything there was to know. That knowledge was tested through endless hours of very realistic full-scale mission simulations, sessions in which unimaginable and unexpected failures were thrown at us time and time again. On days between simulations, it was back to the drawing board to fill the gaps in our knowledge and refine our techniques. Training under such pressures made us keenly aware of where knowledge was lacking. Just as important, we became comfortable in taking action when needed. Not everyone was cut out for this kind of work and some soon moved on. But for me and most other team members, such preparation and effort was not work—it was our passion. Such teamwork successfully paid off many times during missions leading up to and including *Apollo 11*.

I joined NASA in 1964. Just five short years later, I was standing outside the Mission Control Center looking at the moon with the knowledge that my coworkers and I had played a key and decisive role in successfully landing two men on the moon, fulfilling a dream of the human race that so long was assumed to be impossible. The mission control team's major challenges and heroics did not end here; much to the contrary, later missions continued to further challenge the team's preparation and capability, including recovering several from the brink of failure.

In *Go, Flight!*, coauthors Rick Houston and Milt Heflin have gone to great lengths to track down and speak with as many of the people who worked in mission control as possible. What you will find in these pages is something far more than a mere recitation of facts, figures, dates, and accomplishments.

Not only is *Go, Flight!* the story of what happened in that room, it is also about the people who worked there. Regardless of your familiarity with the technical details, readers will find it a great read, and when finished, you will very much feel like you were there with us. History will always remember the names of the astronauts, but back on the ground in mission control, we like to think we were the story behind the story.

John Aaron

Introduction

I walked into the room completely unprepared for the reaction that was about to wash over me.

There on the third floor of Building 30 at Johnson Space Center in Houston, I was transported back in time to the late 1960s and early '70s. As soon as I entered, I was hammered with an overwhelming sense of what had once taken place in this very room. Tears literally welled in my eyes, and I felt unworthy to stand on this hallowed ground. My friend Milt Heflin was a step or two ahead of me and entered before I did, and I was glad of that. I was embarrassed to be standing there like that, but I could not help it.

There was the Trench, and just above it a row of systems consoles. Just across the aisle from the EECOM console on the second row was the capcom station, where Charlie Duke sat as he helped talk Neil Armstrong and Buzz Aldrin down to the lunar surface. Up a row was the throne itself, the flight director's console. Chris Kraft, Gene Kranz, Glynn Lunney, Gerry Griffin, and Milt had all held court there once upon a time. Amazing.

It was in those few moments when the concept for this book was born. Countless stories about human spaceflight have been told from the air-to-ground perspective, that is, mostly from the viewpoint of the astronauts whose flights this room controlled. A handful of people became relatively well known to the public at large due to what they did here—Building 30 is now named after Kraft, the godfather of all things mission control, and actor Ed Harris made Gene Kranz all the more legendary with his portrayal and "Failure is not an option" line in the blockbuster movie *Apollo 13*.

Those are just two of the hundreds of people who toiled here, who were among the very best and brightest of their generations, who could make split-second decisions that determined the success or failure of a spaceflight. If the nation's astronauts were soldiers on the front lines, the denizens of the Cathedral were the personnel behind the scenes directing the whole thing. None—*none*, not a single one—of NASA's storied accomplishments would have been possible without these incredible people.

Yet the majority of them have lived in relative anonymity, legendary superstars within the close confines of the NASA community who could walk down a public street and go completely unrecognized. What a shame, because they deserve the recognition. The willingness of those who took part in this grand adventure to contribute was just one of the many, many true joys of putting this book together. More than one former flight controller answered interview requests by taking the initiative of pounding out lengthy and detailed descriptions of their careers. Jerry C. Bostick became a friend, and read drafts of virtually every chapter and made well-intentioned and helpful comments along the way.

Dave Reed was a fount of information. Dave is a stickler for details, and when we encountered some confusion over a long-ago line from a mission transcript, the lengths to which Dave went to set the record straight was simply awe inspiring. Dave and Rod Loe presented me with unexpected items that have become some of my most prized possessions—Dave passed along one of the matchbooks members of the Trench had made up, while Rod sent pristine temporary access badges for the flights of *Apollo 16* and *17*.

When I called Steve Bales at the appointed time for our interview, he began the conversation by saying that he had already ordered a couple of the NASCAR-related books that I have written and asked if I would sign them for a friend of his. Wait a second. Steve Bales—*the* Steve Bales, of *Apollo 11* lunar descent fame—was asking *me* for *my* autograph? Then, when Steve read a draft of the *Apollo 11* chapter, he again surprised me by sending me a lengthy e-mail describing in detail what he had liked about it. I immediately printed it out and placed it next to my computer screen.

Others dug into old mission reports and research material to refresh their memories. One did so at his wife's hospital bedside, as she recuperated from surgery. I sat next to Bob Carlton at his console for nearly two hours one afternoon, listening to him tell war stories and watching as he drew a detailed diagram of the Lunar Module (LM)'s ascent engine and thrusters. I played a few minutes of audio from the *Apollo 11* landing, in which Bob can be heard giving his famous low-fuel calls. As I listened to those long-ago voices echo through that room, I was once again reminded that this

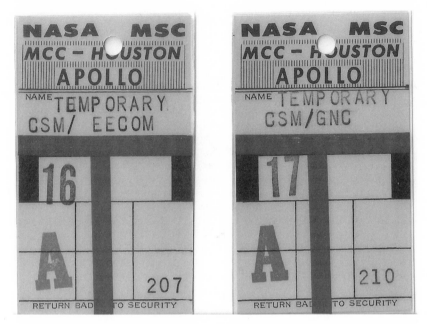

2. These badges, which allowed temporary access into the MOCR during the final two lunar landings, were gifts from Rod Loe to author Rick Houston. Author's collection.

was hallowed ground. After commenting that the moment had given me chills, Bob's quiet reply took me aback.

Me too.

Bob's passion for human spaceflight was as alive and vibrant in 2013 as it was on that summer day back in 1969. In that, he was far from alone. Decades after laying down their headsets and pocket protectors in mission control for the last time, many seemed almost eager to have their stories told. Well after the last "official" interview question was asked, more than a few continued right on reliving the good ol' days—but not in some sad, woe-is-me sort of way. What they accomplished meant long hours in an ultra-high-stress environment, but, by gosh, they were working toward putting people on the moon and in orbit on board the Space Shuttle.

What job could ever possibly be better than that?

It is that very kind of deeply felt dedication that *Go, Flight!* honors. As a direct result of working on this book, I no longer see just Neil Armstrong, Pete Conrad, Alan Bean, and Charlie Duke when I look up at the moon. I also see the people who worked in that magnificent room so long ago.

3. Coauthors Milt Heflin (left) and Rick Houston visit the historic third-floor MOCR. Author's collection.

How do I feel about them? Lee Briscoe, the former Apollo back roomer who made it all the way to the flight director's console during the Space Shuttle years, put it best. "The people who inhabited that room while all this was going on were amazing people, and they did amazing things," Briscoe said. "It's just a shame that you can't preserve those people like you're going to preserve that room. Those people deserve that kind of place in history." If this book could be boiled down to just three sentences, those would be the three.

I also see Milt Heflin when I look at the moon or spot a picture of the Space Shuttle, because he has become the best long-distance mentor I have ever had. Although we have met face-to-face on just a handful of occasions, I would consider him to be a good friend. Maybe it is just a coincidence, but Milt was born in 1943, the same year as my father. Daren is his oldest son with wife Sally. He was born in 1967, same as me. Matt, the younger of Milt and Sally's two children, came into the world in 1973. So did my kid brother.

Living more than a thousand miles from Houston, Texas, I am no NASA insider. Not once—even at the craziest, silliest, or dumbest question—has Milt ever treated me with anything less than a genuine respect. His contributions to this book in opening doors, checking facts, and obtaining just the right information has made it far better and far more complete than it would have been had I flown solo.

I would also here like to express my deepest gratitude to Keith Haviland, Gareth Dodds, Mark Craig, and David Fairhead for their belief in this project. I cannot wait to see what the coming months hold. The same thanks go to series editor Colin Burgess and the staff at University of Nebraska Press—Rob Taylor, Martyn Beeny, Sara Springsteen, and the one and only Colleen Romick Clark, who served as copyeditor for this book. I have come up with the perfect compromise to our capitalization debates. How about we cap certain words in the third through fifth paragraphs of odd-numbered pages in even-numbered chapters?

I will forever be indebted to collectSPACE.com's Robert Pearlman; and Emily Carney, creator and chief comment mocker of the Space Hipsters Facebook group. Their sites are wonderful resources for space geeks like me. I deeply appreciate the artwork provided by NASA photo historians J. L. Pickering and Ed Hengeveld. Thanks also go to the Estep family—Sandi, Joe, and Jennifer; as well as the Knights—Fred, Judy, LeeAnn, and Joe; and the Reynolds—James, Lib, Jamie, and Amy. Without their support and encouragement all these years, this book would not be happening.

Also contributing in one way or another were Charlene Hubbard, Gene and Emma Hubbard, Stephen Slater, and Craig Scott. Almost every writer has a particular reader in mind when he or she puts words to paper. For this book, that person is Craig, who is the most enthusiastic MOCR fan I have ever encountered.

Finally, I want to thank my Lord and Savior, Jesus Christ. Without Him, I am nothing. My wife, Jeanie, is my best friend. Jeanie; our twin sons, Adam and Jesse; and Richard, my son from my first marriage, are my reasons for being.

Rick Houston
Yadkinville, North Carolina

I am still trying to figure out how Rick convinced me to be a coauthor of this book. After nearly forty-seven years in the spaceflight business and now retired, I have done my best to stay away from stressful activities, the non-physical kind. So I was leery of engaging in this project. However, having recognized Rick's uncanny ability to reach into the heart and soul of his subjects in telling their stories, I agreed.

I agreed because I wanted to help Rick illustrate that what we have done in manned spaceflight was actually quite difficult and that indeed many "unsung heroes" are responsible for "snatching victory from the jaws of defeat." If we can introduce some of these people to the public, then count me in. Often we made our accomplishments look easy although many times it was anything but. I predict several of my colleagues will be surprised with some of what they find in these pages. I can tell you that I certainly was.

I got to experience some of these moments, having been privileged to work in the third-floor mission control room three times as a flight controller and four times as flight director. My feelings about this place can best be characterized by the word "reverence." Chris Kraft referred to this place as "this palace." Gene Kranz called it a "leadership laboratory." I would later introduce it as a "cathedral." I think we are all correct.

Getting to where I was qualified to plug a headset into one of the Palace's consoles took help from a handful of folks teaching, pushing, lobbying, and cheerleading on my behalf. I would not be here today fretting over coauthoring this book without support from Rod Loe, who wanted to make me into a flight controller; Bill Peters, the manager assigned to get me there; Jack Knight, my MCC console real-time ops mentor; Don Puddy, who trusted me to operate in a prime MCC position during portions of the orbiter Approach and Landing Tests; Bill Moon, who accepted me as his prime backroom support for the first Space Shuttle launch, STS-1; Gene Kranz, who selected me to be a flight director in the class of 1983; and finally, Tommy Holloway, who gave me very tough love, preventing me from washing out.

Then there was Randy Stone, one of my dear colleagues during the Apollo Landing and Recovery days. He was a close friend. We lost him on 25 November 2013. If there was one individual I owe my many Mission Control Center experiences to, it is Amber Flight. My career path during and after my MCC years has his footprints all over it. He went above and beyond lobbying for me to take on some new challenge. I cannot think of anyone else who was so steadfastly in my corner, even when I didn't know I needed somebody there.

Throughout this career, which began on 6 June 1966, I have been fortunate to enjoy the companionship and support of Sally. She along with our sons, Daren and Matt, graciously tolerated my absences and mood swings as I dealt with riding recovery ships supporting Apollo splashdowns and learning to work in mission control. Their love and understanding enabled me to experience the roller-coaster ride through the triumphs and tragedies of manned spaceflight.

Rick was thrilled by the responsiveness of those unsung heroes who agreed to be interviewed. I think what impressed him most is that each of them made it clear that if he needed anything else, then they would be more than happy to accommodate him. He used an impressive number of interviews to piece together the stories, some known, many revealed for the first time. He was so impressed by everyone's kindness and willingness to talk about their experiences it made him work that much harder to tell their stories. Way to go, team!

Milt Heflin
Houston, Texas
Sirius Flight, EECOM, EGIL, THERMAL, EPS, SMOKHEE

Go, Flight!

1. Who Did What

At first glance, the room appears to be just another auditorium in just another office building. There are nondescript spaces like it in a million different places all over the world. The carpet is old and a bit bunched up here and there. A few stains dot the floor, the result of who knows how many spilled coffees over the years. There is also a distinct smell to the place, not quite musty and not really even a hint of the tobacco smoke that once hung over the room. Maybe it is a faint remnant of the electronics that once hummed and buzzed here. The odor is neither pleasant nor unpleasant. It is just—distinct.

The four rows of consoles facing the front of the room are almost quaint in their simplicity—workstations feature a rotary dial phone. And canisters, too, to send messages to back rooms via pneumatic tubes, the very same kind of transport system featured at your local bank's drive-through window. No email or instant messaging here.

Yet if there's a temptation to dismiss the room out of hand, images of events past begin to sink in and the sheer enormity of everything that took place here hits like a ton of bricks. Only a handful of places inspire such an overwhelming sense of history.

Independence Hall.

Gettysburg.

Westminster Abbey.

Ford's Theater.

Pearl Harbor.

Normandy.

Jerusalem.

Hiroshima.

Dealey Plaza.

Battles were fought and presidents were murdered at most of these locations, but not in this average-sized room on the third floor of what was once known as Building 30 at the Manned Spacecraft Center (MSC) in Houston. It was only after the end of Apollo's lunar landings that the complex was renamed the Lyndon B. Johnson Space Center (JSC). Although there was no great bloodshed here, it served as a critical battleground of the Cold War with the Soviet Union. Had it *not* been for the Russians, it is quite likely that the events that took place here would never have happened.

Officially, the room was known by two different names while it was in service from 1965 to 1992—it was the Mission Operations Control Room (MOCR, pronounced "MOH-ker" in NASA-speak) during the Gemini and Apollo era and the Flight Control Room (FCR, pronounced "FICK-er") during the first decade or so of the Space Shuttle era. It has also been called "the Cathedral" in tones that border on pure reverence because of the things that happened here, as if it were actually a church. Others refer to it simply as "the Palace." Gene Kranz, on the other hand, called it a "leadership laboratory." Either way, the point remained the same. So important were the events that took place in this room, it is now listed in the National Register of Historic Places.

Think of the words that were first uttered to and from this magnificent room.

You are go for TLI.

Until December 1968, never had a human being left the bonds of Earth's gravitational influence. Michael Collins was the capcom sitting right there in *that* seat on the second row, when he gave the call that began the crew of *Apollo 8* on its journey to lunar orbit.

Houston, Tranquility Base here. The Eagle *has landed.*

And then later . . .

That's one small step for man, one giant leap for mankind.

When Neil Armstrong called out those instantly iconic lines, he was talking to this room, and through this room, to hundreds of millions of people watching around the world.

Houston, we've had a problem.

When the crew of *Apollo 13* announced their dire circumstances in hurried yet never panicked voices, they were talking to this room. And it was the men in and around this room who, over the next three and a half days, spearheaded a massive effort to save the lives of astronauts James A. "Jim" Lovell Jr., Fred W. Haise Jr., and John L. "Jack" Swigert.

Roger, go at throttle up.

As momentous as the events of *Apollo 8*, *Apollo 11*, *Apollo 13*, and so many other Gemini and Apollo missions were, this room is also where some of the darkest moments in NASA's history began to unfold on a January morning in 1986. When STS-51L commander Francis R. "Dick" Scobee spoke the last words he would ever speak, he was talking to this room.

Most of the people who worked here during the Gemini and Apollo eras were born just as the country was coming out of the depths of the Great Depression, only to find itself embroiled in the even greater agony of World War II. They were from small-town America—one of their hometowns no longer exists—and a good many were the first in their family to graduate from college. And in fact, college had not been all that long ago. Their average age was in the mid-to-late twenties, and there they were, helping to land people on the surface of the moon.

Who were they, and what kind of work did they do here?

There it was, the very first thing anyone who walked in the main door on the left-hand side of the MOCR would see.

The Trench.

The way the folks who worked in the Trench sounded once in a while, that was all anyone *needed* to see. It was a Trench world, they seemed to figure, and every other controller in the MOCR just so happened to be living in it. The home of the Flight Dynamics Branch might have been on the lowest of four stair-stepped rows, closest to the front of the room and the huge screens that dominated it, but that was just a function of location and darn sure not mission priority. Although Flight Dynamics did not fire the gun at launch, it certainly aimed the trajectory of the bullet wherever it needed to go.

"We were a proud bunch, okay?" said Jerry Bostick, the chief of the Flight Dynamics Branch throughout most of the Apollo program. Then, Bostick invoked the memory of one of the Trench's biggest legends among its own. "As John Llewellyn used to say, 'If it's the truth, it ain't bragging,'" he continued. "We had a deep appreciation for what the systems guys did, but, of course, we thought all they were doing was providing us with the hardware to do the real job, which was to get them there and back."

The left side of the first row was technically *in* the Trench but its positions were not exactly *of* the Trench. That space was reserved for the booster and tanks station during the Gemini years and then consoles for booster systems 1, 2, and 3 in Apollo. On *Apollo 9* and *Apollo 11*, extravehicular activity (EVA) spacesuits were also monitored from there once the booster controllers vacated not long after launch. The tanks controller watched propellant pressures and temperatures, and was usually manned by a young eager-beaver astronaut. Eugene A. "Gene" Cernan walked on the moon during his command of *Apollo 17*, but nevertheless he wanted to know why he had not been asked to tell the story of his tanks duty on the unmanned flight of *Gemini 2* as well as *Gemini 3* and *Gemini 4* in the Trench's self-published book *From the Trench of Mission Control to the Craters of the Moon.*

A booster 1 controller like Frank Van Rensselaer did not have much responsibility at all, other than to oversee the mammoth 363-foot-tall Saturn V, from about twelve hours before launch all the way through docking of the Command and Service Module (CSM) with the Lunar Module (LM). After that, commands were sent to the spent S-IVB third stage to target it for an impact on the moon near a previous landing site. That way, instruments deployed by astronauts on the lunar surface could pick up vibrations from the impact and possibly allow analysts to determine the moon's composition in the area.

Booster 2 monitored the S-IVB third stage, while booster 3 kept an eye on the launch vehicle's Instrument Unit. Their next-door neighbors in the Trench joked with those on the booster consoles, calling them their guests and insisting that they shape up lest they be forced to ship out and move elsewhere in the MOCR. That kind of joking was fine with Van Rensselaer. Although he lived in Houston, the Tennessee native was not technically an employee of the MSC. Van Rensselaer was instead employed by the Marshall Space Flight Center in Huntsville, Alabama, home to the Saturn V and the adopted home of the legendary German rocket scientist Wernher von Braun, who designed it.

There were, to be sure, rivalries between Marshall and Houston. "Early on, there was *some*, let's say, pushback when we were doing mission rules," Van Rensselaer said. "The guys at Marshall, their attitude was, 'Don't touch the booster. It'll be fine.' The guys in the control center were saying, 'Well, if there's anything you can do about it, let's get ready for it.'"

After substantial issues developed during an April 1968 unmanned test of the Saturn V, however, working for a solution finally helped everyone onto the same page. The acceptance from the rest of the MOCR in general and from the Trench in particular from that point on seemed to be "just fine," Van Rensselaer said. He then continued, "We went through all the sims with them. We were part of the Trench, still are. We have gatherings every now and then, the Trench does. Even though we were the booster guys, they considered us part of the Trench."

Next were spots for retrofire, abbreviated to retro (just the way all things NASA are always shortened as much as possible); flight dynamics, or FIDO for short; and guidance officers, who were sometimes referred to as guidos—the three positions for which there was no debate as to whether they were members of the Trench. The people who worked this particular trio of consoles had an esprit de corps about them, an air that said they were the ground pilots of these grand spaceflight adventures. Were they maybe just a little bit cocky? Oh, absolutely. There were "The Trench" matchbooks scattered about the control room, and years later, members of the Trench put together a book, DVD, and website to commemorate their work.

That is not all. Kenneth A. "Ken" Young, a rendezvous specialist who once trained as a FIDO and was named an honest-to-goodness honorary member of the Trench, became the MOCR's unofficial poet laureate by penning a number of original and parody poems through the years. The first stanza of his work "The Trench" read:

> Since the very first days of Houston mission control
> There has been a unique front row of spaceflight consoles;
> Although these vital positions never got much publicity,
> The flight operators there controlled the spaceflight trajectory.
> This row of three positions, labeled: retro, FIDO, and guido
> Began with Gemini and rose to prominence during Apollo.
> These crucial controllers, always under fire, yet never known to flinch;
> Soon began to call their front-row position as, simply, The Trench!
> How The Trench got that name is uncertain but it really makes sense;
> For controllers it formed a space mission's first line of defense!

John the Legend worked the retro console, Young continued, while FIDO had Big Red, the Not-Always-So-Jolly Mental Giant, Bones, Fast Eddie,

Stump, and one that rhymed with Super*duck*. Last came the Fox, Mother, and Gonly at the guidance console.

They *were* the Trench.

Just to the right of the booster consoles was the retro officer's domain, and retro was responsible for continually calculating both planned and unplanned maneuvers that could be executed by in-flight astronauts to return the spacecraft to Earth. Jerry Bostick had been a retro, and so were Bobby T. Spencer, Dave Massaro, Thomas E. "Tom" Weichel, Robert White, Charles F. "Chuck" Deiterich, Thomas F. "Tom" Carter, Jerry C. Elliott, William "Bill" Gravett, and James E. "Jim" I'Anson. However, there was one man every fellow retro, every Trenchmate, and everyone else in the MOCR respected and, yes, maybe even feared a little, and that man was the late, great John S. Llewellyn—his middle name was Stanley, but to his NASA coworkers, the "S" stood for "Star," because that was what he was to them. A star.

Years before joining NASA, Llewellyn experienced things as a member of the U.S. Marine Corps during the Korean War that no human being should ever experience. He was still a teenager when he hit Red Beach during the crucial Battle of Inchon on 15 September 1950, and then was part of a vicious fight that began at Chosin Reservoir two months later. United Nations forces wound up encircled by Chinese troops during that sixteen-day clash, which was fought over some of the worst terrain and in unspeakably terrible freezing conditions. "The Chinese . . . their bugles . . . I could see them coming," Llewellyn told friend and longtime MOCR coworker Glynn Lunney during an interview for the short booklet *From the Trenches of Korea to the Trench in Mission Control*. "I saw them when they stopped all their running around in circles like ants down there. I couldn't believe there were that many people. And I just looked at it. I never saw anything like it in my life."

The booklet goes on to describe Llewellyn hearing the click of an empty Thompson submachine gun, and then coming face-to-face with the Chinese soldier holding it. Llewellyn killed him, and then spent the rest of the night in the foxhole with his dead foe and hearing other enemy troops passing nearby. The experience impacted Llewellyn in ways few could ever imagine or comprehend, and it was only once in a great while that he might mention the war to his coworkers. Much later in his life, Llewellyn admit-

4. John Llewellyn (foreground), Jim I'Anson, and Chuck Deiterich chat in the Trench. Llewellyn, widely known as John Star, was a Korean War veteran who excelled at NASA despite struggling with severe post-traumatic stress syndrome. At the end of the row are Jerry Bostick (sitting) and Bill Boone (standing). Jerry Elliott is seated behind Llewellyn. Courtesy NASA.

ted to those around him that he had struggled with post-traumatic stress disorder (PTSD). "I guess deep down, there was always kind of a sorrow that I felt for the guy that he had been through all he had been through in the Korean War," Bill Gravett said. "He had terrible PTSD, and he bore that burden all those years. Occasionally, he would give us a glimpse of that horror that he went through at the Chosin Reservoir. I used to think about that and wonder, 'How did he survive that?' I had a lot of respect for the man, I really did."

Most credit Llewellyn for the Trench's nickname, either in whole or in part. It was during the flight of *Gemini 6* that pneumatic tubes from the messaging system began piling up around him on the first row, and he thought they looked a lot like empty 105-millimeter howitzer shells he encountered in the trenches back in Korea. If that did not seal it, Llewellyn once issued a challenge to the simulation team during a particularly testy debriefing.

Why don't you come on out here in the trenches and see how tough this really is?

To many, John Llewellyn was a larger-than-life force of nature. He was known to down his fair share of drinks. He could be profane. He spawned countless stories—a good many of which were true.

Some were relatively tame. He could sometimes get the numbers out of order during countdown to retrofire for reentry into Earth's atmosphere.

10, 9, 7, 6, 8, 4, 5, 3, 2, 1 . . .

That was the kind of thing, though, that could have happened to anybody. What others might not have done was challenge astronaut Virgil I. "Gus" Grissom to a drag race on the beach, Grissom in a gleaming new Corvette and Llewellyn in an old "Official Use Only" Plymouth. Afterward, Llewellyn promptly drove his losing car straight into the surf. When the Soviet Union established some new high ground in the space race, it was John Llewellyn who came banging on the door of Glynn Lunney's home early in the morning, demanding that the both of them go into work right then and there to do something about it. Legend also has it that while in Australia for work at a tracking station during the Gemini program, Llewellyn was caught trying to sneak into his locked motel. When told by the manager that if he did not like the rules that he could just buy the motel, Llewellyn apparently responded by doing just that.

Then, there was the time he overslept for a shift during the flight of *Gemini 5*. He raced into work, and after not being able to find a parking spot for his Triumph TR3, drove up the steps to Building 30 and parked directly in front of the door. That stunt got his car pass yanked, but Llewellyn was not deterred in the least. He responded by parking a horse trailer across the street from the main gate and absolutely, positively rode his horse into work. That was Llewellyn, born a hundred years too late, a Wild West devil-may-care gunslinger if ever there was one.

Llewellyn was known as a force in the MOCR as well. "John was somewhat on the short-tempered side against those people that he considered 'pogues,'" remembered Gene Kranz, who competed in judo with Llewellyn and Dutch von Ehrenfried. "Pogues were people that in his mind did not measure up at being steely eyed missile men. This was particularly noticeable shortly after we moved into the Houston area, when we had a bunch of people who were trying to be flight controllers, but really didn't have the background for it. I always had to keep John separated from our pogues at the beer parties."

Peel back a layer or two, though, and the respect his peers had for

Llewellyn was as much the result of his service in the MOCR as it was for the agony he endured in Korea. He was an enigma, to be sure. "John and I liked to party, and he partied a lot," said Jerry Bostick, who along with many others served as an understudy to Llewellyn early in his career. "I lived with this for many years, and many people find it hard to believe, but let me tell you—when John walked into the control center, he was a different person. There was no slouching about him. He was very, very serious. He was dedicated, insisted on doing the right things, very knowledgeable. But then you go to a splashdown party after the mission, and he's doing cartwheels off the diving board into the swimming pool."

Asked what he would like for people to remember about Llewellyn, FIDO H. David "Dave" Reed paused and then said with emphasis, "He was unique." Reed went on to add, "John was, in his own right, a bit of a hinge point for a lot of us. If John started in on a debriefing, look out. You had no idea what's coming. People would sit back and just wait for it." On the other hand, Reed continued, "John Star" was also "brilliant. If you looked at him and listened to him, you're talking major hayseed here. He could come up with some of the more off-the-wall things, but there's no doubt that in the MOCR, no matter what he said about anybody else, John Llewellyn will always stand out as exceptional in his own right."

It was true that John Llewellyn's exploits sometimes overshadowed his gifts while at work in the MOCR, and that was a shame. "I think the thing to be recognized in John's case was that, yes, there are plenty of stories and plenty of things that he did that were attention-grabbing things," began Glynn Lunney. "But he was as sincerely dedicated to winning the competition that we had in the Sixties to do the landing as anybody on the team."

John Llewellyn died 8 May 2012, and his ashes were buried with full military honors in Arlington National Cemetery. Shortly before Llewellyn's passing, Lunney wrote that dealing with the trauma of Korea and its aftereffects "ultimately led to profound changes in John, and all for his own good. He has earned an understanding of himself and sees his life much more clearly. He is also at peace with the past and with himself."

Next in line on the front row of the MOCR was the FIDO console, where men like Jerry Bostick, Dave Reed, Jay H. Greene, Philip C. Shaffer, George C. Guthrie, Edward L. Pavelka Jr., William J. "Bill" Boone III, Maurice G. Kennedy, and William M. "Bill" Stoval labored. Essentially the quarterback of the Trench, FIDO was responsible for the trajectory of the spacecraft from liftoff to splashdown. Tracking the position with ground-based radar and onboard guidance systems, FIDOs calculated the maneuvers that had to be made in order to get both the CSM and LM where they needed to go. It was the only other position in the control center besides booster 1 and the flight director that had the ability to directly call an abort during launch.

After working briefly at Langley, Jerry Bostick moved to the Mission Planning and Analysis Division (MPAD) in Houston and also supported Mercury retro officer Carl R. Huss from a back room at Cape Canaveral in Florida. When Huss suffered a non-life-threatening heart attack shortly after the last flight of the program, Bostick leapt at the opportunity to move into the front room and serve as an understudy to new prime retro John Llewellyn for the first three unmanned and manned Gemini missions. Beginning with *Gemini 4*, which shared flight control monitoring between the Cape and Houston's new Mission Control Center, Bostick switched over to work as a FIDO. "I just thought it was kind of a no-brainer," Bostick said. "It was a step up. The FIDO is really the team leader in the Trench, over the retro and the guidance officers. I wanted to do it."

Dave Reed seemed to be a perfect fit for work as a FIDO. Bill Stoval once said that nobody had ever prepared for a mission like Reed did, and he definitely had a point. Checklists? Reed put together his own detailed masterpieces for virtually every phase of a flight. Most everybody prepared similar lists in some shape, form, or fashion, but that was just one facet of Reed's preparation regimen. "I spent a lot of time going over all this stuff and drawing up my own," Reed said. "I don't know exactly what Stoval would be referring to, but I know Maurice Kennedy made a similar comment. I don't know what in the hell they saw, but I always have been a stickler for detail, I guess. I wouldn't quit until I felt I knew that entire checklist by heart." The Wyoming native's attention to detail also manifested itself in debriefs following mission simulations. If Reed felt he had something to discuss, he was going to discuss it until he felt the subject had been covered to the fullest. "His debriefings during the simulations would go on and on and on and on," Chuck Deiterich remembered. "We [those in the Trench] always went first, so the systems guys didn't get as much time to talk as we did."

Not only were the men of the Trench a proud bunch, but they also took care of their own. When Glynn Lunney and his family spotted Bill Stoval walking along the road in front of MSC on a hot and humid day in early July 1967, the newly hired FIDO had apparently not yet exchanged the wardrobe from his native Wyoming for one more suitable to Texas summers. Stoval, wearing a wool shirt and thick corduroy pants, was taken in by the Lunneys. He would go on to find Fruit Loops cereal in his beloved Corvette after babysitting for Lunney, and he became a target for water balloons and eggs as the "rug rats" grew older. One of those rug rats was none other than Lunney's son, Bryan, who would also go on to work the flight director's console.

The right end of the first row was reserved for the guidance console, manned by flight controllers such as Raymond F. Teague, Neil B. Hutchinson, Kenneth W. "Ken" Russell, Granville E. "Gran" Paules, William E. "Will" Fenner, J. Gary Renick, C. Roger Wells, Willard S. "Will" Presley, Stephen G. "Steve" Bales, Jerry W. Mill, Jonny E. Ferguson, and B. Randy Stone. Guidance officers stood vigil over ground-based and onboard navigational systems and guidance computer software, and were also responsible for maintaining the onboard attitude reference system. If any of them ever got stuck for an answer, the first logical thing to do was check with their section head, Charley B. Parker. He was, after all, the original guido.

Parker was born and raised 120 or so miles northwest of Houston in the tiny hamlet of Concord, Texas. After the war, the train stopped coming through and Concord dried up just like that. Trying to find it on the map today is impossible, because it is not there, swallowed up by the surrounding towns of Centerville, Juet, and Marquez. Hardscrabble sharecroppers, the Parkers had little to no money, but neither did anyone else they knew. His father, Floyd, never went past the eighth grade, while mother Ora Bell—known as Jack, although even she was not quite sure why—made it through high school. Despite their meager means and educational background, Parker had been expected to go to college and get a degree for as long as he could remember, almost as if he did not have a choice in the matter. After a lackluster first couple of years at Lamar University in Beaumont, Texas, a stint in the army was all it took to convince Parker that school was not all that bad an option after all. Refocused, he graduated with a degree in electrical engineering.

Like so many others who went to work in Houston in the early 1960s, Parker was in the right place at the right time. A digital guidance computer was onboard the Gemini spacecraft, and it could take over and fly the Titan II launch vehicle during ascent in case the primary system failed. The guidance computer then acted as the primary system during descent and flew the two-seater spacecraft back into the earth's atmosphere. With such newfangled gadgetry on board, somebody needed to monitor and update it all back in the MOCR. The solution was to add a new position in the sparkling new, state-of-the-art control room—the guidance officer. The contractor TRW had done a study on how to monitor the guidance systems during ascent.

"I was *the* guidance officer when I got there," Parker said. "There was nobody else in the branch working on that problem when I got there. Using [TRW's] study as a basis, I just built on it to develop the console." The console would be a fairly special one with three display tubes instead of the standard two. Strip charts went on the left and right monitors, with a digital display shown on the one in the middle.

Together, the three Trench positions formed such a close working relationship in the MOCR that it might help explain the first row's camaraderie away from it. "Those three positions were almost interchangeable," Parker continued. "We understood what the other person was doing, and understood what their problems were. It was really almost one position, with three people operating. We kind of had a motto that the Trench was where the action was, and the other people, oh, they were just systems geeks. We were actually kind of an insufferable bunch."

Proud? Yes. Cocky? Probably. Insufferable? When it came to the Trench, like beauty, that was in the eyes of the beholder.

Like a line of demarcation, the aisle to and from the back of the room that began a third of the way down the second row separated two decidedly non-systems-oriented positions from those that dealt with the inner workings of two spacecraft.

The left-most workspace on the second row belonged to the flight surgeons, who were responsible for the health of the in-flight astronauts. Doctors Charles A. "Chuck" Berry, Willard R. Hawkins, John F. Zieglschmid, Kenneth M. Beers, George F. Humbert, and Sam L. Pool watched over their flock like mother hens, but even distinguished physicians like them could get tripped up once in a while. Although there was usually not a lot going on at the surgeon console during a simulation training exercise, the physicians had to be there and paying attention just in case. On at least one occasion, however, the physician on duty got caught napping during a test. "It was extremely boring during the simulations for them to be in mission control, so the training people decided they would do something," said Joseph N. DeAtkine, a longtime systems flight controller. "They went to one of the hospitals in Houston, and they got the EKG of a real patient having a heart attack, and, I think, dying. They brought that back and programmed it into the simulation. During the launch, they played this for the surgeons into their console."

The doctor, as it happened, missed the foreboding reading. Afterward came the sim team's turn to drop its bombshell. "The training people came online and said whether you did right or did this wrong, or you missed that or you did that right," DeAtkine continued. "But when they came to the surgeon, they said, 'Oh, by the way, astronaut so-and-so died.' Of course, all of mission control just busted out laughing. It was very embarrassing for the doctors. I think from then on they paid attention during the sims."

The console between flight surgeon and the aisle was where the capsule communicator (capcom) took up residence. With only four exceptions during the four-shift flight of *Apollo 12*—when Dickie K. Warren, James O. Rippey, James L. Lewis, and Michael R. Wash took over—capcom duties were handled exclusively by astronauts during the Gemini and Apollo programs. The theory was that pilots could communicate better with fellow pilots, whether they had actually yet flown in space or not. Their training and language were the same. If some felt that landing a capcom assignment meant that they were one step closer to a flight assignment of their own, that was not the case for Thomas K. "Ken" Mattingly II.

"I suspect everybody's got a different answer," Mattingly said with a chuckle. "In my case, I had no aspirations whatsoever that I was going to get to fly in Apollo. Our class had the moniker of being the 'Excess Nineteen,' and it certainly appeared to me that was the case. So *any* job that got you involved in activities that were current or that would give you some insight was a plum assignment in my book." After being bumped at the last minute from the ill-fated flight of *Apollo 13*, Mattingly flew as the Command Module pilot on *Apollo 16*.

Along the way, the voices of the men who served as capcom became part of history. It was an astronaut capcom who sent *Apollo 8* on its way to the moon; who talked *Eagle* down to the lunar surface, and another who talked Neil Armstrong down its ladder; who passed a fix up to the lightning-struck crew of *Apollo 12*; who talked the crew of *Apollo 13* through the first few minutes of its crisis; and who spoke the final words a Space Shuttle crew would ever hear from the ground.

Just across the aisle to the right of the capcom console rested the first of four systems consoles—two for the CSM and two for the LM. The systems monitor had been responsible for almost all of the tiny Mercury space-craft, while an environmental observer worked closely not with systems, but with the flight surgeon. "Most of the people recognized that this was sort of an aberration for how the Mission Control Center should work," Gene Kranz remembered. "It was not surprising, because to a great extent, the teams we fielded down at the Cape were like sandlot softball. Basically, we didn't know who would be the team members from the systems side of the house until we got very close to launch. Then, we'd borrow them from somewhere. It was sort of a part-time job for them." With so much more telemetry streaming down from the Gemini and Apollo spacecraft, con-trollers were dedicated to watching over their innards.

The first systems console in Houston was reserved for the CSM's envi-ronmental, electrical, and communications (EECOM) officer. The spot was responsible for communications through the flight of *Apollo 10*, and while those duties were consolidated into another position in the MOCR, the "COM" in EECOM remained. William C. "Clint" Burton, John A. Delmont, Charles L. "Charlie" Dumis, Richard D. "Dick" Glover, Lloyd V. Howard, Thomas R. "Rod" Loe, Seymour A. "Sy" Liebergot, J. Steve McClendon, William J. "Bill" Moon, and Craig Staresinich all sat the EECOM console at one time or another. And then there was John Aaron, who described the duties of the job as being "in charge of all the utilities that support the enterprise." Things such as power, environmental control, thermal con-trol, life support, docking system, abort systems, pyrotechnics, sequencing, and instrumentation—it was all included in an EECOM's job description.

Aaron knew the job inside and out, up one side and down the other. Better yet, he was secure in the knowledge of how his job impacted oth-ers in the control room. That is precisely where he gained the monumental respect of his coworkers. "If you polled all the flight controllers as to who they thought was the most capable and competent guy that ever sat in the control center, besides Chris Kraft, they were going to say John Aaron," remarked Jerry Bostick—and this, from the head of the Trench. "I still believe that. It was very satisfying to see when you were on the same shift as John, because you knew he knew what he was doing and knew how his job interacted with mine."

The truly amazing part of Aaron's story at NASA was that almost as soon as his feet hit the ground in Houston, he was ready to pack up and head back home. Surely, it had all been a mistake. Aaron was a farm boy who grew up in rural Oklahoma, almost completely unaccustomed to the bright lights and big city of Houston. The climate was arid back in Oklahoma, a far cry from his new home's heat and humidity, not to mention its mosquito-ridden plains and marshes. It was hard enough to cope with such problems, but over and above that was the very real fact that Aaron essentially had no idea what the space program was all about. He had been in a bubble in college, trying to make ends meet and working toward becoming a teacher so he could afford the herd of cattle he wanted to build up.

Aaron showed up for work at NASA only to find that his new coworkers were speaking what seemed like a foreign language in one strange acronym after another. The air conditioning was broken in the building to which he reported—this was during construction of the MSC campus down on the prairies south of town, when the agency was spread all over town—and people seemed to be piled on top of each other.

As if that was not enough, Aaron's father was getting older and was very ill at the time. As the only son—and next-to-the-youngest child—in a family of eight children, he felt a deep-seated need to do his duty and return home to help on the farm. Houston seemed as far from there as it could possibly have been. Aaron was thinking of leaving, and he tried rationalizing the move with his parents, John and Agnes.

Dad and Mom, you guys are in your seventies and you're having a hard time here. What do you think about me just coming back for a couple of years and helping you transition this operation?

Their response stuck with Aaron for more than half a century.

Son, we are in the September of our life. Do not worry about us. You should carry on and pursue your life. You've got a very bright future in front of you.

*Don't feel like you've got to come back here to help us, because that would be
the wrong thing for you and your family to do.*

Cheryl Aaron, John's wife, was even more to the point.

We're not going back.

That was that. And if members of the Trench ever deemed a systems
controller fit for honorary membership, it would more than likely be Aaron
and for precisely an attitude like this one: "If we had a good day, we all
knew that you don't even need ground controllers like me," Aaron began.
"The crew had good knowledge of the spacecraft. They had canned procedures and so on. We were there for insurance. The crew depended on the
ground to get certain trajectory information. As an EECOM, I was there in
case they had a bad day because they could basically fly the thing to the
first element of surprise without much help from me. That was the moti-
vation. My real job was to be able to be there with the right answer when
the unexpected happened."

Just to the right of EECOM on the second row was the flight controller who took care of the guidance, navigation, and control (GNC) hardware in the CSM. Those men included Gerald D. "Gerry" Griffin, Gary
E. Coen, Richard B. Benson, John A. "Jack" Kamman, Briggs N. "Buck"
Willoughby, Lawrence S. "Larry" Canin, William J. "Bill" Strahle, Raymond S. "Terry" Watson, Neil Hutchinson, Joe DeAtkine, Richard Fitts,
and Ronald Lerdal.

DeAtkine, an army brat whose brother David also worked at NASA for
years in the MPAD division, started out as an instrumentation and communications (INCO) officer during the October 1968 flight of *Apollo 7* and
then ventured halfway around the world to the tracking station in Carnarvon, Australia, to work as EECOM for the unmanned *Apollo 4* Saturn
V test a month later. That was only a temporary move, and he found himself comfortable as an INCO through the first lunar landing. It was then
that the INCO position was consolidated. DeAtkine moved—when he *got*
moved, according to him—over to GNC for the flights of *Apollo 14* and *15*.
"If I had any say in it, which I did *not*, I would've gone with the INCO job
over in Ed Fendell's area," DeAtkine said emphatically. "But they moved
me over there, and GNC is actually more interesting, really. It got me into
an area I'd never worked before."

DeAtkine described work on the GNC console as "mundane" as much as

95 percent of the time during a flight. Beforehand, though, the sim teams had long put him and other systems analysts through the wringer. "They would put these failures in, and then we would look at the mission rule and see what to do," DeAtkine said. "Sometimes, it turned out the mission rules weren't quite what they should be." Along with mission rules came malfunction procedures that DeAtkine compared to an automobile repair manual.

If the problem is this, then do that.

If it is not *this, then try that other thing.*

If it is neither of those, then try something else altogether.

If all else fails, just keep looking.

As in the Trench, the two CSM systems controllers had responsibilities that were quite connected. "The systems officers sat side by side and worked closely together, because quite often, an electrical problem would effect a navigation system or vice versa," Gerry Griffin concluded.

The same went for the next two positions on the second row. These oversaw the guts of the Lunar Module during the Apollo years, while in Project Gemini, that space was occupied by navigation and systems controllers for the Agena docking target. A handful made what seemed to be the perfect transition, Gemini to Apollo, Agena to the LM. "We had two spacecraft in Gemini—we had the manned spacecraft and the unmanned spacecraft," explained Bob Carlton. "When we moved into Apollo, you had kind of a similar situation with the CSM and the LM. The guys who had worked on the Agena kind of naturally fell heir to the LM."

The responsibilities during Apollo were so similar to the Command and Service Module, the two new LM sections were actually referred to as GNC and EECOM in a 9 June 1967 announcement. The jobs were close in duty *and* proximity. To the immediate right of the CSM's GNC console was that of the LM's telcom/telmu officer. The telemetry, electrical, and communications (telcom) position was renamed telmu following *Apollo 11* when responsibility for the moonwalkers' Extravehicular Mobility Unit (EMU) was added and communications moved to the consolidated INCO position. The EMUs had until then been monitored down on the far left-hand end of the Trench, after the spots were vacated by the booster controllers. William L. "Bill" Peters, Donald R. "Don" Puddy, Jack Knight Jr., W. Merlin Merrit, Gary C. Watros, and Robert H. "Bob" Heselmeyer all worked the console.

Bill Peters sat the telcom console during the flights of *Apollo 9* and *10*, and then moved down a row to watch over *Apollo 11* Lunar Module pilot Buzz Aldrin's EMU during the first moonwalk. After that, it was back up to the merged telmu position from there on out. "It wasn't that much additional effort," Peters said. "While the Lunar Module is sitting on the ground, you're not worried about things that happen while it's flying. So you transition your workload effort over to the suit."

The last spot at the right end of the second row belonged to the control officer, who handled guidance, navigation, and control systems for the LM. Harold A. "Hal" Loden, Jackson B. Craven Jr., John A. Wegener, Richard A. "Dick" Thorson, and Larry W. Strimple served as control at one time or another, and it was Bob Carlton who was their section head early in Apollo. New hires were coming on board almost daily, it seemed, with branch chief James E. "Jim" Hannigan heading out on recruiting trips to college campuses and Carlton working the phones to staff the front and back rooms. "I ended up with close to thirty people after we got all powered up for Apollo," Carlton said. "Here a whole bunch of newcomers came in, don't know nothing from nothing, kids fresh out of college."

Add in a few that had been handpicked from the air force, who were bright and the cream of the crop but inexperienced in flight control and systems expertise, and Carlton had his hands full in trying to get everybody all trained up and ready to go. "The training of all those people was a mind-boggling task," he said. "You were trying to teach them how to understand the engineering aspects of their systems details. They were responsible for the propulsion system, the guidance system, the RCS system, et cetera. They didn't know what an RCS system was."

Slowly but surely, the new hires learned. One of Carlton's favorite teaching methods was to have them draw and diagram systems overseen by the control officer. "We had to troubleshoot things in a matter of seconds for problems, and the old set of drawings they used in engineering just wouldn't cut it," Carlton said. "So I used the drawing system that we had as a double-barrel sort of a tool. I would put a new engineer on there and say, 'Okay, you're an RCS man and I want you to upgrade our drawings here for the RCS system. I don't like it. I want you to redo it.'" What Carlton was actually after was an improvement on the drawings, but also for the new guy to understand the system in the process. "When he drew it, he learned it," Carlton concluded. When delivery of the Lunar Module was delayed, some within NASA found themselves frustrated. That was not the case for Carlton. "It was a lifesaver," he admitted. "I was so far behind the power curve, working until midnight, didn't see how in the world I was ever going to make the schedule. Every time the contractor came in and said we can't make the schedule, *deep* down, I rejoiced."

The task at hand—landing men on the moon before the end of the decade—and Carlton's responsibilities within that task sometimes got the best of him. Though he mellowed considerably following his NASA career, he could sometimes be a pill during it. "Sometimes, you had individuals that had an abrasive personality, and you're probably talking to one of them right now," Carlton granted. "In retrospect, it's almost a little embarrassing to think back to how overbearing I was and how cocky I was. I rubbed a lot of people the wrong way." A time or two, Carlton continued, he and a particular FIDO would "draw sparks" on each other in disagreement. "It was a two-way street, probably more my fault than it was his," he added. "Some of that was personality. Some of it was difference in opinion on how you should be doing things and so forth."

Overall, there was what Carlton called a "stupendous harmony" among controllers who were all working toward the same goals of mission success and safety. Generally, though, disputes arose over such things as mission rules and what-if situations. "*That's* where you had differences of opinions, and *that's* where you drew sparks," Carlton said. "The whole team would get together and we'd have great debates about how we should react to various problems. Then we wrote those decisions down as mission rules. Emotions ran high during those debates about mission rules." The important things to remember, though, are that these debates took place outside the MOCR, before a flight, and that input came from several sources. According to Gene Kranz, nearly 30 percent of pre-mission planning was spent on developing mission rules, which represented "a meeting of the minds between the flight director, mission controllers, flight crew, and program office."

Once on console, those sometimes heated conversations were over. "After we got through wrestling over all those mission-rules debates, there would be a decision made," Carlton said. "The flight director would say, 'I hear you, Carlton, but shut up. This is what we're going to do.' Once that decision was made, you laid aside any discussion from that point on. I think there was whole-heartedly an attitude in all of the team that once you got the mission rule resolved, then you went and implemented it."

If ever anybody in the MOCR could have come close to matching John Llewellyn in terms of sheer force of personality, it almost certainly would have been Edward I. "Ed" Fendell.

His was a journey to mission control and the INCO console on the far left of the third row that was one of the most unlikely of them all. Fendell graduated in 1951 from Becker Junior College in Worcester, Massachusetts, with a degree in merchandising, of all things. The two-year degree was as far as the man who would one day be head of the Apollo Communications Section would ever go in terms of formal education outside NASA.

Fendell joined the army reserves as an artillery spotter while still in junior college, and when he tried to join the coast guard after graduation, the waiting list was several months long. Instead, he walked just a few doors down the street and signed his papers for the air force. He was given an IQ test shortly thereafter that changed the course of his life. "That's no shit . . . that's the truth. I wasn't interested in school. I wasn't interested in anything," Fendell said in his distinctive tell-it-like-it-is manner. "When they gave all this IQ test that they did, I was up at the top. I didn't know I was smart. I had no idea. I got into air-traffic control, and the next thing I knew, was first in my class."

Specializing in talking aircraft down in bad weather, Fendell landed at the Federal Aviation Administration after leaving the military. When he turned up at the Cape at one point, he landed a job offer from NASA to serve as a remote-site capcom. His learning curve was a steep one. In the early 1960s, there was no preexisting knowledge base on how to go about getting up to speed in the human spaceflight business. "If you had a question about something, if you didn't know an area, you couldn't go to a library and get a book. There was no book," Fendell said. "There was no training program. There was no workbook for someone like me who didn't know orbital mechanics from a frickin' hole in the ground." That meant when Fendell needed to better understand something, he had to go find somebody to explain it to him.

It was hard enough to comprehend the complexities of building a human spaceflight program from scratch, but just imagine what it must have been like to be in Fendell's shoes in those days. He was *not* an engineer. He did not have so much as a degree from a four-year college. Yet there he was, right in the thick of it all. "Everybody was your friend and you were everybody else's friend," Fendell continued. "Everybody worked together, and when you screwed up, everybody *told* you that you screwed up." Official post-simulation debriefings were an important part of the learning process, but it was post-mission parties at the Hofbraugarten German Village Restaurant in Dickinson, Texas—about ten miles from the MSC campus— where flight controllers really got down to business.

"The only people who went to that party were the flight controllers and the astronauts—no one else," Fendell began, as if warming up to the story. "There was no, 'I'm bringing my friend or my girlfriend.' You went down there, you drank beer, and everybody talked about you and they talked about *all* the shit that you did wrong. Everybody listened and heard when somebody stood up there and said, 'That damn Fendell did the following thing, and that was the dumbest son-of-a-bitching thing in the world . . . tah-dee, tah-dah, tah-duh, tah-dumb.'" And this . . . this was the most important part. "You stood there and took it, or you packed up and you went home," he concluded.

Work became a way of life for Fendell. He would never even know if he or anybody else for that matter got paid overtime, not that he cared much one way or the other. That is not to say, though, that he was *all* work, *all* the time. "One day, I picked up this chick and we spent the night," he remembered.

The morning after, their conversation went something like this.
Where are you going?
I'm going to work.
Fendell's date was incredulous.
You're what? Today's Saturday. What am I going to do?
This is what it was like to be around Ed Fendell back in the day, because his response was so classically him.
Well, you can either stay here, or you can get your ass up, go home, and I'll call you later. You understand what I'm saying? I'm going to work. I write mission rules on Saturday morning.
After Gemini and his service at various remote sites around the world,

Fendell headed back to Houston to serve as assistant flight director before assuming responsibility for the INCO position following the fateful flight of *Apollo 10*. The move saved Fendell's career at NASA. He had so despised the role, he came close to leaving the agency not once but twice. The first time, he had an offer from TRW in Los Angeles, and the other, from a proposed National Hockey League expansion franchise in Seattle, Washington.

He stayed to oversee data, voice, and video communications and the group of INCOs, which in Apollo came to include Joe DeAtkine, Earl W. Thompson, Richard T. "Dick" Brown, Thomas L. Hanchett, James R. Fucci, Harley W. Weyer, Granvil A. Pennington, Alan C. Glines, Gary B. Scott, Harold Black, and Lawrence L. D. "Larry" Armstrong. Several— including Thompson, Weyer, Pennington, and Armstrong—had moved just one spot to the left from the operations and procedures console. Fendell stayed on through the early years of the Space Shuttle program, serving all the while in communications.

The operations and procedures (O&P) officer was primarily responsible for data configurations and the extensive O&P handbook that had been compiled from each of the various branches in the control room. "During the flight, we were responsible for any changes or updates that were necessary because of something that came up during the flight that we hadn't foreseen," Gary Scott said. "We were responsible for making sure that was coordinated with the proper people and sent out to whoever needed to see it. We also kept up with making sure the data retrieval procedures and configurations were correct for whatever phase of flight we were in." Along with those who eventually moved to work as INCOs, Larry W. Keyser, David F. Nicholson, Axel M. Larsen, William Molnar Jr., James O. Covington, Joe M. Leeper, Joseph Lazzaro, Joseph G. Fanelli, Harold Black, Richard B. Ramsell, Kim Anson, Alan Glines, William B. Wood, and Maurice Kennedy all served at the O&P console at one time or another during Apollo.

Next to procedures was the assistant flight director (AFD) console, and if the title sounded relatively self-explanatory, it nonetheless became one of the MOCR's most controversial positions. The role was the brainchild of Gene Kranz, who had worked procedures under original NASA flight directors Chris Kraft and John D. Hodge during the early Mercury days. "This goes back into, I think, the difference between myself and some of the other flight directors," Kranz said. "Throughout my entire life, I never minded anyone looking over my shoulder, willing to give help. I considered him my co-pilot. When I was getting ready to make tough decisions—they're short term, they're quick, they're irreversible—I liked to have somebody saying, 'Yeah, I think that's the way we ought to go.'"

Manfred H. "Dutch" von Ehrenfried served under Kranz in that capacity during a handful of Gemini flights, early in Kranz's career at the flight director's console. Von Ehrenfried would come to respect the man as a friend, mentor, and brother. "You start spending eight to sixteen hours a day with Gene Kranz, you're going to learn something," von Ehrenfried said. "Many times, we would work so hard, I would just kind of hope he would faint or something so I could get a break." To von Ehrenfried, who also worked as a judo partner with Kranz, the AFD's job was as simple as getting the flight director the information he needed when he needed it.

Gene Kranz considered the AFD a safety valve, a wingman, he said, to keep watch over his six. He had flown the demilitarized zone in Korea and the Taiwan Strait during his time in the air force, and he was glad to have somebody watching his back. He sometimes flew in air shows, and he always had someone calling off altitude, airspeed, and show sequences. Not all wingmen made element or flight leader, but they were still good wingmen. They checked their egos, just as Kranz tried to do when he crawled into the cockpit or sat down in his chair at the flight director's console in mission control. If he needed help from a wingman in either arena, so be it.

To more than one of the men who served in the position, however, there sometimes seemed to be a rather large difference between working as an assistant flight director and as an assistant *to* the flight director. Gerry Griffin felt whatever difference that existed was the result more of the personalities involved and how they utilized the AFD than of any outright political motives in the MOCR. He had a point. The men who served as flight director were different, and they did approach their jobs in different ways. Gene Kranz took fastidious notes, while Griffin took few. Others joked with Glynn Lunney and told him to slow down, that they were not quite as smart as he was.

Griffin did not mind the help of the AFD, using John H. Temple as much as possible, but that was not the case for other flight directors. "My problem with this subject was the surmise that it was the preferential position in the competition for—or even be the main path—to being selected for flight director," Lunney said. "Since all the AFD came from the same branch—one of four or five in the Flight Control Division—it was an accident of where one entered the operations division. This seemed a poor prerequisite for flight director. There was lots of talent in the other branches, and I could not imagine deselecting that pool. Plus, the help I got was widely different, depending on who the AFD was."

Neither was Sy Liebergot a fan of the position. "Quite frankly, the positions of operations and procedures officer and assistant flight director were pretty much non-positions," said Liebergot, who served in both jobs during unmanned Saturn launch vehicle tests before moving down to the second row and the EECOM console. "The assistant flight director position was . . . nothing more than a 'go-fer.' In fact, it was that reason that I ended up being an EECOM because Lunney on [the *Apollo 4* Saturn V test] called me over to his console and told me very clearly that if I thought that if he couldn't perform his duty as a flight director that I had another thought coming. He said, 'I will crawl over broken glass to keep you from taking this position. You ought to find something else to do.'"

Liebergot concluded by recalling how members of the Trench would sometimes phonetically pronounce the position's abbreviation as "aphid"—which he noted is "a small, sucking insect."

Charles S. "Charlie" Harlan started his NASA career at the agency's headquarters in Washington DC before moving south to Houston in March of 1964. While he took a little bit of heat early on from coworkers over making the transition from HQ, Flight Operations was the place to be. He threw himself into doing double-duty by monitoring the Gemini program's Titan II, and after launch, moving up to the AFD console. Although that was his home throughout most of Apollo, Harlan was aware of the position's limitations. "It was thought to be an infringement on the flight directors by some. Others, it was thought to be not substantive in nature," he admitted. "I could count on coming to work and getting a ration from somebody."

During Apollo, the AFD duty fell to men like Harlan, Liebergot, Fendell, Temple, Harold M. Draughon, Jones W. Roach, William E. Platt Jr., Perry L. Ealick, Charles R. "Chuck" Lewis, Larry Keyser, David E. Nicholson Jr., James Covington, Howard C. Johnson, Joe Leeper, and Barry Wolfer. Of all the men who sat the AFD console during Apollo, only Lewis and Draughon ever became flight directors themselves.

Back in Mercury, Lewis had gone to school on spacecraft systems and learning Morse code before he was thrown out into the world at the tracking station in Zanzibar, East Africa. Traveling to the different sites he worked and seeing the world the way that he did turned out to be what he called one of the better parts of his career. "I wasn't trying to promote myself into a control-center position that time," Lewis said. "I wasn't even thinking about it." Fate soon intervened, and he was pulled back to Houston to work on Apollo requirements for the control center. One thing led to another, and Lewis found himself in the position of AFD. "In my opinion, the AFD role was primarily preflight," Lewis said. "We did a lot of mission rules work, reviews, following up on action items for *some* of the flight directors. Some didn't want you involved that much. I really felt the emphasis was probably preflight, as opposed to support during the flight."

During a mission, Lewis might occasionally mention it being a minute to loss of signal or some such—and not even over the comm loop, because their consoles were right next to each other. Other than that, however, that was just about the extent of it. "I don't recall a case where he left and left me in charge, so to speak," Lewis said. "If he was not at the console and somebody called him, I said, 'This is AFD. Flight's not here. I'll pick it up if you like, or you can hold for Flight. He'll be back in a couple of minutes.' I never did feel comfortable trying to step into the flight director's shoes when I was assistant flight director, because you can't have two quarterbacks on the field at the same time."

If there was doubt over the AFD's duties, the same could not be said for the flight director. Separated by a narrow aisle on either side, as if to fully designate the spot as the throne of all thrones in the room, the very next console in the MOCR was reserved for the flight director. Written by Chris Kraft, this job description was easy enough to comprehend.

The flight director may, after analysis of a flight, take any action necessary for mission success.

Kraft was everything that it meant to be a flight director during Mercury, even as the job steadily evolved into the one he envisioned. John Hodge joined the exclusive club for the final flight of the Mercury program, that of *Faith 7* and astronaut Leroy Gordon Cooper Jr. in May 1963. Those ranks were exactly doubled, to a total of four, after it was announced in a 4 September 1964 press release that Gene Kranz and Glynn Lunney had also been named as flight directors. They were, the announcement read, "responsible not only for making operational decisions involving spacecraft performance, but also for seeing that flight plans are followed and that crew safety is assured."

Regardless, Glynn Lunney's role model for the new job was none other than his mentor, Chris Kraft. "That was a *very* big deal," said Lunney of his promotion. "Chris Kraft had become a legend by the time we got to that point. We worked with him through the Mercury flights, and we saw his leadership. We saw how he managed things. We saw how he delegated and trusted people, but then made sure they did the job. He trusted us to do big things."

The kind of faith that Kraft showed toward his charges—as stern as it could be at times—was returned in full at virtually every turn. "He was the model that most of us sought to emulate—certainly I did and other people did, too," Lunney continued. "We had a chance to do some of this stuff that looked almost magic. We didn't have leadership courses or anything like that. We had leadership examples flowing all the way through this entire organization. We were immersed in leadership models and examples, and we learned from it. Most of the people who did well said, 'I want to be like that guy. I want to be able to do what he does. He's always able to tell what's coming and be ready for it.'"

Gene Kranz was certainly one of the most well-known flight directors of them all. Kranz's fame was due in no small part to his trademark crew cut; the familiar vests he wore during missions; his autobiography, *Failure Is Not an Option*; and his portrayal in the blockbuster movie *Apollo 13* by actor Ed Harris. Early in his career, Kranz saw the qualities of his contemporaries at the flight director's console and tried to incorporate the best of each into his own manner—Kraft, he said, was utterly brilliant and became a gifted leader; Hodge was a great listener who had flight-test experience; and Lunney was ahead of everything he ever did.

Kranz never trusted his memory, so he became a fanatical note taker. The data books he developed became indispensable parts of that preparation, having gone through every schematic in the entire spacecraft, every mission rule, every flight plan, everything. Terrified that he might somehow misplace one of the books, he placed pictures cut out of *Sports Illustrated* on the outside of the blinder so that people would know immediately that it was his. "Basically, I just relied on organization, personal checklists, and training so that I had my mind made up as to what I would do in the first sixty, ninety seconds of a crisis," Kranz said. "There were some guys like Lunney who could wing it. He was absolutely gifted. Kraft could always find his way through to an answer by asking the right questions, and he already almost always knew the answer. He was just trying to get people to agree with him."

Another skill that Kranz worked to develop was the ability to listen to his troops, like a quarterback running the two-minute drill. The flight director's only consumable, he knew, was time, and under no circumstances could any controller afford to run out the clock. And not only would Kranz listen to what the controllers were telling him, he would listen to the tone of their voice, the inflection of how they were saying it. As time went on, trust developed. "There were many times when the controllers would take a direction and wouldn't even bother to tell me, because they had confidence I would support them," Kranz said. "This is, I think, very critical when you're in time-critical situations. It was a question of getting to know the people, and more so, having an intense feeling for the challenges they had when they were trying to give you answers."

The beauty of the control room, Kranz continued, was that issues were always black and white. There was no gray—calls were either go or no go. Maybe was not good enough. Flight directors had to trust their controllers, and the controllers had to trust their flight directors to do exactly the right thing at exactly the right moment. It was a bond forged in countless hours of simulations and actual missions. Building trust in the ranks meant knowing the strengths and weaknesses of each, and some had more of one than the other. "There were some people who were very good, and there were some people that were not very good at all, but they were still good team players," Kranz continued. "So you had to work extra hard with them, and a couple of them on my team were really a challenge. If I had John Aaron, I could get an answer in ten seconds. If I had another guy, it'd be three or four minutes. Basically, you had to develop that kind of relationship with them."

The thing that stuck out about Kranz to control officer Hal Loden was his bearing in and around the MOCR. He had this air, the perfect leader who had a knack of getting people to perform above and beyond their capabilities. As one memory after another came back to Loden, he began to tear up. "He was one of a kind," Loden said, strong emotion tinting every word. "There could not have been a stronger task master. He's like Glynn. He knew the system as well as you did, and in some cases, probably better than you did. He was what I would call the ultimate flight director. There's nobody who could touch him when it came to getting the job done. He commanded the utmost in respect from everybody, I believe. He certainly did from me."

Not everyone took to Kranz in the end, but that much could have been said of virtually anybody in any walk of life, in any position of authority. Lop off the scores of those who all but worshipped the man as well as those of the handful who did not care for Kranz in the least, and what remained was probably the best indicator of the kind of man and flight director he actually happened to be.

Charles L. Stough, Tommy W. Holloway, William M. Anderson, Ted A. Guillory, John W. O'Neill, Spencer H. Gardner, Turnage R. Lindsey, Elvin B. Pippert, Raymond G. Zedakar, John H. Covington, and R. R. Cain all worked the flight activities officer (FAO) console to the right of the flight director's console. It was located there because Glynn Lunney wanted it that way.

Tommy Holloway never had any grand vision of going to work in the space program before he landed there in February 1963, and the FAO's responsibilities were basically an extension of the planning he did before a mission. He worked on flight plans and crew schedules, and backup plans for things such as cutting a flight short in case something went wrong. Another job was procedures development and putting together the crew's Flight Data File—the books of checklists and cue cards carried on board the Command Module weighed a total of 110 pounds, and there were thirty-five pounds of books inside the Lunar Module. If the plans needed any updating during a flight, Holloway would take care of it.

During the first several flights of the Gemini program, the FAO position was part of the Flight Crew Operations Directorate, and in that realm, astronauts were king. The problem was that the astronauts had not been immersed in the kinds of planning Holloway had done and sometimes came into the training flow late due to their other responsibilities. Lunney's debut as lead flight director came during *Gemini 10* in mid-July 1966, and when too much fuel was used while maneuvering into position with the Agena docking target, it had been Holloway who had worked on those contingency plans. Lunney wanted him close by during the flight, and from that day forward, the FAO was in the front room. "Glynn Lunney was really instrumental in getting that changed and getting the flight activities officer put in the front room," Holloway said. "In my view, and of course I'm biased on the subject, that was a master stroke."

Finally, the last console on the third row belonged to the network controller, who was responsible for the worldwide series of ground stations. George D. Ojalehto, John A. Monkvic, Ernest L. Randall, George M. Egan, Douglass R. Wilson, Lawrence D. "Larry" Meyer, David A. Young, Ronald L. DeCosmo, Charles M. Horstman, Earl Carr, Robert Gonzales, Joseph R. Vice, Fred H. Wrinkle, Walter Soetaert, Julius M. "Julie" Conditt, Thomas W. Sheehan, and Donald H. Baerd worked Apollo from this position. Richard J. Stachurski was there, too, on assignment from the U.S. Air Force. Born and raised in Queens, New York, Stachurski went to high school in Brooklyn—within walking distance of the famed Ebbets Field, home of the Dodgers, although he was a die-hard Yankees fan—and college for the first time in the Bronx. With a degree in history and after a stint in the Reserve Officers Training Corps, he wound up in the air force. "I went in search of adventure, and it found me," Stachurski said. "It was just an enormous set of quirks and coincidences. I came away from the whole thing with the feeling that if you ever think you're in control of your life, forget it. It doesn't work that way."

It was in 1965 that he got a notice to report to Houston for an interview. What in the world did NASA need with a history major? Stationed at the time at Ellsworth Air Force Base just outside Rapid City, South Dakota, it was a heck of a lot warmer down in Texas, so Stachurski figured, why not? Surely, somebody would come to their senses and realize that this had all been some sort of mistake, but maybe not before he could take a couple of days' worth of vacation.

Six years later, Stachurski was still in Houston.

Henry E. "Pete" Clements was the air force lieutenant colonel who had proposed the loan of 128 officers to train for that military branch's manned spaceflight program—which never actually came to fruition—while at the same time supporting NASA's efforts during its early manpower crunch. That was how Stachurski had made it to Houston in the first place. "Henry was quirky, to say the least," Stachurski remembered. "Henry would refer to himself in the third person. He would say things like, 'You may come in now. Henry is prepared to speak with you.' The guy was a real character." When Stachurski asked Clements how he had been selected for duty in Houston, the answer was direct and to the point. "He said to me, '*Well*, I thought it would be interesting to see how a liberal arts puke made out in this environment,'" Stachurski continued. "Coming from him, you can believe every word of that. That's the kind of person he was. He thought that would be funny, and I'm glad he did."

Initially, he was put in operations scheduling before being moved over to the network console. He was on duty 16 July 1969 as *Apollo 11* lifted off. "We were responsible for seventeen tracking stations around the world, eight aircraft, four ships, and all communications that connected them," Stachurski said. "Everything on the ground belonged to us. We were plumbers. Our job was to keep the circuits up and functioning throughout the mission." He was amazed to have such an opportunity, working as prime network controller on mankind's first lunar landing. He was an air force officer, and a history major on top of that. "My sense was even stranger than that," Stachurski said. "What the hell is a history major doing sitting here in the middle of all of these astrophysics and engineering and whatever guys? I was hustling all the time to make sure I understood what I had to understand."

Tradition dictated that a plaque for each mission be hung in the MOCR following its successful conclusion. After *Apollo 11*, that duty fell to Stachurski. "I damn near fell off the ladder," he joked. "It was a priceless adventure. And it was scary at the time, because I was feeling a little insecure."

After leaving Houston in 1971, Stachurski headed to Wright-Patterson Air Force Base in Ohio where he helped develop some of the first remotely flown drones. Over the course of his twenty-six-year career in the military, he also served as deputy program director for the Ground Launched Cruise Missile (GLCM) development program and later served as commander of a GLCM wing in Sicily. Stachurski had, after all, gone in search of adventure.

Finally, the fourth row in the room was staffed by the public affairs officer, as well as upper-level management and officials from the Department of Defense. The fourth row became Chris Kraft's perch once he left his flight director's console midway through the Gemini program. He was there for consultation, and no longer in direct control of the flights.

That was a job he left up to the first three rows.

As capable as those who worked the front room were, their success would not have been possible without the Staff Support Rooms (SSRS) that lined the opposite side of the hallway just outside the door to the left of the MOCR. The position was an outgrowth of Kranz's time in the air force, when he used a Strategic Air Command (SAC) hotline as a B-52 flight test engineer to work out solutions to problems he encountered. Following the fiasco that was the launch of *Mercury-Redstone 1* on 21 November 1960—in which it lifted just four inches off the pad and jettisoned its escape tower—Kranz convinced Chris Kraft to set up a hotline to McDonnell Aircraft Corporation and get a couple of engineers assigned to help in the event of the anomalies that were sure to come. By the end of Mercury, the position had been formalized to provide rapid and direct communication with the design and test teams.

The duty of the SSR was just that—support, and in essence, making smart people smarter. "It was a matter of having specialists in the Staff Support Room," said John R. "Jack" Garman, who staked his claim to fame as an SSR legend during the dicey computer alarms that plagued the moon landing of *Apollo 11*. "The guys in the MOCR weren't expected to know everything that the guys in the Staff Support Rooms knew. If you viewed it hierarchically in terms of knowledge, the further down you went, the more knowledge you had."

Bob Carlton, for instance, had all kinds of support during *Apollo 11* as he worked the control console in the MOCR—Robert S. "Bob" Nance Jr. watched over the ascent and descent engines and the mechanical workings of the Reaction Control System; William E. "Bill" Sturm was an employee of the Philco Corporation who was responsible for the Attitude Control System; and John L. Nelson took care of the Primary Guidance and Navigation System. Quite often, the SSR would spot an issue before the operator in the front room did and would bring it to his attention. That was the way it was supposed to work; the front room had responsibility for every system, while each person in the SSR focused on just one or two and could therefore concentrate on them more in depth. "You can't hardly talk about the MOCR without talking about the SSR, in my opinion," Carlton said. "The SSR monitored my systems at all times, and if I asked them a question, I instantly got an answer. If the flight director asked me a question, most generally, if I kind of stumbled a minute, the SSR would come in. I didn't even have to ask him. He was listening to the flight director."

A good many flight controllers began their careers in the SSR before moving over to the front-room MOCR, but others were content to stay put. Ken Young grew up in MPAD but began FIDO training late in 1963, before choosing to stick with the planning group full time. Rather than riding a console and going through an endless training cycle for the next few years, Young instead supported the Trench's navigation and rendezvous efforts from the SSR. "MPAD just appealed to my planning nature," Young said. "We started on most missions three to four to five years before we actually flew them. Of course, we did all kinds of modifications along the way when certain things didn't work out. I enjoyed that more than sitting on the console and training procedures, which of course are highly important, and all this rapid real-time decision-making stuff. Not that I couldn't make it. I just didn't want to spend endless hours in the control center doing the procedures stuff."

The front and back rooms were a formidable partnership, and one that was strengthened by the simulation team located in a windowed area to the right front of the MOCR. Flight controllers and the sim team formed the perfect example of a love-hate relationship, in that while training exposed many a flaw and embarrassed many an operator over the years, it was fully understood that preparing in such a brutal manner was an absolute critical necessity. The mistakes themselves that were made in training were bad enough, but then they were discussed at length in front of God and everybody once the sessions were completed. Talk about pressure; it was the sim debriefs that derailed many a prospective flight controller. Own up to an error, go over it honestly, and folks were usually good to go unless the gaffes continued to pile up. Those who continually tried to bluff their way out of a misstep were almost always gone as quickly as Chris Kraft could shove them through the closest available door.

"You had a group of people there who either trusted you or they didn't," said John Aaron. "They were not very politically correct about what their concerns were. If you weren't making the grade, if you screwed something up, you got razzed about it. We had confessional every time we made a training run. We would start out at the left-hand front row and all the consoles had to report what they did, why they did it, and whether it turned out to be the right thing to do or the wrong thing to do." After the MOCR operators consulted among themselves, it was the sim team's turn and that is when things tended to get really ugly. "Nobody was able to bluff in that room," Aaron continued. "It was like a poker game. Everybody's cards were face up. You couldn't bluff, and you surely didn't want to get caught bluffing."

Harold G. "Hal" Miller reported to Langley Research Center on 7 July 1959, after turning down a better offer and accepting $5,430 a year from NASA. He joined the Simulation Task Group and stayed in Virginia through M. Scott Carpenter's Mercury flight before heading to Houston. Staying with the sim group until leaving the agency in August 1970, the native of Vanleer, Tennessee, knew the qualities of a good flight controller as well as anyone. He had seen it all.

First, good flight controllers were very quick to think on their feet. They would have made good debaters, Miller added.

Second, although intelligence and great memory were clearly important, there was more to the job than just being smart. Check back to the first quality to begin understanding why. "You could take some really smart people and they would wash out in a heartbeat," Miller said. "I would've *never* made a flight controller. I don't think on my feet fast enough."

Third, capable MOCR operators were confident, almost to the point of being cocky. Who? The Trench? Cocky? Never!

Fourth, it was important to have a good sense of humor. Most did, because if they did not, the unofficial debriefs at some local watering hole could sometimes get downright wicked. Those who knew what was good for them laughed it off when they went down the wrong path in training, but at the same time, they also made a mental note to never, ever do it again.

The theory behind it all was this—simulations were a means of exercising procedures, human and hardware interfaces, mission rules, and so forth. They did not teach systems. That was done elsewhere—or else. They screened flight controllers, to weed out those who were not adept at real-time operation, although grades were never given or even implied. It was up to the flight director to determine who was ready and who was not.

Finally, catastrophic failures were not allowed in simulations. Virtually anything else was fair game. "There had to be a way out," Miller concluded.

With a few notable exceptions—*Apollo 13* comes to mind—training was almost always far more difficult to negotiate than the actual flights. The principle was the same as the one employed in sports, where an athlete prepares for an event with ankle weights or some such. Once a game, match, or race takes place, the weights come off and the athlete is faster, more nimble, lighter, better. The sim team would sometimes go to great lengths to prove a point. "Harold Miller wanted to find out what a flight dynamics officer would do if he lost power on his console," remembered Dave Reed. "He gets some rope, opens up the hollow floor, and has somebody crawl underneath these hollow floors. He gets the rope up underneath my console and ties it onto the circuit breaker." What happened next was not hard to imagine—the sim run started, and pop, just like that, the string was used to pull the breaker. Suddenly, Reed's console was without juice and totally blank.

What was Reed supposed to do? Alert the flight director? Let his SSR handle things until power was restored? No way, not Dave Reed. He unplugged from the FIDO console, *ran* to his back room, and kept right on going. "I guess Harold was happy with that," Reed said with a laugh.

He was not alone. Bob Carlton could not remember the flight for which he was training, not that it really mattered. What was important was that no one would ever let him forget the sim itself. It never failed. He would get together with his former coworkers at a reunion somewhere, and sure enough, somebody would mention it "every dadgum time."

Hey, Carlton . . .

From the tone of their voice, he could probably already tell what was coming.

You remember that Agena burn you simmed that time?

He remembered, all right. The Agena had its share of troubles leading up to the three-day flight of *Gemini 10* in July 1966, but for that one fateful warmup at least, it was Carlton who was the source of the difficulties. Because it was an unmanned vehicle, control commands came from the ground. Carlton was to initiate a short burn of as little as a second and a half, maybe, during the sim. How in the world was he supposed to clock that short an amount of time? The solution he came up with was to hold a stopwatch in his left hand, and at the same instant use his right to press a button to send an initial arm command as well as to actually start and stop the burn.

That was the plan, and it had gone well plenty of times before. Not *this* time, though. He got the Agena's engine going, but instead of starting his stopwatch, he pressed the command button again to instantly kill the burn. He knew immediately that he had screwed up.

Oh no. No. No.

A fleeting thought came to Carlton. He looked at a light on his console. *Maybe the command didn't get to the bird.*

Just then, the command went in and he saw the engine's thrust drop to zero. Not that anybody needed to confirm it for him, but Bob Nance was on the loop from the SSR.

Bob, we quit burning! What's going on? The engine ain't burning!

The FIDO on duty was no help either.

We're not seeing velocity accumulating here. I don't know what's going on. It doesn't look like we're burning.

Gene Kranz was the flight director.

Bob?

Carlton laid his head on his console, his hands on the back of his neck in a sign of complete surrender. He had blown it.

And then there was the time . . .

Carlton was brimming with confidence in his LM control group as the momentous flight of *Apollo 11* approached. He just knew that his section was the best trained, most capable, most competent, most knowledgeable team of people who ever stepped foot in the control center, and so he actually asked the sim team to put them to the test.

Go ahead. Throw it at them. Let us see how good you are. We can handle anything you've got.

Rather than spread the problems out among his team, the issues were instead focused on its boss a few weeks after his bold statement. The legend of the Kill Carlton Sim was about to be born. It had already been a long day when out of the corner of his eye, Carlton noticed Clifford E. "Cliff" Charlesworth drift over to the flight director's console, then Glynn Lunney too, and they gathered around Gene Kranz. Dick Thorson entered and nonchalantly plopped down right next to Carlton. Although he did not know it, something was up. When Carlton asked if he could get rookie control officer Larry Strimple some seat time at the console, Kranz demurred. "I thought, 'Well, crap,'" Carlton said.

The lunar descent simulation began, and seconds before *Eagle* appeared from the lunar far side, telemetry mistakenly showed up on Carlton's monitor. That gave him a small head start on the problems that were about to come hurtling his way. Thorson was evidently in on the ruse, and remarked that his MOCR neighbor was one lucky son of a gun who could walk through a barnyard and still wind up "smelling like clover." After that, a thruster failed. Then another, and another. It was one long string of issues. "I had a *good* SSR team," Carlton said. "I mean, they were sharp, and as fast as the problems came, we figured out what to do. We handled every single warning. Nothing fazed us, and we landed." As well as the situation had been handled, Carlton was nevertheless worn to a frazzle, his shirt soaked with sweat. It had been the most intense sim of his career, and as he walked out, Charlesworth caught his attention. "He said, 'Bob, I don't think there's anything I'll ever doubt you about again,'" Carlton remembered. Not until he had a chance to mull things over did Carlton realize that he had nearly been had.

Hal Miller never sat a console in the MOCR during a spaceflight, but he had nevertheless been a vital part of making it all happen. "The guys in simulations got great pleasure and tremendous satisfaction by seeing those flight controllers handle real problems," he said. "That was a great source of pride. The sim guys felt as much pride in that as the controllers did in actually flying the mission."

Incredibly, though, Gene Kranz estimated that controllers spent less than 20 percent of their time in pad tests, sims, and actual missions. The majority of their time was spent in developing materials that they and the crew would use to conduct the flights, and the material was entirely homegrown. Nobody did it for them. Spacecraft manufacturers provided raw data such as design schematics, test results, program listings, and so forth. The flight controllers then consolidated the information and turned it into integrated schematics as well as normal, emergency, and malfunction procedures.

Expanding the support network even more were the Spacecraft Analysis (SPAN) and Mission Evaluation Rooms (MER), not to mention the Real-

Time Computer Complex (RTCC) down on the first floor that powered the whole operation. SPAN was located right across the hall, and it was there where various branch chiefs took on the role of liaison between the MOCR and contractors responsible for building the spacecraft and its myriad of components. "The SPAN room played a very important role in the Apollo program," said Arnie Aldrich, branch chief over the CSM's systems. "That's where the senior leaders of North American and Grumman [builders of the CSM and LM, respectively] came for the missions. They weren't able to engage the attention of the people operating the flight, but Jim Hannigan and I and the people that did that job on the other shifts were the interface between not only North American and Grumman, but also the NASA engineering organization in this thing they called the Mission Evaluation Room. All those people were needed by the flight control teams so they could ask questions about anything that came up."

Some who moved to the SPAN room missed being front and center in the MOCR. They saw the control room as something of a battlefield, while SPAN meant heading to the rear with the gear. Former front-room flight controllers heard their replacements doing things differently than they would have, and even though they might now be in charge of the section, not a lot could be done about it during a mission. The majority, though, saw working in the SPAN room for what it was—when flight controllers moved there, it generally meant that their careers were advancing up the management chain.

There was a part of Charley Parker that longed for the action of the front room, but he was proud of the guidance underlings who came after him. Steve Bales . . . Ken Russell . . . guys like that were his prodigies. When *Apollo 11* landed on the moon, Parker had turned thirty-five years old just five days before. He was an *old* man by MOCR standards, so he thought it was time once and for all to turn the console over to his guys. That was not to say that he took it easy on them. He prodded them with a lot of questions, playing devil's advocate as much as he possibly could. Parker was the original guidance officer, and now, he was the original guidance mentor. "I have always enjoyed and appreciated teaching," he said. "I guess I would've been a teacher if I hadn't been an engineer. The guidance group was just a fantastic group. To see them come along, to see them mature, I really liked it."

The MER was basically one big room located in Building 45, next to the MCC. It was one more safety net, one more area of expertise upon which to draw in the event of an anomaly. It was the domain of Donald D. Arabian, the MER manager. "If everything did what it was supposed to do, you said, 'Okay, everything's fine. A-okay,'" Arabian explained. "If something wasn't right, then you had to determine what that meant, whether something had to be fixed or it was okay, just didn't understand the design, or whatever, but it had to be assessed."

The Mission Evaluation Room's role was to do just that, evaluate the spacecraft designs, what went right, what went wrong, and if something went wrong, what could be done about it. "It was the designers evaluating the system," Arabian added. "As a result, when something happened, they were the ones that come up with what to do."

Close to the MOCR was the Recovery Operations Control Room (ROCR) staffed by members of MSC's Landing and Recovery Division (LRD). This support room kept track of the dedicated recovery forces scattered around the world on ships and at aircraft staging bases. Within LRD were two distinct groups. One took care of planning and executing recovery operations, while the other developed and tested recovery hardware and procedures.

Each area had somewhat of a Trench attitude toward the other, so much so that each thought the other "just a bunch of turkeys." Taken as a whole, however, their motto was a Trench motto if ever there was one.

Lord, it's hard to be humble when you've been a part of LRD.

The people who worked in the third-floor control room during Gemini, Apollo, and the early years of the Space Shuttle were among the best and brightest of their generations. Together, they accomplished marvelous things. "The attitude and the drive was pretty much consistent across all of us," Dave Reed said. "We just went at it. Nobody said we couldn't do it or that this was tough. We knew we had a job to do, and we would just go at it. There were no pep sessions required to fire these kids up. No. It didn't happen. It was balls to the wall, get it done as quickly as you can, and move on."

2. Tampa, Tranquility Base Here . . .

On 25 May 1961, President John F. Kennedy stood before a joint session of Congress and uttered the thirty-one most important words in NASA's history.

First, I believe this nation should commit itself to achieving the goal, before this decade is out, of landing a man on the moon and returning him safely to the earth.

No single sentence ever moved the agency further and faster. There was no fuzz on the mandate, no chance of misunderstanding its meaning. The goal of going to the moon was clear and concise, with a firm deadline front and center. Kennedy had just told NASA *where* to go and *when* to get there, but there was a catch—there was no mention of *how* it was going to get done. That was the biggest challenge of all, and for somebody else to figure out.

There would most likely have to be some sort of rendezvous involved, or maybe it would just be a direct shot to the moon. Rendezvous might take place either in Earth orbit or around the moon. Important pieces of the technological puzzle that nobody yet realized were needed were far from being invented. The sum total of the nation's experience in human space-flight was a single fifteen-minute suborbital hop by Alan Shepard flown just twenty days before, leaving it woefully behind the Soviet Union in the Cold War space race.

None of that seemed to matter to the influx of NASA hires heading to Houston, who seemed to share one trait in particular. They did not know that it could not be done.

For a time, nobody knew *where* it would be done, either. Houston had almost always been a candidate for the Manned Spacecraft Center, but not necessarily the favorite once NASA officials decided once and for all in early 1961—before an American had ever actually flown in space—that the Space Task Group (STG) would not remain headquartered at Langley Research

Center in Virginia. There were plenty of other possibilities, and given the momentous events and iconic lines that were to come, what might have been can seem something just short of sacrilegious.

Try this one on for size.

Tampa, Tranquility Base here . . .

Or maybe this one.

Bogalusa, we've had a problem . . .

So why Houston?

STG had been attached to Goddard Space Flight Center in Greenbelt, Maryland, and that appeared at one time to at least be in the running for its permanent base. It was a bad political move for STG, leaving its head Robert R. "Bob" Gilruth reporting to Goddard center director Harry J. Goett rather than directly to NASA headquarters in Washington. It was not long before the concept for a separate $60 million complex that would employ an initial estimate of three thousand people came into being.

Even then, the location of a permanent MOCR remained in doubt. Would it stay at the Cape, closest to where the country's crewed spaceflight missions would begin? Surely, that would be the best bet. Goddard, maybe? That was where NASA's earliest computers were located, plus it was a bonus—to some, at least—that it was located so close to the bosses down in DC. Or, finally, should the MOCR go where the rest of STG went and keep everybody in one place? However, there might have been another factor at play—good ol'-fashioned hardball politics—when Chris Kraft made a pitch for mission control to stay put in Florida. "Chris wrote a letter to Gilruth that said essentially, 'It doesn't make any sense for us to go to Houston. We need to go to the Cape—what's more, the flight crew,'" remembered John Hodge, who took over for Kraft as chief of the Flight Operations Division a year after arriving in Houston. "And Gilruth said, 'Absolutely not. I don't care how logical it is, how much it makes sense. If I own the astronauts, I own the program. And we're going to Houston.'"

As closely as Kraft and Gilruth would work, and as powerful as Kraft was already, he was evidently overruled when it came to the location of the MOCR. Gilruth was as respected an individual as there was at NASA in those days, but he was not the sort who was going to be run over very easily. "Gilruth always comes across as, you know, a nice, quiet old man," Hodge continued. "Gilruth was not a nice, little old man. I mean, he was a real tough cookie. He was a nice tough cookie, but he played politics with the best of them. That was one example where there was absolutely no question."

The hunt was on for STG's—and mission control's—new home. To be considered, sites needed to have certain criteria in place:

Access to waterways big enough for large barges. Houston had that, of course, located on the shores of the Gulf of Mexico.

Commercial jet service. With one major airport already in town and another not far off in the future, Houston had plenty of passenger planes coming and going.

A well-established industrial complex. Houston was located in the heart of Texas oil country.

A culturally attractive community with institutes of higher education. Check.

A strong electric utility and water supply. Check again.

At least 1,000 acres of land. If there is one thing Texas had plenty of, it was land.

A moderate climate. Houston was hot and humid in the summer and prone to hurricanes that came in from the Gulf of Mexico, so if there was a mark against the area to be found, its weather might very well have been it. Other than that, Houston fit the bill almost perfectly.

The proposals that inundated Congress were at first whittled down to nine locations—Houston; Jacksonville, Florida; Tampa, Florida; Baton Rouge, Louisiana; Shreveport, Louisiana; Victoria, Texas; Corpus Christi, Texas; San Diego, California; and San Francisco, California. With the addition of four other possibilities near St. Louis, Missouri; two more in Houston; Bogalusa, Louisiana; Liberty, Texas; Beaumont, Texas; Harlington, Texas; Berkeley, California; Richmond, California; and Moffett Field, California, a NASA selection team had plenty of sites from which to choose. Each was visited between 21 August and 7 September 1961, and the front-runners soon became MacDill Air Force Base in Tampa, Florida, followed by the site donated by Rice University in Clear Lake, in southeast Houston. The Benicia Ordnance Base near San Francisco was third.

That all changed when the air force opted to keep the doors open at MacDill. Houston moved to the top of the list, and there were plenty of high-level and powerful Texas politicians turning up the heat to bring the center to their state, including Lyndon B. Johnson, vice president of the

United States and chairman of the Committee on Aeronautical and Space Sciences; Albert R. Thomas, chairman of the House Appropriations Committee, who had lobbied for a NASA "laboratory" in Houston as far back as October 1958; Robert R. "Bob" Casey and Olin E. Teague of the House Committee on Science and Astronautics; and Speaker of the House Samuel T. "Sam" Rayburn. On 19 September 1961, a thousand-acre plot just south of the city donated by Rice University was officially announced to the public as the site of NASA's new Manned Spaceflight Center.

The decision was met with indifference, if not an outright coolness, by some in the Space Task Group. Some were understandably hesitant to leave their homes in Virginia, but others were left in stunned amazement by the aftermath of Hurricane Carla. A category 4 storm when it struck with winds of 145 miles per hour on 11 September 1961, just eight days before the announcement, Carla left forty-three fatalities and more than $325 million in damages in its wake. "There were boats in the trees and snakes," remembered Arnie Aldrich, who briefly considered staying at Langley. "The hurricane didn't just hit Houston. It hit Clear Lake. It hit the very area where the Johnson Space Center is located. It was interesting in *Life* magazine to see that."

Another 620 acres adjacent to the property was soon acquired, and construction on underground utilities and roadways began in earnest in March 1962. The area where MSC would be located was home to a cattle ranch, a simple two-lane paved road leading into and out of the area that would one day become NASA Road One, maybe an oil rig or windmill here and there, and not much else. One reporter showed up at the site and promptly came across a coyote hunter. Picture every deserted setting from every Western B-movie ever made, complete with tumbleweeds blowing across the screen and a lonely dirge for background music, and that was pretty much the original setting for MSC. One of the first things Jerry Bostick did when he hit town was to drive down and check out where he and his family would be living. He came away with the distinct feeling that it was out in the middle of the boondocks, and if the truth be known, that is exactly where it was.

This was where NASA was going to base its manned spaceflight program?

The Bosticks' house was one of the first in Nassau Bay, a subdivision located across the road from the center and just one of several communities that sprang up in the area. Within months of the formal announce-

ment, Gene Kranz dispatched Dutch von Ehrenfried to Houston to scout
the area's real estate situation. Housing had to be adequate but relatively
inexpensive, with down payments no more than $250. He wound up report-
ing back to Kranz that three-bedroom houses could be had for $16,500.
"Dutch did not own a home in Virginia and was as eager as any of us to
get his family resettled," Kranz wrote in his autobiography. "He did well
as a real estate scout." Ten families eventually moved into houses picked
out by von Ehrenfried in an area that came to be known as Flight Controller Alley. The development was a few miles north of MSC, and von Ehrenfried borrowed $250 for his down payment on a corner lot. With a salary
of nearly $7,000 a year, he thought he could swing it.

Glynn Lunney had not been wowed by his time in Virginia, so he was
not tied to the area. If NASA needed him to move to Houston, Texas,
that was fine by him. "There are all these clichés about the Texans, but
they really were gregarious, outgoing, and so happy that we were here,"
Lunney said. "The people in Houston just turned out and were very, very
helpful. They gave all the help that they could to our people for settling
in here and doing things for them, putting priority on roads or whatever they had to do." It was that kind of attitude that most impressed
Lunney. "They're a very can-do people," he continued. "They tend not
to sit around and wait for somebody to tell them what to do, and they
get after it. They like to be independent. It was such a change from what
we'd just come out of [in Virginia], where we were sort of tolerated as
opposed to embraced."

A huge Fourth of July barbeque welcomed NASA to Houston in 1962,
with a sixty-car parade taking dignitaries from the Sam Houston Coliseum
and back again. A little more than two months later, an even grander NASA
welcome took place when 25,000 people greeted President Kennedy at the
airport on 11 September. A day later, 200,000 lined city streets as the man
who had set the nation on its path to the moon made his way to Rice Sta-
dium. The speech Kennedy gave that afternoon in the baking Texas heat
was iconic, ranking right up there with the one before Congress more than
a year earlier.

*Why, some say, the moon? Why choose this as our goal? And they may well
ask why climb the highest mountain? Why, thirty-five years ago, fly the Atlantic? Why does Rice play Texas?*

It was then that Kennedy really lowered the boom, as he was interrupted by applause.

We choose to go to the moon. We choose to go to the moon. We choose to go to the moon in this decade and do the other things, not because they are easy, but because they are hard.

Future flight controllers and other MSC and contractor employees continued to move into the area, one family right after another, almost faster than anybody could possibly ever count. By July 1962, there were 1,600 people working at the center, and that number had doubled just a year later. Another thousand were on site by the end of 1964. Many of the fresh, young engineers who would be manning the MOCR were straight out of such far-flung universities as Montana, Louisiana State, Texas, Texas A&M, Iowa State, Southwestern Oklahoma State, and Mississippi State, among plenty of others. In the Trench, they came to NASA at the rate of about one a month for a year and a half. Glynn Lunney liked to say they simply showed up and hired themselves, and better yet, did not sit around and wait for a job description. That, they pretty much wrote themselves. Many interviewed, if you can call it that, and were employed over the telephone having never before stepped foot in the Lone Star State.

As construction continued on MSC, temporary office space was leased at a dozen or so locations scattered throughout Houston. Gilruth hung out his shingle at the Farnsworth and Chambers Building, the center's interim headquarters, on 1 March 1962. A mile away on South Wayside Drive, just across the Gulf Freeway, was Site Five—which included the temporary base of Flight Operations and mission control, located in the 12,600-square-foot former Stahl and Myers Discount Appliance Center, while several had offices right next door in the Houston Petroleum Center.

That is where Jerry Bostick had his, and it was from there that he watched as President Kennedy's motorcade passed by on the freeway on 21 November 1963. One day later, the president was dead. "Homer Scott, an aide to Chris Kraft, came running into our room screaming, 'The President has been shot!'" Bostick remembered of that terrible day. "We listened to the radio for a while, then I went home. I had just pulled in my parking spot when I heard that the president had died."

The accommodations at the Stahl and Myers building—which not only housed Flight Control but also served as a warehouse for the Oshman's

Sporting Goods Company—were something less than posh. "We were on the second floor, and we had to climb stairs to get up to it—no elevator," Charley Parker said. "The stairs were creaky. I mean, you walked up those stairs and they creaked every step you took. The wooden floor on the second floor, it creaked. Everybody thought it was going to fall down one day, but you know, that building stood for years and years and years before it was demolished."

The best of the young guns coming on board had an innate ability to make accurate split-second decisions, while others were able to pick it up through the relentless grind of simulations and studying on their own. Some thrived in that kind of environment, and there were those who eventually decided—or had it decided for them—that being under such pressure was not their particular cup of tea and moved on. "At the time, it was a very, very rewarding thing," remembered Lunney, who not only was chief of the Flight Dynamics Branch but a flight director as well by the early mid-1960s, just as Project Gemini was gaining a full head of steam. "We brought young folks in there, and I can't give myself credit. I had another job besides running a branch, building it up, teaching a whole bunch of new people what all this trajectory, guidance, going to the moon, and rendezvous was going to be all about."

Spaceflight was obviously a new venture, which meant that everyone was learning the ropes. What NASA wound up doing in many cases was the next best thing when it came to hiring experience and laying a foundation for Flight Control. Tech reps were brought in from the Philco Corporation to build the agency's worldwide tracking network during the Mercury program, and they eventually also designed, built, and installed the MOCR's consoles in Houston. Then, when Avro Canada found its contract for the CF-105 *Arrow* canceled in February 1959, thirty-two of the company's Canadian and British engineers came south to Langley. Among them were John Hodge, the future flight director and chief of the Flight Control Division; and Tecwyn "Tec" Roberts, who served as an original FIDO before becoming a force behind the design of the MOCR in Houston.

It was that kind of knowledge base upon which much of the rest of the control team was built. Lunney had worked his first flight as a FIDO under Roberts on 20 February 1962, for John H. Glenn Jr.'s famed three-orbit journey. He soloed at the Cape console for M. Scott Carpenter's 24 May 1962 flight, and then took Cliff Charlesworth under his wing for L. Gordon Cooper Jr.'s May 1963 Project Mercury finale. John Llewellyn and Jerry Bostick were gaining steam on console too, and together they all stretched the newer guys, throwing them into the deep end of the pool to sink or swim, and then some.

Okay, you're now in charge of flying the Apollo launch phase out of Houston's new control center. Go figure out rendezvous, guided reentries, and retrofire calculations.

Hired in droves, fresh-faced rookies became grizzled veterans who were making life-or-death decisions on console in the span of a year, eighteen months, max. "It was a wonderful time, a really wonderful time," Lunney continued. "It was a very great pleasure to see how rapidly these young people just jumped in and learned what they had to learn. They were very, very aggressive and hard-working guys."

They were aggressive and hard-working, yes, but what some also wanted was a piece of the action in this grand adventure of space travel. Steve Bales had been incredulous when the Soviet Union launched Sputnik on 4 October 1957, and that, combined with a Walt Disney–produced television program on the future of human spaceflight changed the course of his life. He landed a gig as a summer intern at MSC from June to August of 1964, giving tours. The place was so new, not a single console had yet been placed in the MOCR when he first walked in. To better acquaint people with what would be taking place in the room, Bales learned the responsibilities of each console by chatting with the controllers who would work them. It was a great way to get the information he needed—and to get his foot in the door as a potential operator himself. He met Lunney, the Flight Dynamics Branch chief; Gene Kranz, who headed up the Flight Control Operations Branch; and Arnie Aldrich, chief of the Gemini systems branch. "You talk about falling into a tub of butter," Bales quipped. "I found out (a) I would like to work there, I thought, and (b) I could pick the branch I wanted to work in. They were staffing up like crazy, and when I applied, they knew at least who I was."

Bales needed a few credits in the fall quarter at Iowa State, and it was during that quarter that he applied to work at NASA full time. His application came complete with a reference from Lunney, and in December 1964 he was hired. Bales had at least a few things going for him at that point.

He came in at the end of preparation for the Gemini program, so he had the chance to sit in a room with a mix of guidance and flight dynamics officers, listen to them talk, and soak it all in. The team had been working on a procedures manual that was not exactly high level with a lot of details, but it at least gave him an idea of where to start. And after only about a month, he could watch sims from a back room. In the beginning, he hardly knew what anyone was talking about, but with plenty of ojt—on-the-job training—he was ready to move onto the guidance console for the June 1966 flight of *Gemini 9*.

The main responsibilities of Gemini's guidance computer came during ascent, rendezvous, and reentry, and there was not much to do otherwise unless there was an emergency. "I had been in the back room and then I had plugged in next to Charley Parker," Bales said. "Charley hardly ever made a mistake, but some of the younger guys who were learning, I'd say, 'Boy, I could have done that a little better.' That's what you think. You might have done one little thing better, but they were doing four and five things at once."

Bales had talked himself into a sense of confidence, but when it came his turn in the hot seat during training for an actual mission, he knew with an almost guaranteed certainty that something bad was going to happen. "You talked yourself into, 'I can do this,'" he added. "But the first time you sit down and it's *you*, and you've got to talk to the flight director; you've got to talk to the computer room; you've got to talk to the flight dynamics officer; your first thought is, 'What am I supposed to do? What the heck do I do next?' It's really hard to get things to slow down. Things just seem to be coming at you real fast." If Bales did not perform, he felt that he would either go back to the end of the line or get out of the line altogether.

Bales was maybe two months ahead of Maurice Kennedy, who had already accepted another job offer in West Palm Beach, Florida. He and wife Trudy were almost literally headed out the door of their married student housing at the University of Texas in Austin for good when the phone rang, and as he went to answer, his first response was one of frustration with his wife because he thought she had already had the phone turned off. Luckily for him, though, she had not. The call was from the personnel office at NASA, asking him to come to Houston for a series of interviews. The first was with Lunney, and afterward, Kennedy immediately asked that the others be canceled. Kennedy, who like several of his soon-to-be MOCR coworkers had built homemade rockets in his youth, had found a home in the Flight Dynamics Branch.

Like Bales, J. Gary Renick had been struck by the launch of *Sputnik* and knew that he wanted to somehow, some way, work in a space program that did not exist back then. When he arrived in Houston in January 1965 to begin a NASA career that eventually led him to the guidance console, he did so at a salary of less than $7,000 a year. It was his dream in life at that point to someday make the unimaginable, astronomical sum of $10,000 a year. If only he could reach that golden ring, he would have it made.

The Trench was getting full, and so was the rest of the room. Still, as many new hires as seemed to be flooding into the place, Arnie Aldrich never figured that there were too many. He needed as many people as he could get for the Gemini Systems Branch set up on the right-hand half of the second row. "We had a blend of people, and they all came in fast," Aldrich remembered. "They would show up. I wasn't out interviewing. I was too busy doing the things we were doing, and we got a very capable, competent group. They all worked well together. We built a fairly large team quite rapidly and supported a lot of flights in a fairly short period of time over those first few years."

Kranz had the task of hiring for the remote sites scattered all over the world, and the controllers would then filter into the MOCR itself. Experience during the Mercury era provided a starting point for remote-site controllers, whether they happened to be in the John Llewellyn or Chuck Lewis mold. "Basically, we could pretty much characterize the personalities," Kranz said. "If the personalities were matched up with a good skill set, then we said, 'Yeah, this is probably a pretty good guy.'"

A psychologist chimed in and told Kranz that what he was looking for was someone who wanted to *do* something rather than someone who wanted to *be* something—in other words, Kranz needed to steer clear of those who were driven by their egos. While other NASA centers concentrated on recruiting new hires in other parts of the country, Kranz had the Midwest. "Basically, I got farm boys, first in the family ever to go to college, so they had a hell of a work ethic," he recalled. "If you take a look at mission control, there were very few people who came in from MIT or Stanford. Basically, we found out that the people at MIT, Stanford, and those kinds of schools were absolutely brilliant, but they weren't great team players. Basically, the people we got were maybe not quite as brilliant, but they were *great* team players and they would work together to solve a problem."

Like the Trench, the systems branch was getting its fair share of quality applicants as well. After getting his degree from Lamar University in Texas in January 1960, Rod Loe and his new bride, Tina, packed up and moved to Seattle. There he went to work for Boeing's engineering development program and eventually pitched in on the company's proposal for the Lunar Module. A transfer meant moving to New Orleans and the Michoud Assembly Facility, home to Boeing's s-ic first stage, in the midst of the October 1962 Cuban Missile Crisis. There was a small problem when he and his expecting wife arrived in Louisiana—nobody was needed in the engineering development program, and there was a long way to go before hardware was going to be ready for testing. Instead, he went to work for what amounted to customer service, writing manuals for the s-ic's ground support equipment. He was not a happy camper.

At Christmas that year, Loe was at home in Beaumont, Texas, when he ran into a friend who worked at NASA. "I remember thinking, 'He's not any smarter than I am,'" Loe said. "I had lost my mom and my dad was living in Beaumont. I was an only child, so he was by himself. This was a good opportunity to get closer to home."

Years later, Loe would jokingly accuse Kranz of putting on a show for him once he arrived in Houston for his interview. The scene is not hard to imagine, given the near chaos of the time. Kranz, standing in front of a blackboard with all kinds of names headed to all kinds of exotic locations around the world, was barking orders into the phone when he motioned for Loe to enter. Somebody was stuck in New York needed a passport, and he needed it *pronto*. Loe was sold, then and there. "That really impressed the heck out of me," admitted Loe, the soon-to-be EECOM. "To think I might be a flight controller looking at these spacecraft that we were working on, that seemed like the ultimate test to me. I said, 'Yeah, I think I'd sure like to come over here.'"

He took the job, thinking he might stay for a couple of years for the experience, and then depending on how his dad was doing, move on to go see some more of the country. He had seen Seattle and New Orleans, and he was on his way to being settled in Houston. Might somewhere in New England be next?

Half a century later, New England was still waiting on Rod Loe to arrive.

John Aaron, another up-and-coming EECOM, very nearly left NASA early in his career. But once he started to get his feet under him, a handful of mentors were instrumental in continuing that growth process. They saw something in Aaron, a quality that would one day fully blossom. They took him under his wing, and he was not alone. There were plenty of new guys on the block being taken under plenty of wings. That is the way it worked in those days. "I think they recognized my potential, and it just grew from there," Aaron said. "Then, I had some real mission experiences being a controller in the Gemini program. I worked all the Gemini flights and made a contribution. The mentors took me under their wing. If it hadn't been for that, I probably would've gotten discouraged and went back to pursue my dream to be a cattle rancher."

One of Aaron's mentors was James F. "Jim" Moser, one of the Philco tech reps who helped him out during an early Gemini simulation at the Kauai tracking station in Hawaii. Moser showed Aaron the ins and outs of the spacecraft, and its communications systems in particular. As always, Aaron was like a sponge. Moser went back to Houston, and, according to Aaron, "had some good words to say about me. That really started the process of being recognized by Gene Kranz, Chris Kraft, and so forth. They took an interest in me and then started mentoring me in all aspects of NASA."

Arnie Aldrich was also there for Aaron early on, beginning what would become a close lifelong friendship. Aaron had never before written a memo when he joined NASA, and when the rookie attempted one on his own, Aldrich was not impressed with the results. The draft was thick with one redline correction after another, so much so that very few phrases remained unchanged. What separated Aldrich was the fact that he did not just hand it back to Aaron and expect him to start from scratch again. The two of them sat down for what Aaron called a two-hour crash course in Technical Memo Writing 101—how to introduce it, how to get the message across, how to get the request, and how to sign it all off.

A friendship might have seemed unlikely between Aldrich, a native of the Boston area, and Aaron, the midwestern country boy. Yet that is exactly what happened. Their children were about the same age, and their families enjoyed many a camping and fishing trip together. "The first time we went camping, I caught fish, fried fish, and made a big pot of beans with jalapenos in it, he fell in love with pinto beans," Aaron recalled with a laugh. "He taught me many things. I don't know that I taught him a whole lot, but I did teach him how to make pinto beans."

Learning how to write a technical memo versus cooking a pot of pinto beans? It was a good trade. "I've been blessed that I have what I would call some very close, *real* friends in my life," Aaron concluded, turning serious. "It's not a long list, but Arnie Aldrich is on it."

Aaron was also forevermore linked with Gerry Griffin in NASA legend for their roles during the launch of *Apollo 12* on 14 November 1969. First, though, they had to get up to speed in their respective roles.

Griffin was commissioned in the air force once he graduated from Texas A&M, but too many pilots and the tight screening process that resulted caused his 20/25 vision to prevent him from being a pilot. He did the next best thing by going to navigator school. Griffin got his wings, underwent radar intercept training, and wound up flying backseat in both the F-89J Scorpion and F-101B Voodoo. When Griffin got out of the military in 1960, he landed first at Lockheed. Classified satellites were already being launched out of Vandenburg Air Force Base, and while almost as many went into the drink as made it to orbit, Griffin nevertheless became an expert on the company's Agena rocket upper stage. He interviewed with Kranz as early as 1962, but when the two could not get together on money, Griffin headed to General Dynamics/Fort Worth to be a part of the company's fledgling initiative to get into the space business.

Griffin's move was a ploy of sorts. Yes, it was a job, but Fort Worth was also closer to Houston—and a space program that was already in existence. Two years later, Mel Brooks heard about Griffin's Agena expertise and reached out to him. He wanted to work at NASA so badly, he took a small pay cut to do just that. Only a month or so after arriving in Houston and some very basic work as an Agena controller, Griffin was asked by Arnie Aldrich to serve as a GNC.

If working as a GNC meant working at NASA and in mission control, that was absolutely fine with Gerry Griffin.

The native Texan was a little bit older and had experience in a control room—albeit it had been for an unmanned vehicle—during his stint at General Dynamics. Although he had never had any courses in orbital mechanics, space systems, or anything of the sort, he took to the GNC assignment with gusto. Being a flight controller in the MOCR was like being in the backseat of a jet fighter in the air force. The technical background had to be there, and so did a couple of other very important factors—confidence and not being afraid to make decisions. "Quite often, you were exposed. There was nobody else there to answer for you," Griffin began. "Being a flight controller was not for everybody. The people who left the control center, went to the back room, or went to another job, they usually eliminated themselves. It was a lot of pressure."

Griffin was not all that much different from the astronauts whose flights he helped oversee. The possibility of making a critical mistake in front of his peers was an all-encompassing driving force for Griffin to keep learning and improving. "Fighter pilots are very much the same. They don't want to ever have it said that they didn't do something right," Griffin continued. "The big fear of the astronauts and flight controllers was that they didn't want to screw up. You didn't want something to happen bad that you caused. We worked long, hard hours. We took hours to understand the systems we were responsible for and how they worked. We went over test data. We went over all kinds of test procedures. It was constant. You just didn't want to make a mistake."

What separated Griffin from those who did not make it in the MOCR was this—he *loved* being in such a predicament, so much so that he eventually became a general aviation pilot with a commercial license and instrument rated on single- and multi-engine aircraft and helicopters. Pressure? What did Gerry Griffin know about pressure? He ate up that kind of stuff. "I still like those kinds of positions where I have to be out front," said Griffin, who was named as a flight director in 1967. "I don't mean that in a boastful way. I still fly my own airplanes. It's kind of the same thing. You've got to make decisions. You've got to make things happen. You're in control, instead of somebody else. Something starts to happen, and it happens in a hurry that you didn't expect. You've got to be able to roll with the punches."

By late January 1963, work on the foundation of Building 30—what was then called the Integrated Mission Control Center (IMCC)—had begun. Plans called for the three-story building to accommodate 805 people and have a total of 245,000 square feet of enclosed floor space, including two nearly identical MOCRs on the second and third floors that measured approximately 4,315 square feet each. Construction costs amounted to $6,940,939. Two months later, a NASA press release announced that a contract had been signed "definitizing" the Philco Corporation's role in fitting the building with its consoles. "Philco will provide the 'pulse' of the IMCC—all the complicated internal electronic flight information and control display equipment," continued the release. It also noted that the contract amounted to a whopping $33,797,565, including a fixed fee, as well as the fact that the first-floor Real-Time Computer Complex would be outfitted by IBM.

What the controllers were getting was an extraordinary leap in capability from the Mercury Control Center. The Cape's facility was as state-of-the-art as state-of-the-art could get when it was constructed, and it worked well during flights—and maybe that was the truly extraordinary aspect of what had been accomplished, given what controllers had to work with. When John Glenn became the first American to orbit Earth during the legendary flight of *Friendship 7* on 20 February 1962, Dutch von Ehrenfriend spent most of the day hustling back and forth between his console at the Cape and a teletype room to send messages to remote sites monitoring issues that plagued the mission. The messages would be written out by hand and taken back to Robbie Robertson, who staffed the teletype room and tapped out the messages. A reply from the other end was just as laborious, and the whole process took minutes to complete. Voice communications, when and where they were available, were often spotty.

Neil Hutchinson went to work for NASA in 1962, just in time to visit the control center at the Cape a couple of times during simulations. To him, tracking a spacecraft in orbit and doing so on a flat map seemed almost like science fiction.

Star Trek never had it so good.

Given the ingenious complexities involved, the group display at the front of the room was something of a Rube Goldberg machine. On the display was a backlit flat map of the world, with expected trajectories drawn pre-mission. The flight's progress was tracked from the left of the map to the right by a miniature spacecraft with a small light bulb at its center, suspended by four wires to move it up, down, right, and left. The light bulb flickered on every time the spacecraft came in contact with a remote site,

5. Although Mercury Control Center was state of the art for its time, it was a far cry from the rooms that would be built in Houston. Courtesy NASA.

but what happened when the plastic spacecraft reached the right edge of the map was the kicker. "So how do you get the spacecraft from one side to the other?" Hutchinson asked. "Well, you run all the servos at full blast, the spacecraft jumps up to the top of the world map, zips back to the left, drops back down to the proper place on the map on the ground track, and it makes a big noise when it does that. It goes zing! Zing! Zing! Zing! And it's back on the other side." His reaction to the whole thing was simple. "I was *awed* by the crudeness of that device," Hutchinson admitted. "I'm sure there were people who were so proud of that thing, that they figured out a way to put a ground track on a flat map and move a spacecraft along."

Compare that to Houston's sparkling new group display, which featured one of the world's first rear-projection systems. If there was a most obvious difference between the two control rooms, that was probably it. A very close second would have been the advent of consoles in Houston that featured digital data displays, as opposed to the Mercury era's analog gauges and dials. The original consoles had room for maybe fifteen to twenty measurements at the most, while the digital possibilities were virtu-ally endless. The RTCC's computers could take a signal from the computer that was new to the Gemini spacecraft, do a few calculations, and turn it into a raw number that measured, for instance, how much fuel remained in either percentage or pounds. A handful of mechanical measurements gave way to hundreds of digital ones, which led to a huge effort to deter-mine such things as what information everyone needed to see versus the requirements of an individual position.

Everyone needed to know Ground Elapsed Time, but FIDO did not nec-essarily care how much propellant remained in the control officer's Lunar Module thrusters. "The difference was night and day," Bob Carlton said. "When I saw this computerized thing and the ability to put your sche-matic on the display, *man*, that was fantastic! I was exuberant. I jumped on board that in a hurry. The beauty of it was, you could have a tremen-dous amount of data where you could see almost every parameter you had on your schematic. When you're troubleshooting a problem, having it laid out like that is a terrific tool."

Others were not quite so quick to accept the change, and went so far as to have computers draw digital meters on their screens before finally mak-ing the switch to all digital data, all the time. "To a great extent, many of the early people that we had in Mercury had very little background or expe-rience in working with computers," Gene Kranz said. "To a great extent, we were technical dinosaurs. Young folks like John Aaron, Phil Shaffer, and Don Puddy, that generation came in with a background with that type technology."

Gone also were the days when von Ehrenfried was forced to trot here and there with messages. Now in place was yard after yard of pneumatic tubes that could zip canisters to and from the MOCR. The dispatches were *always* of the utmost importance—or not. "People would start putting all kinds of crap in there, not just messages," von Ehrenfried said. "They would put a hot dog in there or a sandwich. We started getting things clogged up, so they said to knock that shit off."

What it all amounted to was this. The MOCR was based very much on the Mercury Control Center at the Cape, with the same basic layout, only expanded. Jerry Bostick thought he had died and gone to Heaven. "The capacity of the computers when we moved to Houston was several times larger," he began. "We had a lot more displays, and they were closer to real time than they were at the Cape. The room itself was probably twice as big." It was a far, far cry from the primitive flight-monitoring trailers—the never-used predecessor to the control centers in both Florida and Texas—that Arnie Aldrich had worked on when he first arrived at NASA. So rudimentary was the task that Aldrich's father, Mark, once asked him when he was going to get a real job.

On 20 February 1964, 280 employees began the process of moving into the MSC's new facilities, and five months later, during the weekend of 6 and 7 June, nearly 80,000 people attended an open house. The relocation from Virginia to Texas had cost the program time, as construction, hiring, and training continued at a lightning pace in Houston. More than a year had passed since Gordon Cooper's Mercury finale, and Gemini would not begin for another nine and a half months.

Plenty of potential controllers had been hired to staff a control center that was ready to roll, and in September 1964, Glynn Lunney and Gene Kranz became flight directors in order to help Chris Kraft and John Hodge oversee it all. The two men joined the fledgling Space Task Group at roughly the same time—Lunney in 1959, Kranz the following year—and a healthy sense of competition developed between them as they became legends at the flight director's console over the next several years.

Members of the Trench tended to gravitate to Lunney because he was one of them, while on the other hand, Kranz was admittedly more attuned to the world of the systems controllers. What developed was *not* necessarily Team Kranz versus Team Lunney—the last thing either of them wanted or needed on their hands was a mission control divided. Kranz called their rivalry friendly but intense, very much the way he had competed for one of two available spots in Fighter Weapons School after graduating from flight training in the air force. "Glynn was *the smartest guy I ever knew*," Kranz said, emphasizing every word. "He was probably the smartest guy who ever worked in mission control. He had an intuitive feel for the job. I think it was an acknowledged competition, but basically, good people compete for jobs. If you don't get it this time, you're going to get it next time. I think the beauty of the thing was that if I was going to launch somebody and got that job, he knew he'd get a launch the next time."

Who might get to lead this or that flight? What about the high-activity phases, like launch or maybe somewhere down the road, a lunar landing? Kranz and Lunney both wanted as much of those kinds of things on their plates as possible, just the way every subsequent flight director did. "The competitive part was only at the very start of the program, because by the time we got into the program, we were so damn busy that we were just glad somebody else was going to pick it up for the next mission," Kranz concluded. "I just respected Glynn because he was so damn smart. He didn't have to run around with three notebooks under his arm all the time."

The 23 March 1965 flight of *Gemini 3* with astronauts Gus Grissom and John W. Young on board was the first manned launch of the program, and it was to be the final mission controlled from the Cape. Controllers in the MOCR on the third floor of the MCC in Houston monitored data and communications. One flight later, the roles would reverse—the third-floor MOCR was prime, the Cape backup. From that point on, through the end of Apollo's epic lunar landings, flights were controlled almost exclusively from the third floor. The only exceptions were three unmanned Saturn IB tests, one unmanned Saturn V shakedown, and *Apollo 7*, all of which were flown out of the MOCR one floor down. Otherwise, it was used for simulations. Why were so many flights flown out of the third-floor control room, leading it to be listed on the National Register of Historic Places, rather than the one on the second? They were, after all, essentially one and the same. Had there been some reason, or had it just worked out that way by chance?

No one seemed to know, except for Kranz.

"The third floor was used for two reasons," he began. "That's where the simulation control area was, and that's where the recovery room was. As a result of that, if you wanted to talk to the sim supervisor, you could walk right out of the room, talk to the sim supervisor, and get back. That facilitated the debriefings. The simulation team could look right out the window at us, see who they wanted to talk to, and call them up. We could walk over to the recovery room and do the same thing. It was generally the location of the three major facilities in one floor."

There you have it.

As advanced as the new Houston MOCR was, spacecraft tracking had not yet caught up with the technological tide. Because of that, a number of tracking stations located around the world were either held over or added since the days of Mercury. Primary sites that gave direct commands to the spacecraft included:

Bermuda, which confirmed orbits and recommended go/no go decisions;

The Cape, from which missions, of course, were launched;

Carnarvon, in northwestern Australia;

USNS *Coastal Sentry*, originally a CI-M-AVI class freighter ship and known in NASA circles as *Coastal Sentry* Quebec—every other tracking station had a three-letter call sign, so the two ships in use had to, as well;

Corpus Christi, located at Rodd Field in Texas;

Grand Canary, located 120 miles off the coast of Africa and 28 miles north of the equator, a critical location had an abort been commanded by Bermuda;

Guaymas, on the Gulf of California in Mexico;

Kauai, the northernmost major island in Hawaii;

Point Arguello, forty miles north of Santa Barbara, California;

Tananarive, located in the Malagasy Republic off the coast of southeast Africa;

USNS *Rose Knot*, known to its NASA inhabitants as *Rose Knot* Victor—if the ships had to use three-letter call signs, nobody seemed quite sure where the "Quebec" and "Victor" came from in *Coastal Sentry* Quebec and *Rose Knot* Victor;

and, of course, the control center in Houston.

It was at best a challenging proposition to coordinate control of a flight between the MOCR in Houston, tracking sites scattered to the four corners of the earth, and a spacecraft whizzing by overhead at a rate of some five miles per second. Windows of opportunity lasted maybe three to five minutes while the capsule was in range, and a lot had to get done in a short amount of time. Timelines were drawn up pre-mission, planning for what could be done and when—an orbit could be updated here, retrofire there. If there were any funnies to check out, a systems controller might ask for a reading on such and such a gauge. "It was very time constraining," said Jerry Bostick, who remained in Houston throughout the Gemini and Apollo programs. "We didn't have any training in this. We just knew that we had a limited amount of time to convey information. So we tried to be as precise and clear as we could, to shorten any questions, any updates or anything."

Overall control of a flight was still exercised out of Houston, but there were mission rules in place that took into account life-threatening emergencies. The capcom, who was in charge at the tracking station, could make just such an emergency call without running it by Houston. "But that was very, very rare," Bostick added. "Otherwise, everything would be run by the flight director back in Houston before they took any action."

The sites were in many cases staffed by newcomers who were getting their feet wet in the NASA universe. Gary Scott was born and raised in Binger, Oklahoma—also the home of Baseball Hall of Famer Johnny Bench, who picked cotton for Scott's father, and Bench's brother, William, was in the same high school class as Scott. After graduating from Southwestern Oklahoma State University with fellow future flight controllers John Aaron and Tom Weichel, Scott set sail out of Puerto Rico; Trinidad; Lima, Peru; and Hawaii; and he worked Carnarvon and Grand Canary as well. "It was an awesome feeling for a country boy," he concluded. "It was really neat getting to travel and see a little bit of the country. Pretty much, you went there and you came back, but you got to see a little bit along the way."

Duty on board the two tracking ships in the middle of the ocean might have been a nightmare for some, but that was not the case for Bob Heselmeyer. He ate it up. Never mind the fact that the *Coastal Sentry* Quebec once had to sail around a typhoon and then get back on station. That was no big deal, at least not to Heselmeyer. "For me, it was great. I *loved* it," he explained. "Ohhhhh . . . that's where I learned that I liked being on ships. It was impressive that the ship could be where it needed to be. I didn't consider that a hardship at all."

And then there was Ed Fendell. Just a few weeks after Fendell joined the agency, Dutch von Ehrenfried dropped a book on his desk. He opened it and one of the first things he saw was an electrical schematic, complete with buses, circuit breakers, the whole nine yards. He asked von Ehrenfried the most obvious question.

What is this for?
The reply was every bit as obvious.
That's the Gemini spacecraft.
What am I supposed to do with this?
You've got to learn this to be a capsule communicator, because when they have problems, you've got to know what they're talking about.

Fendell could not believe what he was hearing. A capcom? No way. Unlike many of the rookies filing into Houston, Fendell had been around the block a few times. That did not mean, however, that he was ready for this gig. Von Ehrenfried was merciful. He told Fendell to get himself a book on basic electronics, copy layouts onto a piece of cardboard, and then use crayons to color the buses yellow, the circuit breakers another color, and so forth.

That was how Ed Fendell learned to read a schematic, with a box of crayons that cost maybe a dime.

As Herculean a task as it might have been, he was at the capcom console in Carnarvon for the legendary four-day flight of *Gemini 4* in early June 1965. Australia . . . Hawaii . . . Mexico . . . the Gemini years were good to Fendell. "The capcom was like the flight director at the site," he said. "When he arrived at the site, even the station manager worked for him. He was like Chris Kraft or Kranz arriving on site. It was an incredibly great job. I mean, it was the best job I ever had." It was easy to get the impression that when a position in the MOCR became available, it did so with Fendell kicking and screaming and not wanting to come back to Houston. He was having too good a time out in the world.

In that respect, Fendell had plenty of company in those who enjoyed life on the road. Working the tracking stations was enjoyable to others, but at the same time, a means to the end of one day sitting a MOCR console back in Houston. Regardless of the circumstances—whether the new guys were in Houston, on the road, or on the road and wanting to get back to Houston—one theme seemed common to them all. They *all* wanted to prove themselves worthy, and they wanted to prove themselves worthy in conditions that were not always the greatest. Many countries in Africa were marking the end of the British Colonial period by engaging in what seemed like almost constant civil war or revolutions. Others on their way to NASA's remote sites had to travel through areas under Communist rule.

Regardless, these were people who had a job to do. "When you went out to those remote sites, you were the only ones that had the data—it was on *you*," said Merlin Merritt, who worked at Carnarvon and chased a few kangaroos before moving to Houston as EECOM for the flights of *Gemini 5, 9*, and *12*. "You didn't have this mass network of the support structure that we had when we were in the MOCR. In a sense, you were kind of proving yourself."

There would be plenty of things to prove during Gemini.

3. Growing Up

If the six manned flights of the Mercury program represented NASA's infancy in human spaceflight and the Apollo era its full maturity, Project Gemini represented the sometimes turbulent teen years.

Over the course of the twenty months between March 1965 and November 1966, NASA began to spread its wings in an all-out effort to meet the challenge of landing on the moon before the end of the decade. As with any teenager, it took time to work through the problems and emergencies that cropped up along the way. No longer would just one American astronaut cram himself into a tiny capsule to circle the earth a few times before splashing back down. This time, there were two astronauts packed into a slightly larger spacecraft, and there was work to be done.

Gone were the days of Spam-in-a-can Mercury astronauts. The Gemini spacefarers actually got in some flying time with their capsules, and not only that, but there were spacewalks and rendezvous to perform and perfect. Before Neil Armstrong could take his first small step onto the surface of the moon, Project Gemini had to make some giant leaps to get him there. "We were stretching ourselves to figure out how the hell we would do this," Glynn Lunney remembered. "How are we going to do a rendezvous? How are we going to go to the moon? How are we going to calculate and ship the burn maneuvers to the spacecraft's guidance system? All that stuff had to be invented."

The sheer volume of details that needed to be sorted out would have been mind-boggling to most mere mortals, down to and including who was in charge at the tracking stations spread throughout the world—the capcom, a controller dispatched from Houston, or an astronaut who also happened to be on site? To Gene Kranz, astronauts were there to observe and help out if needed—"if needed" being the key phrase. Try telling that to Pete Conrad, who showed up at Carnarvon during preparations for the launch of *Gemini 3* under the impression that he would be calling the shots instead of capcom Dan Hunter. "We had two very strong-willed people out at the tracking station," Kranz said. "They were competing as to who was going to be in charge of the station. Well, my guy was in charge of the station because he was the only guy who knew how to run it, but Pete Conrad had to assume his authority because he was a brand-new astronaut within the system. It was a very dicey situation out there."

That was an understatement. Hunter's response to Conrad, who was two months away from his first spaceflight on *Gemini 5*, was succinct.

Kranz put me in charge, and if you give me any more trouble, I want your ass out of the control room.

The confusion led to quite a ruckus, in Australia and at the Cape, where the Mercury Control Center was about to assume primary responsibility for a mission for the final time. Kranz, who shared a Florida apartment with Chris Kraft before they headed to Houston, had already gone to bed when he was awakened by a commotion. Kraft and Donald K. "Deke" Slayton, one of NASA's seven original Mercury astronauts and the director of Flight Crew Operations, were about to go at it tooth and nail. What a sight it must have been. "Kraft and Slayton were in a heated argument," Kranz wrote in his autobiography. "Deke was exclaiming, 'Dammit, Chris, get your guy under control!' Kraft then went nose-to-nose with Slayton. I felt that within seconds the dispute would escalate beyond shouting. Then, magically, both realized it was time to de-escalate but not back down. Like two junkyard dogs, they circled." Just two days remained before the flight.

The idea of a compromise was floated, but it did not sit well with Hunter. He was to take care of site operations, while Conrad would be in charge in "real time"—during the mission itself. The day before the flight during a final review that included the Cape control center and the entire world-wide network of tracking stations, Hunter asked for a clarification. When he got it straight from Kraft, he was something far less than pleased. "Dan Hunter comes up and says, 'Chris, I don't understand this message you sent me. Will you please explain it?'" Kranz continued. "Kraft went through this long explanation that didn't resolve anything, and Hunter says, 'When I get home, I'm going to frame it and hang it in my crapper.'"

It went without saying that nobody, but nobody, spoke to Chris Kraft that way. Still, Hunter had support from none other than friend John Llewellyn, and when John Star had somebody's back, his back was covered. The near-fight between Kraft and Slayton was just round one.

The crew of *Gemini 3*, Gus Grissom and John Young, had already invited a select few to what was supposed to have been their good-natured send-off the night before launch. Kranz was there. So were Kraft, Slayton, Llewellyn, and Alan Shepard. What Kranz termed a "pretty good party" developed, and Grissom—who knew nothing of the issues at Carnarvon—mentioned how glad he was that it was time to go fly his mission. Someone brought up the Hunter-Conrad rift, and it was at that point when it hit the fan all over again. The fact that the controllers already had a "few beers" under their belts only added fuel to the fire. "About this time, Al Shepard stands up," Kranz continued. "He says, 'Yeah, they had this wise-ass controller who told Kraft off down there.' This got Llewellyn in Alan Shepard's face. Llewellyn was telling him about how many Purple Hearts and medals he had, and he basically was ready to poke him out." Somehow, Kranz managed to steer Llewellyn away from the escalating confrontation without any punches being thrown.

If the fight between Llewellyn and Shepard had happened, though, smart money would have been on John Star.

The episode resulted in what amounted to a house divided for the next day's nearly five-hour flight—flight controllers on one side, astronauts on the other. "Dan Hunter, during the mission, laid back and the Carnarvon site did not perform its functions properly," Kranz said. "Basically, that kind of performance that happened out at the site was absolutely intolerable, but also one other thing happened. The astronauts never went out to the tracking stations again." Hunter won the battle, but essentially lost the war when he was reassigned to management of an Apollo tracking station in Madrid, Spain.

Although capcoms were in charge at the tracking station after the episode, there were still plenty of other issues to sort through.

Soviet cosmonaut Alexei A. Leonov became the first human to do an EVA on 18 March 1965, just five days before *Gemini 3* flew. Although NASA was within striking distance of just such an objective, facts were facts. The Soviet Union had trumped American interests in space yet again. Although

Leonov's twelve-minute spacewalk was another in a long line of successes, Americans had no way of knowing that it would be the Soviets' *last* space success for quite a while. The Russians were experiencing their own set of growing pains.

The USSR's cosmonauts would not fly again for more than two years, and for NASA, the time was *now*. Not only was the stalled Soviet effort an opportunity to catch up in the space race, it was the best chance ever to actually take the lead. "I wanted to beat the Russians," Gene Kranz said. "I didn't like Russians. I'd seen their airplanes over in Korea. I'd seen them over the Formosa Straits, and, to put it bluntly, it was a battle for the minds and the hearts of the free world. So, space was not just something romantic to me. It was the battleground with the Soviet Union at that time."

Gemini 4 was a flight of firsts, the most ambitious flight plan NASA had ever attempted to that point. Flown 3–7 June 1965 by James A. "Jim" McDivitt and Edward H. White II, *Gemini 4* was the first with primary control out of the sparkling fresh MOCR in Houston. At just over four days, it was NASA's longest mission to date. Shifts in the control room were necessary due to the length of the flight, and because of that, Gene Kranz made his debut at the flight director's console with his White Team sandwiched between Chris Kraft's Red and John Hodge's Blue. A rendezvous with the Titan II launch vehicle's spent second stage—the first ever attempted in space—was planned but ultimately failed.

The mission's other major objective did not.

Ed Fendell had been in his Houston office when Kranz asked him to step into the hallway. Unlike others Kranz and Fendell would have over the years, this conversation was hushed. Kranz had been in on the secret since about a week after *Gemini 3*, and he was about to expand the tightly guarded circle by one more person.

What I'm about to tell you, you're to tell no one.

If ever there was a way to get somebody's attention, that was it.

When we get done here tonight, go get yourself something to eat. After that, be at the back entrance to Building 30.

When Fendell returned from his meal, a security guard checked his badge and allowed him into the building. The briefing that followed went over details for an EVA that White might perform, as well as details on the Hand-Held Maneuvering Unit and Portable Life Support System backpack he would use. "We get briefed that we are planning a possible EVA on *Gemini 4*, and that this is supposed to be kept in secret," said Fendell, who served as the Carnarvon capcom. "Our job was to get this flight plan together."

Its code name was something straight out of a James Bond movie, intriguing if not particularly imaginative.

Flight Plan X.

Fendell would be responsible for giving the go/no go decision as the Gemini capsule passed over Australia, while White was to venture outside over Hawaii. "We'd finish our work here during the day," Kranz recalled. "We'd go home, we'd eat, and then all the Plan X people would come back. We'd work generally from about six or seven in the evening until one or two in the morning, building the equipment, validating it in the chamber, developing mission rules, et cetera, et cetera, et cetera." About a month before the flight, other remote-site capcoms were handed sealed envelopes and told in no uncertain terms not to open them until directed to do so. If no word came, the envelopes were to remain sealed.

Assistant flight director Dutch von Ehrenfried was taking part in top-secret meetings of his own a month or so before the flight. "The first secret meeting I ever went to was with Ed White, General [Carroll H.] Bolender, a crew systems guy, and me," von Ehrenfried said. "It was a room where there were five or six of us, with a guard outside. Others knew that it was going to happen, obviously, but that was the first time that I knew about it because we had to coordinate with Ed on what the mission rules were."

A cover letter containing a list of general instructions accompanied the flight plan, and the first of those was that the mission supplement was to be treated as classified material. Each prime capcom was to keep it in his personal briefcase, and three copies would be provided to each remote-site team. The fourth item laid it all out.

The prime capcom will brief the remainder of his flight control team at a time specified (probably F-1 day) by the flight director (MCC-H). Supplements will not be opened for any reason prior to this time. This briefing will be conducted in a secure area and information contained in this supplement will not be discussed with other station personnel.

There was no mention of the proposed spacewalk until the third page, on a map of the Gemini Tracking Network. There they were, three little letters—EVA, directly over the continental United States—that said all that needed to be said. The next page was even more explicit.

These mission rules are to be used in conjunction with the GT-4 rules you already have, however these rules cover flight plan activities you have not considered, i.e., booster rendezvous and extravehicular activity.

The rest of the document outlined primary and secondary test objectives; environmental, medical, control, and communications go/no go criteria; a timeline; a familiarization and training document for the Ventilation Control Module on White's suit; an analysis of various failure modes and effects; system schematics; and procedures for the spacewalk going as planned and in the event of an emergency. Despite all that work, however, there had been no official directive that White's EVA would go on as planned. The *Gemini 4* press kit mentioned the possibility of a spacewalk in the iffiest language possible: "No decision has been made whether in the *Gemini 4* mission the crew will engage in extravehicular activity. This will depend on the qualifying of the extravehicular space suits and the hatch. During their training the *Gemini 4* crew performed a simulated extravehicular test in the vacuum chamber at McDonnell Aircraft Corp., at a simulated altitude of 150,000 feet. A decision to undertake the extravehicular test can be made as late as the day before the launch."

That was it. There was no denial that an EVA might take place, but it certainly was not a confirmation, either. A final confirmation of the spacewalk came down on 25 May, the same day it was officially announced to the press. "Everybody was going berserk, 'What the hell is Flight Plan X?'" Fendell said. "I handed out these things, and the doctors went berserk, because they hadn't been brought in. The majority of people didn't even know anybody was working on it. There were a million astronauts over there who didn't even know what was going on. It was quite a shock to an incredible amount of people when they said, 'Open Flight Plan X.'"

The EVA was not the only thing on Jerry Bostick's mind as the flight approached. Alan Shepard had angered John Llewellyn in March, and just before *Gemini 4*, Bostick took Shepard on as well. Scheduled to monitor the mission from the Cape with a skeleton crew just in case something went wrong with the new digs back in Houston, the young controller found himself a chair on wheels that he could use to literally scoot back and forth between the retro, FIDO, and guidance consoles.

Bostick and the rest of the team, which included Cape flight director Glynn Lunney and systems overseer Arnie Aldrich, spent a week or two in sims for the flight. Shepard, on the other hand, did not show up to prepare for his duties as capcom until the morning of launch. Some changes had been made to the console, and when Bostick attempted to explain them, Shepard never so much as glanced up at him. Finally, Shepard icily asked the young flight controller, "Do you know who I am?"

The gruff Shepard might have intimidated Bostick, but he was determined not to let it show. "I still can't believe I said it, but it really pissed me off, to be frank," he admitted. "I said, 'Yes, sir, I know who you are, but if you don't do this right, you're going to fuck the whole thing up!'" Apparently impressed with Bostick's chutzpah, Shepard relented and allowed Bostick to take him through the changes.

Chalk another one up for the members of the Trench.

After launch on 3 June, problems with the failed rendezvous delayed White's EVA from the second to third orbit. Three hours, fifty-eight minutes, and thirty-five seconds into the flight, Fendell began the exchange that would send White out the hatch.

What's your status on EVA?

McDivitt's response was equally as short. There was no time for chit-chat.

The status is go for EVA.

Okay. You're go for EVA from here. Stand by for decompression—correction, depressurization.

Twenty minutes later, the hatch was opened, and twelve minutes after that, White was floating nearly free of the spacecraft, attached only by his umbilical. He was as excited as an astronaut had ever been in flight.

I feel like a million dollars.

Communications, however, were already an issue. Gus Grissom, at the capcom console in Houston, repeatedly tried contacting McDivitt and White.

Gemini 4, Houston capcom.

Gemini 4, Houston capcom.

Gemini 4, Houston capcom.

Gemini 4, Gemini 4, Houston capcom.

New to the Gemini spacecraft, the Voice Operated eXchange switch—known as VOX—was not working correctly. Finally, McDivitt turned it off and made contact with Grissom.

Gemini 4, *Houston capcom. Has he egressed?*

He's out, Gus, and it's really nifty. Listen, our VOX *doesn't work very well, and I don't seem to read anybody. You will have to relay. The gun works swell. He's been able to maneuver all over—out front, back under the nose, and he's back out again.*

Grissom still wasn't hearing clearly and talked over McDivitt.

Say again.

McDivitt began repeating his message, and that time, Grissom evidently heard well enough.

That's great!

Less than two minutes later, the MOCR briefly heard White. He was clearly having the time of his life.

That's right, capcom, it's very easy to maneuver with the gun. The only problem I have is that I haven't got enough fuel. I've exhausted the fuel now and I was able to maneuver myself around the front of the spacecraft back and maneuver right up to the top of the adapter. Just about came back into Jim's view. The only thing I wish is that I had more. This is the greatest experience I've—it's just tremendous! Right now I'm standing on my head, and I'm looking right down, and it looks like we're coming up on the coast of California. I'm going into a slow rotation to the right. There is absolutely no disorientation associated with it.

The communications link between space and Houston was not permanent, and once again, Grissom tried in vain to make contact. Fifteen minutes into White's spacewalk, it was McDivitt's turn to try Houston.

I'm going out to Push-to-Talk and see what the flight director has got to say.

Grissom's order came straight from Kraft.

Gemini 4, *get back in!*

McDivitt sounded for all the world like a parent trying to coax his child to bed, and White like the child who wanted to do anything but.

Aww, Cape. Let me just find a few pictures.

No, back in. Come on.

Coming in. Listen, you could almost not drag me in, but I'm coming.

White was not finished procrastinating just yet.

It's no sweat. Actually, I'm trying to get a better picture.

No, come on in.

I'm trying to get a picture of the spacecraft now.

6. Patricia White (left) and Patricia McDivitt chat with husbands Ed and Jim, respectively, during the momentous flight of *Gemini 4*. Courtesy NASA.

Ed, come on in here!

All right. Let me fold the camera and put the gun up.

Von Ehrenfried was standing next to Kraft as the EVA wound down, and the assistant flight director was listening intently to the brief air-to-ground exchanges. A nighttime pass was coming up and White had bested Leonov's time outside, so there was really no need to continue. It was, in fact, time to get back inside. "Enough was enough," von Ehrenfried said. "We proved the concept, no use pushing it." As the EVA concluded, White was not finished with his commentary. Simple yet poignant, it was a statement that spoke volumes about White's experience.

This is the saddest moment of my life.

Most of the rest of the flight was spent on eleven different experiments, but a day after White's EVA, the monotony of day-to-day life on board a cramped Gemini spacecraft was broken up with a call from Grissom. The wives of the crew, Patricia McDivitt and Patricia White, as well as the Whites' children, Bonnie and Eddie, were in the MOCR. They were about to have a memorable if not somewhat awkward air-to-ground chat.

Patricia McDivitt was up first.

Jim? Jim?
What?
Do you hear me?
Roger. I can hear you loud and clear.
Boy, you're doing great!
She evidently got past whatever case of the nerves she might have had.
Get yourself over Texas.
I'll be over Texas in about three minutes.
Hurry it up.
Just before handing over her headset, she added more piece of instruction.
Be a good boy now, kid.
When his wife took over, White talked her through the process of keying her microphone.
You've got to push the button, honey.
A few seconds later, he tried again.
You have to push the button when you talk and let it go so I can talk.
That did the trick.
It looks like you were having a wonderful time yesterday.
Quite a time we had. It was quite a time.
I can't wait to talk to you about it.
How are Eddie and Bonnie, honey?
Fine.
Okay, honey. I'll see you later.
Okay. Have a good flight.
Thank you, honey. Bye-bye.
Bye.

Before the flight, the Trench worked with McDivitt on reentry alternatives that provided the most accurate way to control the landing point location in case its guidance computer failed. There were at least a couple of choices—a rolling reentry that had been standard in Mercury or one that put the capsule into a ninety-degree bank in one direction and then maybe reversing to ninety degrees in the other. Either way, the end result of zero lift was basically the same.

The preflight conclusion was to go with the bank–reverse bank reentry, if and when the computer went down. Forty-eight orbits into the flight, it did, and another John Llewellyn story was about to be born.

Chris Kraft was on duty for the 7 June conclusion to the flight, and he called for the rolling reentry because he was not comfortable with the alternative. As retro officer, responsibility for reentry fell squarely on Llewellyn's shoulders and he took it seriously. He told Kraft about the agreement with the crew, and then told him again. Other members of the Trench chimed in as well, but Kraft was having none of it. Llewellyn was about to try one more time when he walked up to the flight director's console. According to legend, Kraft stood up, looked over the console, and put a stop to the discussion then and there.

I have your technical input, Mr. Llewellyn. Sit down!

Llewellyn sat down.

Nobody talked to Chris Kraft the way Dan Hunter did from Carnarvon, and few ever tried addressing Llewellyn the way Kraft just had. Nevertheless, it was too good an opportunity for members of the Trench to pass up. Somebody—Charley Parker would not say who—prompted McDivitt to ask Llewellyn about what had happened with the reentry at the post-flight splashdown party. McDivitt took up the challenge and proceeded to bedevil the fiery retro. Like Kraft, Llewellyn could only take so much. According to Parker, Llewellyn jumped onto the center of a table and proceeded to defend his honor.

McDivitt, I damn near got myself fired over that! I don't want to hear anything else about it!

The beauty of the Gemini program was how each flight stood on the shoulders of those that came before it, in order to reach ever more challenging new heights.

Gemini 4 held the American endurance record right up until the point *Gemini 5* came along two and a half months later. Gordon Cooper and Pete Conrad, fresh off his tracking-station encounter in Australia, stayed in orbit for nearly eight full days—a goal heralded on one version of the crew emblem that included the slogan "Eight Days or Bust." The flight was almost twice as long as *Gemini 4* and the same basic amount of time that an Apollo crew would take to travel to the moon, land, explore, and return to Earth. Better yet, it bettered the world mark held by *Vostok 5* by three full days.

Although the Americans had never before been able to boast such an achievement, the flight was not without its healthy share of problems. Flying for the first time on *Gemini 5* were two fuel-cell sections, each of which contained three stacks that converted the reaction of hydrogen and oxygen into electrical power for the longer-duration mission. Half an hour after launch, the cryogenic oxygen tank heater wiring failed due to a short circuit. Without the heater, pressure plummeted from 850 pounds per square inch (psi) to just 65 less than four and a half hours into the flight.

What now?

The critical rendezvous practice with the radar pod was out of the question, and a pointed discussion developed over whether or not to end the flight early. John Aaron, the EECOM on Kranz's White Team, had worked quite a bit on power profiles during his brief fifteen months at NASA, focusing specifically on just how long the spacecraft could fly solely using battery power in the event the fuel cells failed completely. Kraft's Red Team EECOM Dick Glover had Aaron brief Kraft, Kranz, and Hodge, all of whom were gathered at the flight director's console just before the shift handover. The spacecraft was placed into a significantly powered-down state at that point in order to minimize demand on the oxygen tank and stabilize its pressure. By the time the operation was finished, at least 30 amps' worth of demand had been shaved off the spacecraft's power consumption.

It was a historic low, hovering at around 10 amps of total usage.

Pressure in the tank leveled out at about 70 psi, and the fuel cells continued to operate normally. Because of that and the fact that there were adequate battery reserves to make it to a primary landing area in the event that the fuel cells went completely kaput, the decisions were made to continue the mission for the remainder of day one and schedule another go/no go decision at the beginning of its second day.

It was up to the White Team to begin figuring out what to do with the rest of the mission. "At the end of each shift, the previous-shift flight director sort of summarizes the status of the system and gives a sense of direction," Kranz said. "Well, Kraft had neither summarized status nor given a sense of direction. And I wanted to know what the hell he wanted to do with this mission."

Kranz was about to get a lesson from the master. "I wanted sort of a game plan from Kraft," Kranz continued. "Well, Kraft wasn't about to give me one. I said, 'Chris, what do you want me to do?' And in a very disgusted

7. Astronaut Jim McDivitt, EECOMS Dick Glover and John Aaron, and astronaut Elliott See (standing, left to right) gather at the flight director's console to brief Gene Kranz (dark vest), Chris Kraft (leaning forward, chin in hand), and John Hodge about a critical power-down procedure during the flight of *Gemini 5*. Courtesy NASA.

[manner], he gets up, looks at me, and says, 'You're the flight director. It's your shift. You make up your mind.'" Kraft was direct, but Kranz added, "a damn good teacher." Kranz's air force flight instructor flew in the back seat right up to the time he decided it was time for the rookie to solo, and Kraft had basically just done the very same thing. Kranz was on his own, solo at the flight director's console.

"So what happened next is even more interesting," Aaron added. "Kranz and I settled into our shift and right away Kranz said to me that it was time to see what the fuel cells could do. So I started picking equipment to power back up, starting in small increments, waiting at each step to see what would happen. By the time of the go/no go the next day, we had the spacecraft almost powered up to a normal level."

Just as important as Kraft's nudge was to Kranz, Aaron appreciated the sense of confidence that Kranz was showing in him. "I have to give Kranz a lot of credit for pushing me," Aaron continued. "Looking back after the flight, I came to the conclusion that the push was likely Kranz's idea solely. In other words, I think he was determined to demonstrate that either the spacecraft could be productively operated or else a decision would be made to come home early on day two. Had it been left to me? I might have just played it conservatively and left the spacecraft in the low power level for the remainder of day one."

The Radar Evaluation Pod (REP) featured instrumentation similar to that of the Agena Target Vehicle, and it was released just two hours, thirteen minutes after launch. The plan was to test the spacecraft and its techniques, but with limited battery, it had a short shelf life before going silent during the trouble with the fuel cell.

Ken Young, a resident rendezvous expert in the flight dynamics SSR, and several others had been sent home when it appeared that the flight might end early. Instead of going home, several headed to the nearby Flintlock Inn to drown their sorrows. They got there at some point that afternoon, and by 10 p.m. there was no pain to be felt. That, of course, was when somebody tracked them down to get everybody herded back to the space center.

Buzz Aldrin—Dr. Rendezvous himself—and Howard W. "Bill" Tindall went to work on developing a "phantom rendezvous" in which Cooper and Conrad would rendezvous and station keep with an unseen object orbiting in space rather than the by-then dead radar pod. All hands were needed back on deck to get it all figured out. "Several of us managed to wobble back, and we worked all night," Young said. "That was pretty funny, wasn't real funny at the time, but somehow, we made it through the night. Dr. Kraft or even Bill Tindall never said anything about wondering why we were in such a good mood doing all that work all through the night. Some of us managed to sober up about dawn." The phantom rendezvous went off without a hitch on the third day of the flight.

Five more days remained, and they were not trouble-free, either. At least a couple more power-downs became necessary when the ship's supply of hydrogen became an issue, as well as managing storage of the high amount of water that was being produced at the higher power levels. A thruster in the Orbit Attitude and Maneuvering System (OAMS) went down. All in all, the last couple days of the flight were spent biding time and not much more.

It was suggested that they do a couple of victory rolls and a loop just after the Soviets' endurance record in space was broken, and if there were two pilots in the astronaut corps who would have loved to have done just that, it would have been Cooper and Conrad. Their circumstances dictated otherwise.

Cooper shot the ground a quick reply.

We haven't got the fuel.

Conrad added his two cents.

All we've been doing is rolling and rolling.

On top of it all, Kranz opted to cut the flight short an orbit due to the presence of Hurricane Betsy in the prime landing location in the Atlantic.

Walter M. "Wally" Schirra Jr. and Thomas P. "Tom" Stafford were all dressed up with no place to go.

Schirra, one of the seven original Mercury astronauts, and the rookie Stafford had already climbed into their *Gemini 6* spacecraft on 25 October 1965 for their liftoff. All that was left was to wait on the launch of the Agena Target Vehicle. This was it, the first planned meeting in space of two independent vehicles. Four rendezvous were planned in all for the two-day flight, and if the long-duration record set by *Gemini 5* did not put the Russians in their place, surely this would. There was only one problem.

The Agena was destroyed just after its engine fired to separate from its Atlas launch vehicle six minutes into flight.

Bob Carlton was incredulous. Data from the Agena flashed across the console screen for a few seconds, and then, poof, just like that, it was gone. Carlton punched a button on the console to grab several snapshots of the now-vanished data, and just like that, printouts zipped back to him via the pneumatic tube messaging system. "I'll never forget this," Carlton said. "Mel Brooks [the head of the Gemini Flight Systems Branch, not the funnyman film director and actor] was on the console, and we don't have any data. Everybody's scratching their head. My SSR was scratching their head, and I was snap-shooting like crazy. Here come the p-tube full of those things. I got down on the floor behind Mel in the MOCR, and I spread those out, where I could see the history of it second by second." There was enough data to show pressure building up in the fuel tanks, and when the engine quit burning, the pressure kept coming. The tanks blew, and "that's what destroyed the bird," according to Carlton.

What Carlton did not know was that he had somehow gotten onto the communications loop going out to the worldwide tracking network. As he tried to explain what had taken place, everybody could hear him.

Mel, this sucker blew up.

Gene Kranz was still trying to hold out hope. "He wouldn't believe it. He wouldn't accept that," Carlton continued. "He had FIDO run the trajectory to see if it made it on into orbit. He hoped we might have just lost telemetry."

As Kranz continued, telling the next remote site what time to expect a signal from the Agena, Carlton looked at Brooks and could not contain himself.

I don't know what he's smoking, but that bird's dead.

With fifty minutes left before it was to have launched, the Gemini flight was scrubbed. Brooks, who passed away 23 November 2000, felt like he had taken a punch to the chin. He later described the failed Agena launch as one of the "most greatest" disappointments in his life. He had worked on maybe twenty Agena launches to that point, with not a single problem. The air force had readied a publicity campaign honoring this particular Agena flight, its 200th, complete with key chains, T-shirts, and so forth. What happened to those trinkets was the least of anybody's concern around NASA. Rendezvous was the name of the game, and it still had not been accomplished.

A day after the explosion, a solution was beginning to take shape. Instead of docking with an Agena, why not have *Gemini 6* rendezvous with *Gemini 7*'s Frank F. Borman II and Jim Lovell, who would be in the midst of a grueling 14-day flight? Two weeks later, on 9 November, the plan was officially announced. Borman and Lovell would light the fires and lift off no earlier than 4 December, and if all went well with checks of the launch pad and the early stage of the flight itself, *Gemini 6* would follow nine days later on 13 December. Borman and Lovell's flight plan remained virtually unchanged, but that was not the case for Schirra and Stafford's. "To me, the decision to do that and the way that launch team responded was more edifying than the fact that we rendezvoused," Gene Kranz said. "I mean, I just liked the way that we seemed capable of taking adversity and turning it to our advantage in those days. It created a feeling within the team that there is no surrender. We're going to look at it and, son of a gun, we're going to find a way out of this thing!" In NASA lore, the combined effort would forevermore be known as *Gemini 7/6*—pronounced by most as "seventy-six."

Before the twin missions, a legendary escapade involving Ed Fendell and William F. "Bill" Bucholz took place at the Hawaii tracking station. Bucholz, a college classmate of Kranz's who drove his wife and eight children around Houston in a rebuilt Cadillac hearse, was an air force captain assigned to the site. Because Bucholz was having trouble getting used to not working off a checklist, Fendell and Philco tech rep John W. Collins hatched a plan to put him to the test during an upcoming simulation. This was no ordinary plot, either.

How might Bucholz react if capcom Fendell had a heart attack during a pass over the tracking station?

The spacecraft came into range during the sim and, sure enough, Fendell came up out of his chair, grabbed his chest in a scene straight out of the classic American sitcom *Sanford and Son*—"*I'm comin', Elizabeth! It's the big one!*"—and fell to the floor. In the confusion that followed, Bucholz actually stepped on Fendell with what he said were size-eighteen feet, every bit as big as basketball star Shaquille O'Neal's. Then, Bucholz keyed the microphone, and in his haste called to one spacecraft as if he were actually on board the other.

Gemini 7, *this is* Gemini 6.

There were two doctors on site, but only one of them was in on the ruse. The one who was not took a look at Fendell and gave the most dire of all prognoses.

He's dead.

Houston was on the loop, asking what in the devil was going on.

Fendell's just had a heart attack!

The training session continued as Fendell's "corpse" remained sprawled out on the floor. It is hard to imagine what Bucholz's reaction might have been when Fendell got up off the floor, dusted himself off, and placed his headset back on for the next pass, none the worse for wear. Yet if his victim at the remote site was torqued off at him, that was nothing when compared to the reaction that was about to happen back in Houston. Collins had gone to his boss, Carl B. Shelley, to clear the decidedly unusual sim. That was all well and good, but somehow, word of the plan had *not* gotten to one Chris Kraft. "When Kraft found out what had happened, he got *pissed*," Fendell said. "He wasn't mad at me, but that's *not* the place you want to be. You'll have to understand, Chris Kraft is one of the most remarkable people you'll ever meet in your life."

As brash as Fendell could be at times, the respect in his voice for the godfather of mission control was unmistakable. In fact, Fendell remembered clearly the first time he ever slipped up and called Kraft by his first name. It was during fallout from the controversial presidential election of 2000, when hanging chads in Florida meant the difference between one candidate and another. They lived near each other at the time, and while Fendell walked his dog one morning, he met Kraft and they struck up a conversation about the election. "I said, 'Chris . . . such and such and so on,'" Fendell remembered. "When I left him, I got about half a block up the street and I said to myself, 'Holy shit, what did you just do?' Everybody else called him Chris, but he was always Mr. Kraft to me."

What Fendell might or might not have known at the time was the fact that *Gemini 7/6* were the last flights Kraft worked at the flight director's console. It was time to turn his attention to duties as the director of Flight Operations, and to Apollo. "I was not anxious to make the change," Kraft wrote in his autobiography. "I was giving up the best job I'd ever had in my life. But I looked forward to *7/6* all the same, partly because of the camaraderie for the crews and partly because I had a gut feel that the rendezvous mission combined with fourteen days of two guys cramped into a Gemini spacecraft was not going to be easy on any of us."

Gemini 7 astronauts Borman and Lovell, who would again fly together almost exactly three years later on *Apollo 8*, got under way for their marathon mission as planned on 4 December 1965. More fuel-cell gremlins led to more caution alarms and lights, which in turn resulted in erratic sleep patterns for the two spacefarers. Eventually, the ground allowed them to turn the alarms off and tape over the lights during their sleep shifts. That was not all. Although Lovell had been allowed to change from his new oversized spacesuit into a more comfortable set of coveralls, Borman was stuck in his because upper management wanted to see how a crew member would react to two weeks in such a garment.

Not well, evidently.

During nightly "UHF-6" tests—the only time during the flights that the press did not have full access to its air-to-ground transmissions—Borman's protest grew evermore "vehement," according to Kraft. Finally, the issue came to a head between Kraft and George Mueller, the associate administrator of NASA's Office of Manned Space Flight in Washington.

I'm going to let them switch off. Borman takes his suit off and Lovell puts his on.

No. That ruins the test.

Mueller's steadfast refusal to budge got to Kraft.

George, you're a brilliant man, but there's one word in the dictionary that you obviously don't understand.

What's that?

Compassion, George. Compassion.

Eventually, Mueller relented and allowed both men to get rid of the suits. Still, the case was not closed. A few members of the press got wind of what had taken place during the so-called UHF-6 tests, and they were peeved. "We caught hell at the next change-of-shift press conference," Kraft wrote. "That damned phrase *the public's right to know* became the issue. Deke and the doctors and I felt otherwise, we argued our case, and we ended up with a compromise." At first, a public affairs officer would listen in on the medical conversations, take notes, and summarize for the media. "On later flights, we just said what had to be said out in the open and let the press have it all. It was one more penalty we all paid for living in this fishbowl environment."

Eight days after *Gemini 7* left Earth, Schirra and Stafford once again hauled themselves into their Gemini capsule for another launch attempt of the flight now known officially as *Gemini 6A* due to its reworked flight plan. The countdown went perfectly.

Five.

Four.

Three.

Two.

One.

Ignition.

The familiar sight of smoke began to billow from underneath the rocket, and in the capsule, the mission clock began running. At the retro console in Houston, John Llewellyn called liftoff and then—nothing.

The Titan II did not leave the pad, and the crew, Schirra with his hands ready to yank on D-rings that would trigger their ejection seats, stayed put. It was later discovered that an electrical tail plug at the bottom of the rocket had fallen out prematurely, but when no upward motion was detected, computers shut down the engines automatically. Had the vehicle lifted off even an inch or two when the engines cut off, it would have settled back onto the ground in a deadly ball of flame and smoke.

Charlie Harlan and Clifton C. "C. C." Williams, the rookie astronaut who lost his life less than two years later in a crash of his NASA T-38 jet, were working the booster and tanks consoles on the left end of the front row. Between them was a red abort switch. If Harlan had detected a serious enough problem after the launch vehicle left the pad, he would have flipped the switch to trigger an emergency light in the cabin of the capsule. Harlan would also have to verbally confirm the abort.

He did neither.

No liftoff.

All four men—Schirra, Stafford, Harlan, and Williams—had just stared down a deadly monster without blinking. "I could tell, mainly from the rhythm of the thing, that it was still on the pad," Harlan said. "We're talking about two or three seconds, max. You get the rhythm of it, and I knew it was on the pad. John had already called liftoff, and I called, 'Shutdown . . . we're still on the pad.'"

Rigging up a plug that would not come out was an easy fix, and that was a good thing because Borman and Lovell had only a few days left in orbit. It simply would not have done to let yet another mission go by without a rendezvous. *Gemini 6A* lifted off three days later, this time without incident, and the plan was for Schirra and Stafford to catch up with their colleagues on the fourth orbit. Clouds obscured Borman and Lovell's view of the Cape, but what they could see was the contrail left behind by *Gemini 6A*'s launch. It would not be long now.

As *Gemini 6A* began its complicated series of maneuvers to close on *Gemini 7* ninety-four minutes into its flight, the mood was expectant in the MOCR. Both flights were being controlled from the third floor—it would have been much more complicated, Jerry Bostick insisted, to have tried working two flights from two floors at the same time. At a little more than five hours into the flight of *Gemini 6*, it was getting real. Schirra called out:

This is Gemini 6. *I have a lighted target at about twelve o'clock.*

He was not quite sure what it was yet, but both he and the ground were hoping.

It may be a star and it may be 7. We'll check her out.

A few seconds later, Stafford spotted the same object.

Hey, I think I've got it! That's 7, Wally.

That's either Sirius or 7.

The spacecraft were still more than sixty-two miles apart, and that was not good enough for a rendezvous. Forty-eight minutes later, they were 1,200 feet part. Then, 1,000 . . . 800 . . . 540 . . . 360 . . . 300 . . . 240 . . . 180.

At last, two spacecraft that were traveling thousands of miles per hour each were station keeping at a distance of just 120 feet. It was 2:33 p.m. in Houston on 15 December. In the control room, capcom Elliott M. See Jr. prompted them for a status update.

Gemini 6, Gemini 6, Houston capcom. Standing by.

Schirra did not answer him, his attention obviously on Borman and Lovell's ship. See tried again.

Gemini 6. Houston is standing by.

Roger, we're all sitting up here playing bridge together.

The MOCR was abuzz. Chris Kraft, Bob Gilruth, and others lit cigars, and there was a special sense of satisfaction down on the first row. This was their baby, their biggest contribution to the space race so far. "For years, it seemed like the Russians were one step ahead of us," said Jerry Bostick, the prime FIDO on *Gemini 7* who also took a shift on *Gemini 6A*. "So the first rendezvous that we did on *Gemini 7/6*, even though we didn't get to dock, was a *big* thing for all of us, especially the guys in the Trench who were in charge of that. It was one of the happiest days of my life, I guess." It was Bostick who had tracked down a load of small American flags for the occasion. Before launch, he went to Kraft for approval.

He got it.

The Americans now had the records for longest flight and the first rendezvous in space. Next up was an Agena docking, but that was a test that very nearly led to NASA's first in-flight tragedy.

The nastiest emergency in the young history of crewed spaceflight began innocently enough on 16 March 1966, when *Gemini 8*'s Neil Armstrong brought his spacecraft in for a smooth docking with an Agena Target Vehicle six hours and thirty-three minutes after he and David R. Scott had lifted off from the Cape.

That elicited yet another round of cheers in the MOCR, but all-out chaos was about to break loose and the ground had absolutely no way of knowing about it.

Twenty-seven minutes after the docking, and during the fifteen minutes of air-to-ground silence as the astronauts passed between tracking stations located at Tananarive and on the *Coastal Sentry* Quebec as it sailed east of Okinawa in the Pacific Ocean, Scott noticed the spacecraft was in an unexpected bank. Armstrong briefly brought it back under control, but when he again released his hand controller, the capsule began to spin on all three axes—roll, pitch, and yaw. There had been all kinds of issues with the uplink of information for the Agena, so the docking target *had* to be the source of the movement. In fact, that had been one of the last things capcom Jim Lovell had told the crew from Houston just a few minutes earlier.

If you run into trouble and the Attitude Control System in the Agena goes wild, just send in Command 400 to turn it off and take control with the spacecraft. Did you copy that?

There was seemingly no other choice. Scott triggered a switch to undock from the Agena, and if the situation had been bad before, it suddenly got far worse. It was not the Agena, but a stuck Number 8 OAMS thruster midway up the side of the capsule itself. The tumble increased to nearly a full revolution per second, and when *Gemini 8* finally came into contact with capcom James R. "Jim" Fucci on board the *Coastal Sentry* Quebec, his blood almost certainly ran cold when he heard Scott's voice.

We have serious problems here. We're . . . we're tumbling end over end up here. We're disengaged from the Agena.

Fucci asked what the problem seemed to be, and Armstrong was quick to respond even as he wrestled with the controls.

We're rolling up and we can't turn anything off, continuously increasing in a left roll.

There was nothing for Fucci to say, other than "Roger." For thirty-seven more seconds, there was an agonizing silence before the capcom again tried the crew.

Gemini 8, CSQ.

Armstrong told Fucci to stand by, and a few seconds after that, Scott was back on the loop. The OAMS thrusters had been completely deactivated, and his commander was now using the capsule's Reaction Control System (RCS) to arrest the tumble.

We have a violent left roll here at the present time and we can't turn the RCS off and we can't fire it and we certainly have a roll . . . stuck hand control.

Again, all Fucci could offer was a brief acknowledgment, "Roger." It took another minute and twenty seconds before Scott at last responded to say that they were slowly regaining control of the spacecraft. Back in Houston, the MOCR had heard it all. The docking had been a success, and controllers on John Hodge's Blue Team were packing up and preparing for shift handover to Gene Kranz's group when Scott's voice shook them all to their core. Hodge's reaction was the same as so many others would be in the control room over the years. "I think it was something like, 'Oh, shit,'" he admitted. "That was really scary. Of course, there was nothing we could do about it." Bob Carlton, working the Agena Systems console, felt totally helpless and called it one of the most terrifying moments of his career at NASA. "I thought they were gone," he concluded. The worst feeling of all for those in the MOCR was the sense of helplessness, that there was nothing at all they could do to help get Armstrong and Scott out of the spin. They were spectators, and not much else, at that point.

Hodge's decision on his first, and last, mission as lead flight director was not so much to end the mission at that point, but where. "It was interesting," Hodge said. "The flight director really was in charge in those days. Nobody came in and said to me, 'Here's what you have to do.' Everybody stood out of the way, which I always admired people for, Gilruth and Chris and those guys. They just said, 'It's your mission. You do what you do.'" Hodge and Kranz got the USS *Leonard F. Mason* steaming to the expected splashdown area, 496 miles east of Okinawa and 620 south of Yokosuka, Japan. Although the landing was spot on, the *Leonard F. Mason* was still another three hours away.

Both of the crew wound up with Apollo commands—Armstrong on mankind's debut on the lunar surface, and Scott during the first extended exploration of the moon. Years later, John Hodge would joke that his contribution to the space program was making sure that Neil Armstrong was around to fly on Apollo.

Planning for *Gemini 9* began with one tragedy, and the flight almost ended with another.

Original crew members Elliott See and Charles M. Bassett II were killed 28 February 1966 when their jet crashed on approach into Lambert Field in St. Louis, where they were to inspect the spacecraft for their upcoming mission. That thrust their backups, Tom Stafford and Gene Cernan, onto the prime crew for the flight scheduled to blast off in just ten weeks.

Gemini 9 marked a period of transition in the astronaut corps, and there was one taking place in the MOCR as well. Chris Kraft's decision to focus his energies on management brought Gene Kranz into the role of lead flight director for the first time during *Gemini 9*. Not only that, but Glynn Lunney and Cliff Charlesworth were ready to make their crewed-flight debuts at the Houston console as well. Charlesworth, announced as a flight director in a 30 March 1966 press release, was a native of Redwing, Minnesota, and was assistant chief of the Flight Dynamics Branch at the time of his selection. Of all the missions he could have trained on, Charlesworth had been John Hodge's understudy during the heart-stopping flight of *Gemini 8*.

Charlesworth would come to be known in the MOCR as the "Mississippi Gambler" for his calm and collected demeanor. "Nothing ever seemed to upset that guy," Kranz said. "I mean, he was about as loose an individual as you have ever seen in your entire life. It didn't matter if he was going to do something for the first time, it was just no big deal—let's just go do it. Cliff was just absolutely almost carefree. Everybody's up here in intensity, and Cliff's way down here. You wonder if he's ever going to get up for the mission, but that's the way he worked."

Lunney, meanwhile, had seat time as flight director on 26 February 1966 during the unmanned, thirty-seven-minute flight of AS-201, the first test of the Block 1 Command and Service Module and Saturn 1B launch vehicle, but flying a manned mission was something else entirely.

Another failed Agena launch on 17 May 1966 meant another launch scrub for Stafford. What it also meant was that NASA would have to come up with a plan B, and quickly, for the flight now officially dubbed as *Gemini 9A*. The result was that the Augmented Target Docking Adapter (ATDA) was pressed into service for launch on 1 June, and almost as soon as it hit orbit, there were still more problems to address. The conical launch shroud covering the ATDA's docking port refused to fully open and separate from the rest of the craft due to some incorrectly installed straps, leaving its mouth agape and looking like an "angry alligator," according to Stafford. Docking was out of the question.

Or was it?

After seeing Stafford and Cernan through their ascent and catching up with the ATDA on 3 June, Kranz felt comfortable enough to head home for a quick shower before returning to MSC. Before heading to Building 30's sleeping quarters, Kranz checked in on the MOCR, expecting to find Lunney on console. He was not. Instead, Kranz's fellow flight director had been summoned to a meeting concerning the next day's spacewalk. Kranz was instantly livid.

What EVA?

He hurried to the meeting, taking steps two at a time to get there. Once he arrived, Kranz found Chris Kraft, Deke Slayton, George Mueller, Project Gemini program manager Charles W. "Chuck" Mathews, and a handful of other NASA higher-ups deep in conversation. Astronaut Buzz Aldrin had presented a plan that was to have Cernan do an EVA the next day to cut the straps that were holding the shroud partially in place, and Mathews appeared to be buying into it.

Kranz was asked for his opinion, and they got it. There was "a hell of a lot of energy" spring-loaded into the strapped shroud, so what might happen when the straps were cut? Would it rebound and strike Cernan or maybe even the spacecraft? The ATDA was not stabilized. While the tethered Cernan was doing his work with no handholds or footholds to keep him in place, Stafford would have to station keep but not dock with the target vehicle. There had only been one other EVA done by an American, and the one planned for Cernan before the flight was difficult enough without throwing this into the mix.

After more than half an hour of discussion, Mathews made his decision. He felt the risk could be made acceptable, so the EVA was a go. Before concluding the meeting, he asked if there were any additional comments. Kranz had some, all right.

It was a stunt, he told the group, and a dangerous and unnecessary one to boot. Somebody was going to get killed attempting it. "This was a new experience for me, to be directed to do something that I didn't believe in," Kranz said. "It also sort of tested the flight director's mandate that is, is he really in charge of this mission or not kind of thing."

As Kranz passed Kraft's fourth-row console in the MOCR, he had had enough.

Chris, this is my last damned mission. I am through.

Kraft's response was no less direct. He had not liked the proposal any more than Kranz had, but a directive was a directive.

You got your orders, now do your job.

"Red-faced, I turned away thinking, 'Screw the role of the flight director. When push comes to shove, the flight director is just another management flunky,'" Kranz recalled in his autobiography. His career, as storied as it was to become, was likely saved the next day when Stafford called down from over the secondary tracking station at Canton Island, a small coral atoll located halfway between Australia and Hawaii, to speak with capcom Neil Armstrong in the MOCR.

Okay. We both just finished talking it over. Right now, we're both pretty well bushed. But I'm afraid it would be against my judgment to go ahead and do the EVA at this time.

A few moments later, Stafford ended the transmission.

Gene and I talked it over, and we think it might be better for both of us to knock it off for a while. Do some experiments and try in the morning, unless you have a specific plan with the ATDA out there where we can do some good with it. I don't see where we can gain a whole lot. Over.

Armstrong turned to look at Kranz up on the third row, and got a big thumbs-up in return. Stafford had estimated that his remaining maneuvering fuel was at 16 to 17 percent, far too little for a rendezvous to get Cernan into position for the proposed strap-cutting EVA.

In his account of the episode in *his* autobiography, Kraft backed Kranz's position without actually mentioning his name. "[The shroud EVA] turned into an intense argument with backup astronaut Buzz Aldrin claiming loudly and not too politely that it was a safe and reasonable plan," Kraft wrote. "The rest of us disagreed. Bob Gilruth turned back each of Aldrin's arguments by pointing out the dangers to Cernan if the shroud flew off suddenly, and by listing the difficulties Cernan would have in stabilizing himself to do the cutting and in just getting over to the ATDA in the first place. We'd already proved on *Gemini 8* that docking wasn't difficult, and we'd have three more Gemini missions to practice it. Aldrin wouldn't budge, but the decision was obvious. It turned out to be the right thing to do."

There was another factor at play during the episode, and that was the tendency of upper management sometimes attempting to interject itself into the operational decision-making process. It turned out to be like mixing oil and water. Glynn Lunney remembered the time early in the Gemini program when Chris Kraft waved off a launch, and while it had been the right call to make, a person dispatched by headquarters in Washington to make the "big decisions" in the control room felt it had been his call. The one problem? He could not figure out how to use his intercom. "Some boss," Lunney wrote in *From the Trench of Mission Control to the Craters of the Moon*. "Later in that day, I inadvertently walked into a conference room, deserted except for Chris and this guy. In the silence, I could immediately feel that the temperature in the room was in the 30s. Chris was in one of his towering 'angries.' I turned right around, left, and never saw that guy again."

Lunney felt that the concept management was floating, and the insistence upon going through with it, was an extension of that busy-body mindset. "Gene was the prime guy for this flight, the lead flight director, so he was carrying that argument to people in our management," he added. "They wanted to do something, but they also did not know how difficult this was going to be. They *almost* had us go over to the shroud and mess with that."

In light of the near-disaster that Cernan faced on his scheduled spacewalk, attempting to do the shroud EVA almost certainly would have been lethal.

With two total spacewalks to that point in the history of human spaceflight, one Russian and one American, there were still countless unknowns. The Russians had trumpeted Leonov's feat to the world, but the life-threatening problems he had encountered with his spacesuit and attempting to reenter the airlock of his Voskhod spacecraft went unreported. Ed White had his own issues cramming himself back into the cockpit and then closing the hatch during *Gemini 4*. White's main objective had been not much more than getting out and then back in again, and while he had done just that, *Gemini 8*'s early termination resulted in the cancellation of Dave Scott's jaunt outside and a missed opportunity to further figure out what could and could not be done during a spacewalk.

Cernan was about to prove once and for all that there was far more to the business of spacewalking than mere sightseeing. The goal was to test the Astronaut Maneuvering Unit (AMU) located at the base of the spacecraft, but as the two-hour, seven-minute EVA wore on, his main concern became mere survival. His suit was too stiff. When he wanted to go one way, he had no hand- or footholds to steady himself and wound up going the other. His heart rate rocketed to nearly two hundred beats per minute, and he was sweating profusely with the supreme effort. His visor became completely fogged, and he could clear only one small spot by rubbing his nose against it. Communication between the crewmates was spotty. Afterward, it was discovered that Cernan's suit had gotten scraped during the nightmarish incident, cutting through a layer or two.

As encouraging as White's excited comments had been during *Gemini 4*, the conversations between Stafford and Cernan had to have been downright shocking for those back in the MOCR to hear. Over and over again, Cernan mentioned his ever-worsening visor situation.

Boy, I'm fogged up. My pressure . . . my pressure reading is fogged up, my visor's fogged up, and I'm in high flow.

And then later . . .

Okay, Gene. How we doing?

I don't know. I'll let you know.

And . . .

Just sit there and rest, Gene. You just take it easy. If we're going to have any trouble with visibility on loosening electrical parts, let's just take our time.

When Stafford asked if the visor was clearing up any, Cernan's reply was gallows humor at its best.

If I don't breathe.

While over the Carnarvon tracking station, Stafford gave the ground a report about Cernan's condition.

We had about four or five times more work than what we anticipated and the pilot's visor is completely fogged over, nearly frozen into him. I'm having him stay there and just relax. Also, our communications are very poor. He has a lot of garble.

Less than five minutes later, Stafford called off the test of the AMU and got Cernan headed back inside, coaching him like a worried parent rather than a stern spaceflight commander.

Why don't you just stand there and relax for a while, Gene? Let me know when you get unfogged.

Cernan apologized for the AMU, but there was no need. The test was not the point, not then. Stafford would later admit his growing concern that Cernan might not make it back inside, and said that while he would not have cut the umbilical loose, the horrifying result was that the spacecraft would have reentered the earth's atmosphere with Cernan being dragged behind.

Back in the MOCR, controllers felt as if yet another bullet had been dodged. "When all was said and done, we were just damn lucky to get through it," Lunney conceded. "It was not a matter of just stopping and going back in for Gene. It was spooky."

Cernan, of course, survived the incident to fly *Apollo 10* and he then became the most recent human to walk on the moon during his command of *Apollo 17* in December 1972. If anything good came out of the shroud EVA debacle and Cernan's problematic spacewalk, it was what Lunney called a "pronounced change in attitude" about management's role in the MOCR. From then on, he concluded, they simply asked to be kept up to date on changes to the flight plan so that headquarters could remain informed. "I think when the flight was over, those guys sat down, talked to each other, and said, 'You know, we almost screwed up royally. We'd better back off from telling these flight guys what to do,'" Lunney said.

Things were moving fast as the Gemini program progressed. Before *Gemini 9A*, Glynn Lunney had never before worked a manned mission at the flight director's console, yet just two months later, he was the *lead* flight director on *Gemini 10* flown by John Young and Michael Collins in July 1966.

How anxious was he? That was a good question. "Let's see . . . what's the best way to answer that?" he began. "I was really pleased with the idea of being a flight director, and felt I was ready to grow into that. It took me a while to go learn all the systems and be comfortable with that side of the business, but *everything* we did was a crash course. I don't know I would say that I was nervous about it. I knew it was a challenge, and I knew I had a lot I needed to be ready for." Not once, Lunney continued, did he ever feel as if he could not handle the responsibilities of the position. Instead, he just wanted to get on with the program.

Get on with it he did. With Gene Kranz gearing up for Apollo, Lunney and Cliff Charlesworth were left to swap lead flight director duties for the remaining three missions of the Gemini program. The most pressing item up for business was getting a handle on these confounded EVAs. If Ed White and Gene Cernan had proven anything, it was the cold, hard fact that nobody knew just how much they did not know about the business of spacewalks. "For all the effort we put on rendezvous and stuff like that, it was EVA that turned out to be the thing that we did not understand as well as we should have in the Gemini program," Lunney granted. "Gemini was quite an eye-opening thing for us, in terms of EVA. It was at that point that people said, 'Oh my God, we've really got to do something. This is a lot more difficult than we thought.'"

Looking back, at least part of the reason for the difficulties was the result of the organization that was in place. In Flight Operations, issues such as ascent, rendezvous, and guided entries were worked in great detail during meetings with Bill Tindall. When it came to EVA, though, such preparation was handled in a different division and catered more to an individual astronaut's own preferences. Leadership for EVA planning changed with each flight, so there was no single go-to manager through Gemini. "When we did the EVAs, they were planned kind of by a handful of people over in Deke Slayton's organization," Lunney said. "It wasn't done in the full glare of the meetings and the reviews like Bill Tindall's outfit did." It was not a criticism on Lunney's part, just a recognition that EVAs were approached differently than most of the rest of the flight. Nobody in the MOCR had come up with the idea for hand- and footholds either.

Collins did two EVAs on *Gemini 10*, the first in which he simply stood up in the hatch to photograph the Southern Milky Way and a plate on the side of the spacecraft. On the second, he had trouble securing a Micrometeorite Collector, and after he finally did get it, the plates soon mistakenly floated out of the cabin as the spacewalk continued. Having rendezvoused with the Agena that Armstrong and Scott had docked with during *Gemini 8*, Collins headed over and tried his best to work with it. When he attempted to use the Hand-Held Maneuvering Unit first tested by White, it quit on him. The spacewalk ended after just thirty-nine minutes. "*Gemini 10* was mostly a free-form EVA, where Mike Collins went over and got some sample plates off the Agena, but in the end, he lost those and we brought him back in the spacecraft," Lunney said. "*Gemini 10* didn't ring our bell with the difficulty of EVA. We'd already experienced that on *9*."

Spacewalks were obviously not the only issues on the table. Altitude records increased gradually until Young and Collins boosted to about 474 miles on *Gemini 10*, but that was barely a drop in the bucket when it came to going to the moon. The plan was for *Gemini 11*'s Pete Conrad and Richard F. "Dick" Gordon Jr. to nearly double that during their three-day flight in September 1966.

Managing successful EVAs and altitude were a couple of items on NASA's to-do list. For one MOCR operator before the flight of *Gemini 11*, navigating a minefield of red tape was another.

Bill Peters made his debut at the Agena console in the MOCR after a practical joke spun wildly out of control. Mel Brooks—the one who was supposed to sit the shifts during the upcoming mission—was an avid Barry Goldwater supporter at the time. When he spotted some cans of Ginger Ale soda rebranded with the political figure's name, Brooks bought a couple of six-packs and covertly placed them on the desks of his supervisors and lead controllers. In mock retribution, someone loaded Brooks's desk down with a pile of Goldwater campaign material and placed a bumper sticker on his car. That would have been all well and good, the joke over and done with, but security spotted it and reported the whole thing. Brooks was accused of being in violation of the Hatch Act, which prohibited federal employees from engaging in political activities. Although Gene Kranz testified that the whole episode had been a joke, Brooks wound up suspended for thirty days without pay.

Just like that, Peters was moved from the SSR to the front room for the final two flights of the Gemini program.

With Charlesworth at the helm for his initial run as lead flight director, Conrad and Gordon docked with the Agena on their first orbit just an hour and thirty-four minutes after lifting off from the Cape. Before hitting the sack for the day, both astronauts got the chance to pull back from the Agena and dock again.

The next day, Gordon did the first of two spacewalks and again, attaching a tether between the Gemini capsule and the Agena proved difficult. One of the most well-known photographs of the Gemini era captured Gordon as he straddled the nose of the spacecraft, just like a cowboy riding a bucking bronco. The sound of his labored breathing stuck for years afterward with Glynn Lunney, who called it a terrible noise and sound. "Dick was struggling," Lunney said. "I could just feel his heart thumping away up there, and I said, 'My God, there's got to be something we can do easier than this or we'll never do it.'" A standup EVA later in the flight went well enough, but that was likely due to the fact that Gordon's photography work did not require much if any physical exertion.

Rendezvous and docking was turning out to be a piece of cake. EVA? Not so much, even on the fourth attempt. There were other considerations as well during the flight of *Gemini 11*.

Gordon eventually managed to get the tether attached for an experiment in which they would attempt to produce artificial gravity. When the Agena began loosely oscillating at the end of the tether during the test, Bob Carlton had his hands full trying to figure out a solution. "Did you ever have a situation where things were going to hell in a handbasket, and it wasn't nothing you could do about it?" he asked with a chuckle. "Everybody's breathing down your back, saying, 'What do we do? What do we do? What do we do?' and you didn't have a clue? That was that situation."

Kraft pressed him for answers. So did his boss, Mel Brooks. Years later, he could laugh about their exchange.

Bob! Tell 'em what to do. Tell them what to do!

There was only one problem.

Mel, I ain't got a clue. I don't know what to do.

"You don't know what the crew is doing, and more than that, you just can't visualize what to do about the dynamics of what's going on," Carlton continued. "The long and short of it was I was helpless. It was a bad feeling, too, I'll tell you. Not very many times as a flight controller did we have a situation where I felt totally helpless, but that was one of them."

Bill Gravett also had concerns during the flight. Back in Dayton, Ohio, his father grew up on the same street as the Wright brothers, Orville and Wilbur. They tended to keep to themselves, his grandfather had told him, but little could any of them have imagined that the adventure of powered flight that the Wrights invented would one day lead to the work Bill Gravett was doing as a retro officer in the Trench.

Using the Agena to boost Conrad and Gordon to an altitude of 850 miles was a huge concern to Gravett, who had been with NASA, officially, for all of twenty months. "The spacecraft heat shield was not designed to reenter out of an orbit like that," he explained. "It really made me nervous, knowing that if something happened with us up that high, we couldn't execute an emergency reentry right away. We had to learn how to play with the

Real-Time Computer Complex reentry processor to get it to come up with a solution for the retrofire. You had to provide it a guess, the best estimate of a time to fire those retro rockets to come out of the orbit." Just talking about it decades later, Gravett could feel his heart start beating faster.

Gravett's fretful concern was for naught. The vista that unfolded far beneath Conrad and Gordon was gorgeous, and they splashed down nearly thirty-one hours later less than three miles from their prime recovery ship, the USS *Guam*. It would not be the astronauts' last spaceflight together, and definitely not their farthest from home.

Buzz Aldrin's doctoral thesis at MIT was on manned orbital rendezvous, and after he joined NASA in its third astronaut class, he never seemed to hesitate to weigh in about anything having to do with the subject. That was the stuff of theory, of classrooms and chalkboards, but Aldrin got a real-world opportunity to put his knowledge to use during the flight of *Gemini 12* on 11 November 1966.

The Gemini capsule's onboard radar refused to cooperate as Lovell started the final phase of the docking process with its Agena target, but that was no problem for Aldrin. He figured out the maneuvers himself, and there were those back on the ground who laughed and joked that the balky radar might not have been an accident. "We never let him forget this," said Ken Young, the rendezvous specialist stationed in the SSR. "His rendezvous radar *allegedly* failed on *Gemini 12*, and he had to do a manual calculation for the terminal phase. We said, 'Oh, yeah. It *really* failed. It was just a coincidence that the only one that failed was on his flight.'"

The rendezvous radar was not the only technical glitch. Fuel-cell stacks failed. A couple of thrusters did not want to work properly. What did work well from start to finish—at long, long last—were Aldrin's EVAs planned for the mission. The first and third were standups in the hatch, but on the second, he easily made his way from one end of the spacecraft to the other thanks to new hand- and footholds. On the ground, he had been one of the first to make full use of underwater training techniques. Gemini's final hurdle had been cleared, and with room to spare. Mission planners, flight controllers, flight directors, and astronauts alike were experienced and ready for the final push to the lunar surface. "We just applied all the lessons we'd been learning all along," Glynn Lunney concluded. "By the time we came out of Gemini, the experience had rippled through multiple people within all of those jobs. They were pretty damn good at the stuff we had to use when we went to the moon. We came out of Gemini like gangbusters. We were ready to do Apollo. We were pretty confident in ourselves, maybe even pushing the envelope a little bit, that we would be able to handle anything that came up."

Until the evening of 27 January 1967, the MOCR had in fact been able to handle everything that had been thrown its way. It took less than fifteen seconds to shake that kind of supreme confidence to its very foundation.

4. We're Going to Make It Right

On the afternoon of 22 November 1963, Dallas businessman Abraham Zapruder excitedly awaited the arrival of President Kennedy's motorcade in Dealey Plaza. In his hands was his trusty eight-millimeter camera, primed and ready to capture a home movie of the big event.

The 486 frames Zapruder shot that Friday lasted a mere twenty-six seconds, but in those six feet of film were images of a gruesome murder, the end of Camelot, and the start of one of the most turbulent periods in American history. *Life* magazine purchased still and motion-picture rights to the film before the weekend was over and published thirty-one frames—excluding the most graphic—in an issue that hit newsstands just three days after the tragedy. More than twenty years would pass before the complete film was viewed by the public at large, and the reaction was one of complete and utter shock.

Few losses of life would ever be recorded in quite so troubling a fashion, except, maybe, for audio of the *Apollo 1* fire on 27 January 1967. No video images have ever been discovered of the accident, but its sounds are nevertheless very deeply disturbing.

The plugs-out test had not gone well that day, and moments before the flame that was to claim his life broke out, command pilot Gus Grissom could not contain his growing frustration.

How are we going to get to the moon if we can't talk between three buildings?

There was no response from Clarence A. "Skip" Chauvin, the test conductor capcom who was located not 240,000 miles away, but a mere handful in the Operations and Checkout Building at the Cape. Ed White, the all-American hero of *Gemini 4* spacewalking fame, was quick with a quip.

They can't hear a thing you're saying.

Grissom was not happy.

Jesus Christ.

Say again?

How are we going to get to the moon if we can't talk between two or three buildings?

Another minute passed, during which possible indications of crew movement could be heard in the crackling comm. At four seconds past 6:31 p.m. on the Florida launch pad, a voice rang out in alarm. Some thought it was rookie Roger B. Chaffee, others White.

Hey!

Two more calls, these likely from White.

I have got a fire in the cockpit!

The next began with either the singular pronoun *I* or possibly the plural *we*, while the next four words seemed unmistakable.

. . . have a bad fire!

The final voice transmission was determined to have come from Chaffee, and it was the most terrible, the most heartbreaking, the most sickening of all. It was a primal howl, perhaps attempting to actually say something or perhaps not, as the side of the Command Module ruptured with the force of the blaze.

Hundreds of miles away in Houston, flight controllers monitoring the test from the MOCR on the second floor heard every brutal second.

If heading into Apollo was not exactly starting over from scratch, it seemed to be something very much like it after the successes of the Gemini program. The way John Aaron put it, things just were not as crisp as the program that had just concluded. McDonnell Aircraft constructed both the Mercury and Gemini spacecraft, while the Apollo Command and Service Module contract went to North American Aviation. Experience in building spacecraft did not carry over from the first two programs to the third, and North American's original Block 1 spacecraft turned out to be what Charley Parker not-so-delicately termed "really a mess."

Gene Kranz was shocked by how far Rockwell's Block 1 capsule had to go before it could fly with the same kind of quality as the Gemini spacecraft. "All of our experience had been with McDonnell, and Rockwell was used to building fighter airplanes, rolling them out of the factories, et cetera, and they weren't about to listen to anybody that wasn't a test pilot, okay?" he said. "So the astronauts were able to influence, to a great extent, Rockwell. We had virtually no influence out at Rockwell on the next system." The people on the ground had to know the craft that was going to be flown, and before the *Apollo 1* fire changed everything, that simply was not happening.

That was only one part of the problem. There were simply too many cooks in the kitchen. Grumman Aircraft Engineering Corporation built the Lunar Module, while the Boeing Company, North American, and Douglas Aircraft Company combined to construct the monstrous Saturn 1B and Saturn V launch vehicles. The Saturn 1B flew three unmanned test flights before the end of the Gemini program. Gemini flight controllers were busy flying missions, while a separate group of planners worked on all things Apollo. The result was that Gemini controllers had experience on console, but little if any background in Apollo systems and procedures. Those who had been studying such things on Apollo, in turn, tended to have comparatively little real-time experience in the MOCR. The two groups mixed as Gemini came to an end and Apollo began, but not very well at the outset.

There were three full years remaining in the decade, but the slain president's deadline was in dire jeopardy. "We had what people thought was plenty of time, but there wasn't," said Bob Carlton, who was making the switch from Gemini Agena flight controller to Apollo Lunar Module control officer. "We were not getting ready fast enough, and it was compounded by a whole bunch of factors. Everything was in limbo."

Then came that horrific night.

Dutch von Ehrenfried left NASA in January 1966 to move to Denver, Colorado for a much better paying job, but after the excitement of *Gemini 8*, he realized just how much he missed flight control. After just four months away, Lunney gave him a job at the guidance console in the Trench.

That was where von Ehrenfried found himself on the night of the accident, alongside Will Presley. John Aaron was working his very first Apollo shift that night, having swapped with fellow EECOM Rod Loe, who was celebrating his anniversary by playing bridge with wife Tina and a few other couples. Arnie Aldrich and Gerry Griffin, both GNCs who would have been sitting right next to Aaron, were in the room as well. Bill Gravett handed the retro console over to Chuck Deiterich and was on his way to a date when he heard. Gravett called Deiterich and asked if he needed to come back in, but the answer was no.

There was nothing he could do.

Gene Kranz was dressing for a dinner date with his wife, Marta, when next-door neighbor and LM branch chief Jim Hannigan knocked at his front door and told him the news. Rushing to MSC, he found Building 30 locked down and got in only after bulldozing his way past a security guard and taking a freight elevator up to the second floor. Glynn Lunney had dinner plans with astronaut William A. "Bill" Anders, Jerry Bostick, and their wives. FIDO Dave Reed had been on an earlier shift for the test, and headed home after grabbing a few checklists from his office. Ed Fendell got off work, too, and went across the street with a few others to hit the bar at the local Holiday Inn. FIDO Jay Greene was in downtown Houston at a joint called the LeCue Pool Hall. Charley Parker, the MOCR's original guidance controller, heard the news on his car radio.

Chris Kraft, returning one more time to the flight director's role that he invented, had also left the second-floor MOCR to catch up on some work in his office. He was still an operations guy at heart, and could take pushing papers for only so long. Around 4 p.m. or so, he went back to the control room.

Like every other person who was there that night, Kraft heard the chaos of the fire unfolding in his headset. Their heads shot up, looking at each other in stunned disbelief. Surely, they had not heard what they had just heard.

What was that?

Did somebody just say fire?

Kraft began praying harder, he said, than he ever had in his life. Part of him wanted to get on the loop to the Cape to ask what was going on, but he did not, knowing that the pad workers already had their hands full. "Around me in mission control, there was an awful silence," Kraft wrote in his autobiography. "Every member of my team sat white-faced and rigid, every ear tuned to the terrible sounds coming from the Cape. We were nine hundred miles away and helpless. This was not an emergency that mission control could handle."

Another test conductor, George F. Page, was in the smoke-filled White Room surrounding the spacecraft. He gave a quick report to Kraft, who could hear the despair in Page's voice. After waiting a couple of minutes,

Kraft could stand it no longer and asked about the crew. Page's reply shot through the MOCR.

Not much hope, Flight. We'll have the hatch open in a minute.

After another couple of minutes, another message from the launch pad confirmed the worst. Kraft could not tell if the voice was Page's or maybe somebody else's, not that it really mattered.

The crew is dead.

"My stomach lurched and I felt sick all over, so weak and drained that I almost collapsed into my chair," wrote Kraft, who served as a pallbearer at Grissom's funeral. "People had these stares, looking at each other like, 'What the hell?'" von Ehrenfried remembered. "It wasn't a big, fast, emotional thing, but by the time I left, I was in tears." Von Ehrenfried was later assigned to the program office as a staff engineer for the flight of *Apollo 7*. He also became an Apollo pressure suit test subject, and in late 1969 he applied to the astronaut office. That night, however, Jerry Bostick found von Ehrenfried in the parking lot outside the building, repeating the same word, over and over.

Terrible.

Terrible.

Terrible.

John Aaron's wife, Cheryl, called Loe and asked if he could go pick her husband up at the control center. He charged out to MSC and found Aaron, who had repeatedly gone over the data from the accident to see if he might figure out a root cause. Emotionally and physically drained to the point of no return, Aaron was in no shape to make the drive home. By Sunday, Loe was on a NASA Gulfstream jet bound for the Cape to assist in the investigation. He heard the cockpit recordings, as did several others. "We'd had a pretty long run of real success in Mercury and Gemini, and it was a bolt out of the blue," said Arnie Aldrich, who was asked by Kraft to review the tapes. "Nobody expected it, and it was devastating. It caused doubts about ourselves we hadn't had before."

On the Monday following the accident, Gene Kranz told John Hodge that he was calling a meeting in a Building 30 auditorium. His initial shock had turned to anger. Three astronauts were dead—astronauts that many in the MOCR knew well—and he had an inescapable sense that the control team had somehow let them down. After a few remarks by Hodge, Kranz climbed the four steps to the stage. Searching at first for words, he began.

Spaceflight will never tolerate carelessness, incapacity, and neglect. Somewhere, somehow, we screwed up. It could have been in design, build, or test. Whatever it was, we should have caught it. We were too gung ho about the schedule and we locked out all of the problems we saw each day in our work. Every element of the program was in trouble and so were we. The simulators were not working, mission control was behind in virtually every area, and the flight and test procedures changed daily. Nothing we did had any shelf life. Not one of us stood up and said, "Damn it, stop!"

As he continued speaking, the passionate fervor in Kranz's countenance took on that of a tent-revival preacher. He did not know what the review board chaired by Langley Research Center director Floyd L. Thompson would determine as the cause of the accident, but Kranz knew what he thought as he continued:

We are the cause! We were not ready! We did not do our job! We were rolling the dice, hoping that things would come together by launch day, when in our hearts we knew it would take a miracle. We were pushing the schedule and betting that the Cape would slip before we did.

The two words Kranz wanted ingrained in everyone's mind from there on out were "tough" and "competent." Those present were told to write them on the blackboards in their offices, never to be erased, as a reminder of the sacrifice that had been made by Grissom, White, and Chaffee. No matter how many people actually obeyed the command, its impact was the same. "When you hear about Kranz and his speech after the fire, that sounds like this great big hoo-rah thing," said Ed Fendell, ever the wordsmith. "That's an unbelievable speech. You've just killed three people, and some guy you work for carries everybody in his organization, even the secretaries, into this auditorium and commenced to tell them that we're *all* at fault. It's not only the vehicle. What kind of an individual does that? Is that an ordinary guy? That's not an ordinary guy."

Fendell's remarks were not a criticism of Kranz by any stretch of the imagination. Fendell went so far as to equate the flight director with Joshua L. Chamberlain, an ordinary antebellum college professor turned Civil War hero who was awarded the Medal of Honor for his actions on the Gettysburg battlefield.

NASA was forced at every level to take a step back and reexamine itself to the point where there was one agency before the fire and an almost completely different one afterward. The first order of business was making the decision to not end the American march to the moon then and there, a move that was actively considered in some corners. "Imagine if it had turned out the other way," Glynn Lunney began. "Suppose Apollo ended with the fire and the loss of three people, and we turned away from the challenge. How would the Cold War have turned out? What would that have looked like if we'd just said, 'We're done. We're getting out of this competition'? How would that have looked in history?"

A specific cause was never determined for the *Apollo 1* fire, but plenty of kindling was found—a cabin pressurized with 100 percent pure oxygen and filled with flammable materials. Never again would those kinds of catastrophic components come together on an American spacecraft. For many, years of reflection and hindsight showed that had it not been for the loss of the *Apollo 1* crew and the top-to-bottom improvements that came with it, Kennedy's end-of-the-decade deadline would probably not have been met. "From our perspective in the control center, we said, 'We're never going to let anything like that happen again. If it's not right, then we're going to *make* it right before we commit a crew to it,'" said Charley Parker. "That's the way we approached it, and I think that's the way a lot of people did."

A 3 April 1968 press release announced that Glynn Lunney had been assigned as lead flight director for *Apollo 7*, the first manned flight of the redesigned program, while Gene Kranz was scheduled at that point to handle the second, *Apollo 8*.

There were no surprises there, but it was the next piece of news that had already raised more than a few eyebrows in and around the MOCR. Joining the ranks of flight directors were M. P. "Pete" Frank III, Milton L. Windler, and Gerry Griffin—Frank and Windler flew jets in the marines and air force, respectively, while Griffin was an air force backseater. At first glance, their time in the air appeared to be the only thing the three men had in common. Frank was chief of the Lunar Missions Analysis Branch in the Mission Planning and Analysis Division at the time, while Windler came to the job from the role of chief of the Operational Test Branch in the Landing and Recovery Division. Technically, both were part of Flight Operations, but neither Frank nor Windler had ever had so much as a second's time on a MOCR console.

For some in the control room, that was cause for, if not outright resentment, then certainly surprise. Definitely, Gene Kranz disagreed. "I believed all flight directors should be selected from the ranks of mission control and was surprised by the selection of two virtual unknowns," he wrote in his autobiography. "Since they would need time to come up to speed, I successfully lobbied Kraft to add Gerry Griffin, a top-notch Gemini controller, to the list so we could get some immediate help."

Kranz knew neither Frank nor Windler, and for Frank at least, all he knew of Kranz was his hard-driving reputation. That gave him more than a moment's pause when approached about the job—could he put up with Kranz? "His personality was totally different from mine," said Frank, who died 22 February 2005 after being involved in an automobile accident. "I'm really pretty casual and not exactly laid-back, but don't get real excited about things and not very intense in dealing with things. Gene is a very intense person. You get that message real quick."

It marked the beginning of an extraordinary journey for Frank, who was initially completely befuddled by the MOCR's intercom system. Observing during a Gemini mission, he plugged in but did not know how to operate the console. "I pushed one of the buttons, and it started flashing," he recalled. "I thought, 'God, what have I done?' I'd punch it again and it kept flashing." If that was his introduction to the control room, his baptism of fire came the day that Glynn Lunney had to be in two places at once—a meeting over in Building 2 and a launch-abort simulation in the MOCR. Lunney went to the meeting and handed the sim off to Frank. Lunney left him with a pep talk. There is nothing to it, he told Frank. The guys know what they are doing, so just respond to their calls.

Frank sat down for the simulation, felt lost, and called it a "horrible day." Despite all that, however, Frank managed to get through it. "I felt like an idiot and looked like an idiot," Frank admitted. "There's these guys that someday you're supposed to be down there running this thing telling them what to do. Here they're seeing you do this and you don't know what you're doing." Frank would go on to sit down with controllers at each of the consoles in the room, learning their responsibilities and problems. After the native of Bryan, Texas, sat his first shift during the May 1969 flight of *Apollo 9*, he came into his own. He was lead flight director for both *Apollo 14* and *Apollo 16*, and by the end of the lunar landings, he was chief of the Flight Directors Office and lead for the Apollo-Soyuz Test Project as well.

From 1974 to 1982, he served as chief of the Flight Control Division—a role once held by Kranz. "I have a lot of respect and admiration for him," Frank said. "Once you get beyond this outward façade that he has—it's not really a façade, he's truly what he says he is—he's also a really kind, decent person behind all that. He's not just a martinet that he runs by, you wind him up, and he does things. He's a real human being."

Windler joined NASA's predecessor, the National Advisory Committee for Aeronautics, in 1954 after graduating from Virginia Polytechnic Institute—Kraft's alma mater, which is now Virginia Tech—with a degree in aeronautical engineering. He specialized in location aids and operational testing in Landing and Recovery, and when he was called in and asked if he might like to be a flight director, Windler did not have to think about it.

Yes.

Windler would insist that he was never aware of any controversy that might have come with his being named to the job. "Among the troops, the people that had been doing that kind of thing, yeah, they probably said, 'Pete who? Milt who?' Most of them probably didn't have any idea who we were, but nobody ever said anything to me," Windler began. "It never really became a factor in my mind." Like Frank, Windler found training to be intense. Griffin had a systems background, and Windler had to get one, not only in the Command and Service Module but also in the Lunar Module and, to a somewhat lesser extent, the Saturn V booster. His first flight on the flight director's console was *Apollo 8*, during coasts to and from the moon. To Windler, the lower-activity phases of the mission were not nearly as exciting as his first solo flight, or the first time he strapped into a high-performance F-86 *Sabre* jet fighter.

That was solo, too, because it had no backseat.

After the fire and during the almost total overhaul of North American's Command and Service Module, Griffin spent most of the next year going back and forth between Houston and Downey, California, and helping remove as much flammable material from its cockpit as possible. Becoming a flight director was not something he sought or even expected, but if somebody had asked him beforehand if he might be interested in the position, his response would have been a rapid one.

You're damn right.

Somewhere along the line, he got a phone call from somebody—it might have been Kranz, but Griffin was not sure—that changed the course of his life.

Hey, we want to make you a flight director.

Griffin mulled the offer over for all of a second or two before responding.

Fine!

Kraft had been the decision maker on every other flight director, but Griffin understood that he had somebody else in his corner, at least when it came to his selection. "Gene Kranz got into it a little, probably even when I was selected, or maybe even quite a bit," Griffin figured. One way or the other, John Hodge was in sharp disagreement with what was taking place, and, in fact, he ended up moving on at least in part because of it. His issue was not necessarily that Windler and Frank came from outside the close-knit circle of MOCR controllers, but rather that he had known nothing of the assignments, experience or not. "I didn't mind at all the idea that somebody was coming from outside," Hodge said. "I was just annoyed that [Kraft] didn't consult me on it. He said he thought I'd disagree with him on it, and I said, 'Yeah. That's what I'm supposed to do. I didn't think I'd change your mind, but my job was to argue with you on those kinds of positions.'"

A 14 May 1968 press release announced that Hodge had been reassigned as director of the newly established Lunar Exploration Working Group, in which he would "be responsible for coordination and direction of all MSC activities relating to lunar exploration" in Houston, at NASA headquarters in Washington, and with other outside groups involved in the Lunar Exploration Program. In his place as division chief went Gene Kranz, who figured that Hodge's decision to move on was partly personal, partly organizational, and partly policy related. In the end, he believed that Kraft felt Hodge was too conservative to be a flight director.

Hodge eventually left NASA in 1970, the highest-ranking member of a contingent that went to work at a new research center in Cambridge, Massachusetts, operating under the auspices of the Department of Transportation. While he returned to the agency in 1982–86, working as director of the Space Station Task Force and as acting associate administrator, some thought there had been more to his departure from the Flight Control Division in the first place. A graduate of the University of London with First Class Honors in engineering, there was no doubting the Englishman's pedigree. He was a nice guy and maybe a little too nice to corral the competitive energies of a go-getter group like those who worked in the MOCR. Other branches within Flight Operations complained about working with a bunch that could at times come across as a bunch of know-it-all prima donnas. Once Kranz took over, it was up to him to make it right. They could either work things out among themselves, or he would step in and make whatever call needed to be made.

Nobody was going to intimidate Gene Kranz, but he did not become an autocratic dictator either. "Kranz always thought that whatever he did was right, and if somebody didn't like to do it his way, that's fine, they could challenge him," said a former flight controller who asked that his name not be used. "He was the first guy I ever worked for that if he came up with some plan, you could tell him right to his face, 'That plan's no good.' He'd say, 'Okay, show me why.' If you did show him why, he'd change it. If you didn't, he won and you went by his plan."

That kind of character trait did as much as, if not more than, anything else to gain Gene Kranz the respect of those who worked under him. He was a tough-as-nails boss, yes, but more important, an approachable one.

From the first time that Bill Gravett sat the retro console late in the Gemini program, he had been confident about the situations and emergencies for which he had trained over and over and over again. Those sims could be rough, no doubt about it. God help you if you sent the wrong command at the wrong time.

The loops would go into bedlam, the Cape, SSR, test conductors, and the flight director all wanting to know what had happened and what was going to be done about it. There was not a hint of sarcasm or irony in Gravett's voice when he said that sims were not a restful, easygoing atmosphere at all. Yet that was where mistakes were supposed to be made, where things were supposed to go wrong. When he made it out to the front room for the last four flights of the Gemini program, there were butterflies to be sure, but he felt sure he could handle virtually anything that had ever been thrown his way in a sim. A nagging question, though, always seemed to be haunting him in the back of his mind.

What about the situations that the real world is going to throw at me for which I have not *received training?*

The unmanned Saturn V test flight of *Apollo 6*—officially known as AS-502—turned out to be exactly Bill Gravett's worst nightmare.

The first time the Saturn V flew, on 9 November 1967, those in the second-floor MOCR had been astounded by how well it performed. The flight of *Apollo 4* was "perfection," Gravett said, getting off the launch pad as though it had been flying a million years. After *Apollo 5*—another unmanned Saturn IB test with a working LM that was controlled out of the second-floor MOCR in January 1968—it was Gravett's turn on *Apollo 6*. "I guess the management said, 'The first one went so good, we'll kind of ease ol' William Gravett in here. We'll let him be on the launch team for the next one, and that should be a piece of cake,'" he said. According to Gravett, he and a handful of others were being groomed for the Moon Platoon, a group of controllers who would handle the early lunar landings, if not *the* first. After Gemini, he had hit the ground running to get Apollo figured out.

How do you do an abort out of a lunar orbit?

How do you do an abort halfway between the earth and the moon to get home?

What kind of computer processors and displays do you need to have to do all that?

He was already scrambling when engineer Jon C. Harpold walked into his office a couple of days before the launch of *Apollo 6*. A glitch had been found in the vehicle's reentry software program.

Oh?

The software was showing the vehicle with more lift than what was actually available, and during the final phase of reentry, the problem was being discovered too late to do anything about it. But do not worry about it, Harpold told Gravett. Multiple failures had to take place in the mission before it would ever actually happen in real time.

Oh?

Come launch day, Gravett was at the retro console in the third-floor MOCR. Next to him was FIDO Jay Greene, with Neil Hutchinson working the guidance console. On the far left of the Trench was Bob Wolf, the booster engineer from Marshall, with backup Frank Van Rensselaer situated between Wolf and Gravett. Wolf smoked constantly and tended to call people "Bud," never by their name. To the rest of the Trench, he became "Bud the Cigarette."

The flight went perfectly for all of two minutes, at which point severe oscillations began to shake the Saturn V so badly that pieces were falling off the area around the Spacecraft/Lunar Module adapter that connected the Command and Service Module to the rest of the stack. The problems did not stop there. Five minutes, nineteen seconds into the flight, thrust on the s-II second stage's Engine Number 2 dropped significantly due to a ruptured igniter fuel line. Just short of a minute later, the eleven-foot-tall Rocketdyne j-2 engine shut down altogether. Less than two seconds after that, Engine Number 3 followed suit. Greene noticed the depressed trajectory and mentioned it to Hutchinson and Gravett. Hutchinson saw the vehicle steering way more than normal, gimbals moving around all over the place, trying to make up for the oscillations and engine cutouts. Gravett heard Wolf talking to his SSR over the comm loop.

You lost what?!? You lost an engine?

Gravett turned to Greene.

Booster is saying we lost two engines on the S-II.

Sure enough, the Trenchmates saw altitude starting to peel off and the vehicle flying "*low* and *slow*," remembered Gravett. Both Greene and Hutchinson had gotten on the loop to let flight director Cliff Charlesworth know what was taking place when Wolf chimed in. "About that time, Bud the Cigarette comes on—and of course, he knew this maybe fifteen or twenty seconds before he said it—and said that, yes indeed, an engine had gone down," Hutchinson remembered, and nearly half a century later, he could afford to chuckle. "I was always proud of the fact that me and the flight dynamics officer—actually, I'm *sure* that we didn't figure that out before Bud, but he was so reticent to get on the loop and say, 'Hey, man, one of my big s-II engines crapped out.'"

Guidance software had been set up to compensate for a single failed engine, but not two. Greene watched the whole episode, knowing that two engines out should have meant an abort. He had the capability to call one, and so did Wolf. "We're sitting there on pins and needles, man," Gravett said. "I kind of had a funny feeling in the back of my mind that said, 'I think it'll be a cold day in hell before Marshall Space Flight Center authorizes an abort on their baby up there.'" He remembered the ensuing conversation between Charlesworth and Wolf.

Okay, booster. It's your call.

Flight, it seems to be flying along. My bosses say as long as it's not a safety problem, let's let her go and see what she'll do.

The range safety officer located at the Cape was seeing the same thing as the MOCR. The vehicle had not violated any limits, so Charlesworth held him off. The loss of the two engines caused the remaining three to burn for nearly fifty-eight seconds longer than normal, and then the third-stage S-IVB also had to burn for an extra twenty-nine seconds. The problems continued to pile up. "The vehicle lofted, and then got on third stage and it started to dive straight at the earth," Greene said. "Based on that, I had a limit line that we were approaching and had my sweaty little fingers on the abort switch. The thing finally straightened out and it made it to orbit. Probably the first time we ever inserted into orbit going backwards, based on the way the guidance missed its target box. It just kept trying until it got there."

The Command and Service Module and S-IVB stack was placed into an oddly shaped elliptical orbit of 107.5 miles by 223.6 miles above the earth, instead of the intended circular orbit of 115 miles. "That S-IVB woke up, and it said, 'I am *very* low, and I am *very slow*, and I've got to get with it,'" Gravett continued. "It went to a super-rich fuel mixture, and it *screamed* up to orbit." Everything looked copasetic, Greene said, and the S-IVB engine was reignited for a boost to an altitude of nearly 14,000 miles so that the Command Module's heat shield could be tested at lunar reentry speeds.

The time came for the partial trans-lunar injection (TLI) maneuver, and the time went. The S-IVB engine would not fire.

This was the worst of simulations unfolding on a real mission. Greene threw a switch to separate the CSM from the S-IVB, and the big Service Propulsion System engine at the back of the service module kicked in the additional 7,000 mph or so needed to get to a suitable altitude for the reentry test. Not enough fuel remained, so rather than hitting the atmosphere at 37,000 feet per second, it could only manage 4,000 feet per second less. One final difficulty was facing Gravett, and as a retro officer, it was perhaps the most serious of all. He could not tell anybody where the capsule was going to land. His landing points were literally all over the map. "One of the tenets in being a flight controller that was taught to us by *the* teacher, Chris Kraft, was you gather as much data as possible and you do not make the decision any earlier than you absolutely have to," Gravett said. He was pressed for a landing point, and then pressed again.

His best guess was that the capsule was going to come down approximately a hundred miles short. On that word from Bill Gravett, the USS *Okinawa* recovery ship lit its boilers and hustled to the new splashdown point. It had already been a long day, a tough one, and Gravett was frazzled as the capsule hit the earth's atmosphere. He listened carefully for word from the radar operator on board the carrier, located where he thought *Apollo 6* was going to come down. The call was *not* the one for which he had hoped.

The spacecraft is directly overhead.

Because the capsule was still reentering the atmosphere, there was at that point no way of telling where it might actually hit water. The carrier wheeled around and headed back to where it had been initially, and Advanced Range Instrumentation Aircraft (ARIA) were sent out to begin a search. One ARIA spotted what was thought to be the spacecraft, but it instead turned out to be a whale. Nearly ten hours after launch, the *Apollo 6* capsule was found fifty miles from where it had been expected. The spacecraft had one last surprise in store—it was in the Stable 2 position, nose down into the water and its heat shield facing up. Three flotation bags automatically inflated, and that, along with the ocean's waves, brought the capsule upright well before the recovery ship arrived.

The date was 4 April 1968, the day civil rights leader Martin Luther King Jr. was shot and killed as he stood on a Memphis motel balcony.

Afterward, Bill Gravett chose to step away from the retro console. How would he have felt, he asked himself, about sitting in the MOCR for a manned mission and getting bit the way he had on *Apollo 6*? He had hurried up to catch up during Gemini, and it was starting all over again on Apollo. Could he emotionally and physically handle it? He called up the simulation team and asked if he might be of use. "I didn't feel nearly the stress that I did," Gravett concluded. "Basically what I would do was come up with training cases to throw at the guys in the Trench. It was still a lot of pressure and a lot of weird hours, but it wasn't the pressure of being out there in that seat."

Apollo 6 was over. The next time a Saturn V left the launch, there were three human beings at the pointy end, headed for the moon.

5. Merry Christmas from the Moon

It was late in the summer of 1968, and Rod Loe had been called into a big meeting in Chris Kraft's office. Arnie Aldrich knew what was coming during the gathering, and told Loe that the two of them needed to be there.

Just keep it quiet.

When Loe arrived, it was readily apparent that something important was going down. Frank Borman was there and so were several other movers and shakers in the NASA world. Kraft wasted no time in getting to the point of it all.

Apollo 8 *is going the moon in December.*

Loe's mind buzzed for a moment, silently racing through the implications. He had not been expecting the remark. The calendar said it was August, which meant that a December launch was just four months away. There were, in fact, plenty of reasons not to commit to a lunar journey. There had never been a crew shot into orbit by a Saturn V, and the last time an unmanned one had been launched and tested that April, things had not gone very well at all. And even that was putting it mildly. No human being had ever left the earth's gravitational sphere of influence. Yet here was Kraft, telling his team that Borman and the rest of his crew would be sent that way in four months' time. There were reservations aplenty, but none that could not be overcome. This was to be on a strict need-to-know only basis, and for the time being, not that many people needed to know what might be on tap for *Apollo 8.*

The moment was a seminal one in NASA's history. The agency could meekly back down from John F. Kennedy's challenge with the excuse that it was too difficult and dangerous, or it could boldly stare down those demons and formulate an audacious plan to send Borman, Jim Lovell, and Bill Anders on their way to lunar orbit. NASA did not back down from the monstrous challenge. Instead, NASA opted to spit in the monster's eye. A lot of time had passed, but the memories of those heady days were as fresh and as powerful as they had ever been for Loe. Remembering Kraft's meeting, he paused, trying to choose his words and phrases carefully, each one coming out slowly. Loe was getting choked up, genuinely moved.

Loe served as an EECOM throughout the Gemini program, and was eventually bumped up to oversee the second row's Communications and Life Support Systems group as its section head. Working as "just" an EECOM meant hour after hour at the console, running simulations. On the other hand, being a section head brought with it the responsibilities of managing people and reviewing people and helping people out. Management was all well and good, but it left little time for work in the front room. As a result, Aldrich had been after him for some time to consider moving over to the SPAN room. Loe resisted, because the MOCR was where the action was. In his heart of hearts, Rod Loe was an EECOM and not a manager.

Following the meeting in Kraft's office, Aldrich and Loe walked back to the Mission Control Center together. Loe was struck hard with a thought. He wanted this flight, and he wanted it badly. He wanted to be a part of its planning and its implementation. There would be almost too many firsts to count. This was going to be the biggest thing in the young history of human spaceflight, and so he made Aldrich a deal. "I can remember walking back over to our building with Arnie, and I remember telling him, 'You let me be the lead EECOM on *Apollo 8*, and I'll go into SPAN, no arguments *at all*,'" Loe said.

Loe got his wish, and the flight turned out to be everything he hoped it would be. *Apollo 8* was tailor-made for the CSM systems folks—it was *their* mission, he emphasized. After all, it would be their systems that took the three astronauts on their epic journey. That was despite the fact, of course, that those who worked on the first row of the MOCR would always insist that it was a Trench mission, because it was the Trench's job to establish the trajectory to and from a moving target. In reality, both were correct.

The year 1968 was one in which the world seemed to be coming apart at the seams, but most in the MOCR were too busy to look up from their consoles to notice.

In January, the Tet Offensive served as proof that the situation on the ground in Vietnam was not good and was getting worse. American troops were facing not just a simple band of guerrillas hiding here and there in the bush, but a well-organized and determined enemy. Civil rights icon Martin Luther King Jr. was gunned down in April, while presidential candidate Robert F. Kennedy—brother of the slain president John F. Kennedy—was murdered in June. Nearly seventeen thousand American military service members were killed in Vietnam that year, by far the greatest yearlong total of the war and a full ten thousand more than were lost just two years later.

Unrest exploded around America. Jerry Mill, who had graduated in 1967 from the University of California at Berkeley, was a member of the simulation team when *Apollo 8* flew, and he remembered clearly having to plow through campus demonstrations to get to his physics classes. "When I finally graduated and got a job with NASA, I felt vindicated," said Mill, who would later alternate between working as a guidance officer in the Trench and in the SSR. "I've never been supportive of those kinds of people or that kind of attitude. I always believed in hard work and the United States of America." In August, full-scale riots broke out during Chicago's Democratic National Convention.

Mill was not the only one at NASA to be touched by the war. Gerry Griffin's twin brother, Richard L. "Larry" Griffin, flew 250 U.S. Air Force missions as a forward air controller in Vietnam and in July 1985 became the first commander of the branch's Second Space Wing. Bill Bucholz, the air force officer involved in Ed Fendell's faked heart attack episode back during preparations for *Gemini 7/6*, flew C-123 transports during the conflict.

Richard Stachurski had a friend in the air force who was killed in the conflict. Jack Knight, in training for his debut on *Apollo 9* and the telmu console, was an air force brat who lived at one time or another in the Philippines for a year or so; Libya for two and a half years; Washington DC, while his dad did a stint at the Pentagon; Montgomery, Alabama; and San Antonio, Texas. Jack Sr. also served a tour in Vietnam. More than one person who worked in the MOCR got a draft notice. The letter NASA bosses wrote on his behalf requesting a deferment almost made it seem that if it had not been for Mill, the whole country would have gone down in flames.

It seemed very close to doing so any way.

And then there were the Soviets. It was impossible to forget about the bad guys on the other side of the world. The Cuban Missile Crisis in October 1962 brought the world to the brink of a nuclear holocaust, and while that scare passed, others remained firmly entrenched. When the Russians established some new high ground in the space race, retro officer John Llewellyn came banging on the door of Glynn Lunney's home early in the morning and demanding that the both of them go into work right then and there to do something about it. "That was the world we lived in, one that was frightening," Lunney said. "There was a lot of uncertainty about whether these guys were really going to do something to us. It was a scary time. A lot of people couldn't do anything about it, but we could, at least in our portion that we were in charge of in the space theater."

In mid-September 1968, the Russian *Zond 5* flew to the moon and back. It was unmanned but did carry a crew of sorts in the form of a couple of Russian tortoises, wine flies, and mealworms. That resulted in the Central Intelligence Agency picking up on talk that the Soviets might follow up by attempting to send cosmonauts to circle the moon before the end of the year. After pulling even during the Gemini program and in many respects ahead, NASA was not about to miss out on yet another first in human spaceflight. Not this time. It was then that the idea came to George M. Low.

Low was born in Austria, immigrated to the United States after Nazi Germany's 1938 occupation of the country, and then served in the army during World War II. By 1968 Low had risen to the influential role of manager of the Apollo Spacecraft Program Office. He knew that the LM was not ready, but if all went well on the October flight of *Apollo 7*, why not send a crew to the moon using only the Command and Service Module? The notion was a "shocker," according to Chris Kraft. The quartet of Low; Kraft; Bob Gilruth, the director of MSC; and Deke Slayton were what Kraft called in his autobiography "an unofficial committee that got together often in Bob's office to discuss problems, plans, and off-the-wall ideas. Not much happened in Gemini or Apollo that didn't either originate with us or have our input."

Once the ball started rolling, it gathered momentum on an almost daily basis. One by one, meetings led to more meetings and others were brought into the highly secretive fold. Kraft felt out Gene Kranz, Aldrich, and Jerry Bostick about *Apollo 8*'s lunar plans before the end of the year during a meeting on Friday, 9 August. Aldrich was sure right then and there that the CSM was ready to take on just such a challenge. "It seemed to me immediately that we sure could do that, and it would be a great thing to do," he remembered. "We never did come up with anything in my discipline that said anything different than that."

Meanwhile, for the first few moments at least, Bostick had the almost overwhelming notion that it was the dumbest idea he ever heard. Although Bostick was on board as well by the time he got back to his office, he knew that there were going to be hurdles to clear. He told Kraft, "That's a bold move, and we don't know if we can do it or not. Give us a few hours, and we'll try to figure it out."

Bostick needed to figure out the minimum requirements for the Trench—what displays and capabilities the retro, FIDO, and guidance positions had to have. That in turn became a question for the implementers and how much they could actually accomplish in time to get Borman, Lovell, and Anders off the ground and doing laps of the moon. Software was needed from MPAD for implementation in the Real Time Computing Complex. A new processor was being developed to calculate the maneuvers it would take to get the spacecraft and its crew back home. On top of it all, Kraft wanted Bostick to return to the retro console after working most of the Gemini program as a FIDO. "I would like to think that Chris had great trust in me," said Bostick, who remained the Trench branch chief. "He understood that one of the risks we would be taking was if we had to abort the mission for some reason, and even if we didn't, we were going to be reentering the earth's atmosphere at a higher speed than we ever had before. He had enough confidence in me to think, 'You're the natural guy to supervise all of that the first time we do it.'"

Bostick was back on the retro console, but he was not technically the position's lead for the historic flight of *Apollo 8*. Neither was the larger-than-life John Llewellyn, the section head. Instead, that duty fell to Chuck Deiterich, who would be working his first manned mission. Consider that for a moment—a rookie taking the lead over two of his bosses, one the branch chief and the other his section head. Bostick broke the news to Deiterich;

Ed Pavelka, the flight's lead FIDO; and Charley Parker, who took on the role of lead guidance officer. Pavelka and Parker were heads of their respective sections—Deiterich was not. "Llewellyn was kind of a strong-willed guy," Deiterich said. "But you could get along with him. He always trusted me. Bostick did the same, or they wouldn't have selected me to do that. So as far as feeling like I couldn't say anything or couldn't tell them what to do, that never occurred to me."

There was another reason for Deiterich's relatively easy transition into the leadership role. Once the door of the MOCR closed behind them as they entered, the hierarchy of the first and second rows all but dissolved. There was the flight director and then everybody else. "The administration level in the office environment goes away," Deiterich said. "When you're in the control center, you work for the flight director. You don't work for your branch chief. So, as far as being intimidated because I had my two bosses working for me, I never once thought that what I did or didn't do would affect my career or my relationship with them when we were back in the office. That just never occurred to me."

Parker might have been known as "the Fox" for his calm, cool, and calculating demeanor at the Trench's guidance console, but he could not stifle a chuckle when asked about his response to Bostick's big news. "My initial reaction was, 'Awww, man, that is a long step,'" Parker said in his rich Texas tone. "I had a lot of misgivings about it at first." His primary concern was whether or not the first-floor computing complex could be readied in time with all the necessary programs to compute lunar orbits and returns.

This would not be just a slingshot trip around the moon, either. John P. Mayer, the head of MPAD, and Bill Tindall, a NASA engineer who was the chief of Apollo Data Priority Coordination, figured the flight could go into lunar orbit. "After we got to looking at it and realized we had the capability to do more, we went back with a proposal that said, 'Hey, we want to go into orbit, map the lunar-landing sites, spend a day in orbit, and then come back,'" Parker recalled. "That was kind of a big surprise to headquarters, and they mulled it over for a while before coming back and saying, 'Go for it.'" Before he knew it, Parker was involved in planning and flight techniques meetings and farmed out some of the work on console and training requirements to Will Fenner. It was all still very much hush-hush, so Deiterich, Pavelka, and Parker each limited engaging others as much as possible.

Glynn Lunney served as lead flight director for *Apollo 7*, which was controlled out of the MOCR on the second floor. Although there had been a near mutiny on the part of the crew during that flight, all had gone well with the CSM. Aldrich's confidence in his machine was nowhere near unfounded—that hurdle to the moon for the next flight had just been cleared. As Lunney was walking out of the second-floor control room following *Apollo 7*'s splashdown, Cliff Charlesworth took him aside. Charlesworth would be taking the lead as an *Apollo 8* flight director, and he broke the news about its flight plan. Lunney's response was one of stunned disbelief, though the possibilities were probably already going through his mind.

"We're going to *what?!?*" he wondered out loud. Lunney came around, and quickly. "Within minutes—*minutes*—it was like, 'That's the best damn idea I've ever heard,'" he admitted. "It was like a bolt of energy flowing through this whole team when the idea that we were going to go to the moon on the next flight was decided." Ever supportive of Low and Kraft, Lunney would eventually wonder why *he* had not come up with such a bold initiative.

A bolt of energy or not, NASA was in the process of taking a calculated risk with its future. Barely nineteen months had passed since a fire claimed the lives of the *Apollo 1* crew, and "go fever" had helped seal its fate. In its rush to the moon, issues were overlooked and three astronauts died as a result. Was the same thing in danger of happening again? The goal of beating the Soviets to the moon was admirable enough, but what might happen if another team of astronauts lost their lives in the process? A successful flight of *Apollo 8* would open the gates to a lunar landing, but that success was an awfully big mountain to clear. "It was daring," Bostick concluded. "A lot of hurdles had to be overcome. I knew it was risky, and we did take risks. Glynn Lunney and I in our old retirement years have sat around and talked about how that was really what we were doing. We were in the risk-management business. We didn't call it that, because we'd never heard that before. But that's what it was. We did take risks, but we were never reckless. I didn't think that on *Apollo 8* we were doing anything that was reckless."

Once he got over his initial shock, Lunney was ready to take the leap of faith. "Here's the deal," Lunney said matter-of-factly. "The truth is, if you're going to go to the moon, sooner or later, you've got to go to the moon. Now, you can hunch around and do little things in Earth orbit and so on and so on, but if you want to go to the moon eventually, then eventually, you've got to go to the moon."

It was not until NASA issued a press release on 12 November 1968 that the orbital flight around the moon was officially announced to the public. The flight would depart no earlier than 21 December, so close to Christmas, yet the release insisted that timing of the launch window was "solely dependent" on technical considerations.

Rod Loe was the prime EECOM on *Apollo 8*, and he worked closely with John Aaron while preparing for the mission. "You couldn't keep John away," Loe said. "He was as excited as I was about doing this." From the time the two of them were told of *Apollo 8*'s ambitious flight plan until launch, Loe and Aaron spent most every Saturday at MSC and a few Sundays, too, with Anders. Although there was no Lunar Module to pilot, the rookie astronaut was designated the flight's Lunar Module pilot (LMP). That put him closest to most of the EECOM-related switches near the Command Module's right-hand couch during launch and reentry. Together, the three of them wrote procedures and mission rules and what-iffed everything they could possibly imagine.

They pictured an oxygen leak in the CSM, and what might be powered down in an attempt to get back home in case of some sort of failure in its power systems. They thought of cobbling together some sort of device to scrub excessive carbon dioxide out of the cabin. The groundwork was being laid for the life-threatening issues *Apollo 13* would face in a little more than a year's time. "The decision was made and we scrambled and got everything together to do it," Aaron said. "That was the surprise of the century to me, that we were going to step off *Apollo 7* and just go to the moon. The *Apollo 7* mission demonstrated that the CSM and its systems were ready, but that CSM was launched on a very mature and different booster. But next, we were going to stack men atop that big and relatively new Saturn V on *Apollo 8* and go. That was an incredible surprise, and of course, it went like clockwork."

When *Apollo 8* launched on 21 December 1968, less than nine months had passed since the *Apollo 6* unmanned test of the Saturn V booster went all kinds of haywire.

If sending a crew to the moon seemed ambitious in the late summer of 1968, doing so on top of a Saturn V might well have been considered downright crazy earlier that year to most outsiders. To Glynn Lunney, however, the gigantic launch vehicle had simply "misbehaved" on its second unmanned test. "It just hiccupped all over the place," he said. "But the Marshall guys did fixes for it, and they were the kind of fixes that said, 'Oh, well, that's going to solve this problem. They'll go away, so let's get on it.' The truth is, if you're going to light a big Saturn V, which is really a big bomb that you're trying to control, you might as well get the most out of it."

One of those Marshall guys was Frank Van Rensselaer, who was assigned the booster systems 1 console at the left end of the Trench for the flight of *Apollo 8*. Van Rensselaer had not been prime on *Apollo 6*, but he was for *Apollo 8* and he knew exactly what was on the line. Would the launch vehicle perform as it had been designed, and would he be able to perform as he had been trained? For each and every person who ever sat a console in the control room, the latter was the question of all questions. "It was a great concern after seeing what happened on 502," said Van Rensselaer, referring to *Apollo 6* by its Saturn V spacecraft designation. "The more sims we did, the more you realized how many things could go wrong. So you just hoped that you had prepared yourself for the failures you think might happen. You're trained to think fast. You're trained to say what you had to say on the loop and then get off. You were trained to know where to go to get help, if you had time to get help. Most of the time during the boost phase, you didn't have time to get help."

Apollo 8 was the highlight of many a NASA career for a myriad of reasons, and Van Rensselaer was no different. Knowing what could have gone wrong and seeing what *had* gone wrong on *Apollo 6*, Van Rensselaer felt most would have given the first manned lunar mission not much more than a fifty-fifty chance of making it to the moon. "Frankly, I was just praying we could at least get the crew in orbit," he continued. "We did plenty of simulations on aborts—aborts off the pad, aborts a couple of minutes into the flight, and on all the way into orbit. I think everybody was probably as nervous as they were ever going to be on that flight."

The only other flight in NASA's history that could begin to approach *Apollo 8* in terms of sheer nerve was STS-1, the 1981 maiden voyage of the Space Shuttle. The stack of the orbiter, External Tank, and twin Solid Rocket

Boosters had never been tested together, much less with a couple of living, breathing human beings in the form of astronauts John Young and Robert L. Crippen on board *Columbia*. "We all knew that if something went wrong in the first two minutes, there was no coming home for those guys," Van Rensselaer said. "To picture them sitting on top of that thing, at least on *Apollo 8*, we had a couple of test flights unmanned. One of them didn't work so well, but we did get them in orbit. No matter what flights we're talking about, those two stand out for me as the real gutsy ones."

For all of Van Rensselaer's concerns—or anyone else's, for that matter—the candle was lit under *Apollo 8*'s Saturn V and it left Launch Complex 39, Pad A, at KSC right on time. It was precisely 6:51 a.m. in Houston, and the ascent was described in one of the most beautiful NASA-speak words possible.

Nominal.

Nothing of any consequence, real or imagined, went wrong. Eleven minutes, thirty-five seconds later, *Apollo 8* was in Earth orbit. So far, so good. The first two of three major commit points had been achieved—launch and Earth parking orbit—while a third, the trans-lunar coast up to the point of braking into lunar orbit, still remained. Cliff Charlesworth was the lead flight director, and he had overseen a virtually flawless flight. Next came checks of virtually every nook and cranny of the CSM's systems, making sure that everything was just right. It was. Charlesworth's Green Team was still on shift two and a half hours after the launch when capcom Michael Collins gave the crew a momentous call—the spacecraft's systems checked out fine. They were all set for the translunar injection burn of the S-IVB stage.

All right, Apollo 8. *You are go for* TLI.

For the first time ever, the bonds of Earth orbit were about to be broken. In his extraordinary autobiography, *Carrying the Fire*, Collins wrote of the moment's meaning.

A hush fell over mission control. TLI *was what made this flight different from the six Mercury, ten Gemini, and one Apollo flights that had preceded it, different from any trip man had ever made in any vehicle. For the first time in history, man was going to propel himself past escape velocity, breaking the clutch of our earth's gravitational field and coasting into outer space as he had never done before. After* TLI *there would be three men in the solar system who would have to be counted apart from all the other billions, three who were in a different place, whose motion obeyed different rules, and whose habitat had to be considered a separate planet. The three could examine the earth and the earth could examine them, and each would see each other for the first time. This the people in mission control knew; yet there were no immortal words on the wall proclaiming the fact, only a thin green line, representing Apollo 8 climbing, speeding, vanishing—leaving us stranded behind on this planet, awed by the fact that we humans had finally had an option to stay or to leave—and had chosen to leave.*

The actual burn began at 11:41 a.m. in Houston, about half an hour after Collins's message. The maneuver lasted five minutes and 17.72 seconds, and ten seconds after it was finished, the CSM had been injected into its translunar coast at a speed of more than 6.7 miles per second.

Apollo 8 was on its way.

One last item of business was left, and that was to separate the CSM from the S-IVB third stage thirty minutes after the start of the TLI burn. After spending another twenty minutes photographing the third stage and station keeping, a tiny burn of the Service Module's Reaction Control System moved the two gently apart from one another—a little *too* gently, as it turned out.

When the CSM was still too close for comfort from the spent S-IVB, FIDO Jay Greene began preparing for a second and larger burn to get away for good. "It was kind of interesting," Deiterich remembered. "Borman didn't like where the S-IVB was. I think they approached to see what the panels looked like or what have you, and when they backed away, he still didn't like it. Jay computed a midcourse correction, which certainly put us far away from the S-IVB."

A couple of potentially serious issues cropped up early in the outbound journey. A midcourse correction took place eleven hours into the flight, at 5:50 p.m. in Houston. The flight's trajectory had been biased off ever so slightly, just so the engine could be tested. While it had been targeted to boost the CSM's velocity by 24.9 feet per second, the burn instead came up more than four feet per second short of that goal. This was the same engine that Borman, Lovell, and Anders were depending on to get to the moon, into and out of lunar orbit, and then back home again. Less than half a day into the flight, it was showing an anomaly. "I haven't seen too much written about it, but there was a glitch," said guidance officer Charley Parker. "The engine had a rough start. It didn't come up to thrust properly. So now we really had a problem. Are we really going to trust this engine to put us into lunar orbit, knowing that we're going to have to use that engine to put us into lunar orbit, knowing that we're going to have to use that engine to come out of orbit? There were some tense times during that period, but the engine people felt like they had it well under control and that we could go ahead. We did, and it worked fine." Helium left in the fuel lines of the SPS back on the ground caused the small burp in performance, so essentially, the engine was fine, none the worse for wear.

If the balky SPS left some mission controllers with a sinking feeling in the pits of their stomachs, Frank Borman was in far worse shape. All three crew members had been a bit queasy after unstrapping from their couches and beginning to move around the spacious—and downright luxurious, compared to the Gemini capsules in which Borman and Lovell had previously flown—Apollo Command Module. Borman, however, wound up sickest of the three by far. After waking up from a fitful sleep sixteen hours into the mission, Borman had a headache and was stricken with the Big Three in motion sickness—nausea, vomiting, and diarrhea. The ground knew nothing of the problem until it was mentioned in a downlinked voice tape. "The spookiest moment was when Borman got sick on the way out," Deiterich said. "We didn't know if it was radiation sickness or what it was. That kind of got us a little on edge." The mission pressed on.

The more Borman, Lovell, and Anders traveled away from their home planet, controllers began noticing something they had never seen before during flight. A command would be sent, say, to switch from one antenna to another to get a better signal, and nothing happened right away. A second or two might pass, and then maybe another. Finally, confirmation would come back that the change had been successful. "The signal would come back to Earth, but it was about a three-second delay," said INCO Joe DeAtkine. "We didn't use to have that. You had to kind of get used to it as they got further and further away from the earth. The speed of light wasn't that fast anymore."

Phil Shaffer was a giant of a man. Standing maybe six and a half feet tall and tipping the scales at close to three hundred pounds or more, Shaffer got tagged as "Jolly Red" by his mates in the Trench and the rest of the MOCR because of his size and what red hair remained around the balding crown of his head.

There was more to Shaffer than just his imposing size, a lot more. To Jerry Bostick, Jolly Red was his deputy branch chief and one of the most exceptional people he ever met. To rookie Bill Boone, who made his debut as a FIDO during the flight of *Apollo 7*, Shaffer and John Llewellyn had served as his unofficial hosts his first week at NASA in June 1967. The three of them went out for a night on the town at the Singin' Wheel, a local watering hole in nearby Webster, Texas. The rest is history, what Boone can remember of it. "I was fresh out of school and thought I could drink beer with anybody," Boone said. "There was no way I was going to dust them. Shaffer piled me in the back of his convertible and proceeded to show me the Gulf Coast at night. I ended up at his place, fertilizing several trees."

In the control center, Shaffer had the ability to ask questions of Boone that helped guide the young operator to solve problems on his own. Shaffer, Boone continued, spent time with shamans in New Mexico and came to believe in reincarnation and out-of-body experiences. The two of them, he continued, once actually shared such an event. "I could talk hours about him," Boone said of Shaffer, who died 14 June 2007. "I miss him. I miss him today, and he's been gone several years. It was just great to pick up the phone, and in about thirty seconds, we'd be right back where we were twenty years ago."

To Bill Stoval, another freshman controller who made his debut at the FIDO console during the flight of *Apollo 10*, Shaffer had the amazing ability to manipulate without anyone actually feeling as though he had *been* manipulated. Stoval joined Shaffer in Mensa, the high IQ society, then promptly dropped right back out again after about a year. They cooked ribs and drank beer together. "He was an incredible man," Stoval said. "When he became a flight director, he would ride me hard. It pissed me off, because he knew more than I did."

As brilliant as Shaffer was, press conferences were evidently not his cup of tea—at least not when it came to attempting to explain the transition from the earth's to the moon's sphere of gravitational influence to a bunch of dumb reporters. A blip in the computers caused them to calculate a sudden difference of a few miles in the spacecraft's positioning as it crossed between the two, and as hard as Shaffer tried to get the point across to the press, it was just not working for him. "Never has the gulf between the non-technical journalist and the non-journalistic technician been more apparent," Michael Collins wrote in *Carrying the Fire*. "The harder Phil tried to dispel the notion, the more he convinced some of the reporters that the spacecraft actually would jiggle or jump as it passed into the lunar sphere."

By then, Collins was having himself a jolly good time, snickering over Shaffer's predicament. "Big as a professional football player, red-faced and sweating, Phil delicately re-examined his tidy equations and patiently explained their logic," Collins continued. "No sale. Wouldn't the crew feel a bump as they passed the barrier and become alarmed? How could the spacecraft instantaneously go from one point in the sky to another without the crew feeling it? The rest of us smirked and tittered as poor Phil puffed and labored, and thereafter we tried to discuss the lunar sphere of influence with Phil as often as we could, especially when outsiders where present."

Collins had so much fun with Shaffer over the incident, he mentioned it during the flight of *Apollo 11*. As the flight began its long journey back to Earth, capcom Bruce McCandless let the crew know when it had left the moon's sphere of gravitational influence. Collins could not help himself.

Roger. Is Phil Shaffer down there?

Negative, but we've got a highly qualified team on in his stead.

Rog. I wanted to hear him explain it again at the press conference. That's an old Apollo 8 *joke, but tell him the spacecraft gave a little jump as it went through the sphere.*

As McCandless began his response, Dave Reed knew exactly what Collins was up to.

Okay, I'll pass it on to him. Thanks a lot, and Dave Reed is sort of burying his head in his arms right now.

Jerry Bostick and Charley Parker passed time during the outbound coast with a discussion of what might happen during the crossover—well out of earshot of any reporters, quite unlike Shaffer. No one was quite sure exactly when the computers would decide that the *Apollo 8* spacecraft had started falling toward the moon, with its gravitational influence greater than that of Earth's. Across the hall from the MOCR in the Flight Dynamics SSR, Jack Garman got in on a pool that somebody drew up over when the event light would flash. It was high stakes too, at a quarter a pop. "I did

8. As famous as the *Apollo 11* lunar landing would become just a few months later, many who worked in the MOCR considered *Apollo 8* every bit as memorable a moment in their NASA careers. Courtesy NASA.

not win," Garman admitted ruefully. Mankind first left the earth's gravitational dominance at 2:29 p.m. in Houston on 23 December 1968, fifty-five hours and thirty-eight minutes into the flight of *Apollo 8*. The spacecraft was 176,250 nautical miles out.

History does not record who won the SSR pool.

It was the wee early morning hours of Christmas Eve in Houston, and less than five minutes remained before *Apollo 8* was supposed to slip around to the far side of the moon.

A lot was about to happen, and nerves were taut in and around the MOCR. Loss of signal (LOS) meant no communications or telemetry until the spacecraft peeked back around to the lunar near side. As if the tension needed to be ratcheted up any more, the lunar orbit insertion (LOI) burn of the SPS engine was slated to take place on the far side. There would be no way of knowing if it had been successful until the signal was once again acquired (AOS). Amid all that, a message from capcom Gerald P. "Jerry" Carr caught Frank Borman off guard.

Apollo 8, *Houston. Five minutes LOS, all systems go. Over.*

Borman responded like the West Point cadet he once was.

Thank you, Houston. Apollo 8.

Roger, Frank. The custard is in the oven at 350. Over.

If ever an air-to-ground message seemed out of place, that was it. Custard? What custard? Borman came back to Carr the only way he knew how.

No comprendo.

The custard was, figuratively speaking, in the oven and it had been placed there by Borman's wife, Susan. Although she had at one time or another been sure that the flight would end in disaster, the custard line was her way of putting up a brave front for her husband. He could take care of his business as a world-famous astronaut, while she stayed behind to stand vigil as the ever-supportive wife. "I remember talking with Susan about it," Carr said. "She said, 'When I would get excited or overwrought or anxious about something, Frank would say to me, 'Why don't you just calm down, go make a custard, and just take it easy?' So I want you to tell him when you get a chance that the custard's in the oven at 350.' I think we caught him completely unawares, because he said, 'Huh?' and then thought for a few minutes before he figured out what we were saying. I don't think he expected to hear that from me."

Carr remembered Susan Borman's message, but he had already forgotten all about fellow rookie astronaut Ken Mattingly. Mattingly had been the capcom on flight director Milt Windler's Maroon Team as *Apollo 8* closed in on the moon, and he did not want to miss out on being in the control center for LOS. But miss out he did. "I had finished up and turned it over to Jerry," Mattingly remembered. "I said, 'Jerry, I'm going to go get some sleep. Call me an hour before LOS so I can come over and watch.'" It was a simple-enough request, but one easily forgotten in the midst of the momentous events that were unfolding. "Well, Jerry got all excited and forgot to call me," Mattingly continued with a good-natured chuckle. "When I woke up, the whole world knew they were in lunar orbit. I was *really* chagrinned."

What Mattingly missed was a hush that fell over the control room as the seconds ticked down to LOS.

Two minutes.

One minute.

Borman announced that he was starting the onboard recorder, and Carr wished the crew well.

Roger. Safe journey, guys.

Anders came on the line.

Thanks a lot, troops.

Then Lovell.

We'll see you on the other side.

And that was it, just before a crackle of static echoed through headsets plugged into MOCR consoles. The signal from *Apollo 8* blinked out right on time, at 3:49 a.m. in Houston, sixty-eight hours, fifty-eight minutes, and forty-five seconds into the flight. The LOI burn would not take place for another ten minutes or so. The whole thing was a tad unsettling to Jerry Bostick. "It was obviously a very critical maneuver that they had to perform on the backside of the moon, out of contact with us," he said. "Everything had to go right, or we would be in a number of bad situations. It was pucker time." Already, Bostick was sorting out his options on what to do if the burn was too long or too short, or if it had not taken place at all. "It was an unknown, the first time we'd ever done this," he continued. "There were a number of possible outcomes, some of which were not very pleasant. It was just a time to really be on guard."

The Black Team was on console for LOS, and with nothing to monitor, flight director Glynn Lunney told his troops that it was as good a time as any to take a break. Take a break? Now? Why not? There was nothing else to do. "Very quickly, I realized that was probably the *smartest* thing I ever heard, because there's not a damn thing we could do," Bostick said. "If we weren't prepared for the consequences, there wasn't anything I could do in the next ten minutes that was going to get me prepared, except go to the bathroom."

Retro officer Chuck Deiterich had virtually the same initial reaction as Bostick to Lunney's suggestion. "As soon as we had LOS, Lunney said the funniest thing that I'll never forget," Deiterich remembered. "He said, 'Take a break and we'll see you back here before acquisition of signal.' I thought, 'Now, that's *really* interesting.' There was absolutely nothing we could do. It was just that walking away when they getting ready to do the first lunar insertion burn seemed kind of strange." That was Lunney, in a nutshell. "Lunney knew all our jobs very well," Deiterich continued. "He would let you do your own job and he would never try to second-guess you. He was probably one of the best flight directors there ever was."

Ten minutes after *Apollo 8* disappeared, the SPS came to life to slow the spacecraft to its orbital velocity of 5,458 feet per second. It burned for four minutes, 6.9 seconds and put the flight into an elliptical orbit that was later refined to a circular one of just sixty nautical miles in altitude above the surface of the moon. Back on Earth in Houston, the MOCR was holding its collective breath. Two clocks were set up in the control room—one that took into account an anomaly, the other a nominal timeline. If the burn had not taken place, the spacecraft would arrive back in range some two minutes before the expected time of acquisition, still speeding along in its free-return trajectory. "Waiting was something we had become used to, but this wait had a distinct edge to it," Lunney wrote in *From the Trench of Mission Control to the Craters of the Moon*. "Most of the flight controllers sat quietly, eyes on the two clocks listening and probably offering a prayer. In due course, the first clock reached zero and there was no communication from the ship. The second clock continued to count, reached zero and almost at the same time, the crew reported that the spacecraft was in lunar orbit."

Carr began his calls to the crew early, in case something had gone wrong.

Apollo 8, *Houston. Over.*

The same thing, repeated time after time.

Apollo 8, *Houston. Over.*

Apollo 8, *Houston. Over.*

Nearly thirty-six minutes after the MOCR had last heard from the crew, public affairs officer John E. McLeish, handling commentary from the control room, excitedly reported:

We got it! We got it! Apollo 8 *is now in lunar orbit! There is a cheer in this room! This is Apollo control, Houston, switching now to the voice of Jim Lovell.*

And there was Lovell.

Go ahead, Houston. Apollo 8. *Our orbit—169.1 by 60.5, 169.1 by 60.5.*

Carr welcomed his fellow astronauts back into contact with the rest of humanity.

Apollo 8, *this is Houston. Roger, 169.1 by 60.5. Good to hear your voice.*

At the flight director's console, Glynn Lunney could not suppress a grin. "It was lunar orbit on Christmas Eve 1968," he wrote. "Playing to an American audience, which was overdue for a reason to celebrate, it choked up all of us. Misty eyes, nods all around, and touches on the shoulders and backs were the shared signs of a decade of work together by the MCC team." Sy

Liebergot, training on the EECOM console, stood up during the celebration and made a rather distinct announcement. "I was excited," Liebergot said. "That little booger came right around from the backside of the moon after the orbit insertion burn, right to the second. I just leaped to my feet and screamed, 'The Russians suck!' I think everybody agreed with me."

The first television transmission from lunar orbit began a little more than two hours later, at 6:31 a.m. in Houston. Almost as soon as it began, the faraway astronauts began calling off craters that had been named in honor of their NASA brethren.

Brand.

Carr.

Mueller.

Bassett.

See.

Their own craters—Borman, Anders, and Lovell—came into view. After that, Anders continued the running commentary.

Okay, we are coming up on the crater Collins.

Carr, who already had his crater, asked about one that was just passing out of the frame of the television picture.

What crater is that that's just going off?

Anders came back.

That's some small impact crater.

Okay.

We'll call it John Aaron's.

Okay.

If he'll keep looking at the systems anyway.

He just quit looking.

Aaron never forgot the surprise of hearing his name called over the air-to-ground loop. "On the way out there, there were a couple of problems with one of our coolant systems pieces of hardware," Aaron remembered. "I had made some recommendations to the crew about what to do about it and so forth, and it kind of stuck in their minds because they knew who the EECOM was on the ground. So they started naming craters after people, and all of a sudden, they named one after me, an EECOM. I mean, I wasn't in management at NASA. I was totally shocked that they would remember me, to name a crater after me."

9. Capcom Ken Mattingly (foreground) listens intently to the memorable Christmas Eve broadcast. Surrounding him are fellow astronauts Jack Schmitt (seated behind Mattingly), Buzz Aldrin (standing), Deke Slayton, and Neil Armstrong. Courtesy NASA.

Aaron had not seen anything yet. *Apollo 8*'s second television broadcast from the moon, which started at 2:34 p.m. on Christmas Eve in Houston, some sixteen hours after arriving in lunar orbit. It was estimated that one billion people in sixty-four countries saw or heard the live broadcast, with another thirty countries added later the same day with a delayed broadcast. By contrast, "only" about 600 million were said to have seen or heard the *Apollo 11* moon landing.

The crew began its banter with capcom Ken Mattingly by describing both the moon's surface and the "foreboding expanse of blackness," as Anders described the sky around it. When the almost half-hour program was nearing its conclusion, the Sea of Tranquility came into the grainy black-and-white view. Years after the fact, the reading Anders began moments later would still send chills through those who had worked in the MOCR during the flight.

We are now approaching lunar sunrise, and for all the people back on Earth, the crew of Apollo 8 *has a message that we would like to send to you.*

Anders continued, reading the first four verses of the King James Bible's book of Genesis.

In the beginning, God created the Heaven and the Earth. And the Earth was without form and void, and darkness was upon the face of the deep. And the spirit of God moved upon the face of the waters. And God said, "Let there be light" and there was light. And God saw the light, that it was good, and God divided the light from the darkness.

Lovell then read the next four verses.

And God called the light Day, and the darkness He called Night. And the evening and the morning were the first day. And God said, "Let there be a firmament in the midst of the waters. And let it divide the waters from the waters." And God made the firmament and divided the waters which were under the firmament from the waters which were above the firmament. And it was so. And God called the firmament heaven. And the evening and the morning were the second day.

Borman took over and concluded with verses nine and ten.

And God said, "Let the waters under the Heaven be gathered together into one place, and let the dry land appear." And it was so. And God called the dry land Earth, and the gathering together of the waters, called He seas. And God saw that it was good.

Flying in space for the second and final time, Borman ended the broadcast with a dramatic flourish.

And from the crew of Apollo 8, *we close with good night, good luck, a merry Christmas, and God bless all of you, all of you on the good Earth.*

That was the moment when the magnitude of what he had just helped accomplish hit John Aaron. The goal all along had been to go to the moon to learn about the moon, and while that did in fact happen during the flight, it also brought back stunningly dramatic images of the earth rising over the lunar landscape—Earthrise. Never before had a single series of photographs captured all of humanity with such clarity, giving him an entirely new perspective on his home planet. For Aaron and so many others in the MOCR that day, the Genesis reading was the perfect capstone for what had to that point been nearly a perfect flight. "They came around the moon and started reading from Genesis, 'In the beginning, God created Heaven and Earth.' Just saying it, talking to you, sent cold chills around me," Aaron said. "Remember, that was on Christmas Eve. I don't believe there was anybody in that room who knew that was going to happen."

This is how strongly the moment touched the EECOM. "It was the most overwhelming thing that has ever happened to me in my life, just because it was not only a surprise, it was *so* appropriate." For a brief second, Aaron appeared to be on the verge of losing control of his emotions. Quickly, though, he collected himself before concluding, "I don't know if it had the same kind of impact on other controllers that it had on me, but I suspect it did."

There was no suspecting to it, really. The audaciousness of the flight plan in general, and the reading from Genesis in particular, had all kinds of lasting impact on the people around Aaron in the MOCR. "The word 'incredible' is not even adequate," said Jerry Bostick. "I had two feelings, I guess. I thought, 'My God, I'm proud to be an American. We've got American astronauts circling the moon. That's just amazing.' The other thought was that it was Christmas, and they started reading from the Bible. I just thought, 'It doesn't get any better than this.' It was very moving. It's something I'll never forget."

All that was left now was to disappear behind the moon one last time, and while on the far side, to perform the trans-earth injection burn to get out of lunar orbit and start the return journey. Beginning at just past midnight on Christmas Day and lasting three minutes and 23.7 seconds, flight director Milt Windler's Maroon Team was on console for the burn that hurtled the spacecraft Earthward at a velocity of 8,842 feet per second. *Apollo 8* had been in lunar orbit for twenty hours, ten minutes, and thirteen seconds, for a total of ten laps around the moon.

Ken Mattingly was once again on duty as capcom. After giving the crew a handful of cursory calls, he finally got a response from Lovell.

Houston, Apollo 8, *over.*

Hello, Apollo 8. *Loud and clear.*

Roger. Please be informed there is a Santa Claus.

It was 12:25 a.m. in Houston. "The next thing, I saw the spacecraft come around the hill," Aaron said. "When it came around from behind the moon, they were on their way home." Twenty minutes later, Deke Slayton was on the horn to the returning astronauts.

Good morning, Apollo 8, *Deke here. I just would like to wish you all a very merry Christmas on behalf of everyone in the control center, and I'm sure everyone around the world. None of us ever expect to have a better Christmas present than this one. Hope you get a good night's sleep from here on and enjoy your Christmas dinner tomorrow, and look forward to seeing you in Hawaii on the twenty-eighth.*

Borman took the mic, sounding positively excited to hear Slayton's voice.

Okay, Leader. We'll see you there. That was a very, very nice ride, that last one. This engine is the smoothest one.

Yeah, we gathered that. Outstanding job all the way around.

Borman then paid the MOCR a compliment, almost like a triumphant NASCAR driver thanking "the boys back in the shop" after a victory.

Thank everybody on the ground for us. It's pretty clear we wouldn't be anywhere if we didn't have them helping us out here.

Moments later, Anders took the opportunity to get in a dig on the MOCR's boss of all bosses.

Even Mr. Kraft does something right once in a while.

Slayton, grinning, gave his reply.

He got tired of waiting for you to talk and went home.

The good-natured banter was not over. Mattingly briefly turned the capcom mic over to fellow rookie astronaut Harrison H. "Jack" Schmitt. "Typhoid Jack," as Schmitt called himself, read up a "gotcha" poem to the crew. The parody of "Twas the Night before Christmas" by Clement C. Moore was one of several written by MPAD's Ken Young, who was in one of the back-room SSRs when Schmitt took the floor. Young wrote several different parodies of Moore's famous poem over the years—"A Visit from St. Kranz" seemed a particular favorite—but the *Apollo 8* version was the only one that ever made it onto the air-to-ground loop. He was taken completely by surprise. "Yeah, it was a thrill," Young said. "Everyone in MPAD was proud of their parts on all these great flights. And as MPAD poet laureate— several threatened to string me up!—I just tried to get some props for the best group of rocket scientists in NASA. We were a fun bunch!"

Schmitt began reading.

Twas the night before Christmas and way out in space,
the Apollo 8 *crew had just won the moon race.*
The headsets were hung by the consoles with care,
in hopes that Chris Kraft soon would be there.

Frank Borman was nestled all snug in his bed,
while visions of REFSMMATs *danced in his head;*

and Jim Lovell, in his couch, and Anders, in the bay,
were racking their brains over a computer display.

When out of the DSKY, there rose such a clatter,
Frank sprang from his bed to see what was the matter.
Away to the sextant he flew like a flash,
to make sure they weren't going to crash.

The light on the breast of the moon's jagged crust,
gave a luster of green cheese to the gray lunar dust.
When what to his wondering eyes should appear,
but a Burma Shave sign saying, "Kilroy was here."

The line about the Burma Shave sign and Kilroy brought down the house. A hearty round of laughter could be heard on the air-to-ground loop as Schmitt continued.

But Frank was no fool, he knew pretty quick
that they had been first; This must be a trick.
More rapid than rockets, his curses they came.
He turned to his crewmen and called them a name.

Now Lovell, now Anders, now don't think I'd fall,
for that old joke you've written up on the wall.
They spoke not a word, but grinning like elves,
and laughed at their joke in spite of themselves.

Frank sprang to his couch, to the ship gave a thrust,
and away they all flew past the gray lunar dust.
But we heard them explain ere they flew 'round the moon,
Merry Christmas to Earth; we'll be back there real soon.

Apollo 8 slammed back in the earth's atmosphere at 9:37 a.m. in Houston on 27 December, traveling at a speed of nearly seven miles per second. Fourteen minutes later, the spacecraft nestled into the waters of the Pacific Ocean in the local predawn hours. After a planned wait for daylight, the crew was helicoptered to the awaiting deck of the USS *Yorktown*.

Frank Borman, Jim Lovell, and Bill Anders were home. The MOCR had done it.

One right after the other, many in the MOCR agreed that *Apollo 8* was the highlight of their careers, even more so than *Apollo 11* or maybe even *Apollo 13*. It represented the light at the end of the tunnel. NASA could, in fact, land a man on the moon by the end of the decade. To Jerry Bostick, the cake was baked at Christmas of 1968 with the flight of *Apollo 8*. The icing was added less than seven months later during *Apollo 11*.

John Aaron concluded that *Apollo 8* was every bit as unlikely an adventure as the famous early 1800s expedition of Meriwether Lewis and William Clark. "Lewis and Clark hauled off on a mission to go across the whole country, didn't know where they were going, and wound up pulling it off," Aaron said. "They only lost one man, due to ruptured appendicitis. It was just like that was meant to be." That was the distant past, but *Apollo 8* represented that same spirit nearly two centuries later. "A lot of things could've happened to us on *Apollo 8*, because it was hanging out," he continued. *"It was hanging out."*

Then there was Rod Loe. "It's the only mission I can ever remember having tears in my eyes, sitting on the console that night when they came around the moon and they started reading from the Bible," he said. "That was really touching."

Again, the emotion was thick in Loe's voice. It took not even a second, and he was back in 1968, about to attend the splashdown party for *Apollo 8* at the nearby Flintlock Inn. He and Aaron took their time before heading to the bar upstairs, and somebody eventually asked why they had not yet made their way to the festivities. His answer was simple.

We're standing here, just proud to be Americans.

"That's the way I felt," Loe added. "I really felt like we had won."

6. Dress Rehearsals

The new-and-improved Command and Service Module worked well during its first two manned flights in late 1968, and the Saturn V launch vehicle performed flawlessly during the launch of *Apollo 8*. It was time to see what the Lunar Module could do.

The LM was so bizarre in appearance, its boxy ascent stage and antenna combined with the gold insulation and four spindly legs actually came across as quite beautiful. This was a flying machine unlike any other, designed exclusively for use in space where it was afterward discarded, never to be returned back to the ground. There would be no museum exhibits for the *Apollo 9* LM, *Spider*, or for its *Apollo 10* counterpart, *Snoopy*—which along with the same flight's *Charlie Brown* CSM were the very best call signs ever for an American space mission.

Columbia and *Eagle* were certainly more proper, more eloquently grand names. But *Charlie Brown* and *Snoopy*—named after the two main characters in the American comic strip *Peanuts*—were in the right context every bit as appropriate. Charlie Brown was always the underdog, just as NASA had been during the early days of the space race with the Soviet Union. Snoopy on the other hand was the highly intelligent, intuitive creature who could overcome any obstacle—such as being a dog—to accomplish any goal, again just like NASA as it erased the Russians' lead and raced headlong toward the moon.

The *Apollo 9* test went no further than Earth orbit, while *Apollo 10* ventured to within a handful of hair-raising miles of the moon's surface. They were bookended by the two most famous missions in the history of human spaceflight. The flights became mere footnotes, and that is unfortunate, because without a shakedown of the Lunar Module, there could not have been a lunar landing on *Apollo 11* or any other mission for that matter.

Plans called for *Apollo 9* CDR Jim McDivitt and rookie LMP Russell L. "Rusty" Schweickart to take the Lunar Module out for its first manned spin, with CMP Dave Scott staying behind to mind the CSM. McDivitt, in particular, was a favorite of Gene Kranz, the mission's lead flight director. All but a war had been fought over control of crew procedures between those in the MOCR and Deke Slayton, the head of the astronaut office. "My guys studied the systems from the ground up," Kranz began. "We built the schematics. We'd write the mission rules, mission strategy. So we had this argument going on between the two players. It was so petty that Slayton would never give a flight set of procedures to the controllers on console. So we were always wondering what the crew was carrying on board the spacecraft." It was no small feat for McDivitt to end the stalemate, what with Slayton being his boss and all. "McDivitt looked at this and said, 'This is ridiculous!'" Kranz continued. "So McDivitt got a hold of his crew procedures people, broke ranks with Slayton, and made sure that every controller, including the flight director, had a set of the onboard crew procedures. And from that day on, we never had a problem."

Kranz led the unmanned test of the LM on *Apollo 5* in January 1968, and with the experience of *Apollo 9* in his back pocket, he felt it would give him a leg up on getting the plumb assignment of all plumb assignments— directing the first lunar descent and landing. Kranz was the boss and he could very well have named himself to the landing, regardless of whether or not he was familiar with the LM. He *could* have done that, but he did not. Gene Kranz was getting his ducks in a row for the *Apollo 11* descent by flying *Apollo 9*. "Every flight director wanted to do the landing," Kranz said. "We were all trying to figure out ways to position ourselves so that we'd be the obvious ones chosen. This gave me an opportunity to really come up to speed now with a manned Lunar Module, and with two Lunar Modules under our belt, I not only knew the spacecraft but also knew the mission control teams that work with them to understand the strategy and the use of the system, to be intimately familiar with not only the systems, but the procedures, the mission rules. So you're really flying missions, but you're also preparing yourselves for the big one."

The first five days of the ten-day flight were to include an all-out simulation of a lunar mission—docking and extraction of the LM from its berth in the S-IVB third stage; undocking, followed by tests of the LM's descent engine, staging, and ascent engine; systems checkouts; burns of the SPS while the two spacecraft were docked; and an extended spacewalk by Schweickart to test his spacesuit and its Personal Life Support System (PLSS) backpack.

Dave Reed was a detail guy, and on *Apollo 9*, there were more than enough elements to sort through, debate, checklist, and execute. With the obvious exception of *Apollo 13*, *Apollo 9* was the toughest flight of Reed's career. From his perspective in the Trench, timing was everything. Maneuvers had to go off like clockwork, taking place at just the right time so they could be tracked over various ground stations around the world.

"We had no problems on *9*, but boy, we had to work," said Reed, the flight's prime FIDO who served on Kranz's White Team during the flight. "You're going to do an entire dress rehearsal of everything that has to go on in lunar orbit. It was a real learning curve, and it was a tough one. If I needed to do a burn at Canary, that burn had to come off at Canary. I had to see it and know what the vector was, because the next maneuver would be someplace around Carnarvon. It was bang, bang, bang. If a slip took place, you could be off-range. You may not have what you need to get the job done the way you want to get it done. It was dicey, in that we really needed to stay on schedule."

Techniques for initializing the LM's Primary Guidance and Navigation System (PGNS, pronounced "pings" in NASA-speak) and its backup Abort Guidance System (AGS) computers had to be practiced, right along with separation maneuvers, rendezvous, and docking between *Gumdrop*, the flight's CSM, and *Spider*. How would the two react to one another in space? "A lot of people were kind of worried about the dynamics between two inertial guidance systems and which was in control or whether they would try to control each other," said Gary Renick, who manned the guidance console for the LM initialization, the docked burns of the LM's descent engine, rendezvous, and SPS burns. "It was like they were fighting each other. One was trying to do one thing, and one was trying to do another thing. The difficulty was just developing all the procedures and techniques to do those things."

Bob Heselmeyer was as anxious about *Apollo 9* as any flight he would fly for reasons similar to Reed's, and on a personal level as well. The mission was *huge*. It was the first manned flight of the Lunar Module but it was also his first back in Houston, where he worked on managing the LM's consumables in the SSR. He was moving up in the world, and if he could continue to progress in his career, the front room was next.

In a sense, *Spider* and Heselmeyer were a lot alike. He had been out to the tracking stations during Gemini, and he had been through many a simulation in Houston, but he was still an SSR first-timer once the flight got under way on 3 March 1969. Like Heselmeyer, the LM was also unproven. "It's the first time it's flying and under fine control," Heselmeyer said. "You just never know for sure how well all that's going to work out. You've got the guidance system, the propulsion system, the environmental control system, and they all needed to work well enough for that vehicle to get docked again. There wasn't a backup. The only out was getting docked."

Heselmeyer wasn't the only rookie on console in Houston. Jack Knight had been in the SSR for a couple of the unmanned Apollo launch vehicle tests, but *Apollo 9* marked the first time he made it out to the front room to man the LM's telcom console. In doing so, he became the latest in a long line of controllers who uttered a version of what had come to be known as Alan Shepard's Prayer.

Dear Lord, please don't let me screw this up.

Of course, a healthy dose of respect for what could go wrong was essential. Those who thought they had everything under control right from the start were the ones you had to watch out for. "That worry was always there for me," Knight said. "After a while, you have more confidence when you've been through a number of flights. I think that's true of most people. You do have a few people that have excessive self-confidence. Sometimes, those people will think they know more than they do and they'll go off and make recommendations for things which they don't really have the background for. They sound like they really know what they're talking about."

After the booster controller moved out of his spot on the left end of the Trench, James A. "Jim" Joki was able to set up shop to watch over the Extravehicular Mobility Unit that was to be worn by fellow freshman Rusty Schweickart during an EVA that was scheduled to last more than two hours. The plan called for Schweickart to use handrails to move from *Spider* to *Gumdrop*, and then stick his upper torso in the Command Module's open hatch to simulate a crew rescue. After that, he was to move back to the LM's porch to do some still photography and television camera work.

Although that was the plan, it was not what actually took place.

Motion sickness had rarely been a problem during the Mercury or Gemini programs, for the simple reason that there had been *no* room to move around. Compared to those tiny capsules, the Apollo Command Module had room to spare. With that, however, came a price. Room to move also meant having to stave off bouts of nausea—or worse. Soon after the launch of *Apollo 9*, Dave Scott left his couch to make his way down to the lower equipment bay for a platform alignment. Almost immediately, he knew that he needed to move his head slowly. There was no nausea or vomiting; he just needed to take it easy. He also experienced some spatial disorientation, accompanied by a bit of queasiness for a couple of minutes. For Scott, the feelings quickly passed.

For Schweickart, they did not.

Schweickart took a Marezine tablet three hours before liftoff and another one ninety minutes or so after reaching orbit, but he was still experiencing what the mission report termed a mild dizziness after leaving his couch and turning his head rapidly. He fought the sensation by turning slowly at the waist, instead of just his head. As poorly as he must have felt, he got into his pressure suit to move over to the LM and was sitting quietly in *Gumdrop*'s lower equipment bay when he suddenly and unexpectedly threw up. Four hours later, he was busy in *Spider* when it happened again. Evidently, that was enough to get whatever ailed him out of his system. Although he began to feel better and could move about freely, he had no appetite and an aversion to the smell of certain foods. For the first six days of the flight, he consumed only liquids and freeze-dried fruits.

Joki was trying his best not to act like a rookie when he came on duty and discovered what was taking place with Schweickart. "He was really a smart guy," Joki said. "He could pick up things faster than anybody else. It was just amazing. Unfortunately, we found out that most of the guys get motion sickness. They may be the best test pilots in the world, but they get motion sickness in space. Rusty was still puking his guts up, but we didn't know that."

Although it started right on time, at about seventy-three hours into the flight, the EVA was shortened to just thirty-nine minutes. Schweickart briefly tried out the handrails, and also stood on *Spider*'s porch with his boots secured by foot restraints while Scott did his own stand-up spacewalk from *Gumdrop*'s open hatch to watch and photograph the whole thing.

"Instead of doing a two-hour EVA, we'll have him put on the equipment and he'll step out into what they called the 'golden slippers' on the porch," Joki said. "He'll wave at everybody, we'll get photographs, they'll communicate, and we'll make a two-hour EVA into whatever it took so he didn't throw up. My first time on console, I got thirty-nine minutes of data. Boy, was I happy as could be."

With the next day of the flight came the first free flight of the LM and joining back up with *Gumdrop*. *Spider* performed almost flawlessly, but at the opposite end of the second row on the control console, Bob Carlton was not exactly satisfied. Rather than being in constant direct sunlight the way it would be on trips to and from the moon, *Spider* was in shade half the time as it orbited the earth.

Shade.

Sunlight.

Shade.

Sunlight.

Shade.

Sunlight.

The issue of thermal control on the thin-skinned LM was one of Carlton's biggest concerns—it really drove him up the wall, he said—and the mission of *Apollo 9* in Earth orbit did not help him solve much. The PGNS platform was very sensitive to overheating. Gyros did not function properly when they got too cold or too hot. Pressure rose in the LM's tanks as their temperatures did. What might happen to them during a lunar mission? How was Carlton going to know what the limits of the systems were one way or the other, too hot or too cold?

The issues, of course, were not limited to matters of too hot, too cold, or just right. What might happen if Carlton was losing the LM's batteries, and trying to get the crew back to Earth? How low could the voltage go and still be able to open the valve for a reentry burn?

It was exactly the kind of information the MOCR would need a year later during the crisis of *Apollo 13*.

Carlton remembered a thermal expert being brought in to predict what the temperatures were going to be in each of several different systems during just such a flight, and the poor guy was not even close on any of them. "After we flew the first lunar mission, it was laughable," Carlton said. "I

10. Gene Kranz's White Team during the flight of *Apollo 9* included Chuck Lewis (2); Bill Molnar (3); Stu Roosa (4); Dr. Willard Hawkins (5); Dave Reed (6); Earl Thompson (7); Dean Toups (8); John Llewellyn (10); Will Fenner (11); Larry Wafford (12); Arnie Aldrich (13); Charles Dumis (14); Jim Hannigan (15); Bill Strahle (16); Neil Hutchinson (17); Hal Loden (18); Larry Myers (19); Bill Peters (20); Bill Johnson (21); Ernie Randall (22); Jack Riley (23); and Tommy Holloway (24). Numbers 9, 25, 26, and 27 are unidentified. Courtesy NASA.

mean, he was so far out of the ballpark, he was embarrassed, just literally embarrassed. I can't remember the guy's name now, but I felt sorry for him." The solution was to "barbeque" the LM by slowly rotating, as if on a spit, just as the CSM had been during the flight of *Apollo 8*. "The Earth mission for the first Lunar Module, it was not a good parallel," Carlton concluded. "It helped, but the real gold mine came when we began to go to the moon."

Dave Reed calculated the burn of the LM's ascent engine that started the process of closing and braking for re-docking with *Gumdrop*. After the numbers were read up to the crew, Reed could not hide his surprise when McDivitt called back down to capcom Stuart A. "Stu" Roosa, who had served as a smoke jumper in the Forest Service before joining the air force.

Hey, Smokey. Is Dave Reed smiling?

Roosa glanced at Reed and grinned.

Well, yes. He's pretty happy, but he's not going to relax until you've finished burning.

Better not.

Reed could not afford to relax just yet, and neither could the rest of the MOCR. McDivitt and Schweickart were out on the ragged edge unlike anyone had ever been before, in a spacecraft without a heat shield. If they could not return to the CSM and dock, they were goners. Ninety-nine hours and two minutes into the flight, *Spider* and *Gumdrop* were once again docked. They had been apart for six hours, twenty-two minutes, and fifty seconds.

Years later, long after his career in the MOCR was over, a question arose over the "Is Dave Reed smiling?" quote. To the best of his recollection, it had been McDivitt who asked the lighthearted question. The official transcript released by NASA, however, attributed the line to Schweickart. It was a problem to be solved, and if nothing else, Reed was a detail-oriented problem solver. He emailed both astronauts, and neither could quite put their finger on it. Case closed, right? Not for Dave Reed, not by a long shot.

He had old reel-to-reel tapes of audio from the mission, and they just so happened to include that portion. Not only did he have them converted over to compact disc by MassProductions in Massachusetts, Reed then used his own spectral analysis software to tentatively determine that McDivitt was the speaker. Even that was not good enough. He got in touch with Digisound Mastering out of Melbourne, Australia, convinced them to do a more extensive check, and that result was, at last, good enough for Reed.

It was, once and for all, McDivitt who asked that long-ago question.

So jovial were McDivitt, Scott, and Schweickart after the docking, they had a surprise in store for Chris Kraft nearly five days into the flight. McDivitt first asked if Kraft was in the room, and when told that he was, the veteran astronaut was quick to respond.

Okay. We've got a message for him.

Scott and Schweickart joined McDivitt on the loop.

Happy birthday to you, happy birthday to you. Happy birthday, dear Christopher, happy birthday to you.

Kraft's birthday was actually 28 February, the flight's original launch date that was delayed due to colds experienced by the crew. Two more choruses planned for their boss, Deke Slayton, and their crew secretary, Charlotte Maltese, did not take place because neither was present for the occasion.

Gumdrop settled into the Atlantic Ocean on 13 March 1969. Another warmup down, one to go.

If *Apollo 10* was going to the trouble of simulating a descent to within fifty thousand feet of the lunar surface, why not just attempt to go the rest of the way and land?

11. Lunar Module flight controllers Don Puddy, Bob Carlton, Hal Loden, Jack Craven, and Jim Hannigan (seated on ledge) gathered during landing and recovery operations following the 13 March 1969 splashdown of *Apollo 9*. Next to them are Ed Fendell and Sy Liebergot (in dark-framed glasses). Larry Canin (back to Liebergot) can be seen chatting with fellow GNC Gary Coen. Visible on the next row up are Richard Stachurski and Ernie Randall. Courtesy NASA.

Really, the question made perfect sense. Glynn Lunney wanted the first lunar landing as badly as the next guy, certainly as much as Gene Kranz, Cliff Charlesworth, or any of the other flight directors active at the time. Lunney was lead flight director on *Apollo 10*, so maybe this was his in. He and others made their case to Chris Kraft, but Lunney's mentor was, he said, the "staunchest advocate" of stopping short of the lunar surface. "He wanted us to have the experience of navigating these two vehicles around the moon, knowing where they are and how fast they're going so that you can get them back together," Lunney said. "There were unknowns associated with flying so low, close to the lunar surface, because the trajectories would be disturbed by concentrations of mass from whatever hit the moon. It would change the orbit a little bit, and that doesn't sound like much, but you can't afford to miss very much when you're doing what we were doing."

As was almost always the case, Kraft won the debate. *Apollo 10* CDR Tom Stafford and LMP Gene Cernan were going to give *Snoopy* a shakedown in lunar orbit while CMP John Young stayed behind in *Charlie Brown*, but that was it. There would be no landing, not this time, for the crew that was NASA's first in which each member had previous spaceflight experience. All three would also go on to command subsequent Apollo missions—Young and Cernan walked on the moon during the flights of *Apollo 16* and *17*, respectively, while Stafford flew the Apollo-Soyuz Test Project. "In retrospect, *Apollo 10* probably could have landed on the moon, but it was a matter of how much do you bite off at a time," Lunney concluded. "The way it came out, *Apollo 10* was absolutely the right thing to do."

The flight got under way to lunar orbit on 18 May 1969, less than two months before the scheduled launch of *Apollo 11*. Nearly seventy-six hours later, the SPS was fired for almost six minutes to place *Charlie Brown* and *Snoopy* into lunar orbit. Later, as the two spacecraft were preparing for undocking, communications problems between them developed.

Communications was not a new issue. There had been substantial problems during *Apollo 9*, and now these. The Command, Service, and Lunar Modules all had communications equipment, and controllers in each branch were responsible for their own gear. It was redundant, to say the least. To Bill Peters, who manned the telcom console for both lunar dress rehearsals, a simulation leading up to the mission underscored the issue. "On *Apollo 10*, I ran the first lunar communications test," Peters said. "There were about ten communication modes on the LM, as there were on the CSM, and we checked all of them out. That was kind of a detailed, aggravating test for everybody involved, because you're trying to coordinate ground switching, MCC switching, and spacecraft switching.

Ed Fendell was an assistant flight director during *Apollo 10*, and it was a job that he loathed. Although he did not know it yet, the comm glitches were going to change the course of his career. "When we went to separate on *Apollo 10*, the mission rule required that the Command Module and Lunar Module be able to talk to each prior to separation, and they couldn't," Fendell said. "They screwed around there for an hour or two, and they finally found out that their switches were out of configuration with each other. Kranz was bouncing off the frickin' wall."

A week or so after splashdown of *Apollo 9*, Fendell was in his office late one afternoon when he got a call from Kranz. "I said, 'Oh, boy. Here we go,' because he and I used to have some incredible battles with four-letter words and referring to ancestry," Fendell admitted and then added as if to spell it out, "We had a different relationship than everybody else."

Fendell sat down in the flight director's office, and Kranz began laying out his solution to the comm issue.

We're going to take every piece of communication equipment and put it under the control of one area. We're going to form a communications section, and we're going to form a position in the control center for this communications position.

When Fendell began wondering why Kranz was bringing this up to him, Kranz dropped the hammer.

And you're going to be in charge.

Fendell could not believe what he was hearing.

What?

Kranz repeated himself.

You're going to be in charge.

Oh, is that right?

Yeah.

That is not my area of expertise.

It is now.

Fendell's new staff was going to consist of representatives from various contractors involved in the Command and Lunar Modules, as well as a few others who had never before worked communications. Kranz then gave Fendell his marching orders.

This is your new section. This is your new job. Get out of my office and go do it.

Bill Peters was sold on the idea. "They started planning to make the INCO position its own independent position, and take it away from the Command Module side and take it away from the Lunar Module side," Peters said. "I think that was a good decision, because there was so much to do on the console anyway."

If the comm problems were frustrating, the next hiccup was nearly catastrophic. An hour and a half after undocking, *Snoopy* began a 27.4-second burn that dropped the LM into a descent orbit to test the landing radar for the next flight's approach into the Sea of Tranquility. Although the closest Stafford and Cernan would get to the surface was 47,400 feet during a low-level pass over *Apollo 11*'s proposed landing site, Stafford marveled to capcom Charlie Duke about just how near to the surface they seemed to be. Maybe they could attempt a landing after all.

Charlie, it looks like we're getting so close, all you have to do is put your tail wheel down and we're there.

Duke was not about to let the pitch go by without a good-natured crack.

Hey, Snoop. Air force guys don't talk that way.

Cernan excitedly called out the moon's geological features as they passed by underneath.

Seems like we're coming up on my side on Taruntius G and I believe Tom's got his Taruntius H there on his side.

Again, communications were proving to be iffy as the air-to-ground link dropped in and out.

Houston, if you read, we have Secchi on my right. We're coming into Apollo Ridge. Here's Apollo Hill, right out the window!

The observations continued until the time came to prepare for staging and rendezvous with Young in *Charlie Brown*. The ascent was to be flown using *Snoopy*'s Abort Guidance System in order to simulate an emergency coming up from the lunar surface, but the danger Stafford and Cernan were about to encounter was all too real.

The AGS had a three-position control-mode switch—Auto; Att (short for Attitude) Hold; and Off. In Auto, the guidance system locked the LM onto the CSM's position and steered it in that direction, while Attitude Hold did just that and held the LM in place. *Snoopy* was supposed to be in Attitude Hold for its ascent, although a cue card used during the flight showed that the proper mode setting was Auto.

The card was in error. "We traced the problem to a switch setting that was wrong on their checklist," wrote Chris Kraft in his autobiography. "That was a checklist that got double-checked twice during the rest of Apollo." Both astronauts later said that the card was not the issue, but they wrote in their autobiographies that Cernan had inadvertently flipped the switch one way and Stafford the other. Regardless of which miscue came into play, it nearly cast *Snoopy* into the abyss. The LM was left searching for a CSM that was on the other side of the moon and nowhere to be found.

At 102 hours, 44 minutes, and 49 seconds into the flight, the LM started to "wallow off" slowly in yaw, but stopped. The unexpected motion left the LM off thirty degrees in roll, and ten degrees in both pitch and yaw from a normal staging attitude. Twenty-three seconds later, the situation got far worse when the Auto mode began searching for *Charlie Brown*. *Snoopy* was pitching about on all three axes, and during the process, staging took place thirty-six miles above the lunar surface.

The now-lighter weight of the vehicle and the AGS's unlimited error signals only worsened the motion of the spacecraft, to the tune of more than twenty-five degrees per second in both yaw and roll. The desired attitude of the LM was overshot, which in turn caused high reverse errors and rates. Both men cursed vehemently, Cernan's going out over the air-to-ground loop.

Son of a bitch.

Stafford was a former test pilot who had been through the heart-stopping launch abort of *Gemini 6*, and he knew that the situation in which he and Cernan found themselves was dire. That he admitted it out loud seemed to be proof of just that.

We're in trouble.

Helpless, Duke got on the loop.

Snoop, Houston. We show you close to gimbal lock.

"Any time you get close to gimbal lock, that's really, I'd say, tense more than scary," Duke remembered. "If you get into gimbal lock, you've lost your platform. You had to be very careful about that, so yeah, we were concerned and focused."

Fifteen seconds after staging, during which time Cernan would say he saw the lunar horizon whiz by his window no less than eight times, the wildly gyrating rotations were at last nulled out. Official reports attributed the "attitude excursion" to human error, but the near disaster was an easy thing to overcome—do not make the same mistake again. It was not the result of some sort of flaw within the AGS or either of its three modes, so there was no need for an extensive redesign that might jeopardize the end-of-the-decade deadline. "It was something they knew quickly how to correct," said Lunney, who was at the flight director's console during the crisis. "The response was very quick and orderly. It got a lot of attention because of Gene's purple response, but other than that, we were just trucking right along."

There were other, less serious issues to deal with the rest of the flight. The Trench had pushed for a definite separation sequence when *Charlie Brown* and *Snoopy* parted ways for good in lunar orbit, but got overruled. "During meetings with Bill Tindall, we said, 'When we get ready to undock, this is what we think you ought to do,'" said retro officer Chuck Deiterich. "Staf-

12. Despite the good-natured presence of Snoopy and Charlie Brown dolls at his console, capcom Charlie Duke and the rest of the MOCR were forced to listen in during *Apollo 10*'s deadly serious attitude excursion. Courtesy NASA.

ford said, 'No, no. Don't worry about it. I can handle it. I'll just get away from it.' Well, of course, you don't argue with Tom Stafford."

When it came time for the two spacecraft to undock at 108 hours, 24 minutes, and 36 seconds into the flight, their separation attitude had the LM pointed toward the sun. A fitting had been incorrectly installed on the docking tunnel vent prior to the flight, and when *Snoopy* was jettisoned, residual air in the tunnel popped it directly into the glare of the sun and momentarily out of the crew's view. "In itself, this would not be a big deal, but the ascent stage was about to send the LM into a solar orbit," said Deiterich, who made sure to be in the MOCR when the moment went down. "It can be a bit unnerving when the exact location of a nearby thrusting vehicle is unknown."

Once the LM was free and clear, its ascent batteries lasted for another twelve hours or so. Bob Carlton finally had his chance. "The questions were exceedingly important in my mind, and the hardest of all to get answers to," he said. "We had the LM in orbit, so we played with it . . . we experimented with it . . . or . . . we tested it. We turned the coolant off to the platform, just to see how hot it could get and still work. We watched the batteries go down to zero, and we experimented to see which valves and equipment quit first."

It was not just in flight where he got help, either. An LM was undergoing a thermal vacuum test at MSC when somebody forgot to turn on the coolant to its guidance, navigation, and control systems. Although they overheated, of course, they continued to work long after their predicted tolerances. "We got our hands on that data and, man, you talk about pleased, tickled, a gold mine—that was a gold mine," Carlton added. The process continued during the next couple of lunar missions, to the point where Carlton felt comfortable with his LM data.

If Stafford and Cernan had found themselves in deep water during the wild gyrations in lunar orbit, EECOM Sy Liebergot also came face-to-face with trouble on the long coast back to Earth. A short caused the circuit breaker for Fuel Cell 1 to trip, and when attempts were made to reset it, it triggered master alarms and undervoltage and failure lights. As a result, the fuel cell was reconnected to its bus only when the skin temperature of the CSM cooled to 370 degrees and then disconnected again when it reached 420 to 425 degrees. It was operational, but just barely.

Liebergot was on duty when the problem took place 120 hours, 46 minutes, and 49 seconds into the flight and he briefed his Orange Team flight director, Pete Frank, on the issue. If it had taken place on the outbound trip to the moon, mission rules would have prevented an undocking. But now? There was no real impact. John Llewellyn, however, had evidently not heard Liebergot's explanation. "We all had twenty-five-foot coiled cords on our headsets so we could move around beyond our console," Liebergot began. "So he leaped out of the Trench, came up to my console, and yelled at me, demanding to know, 'What the hell's this thing about a fuel cell?'" Liebergot very carefully told Llewellyn that he had just explained the situation over the flight director's loop. According to Liebergot, that set Llewellyn off: "He got right in my face and said, 'Look, you son of a bitch. If you don't tell me what I want to know right now, I'm going to kill your ass right here.'" Liebergot's recollection begged the question—did he go over the fuel-cell problem again with Llewellyn?

Absolutely.

Charlie Brown reentered the earth's atmosphere traveling an astounding 36,314 feet per second—at approximately 24,760 mph, it was the fastest any human beings had ever traveled before or since. The Command Module splashed down just a mile and half from its target point, and just 3.3 miles from its recovery ship, the USS *Princeton*. Future GNC controller Terry Watson was working in the Landing and Recovery Division at the time, and when Milt Heflin offered to let him power down the spacecraft, he jumped at the chance. At the same time, however, he also wondered if there might be something else he could be doing. "Milt gave me all the manuals and stuff, and so I got to climb in the Command Module and pull all the waste management stuff out and all the suits and pack up all that stuff," Watson remembered. "When I did all that, I thought, 'Is that all there is to this job?' When I got back to Houston, I just said, 'I think it's time to move on.'"

It was, in fact, time to move on for not only Watson but NASA as well. Looking back, it is hard to comprehend just how far the agency had come in such a relatively short amount of time. There had been plenty of highs, and plenty of lows:

President Kennedy's speech before Congress, saying that he believed the nation should commit itself to the goal of landing a man on the moon before the end of the decade.

Being one-upped so many times by the Soviet Union.

Mercury's baby steps.

The bridge built by the Gemini program.

The devastation and doubts cast by the *Apollo 1* fire.

A gutsy gamble to send *Apollo 8* to lunar orbit.

The dress rehearsals of *Apollo 9* and *10*.

All of it had led to this very point. It was go time.

7. A Bunch of Guys about to Turn Blue

After the first four Apollo crewed missions, there was nothing left to accomplish other than the grand prize itself.

As momentum built following each of the flights, those who worked in and around the MOCR were looking forward to the next before the Command Modules ever finished dripping on the recovery carriers after splashdown. "Everybody worked as if they knew this was a noble thing to do," remarked Glynn Lunney, on tap to serve as flight director for *Eagle*'s lunar liftoff. "It was something where people came because they *wanted* to participate. When it came time to land, we'd been working on this for a long time—say a decade. The truth is that mankind had been waiting for this for thousands of years. Imagine all those people sitting around their fires, coming out of their caves. The moon had to be a big mystery to them—this great, big ball right up there."

The Wright brothers had managed the first powered flight just thirty-three years before Lunney's birth—Orville was still living when young Mr. Lunney made his debut into the world. Lunney knew of outhouses, iceboxes, and wicker lamps in his youth, and his family did not own a car until after World War II. Barely more than three decades after Kitty Hawk, Lunney helped to land human beings on the moon. The Apollo program in general and *Apollo 11* in particular, Lunney concluded, represented the pivot point from the horse-drawn past to the supersonic future.

Who could argue the point? Certainly not Dave Reed, the twenty-eight-year-old FIDO who drove a green-and-black 1929 Model A Ford sedan with straw-colored wheels and whitewall tires to work.

To INCO Ed Fendell, the uproar kicked up by the flight was a moot point. A fifty-fifty shot at landing might have been the opinion of most of his coworkers, but it was not Fendell's. There was no way, none whatsoever, that *Apollo 11* was going to make it down to the surface. "Hell, no," Fendell began. "How many things have to work right to make that happen? You start with this incredible rocket that has to stage and the next thing has to burn. Then, it has to stage the S-IVB burn. Then, you've got to get into the right orbit. Then, you've got to burn the S-IVB again to get you going out toward the moon."

Fendell was not finished. The CSM *Columbia* would have to perform all but flawlessly, and so would the LM *Eagle*. The procedures would have to be spot on. Something somewhere, he was sure, would go wrong and prevent Armstrong and Aldrin from sticking the landing. "You're telling me you think you're going to make it the first time?" Fendell concluded. "Not if I'm in Vegas. Not with my money you ain't. I ain't turning you loose with *my* American Express card."

Fendell was not even sure if *Apollo 12* would be able to make a landing. Or *Apollo 13*. If NASA was lucky—really, really lucky—a landing might finally be accomplished on the fourth try. Maybe.

Steve Bales was on the hot seat, and he knew it.

Training for *Apollo 11* began in earnest a month or so before the launch of *Apollo 10*, and as the very first powered descent simulation was about to begin, Bales heard someone plug into a spare port his console. It was probably just branch chief Jerry Bostick or section head Charley Parker, checking in to see how things were going. When he saw who the visitor actually was, Bales's heart skipped a beat. It was the godfather himself, the one and only Chris Kraft.

Bales was already keyed up for the test. Protecting the ability to abort placed several critical scenarios squarely in the guidance officer's lap. The theory was this. If the capability to abort on the primary guidance system was either lost or about to be, then the landing would be called off. This was a system that contained what in the twenty-first century would be considered a measly thirty-six thousand words of fixed read-only memory, plus another two thousand words of erasable random-access memory. Between the guidance computer in *Eagle* and an identical one in *Columbia*, the combined onboard computer memory of the two spacecraft that made humankind's first lunar landing possible was dwarfed by that of just one ordinary smartphone decades later.

And then some.

Miniscule computing power was just one of many issues that made protecting abortability an iffy proposition, and it was open to all kinds of debate. According to Bales, "The first question would have been, 'You guys aborted this first chance to land on the moon, this multibillion-dollar program that was a symbol of America's prestige? Why? Because the computer couldn't have done an abort? Could it have landed safely?' Well, possibly, yes."

The descent to the lunar surface, Bales knew, presented few if any great choices. An abort was risky. Going on was risky. He had a lot on his mind while getting geared up for the flight's initial trial run, and now, the whole back row was filled to the brim with management types. The VIP viewing room was nearly full as well, and Kraft was front and center in the Trench with Bales. He almost always simply listened in on a squawk box installed in his office or positioned himself with the rest of management in the room's uppermost row, but not now.

Gulp.

"I almost said, 'What the hell?' but I didn't," Bales remembered with a laugh. The simulation began, and sure enough, his velocity numbers on the LM's descent started rising. Then, they rose some more. Finally, they got to the point where he had no other option than to call off the landing. It turned out to be exactly the right decision to make. If he was going to be replaced by his section head, Charley Parker, a mistake in the first sim would have been cause to do it. There was a lot riding on Bales's actions that day, and he nailed the abort call with Kraft sitting right there next to him.

Kraft slapped Bales on the shoulder, told him that it had been a job well done, and then returned to his perch in the back row. It is not hard to imagine the relief that must have coursed through Bales.

While the final couple of weeks of training did not turn out nearly as well initially, they went a long way toward making the actual landing possible. Simulation supervisor Richard H. "Dick" Koos, according to Kranz, "kept beating us up and beating us up and beating us up." One day, Kraft called Kranz on a phone behind the flight director's console. "There wasn't any help this guy could give me," Kranz said. "I mean, there was nothing. The only help he could give me was to maintain his confidence that I was going to get it all together." Kranz responded to the call by turning the ringer off on the phone. "At times, it got so bad that the prime crew, *Apollo 11* crew, Armstrong and Aldrin, just didn't want to train with us anymore, and we didn't want to train with them, to the point where they'd go off in a different simulator and we'd work with the backup crew or work with the *Apollo 12* crew."

The final sim was on 5 July 1969, and with the prime crew already in Florida preparing for launch, the training session was left up to Pete Conrad and Alan L. Bean of *Apollo 12*, and their backups, Dave Scott and James B. "Jim" Irwin. Late in the afternoon, with several successful runs already under their belt that day, Gene Kranz felt his team was primed and ready to go.

Dick Koos was about to throw the control team a wickedly breaking curveball with the count full, two out, and bases loaded in the bottom of the ninth inning of the World Series. A few minutes into the descent, a computer program alarm cropped up. Bales remembered it being a 1210 alarm, Kranz a 1201. Whatever it actually was, the alarm was about to wreak havoc in the control room.

"1210 meant two users were trying to access the computer at the same time," Bales explained. "I've never thought that was a planned failure. I think something went wrong with the simulator. They never 'fessed up to it, nor would they. It didn't matter if it was planned or not." That might not actually have been the case, because Jack Garman had been working both sides of the fence by helping the sim teams come up with various computer failures to throw in during training. Just like that, Bales was struggling to figure out what to do with an issue very similar to what Garman had suggested.

On what had long been considered graduation day in the MOCR, Bales made up his mind.

Abort!

Kranz confirmed, and Scott and Irwin were off to the races in exactly the opposite direction they had planned to be going. If the abort was a frustrating decision to make, the post-sim debrief was even more so when Koos made it abundantly clear that the landing could—and *should*—have continued. "I felt that we had made the right, necessary call, but I was really unhappy with Koos," Kranz wrote in his autobiography. "Dammit, we should have finished our training with a landing on the surface."

"We were very young," Garman added. "It wasn't funny, particularly when Gene Kranz started bawling out the sim guys, saying they never should have given us a sim like that and the sim guys turned around and bawled out Kranz, because it was supposed to be a survivable kind of an issue."

When the smoke cleared, Kranz asked Bales to come up with a list of computer alarms and to note which ones would require an abort and which would not. Bales did not want to do it, because he already had a mountain of work to plow through before the actual mission began. Instead, Bales went to Garman. Computer software was Garman's specialty, and he knew and worked with MIT virtually every day. Bales took Garman's findings and added a list of program alarms to his mission rules that would mean an abort.

1201 and 1202 were not among them.

Garman also developed a handwritten cheat sheet list, placed one under the glass at his console in the SSR, and gave one to Bales. "Thank the Lord he did," Bales admitted. "I thought we'd never use the sheet. I thought that was just the biggest waste of time." Bales stopped, then reconsidered what he had just said. "Not that it was a waste of time, but I thought it wasn't the top priority thing we needed to be doing at the time."

Bales and Garman would be forever thankful for that little slip of paper come landing day.

Over his comm loop, FIDO Dave Reed sounded ever so poised and confident as the launch of *Apollo 11* approached on 16 July 1969. His callouts were crisp and precise, just the way he had always done them.

From the sound of it all, there was also no sign that he was deeply disappointed in not being assigned as the FIDO on the flight's lunar descent team. The plum role went instead to Jay Greene. Although Reed was lead FIDO on the next three flights and got to do lunar landings on both *Apollo 12* and *14*, there would never again be a *first* landing. "After having formed my career around the Lunar Module and having flown *Apollo 9*," he said, "I was at the very least confused why Jay would get that role given that he wasn't at all that familiar with the LM. Made no sense."

The call was made by the head of the FIDO section, Ed Pavelka, who would later insist that the decision had nothing whatsoever to do with choosing one operator over another. He felt it was just another shift that had to be staffed, and Reed had been buried in work as lead FIDO on *Apollo 9*. According to Pavelka, he had not considered the implications and said that when the manning list went out, Reed was furious. "He could not stand it," said Pavelka, who died on 26 August 2005. "He was going to be

APPLICABLE TO: IN DESCENT, AVERAGE-G ON

ALARM CODE	TYPE	PRE-MANUAL CAPABILITY	MANUAL CAPABILITY
00105 MK ROUT. BUSY	POODOO	PGNCS GUID. LOST,	PGNCS GUIDANCE NO/GO
00430 CANT INTG. SV.	"		(PGNCS GO for
01105 CCSHOLE- PROG. BUG	"		TAPE METER, CROSS-POINTERS,
01204 NEG. WAITLIST	"	PGNCS/AGS ABRT/ABRT STG	CONTROL,
01206 DSKY, TWO USERS	"		ABORTING)
01302 NEG. SQ, ROOT	"	(decision how on	
01501 DSKY, PROG. BAD	"	current rules)	
01502 DSKY, PROG. BUG	"	(NO LR DATA)	(NO LR DATA)
00607 LAMB. NO SOLN	"		
"O.F." = Overflow, too many. CONTINUING OCCURRENCE OF:		DUTY CYCLE MAY DESTRESS PGNCS (AGS CONTROL MAY HELP- SEE BELOW)	SAME AS LEFT
01109 DELAY ROUT. O.V.	BAILOUT	(WATCH FOR OTHER CUES)	(except "other cues"
01201 EXECT. O.F (VAC)	"	PGNCS CONTROL UNCERTAIN,	which would otherwise
01202 EXECT. O.F. (CORE)	"	DSKY MAY BE LOCKED UP,	be cause for ABORT
01203 EXECT. O.F. (TASK)	"	DUTY CYCLE MAY BE UP	PROBABLY ABRT'N),
01207 EXECT. O.F (CHRG)	"	TO POINT OF MISSING SOME	INSTEAD IT WOULD
01210 TWO USERS	"	FUNCTIONS (NAV. LAST TO DIE)	BE PGNCS GUIDANCE
01211 MRK ROUT. INTRPT	"	SWITCH TO AGS (FOLLOW FDAI	NO/GO — COMPLETE NORMAL
02000 DAP O.F.	"	NEEDLES) MAY HELP (REDUCES PGNCS DUTY CYCLE SIGNIF)	LANDING IN AGS.)
ESS WARNING WITH:			
00777 PIPA FAIL	LIGHT ONLY	PIPA/CDU/IMU FAIL	
03777 CDU FAIL	"	DISCRETES PRESENT	Same as left
04777 PIPA, CDU FAIL	"		
07777 IMU FAIL	"	(Other mission rules	
10777 PIPA, IMU FAIL	"	suffice; alarm may help	
13777 CDU, IMU FAIL	"	point to what rule will	
14777 PIPA, CDU, IMU FL	"	be broken)	
00214 IMU TURNED OFF	LIGHT ONLY	AGS ABRT/ABRT STAGE	SWITCH TO AGS PGNCS NO/GO on GUID C (poss. NO/GO on NAV.)
01107 E-MEM. DESTROYED	FRESH STRT	AGS ABRT/ABRT STAGE	SWITCH TO AGS PGNCS NO/GO! (IMU as ref. okay)
CONTINUING 00402 BAD GUID. CMDS	LIGHT ONLY	IF ALARM DOESN'T STOP: Same as "POODOO's" ("ABRT.")	IF ALARM DOESN'T STOP: Same as "POODOO's
CONTINUING 01406 GUID. NO SOLN 01410 GUID. O.V.	LIGHT ONLY	PGNCS GUID. NO/GO AS LONG AS ALARM OCCURRING (ATT. HOLD, CONST. GTC, CONT. K) (ABRT WILL PROB. COME FROM CURRENT RULES e.g. GTC vs. V) WATCH GTC	Same as left (except prob. no abort)

13. After taking a shellacking during simulations for the flight of *Apollo 11*, Jack Garman put together this cheat sheet to have on hand back in the SSR. As it turned out, the sheet came in very, very handy during the landing. Courtesy Jack Garman.

on console for the first landing, and he went to my boss. We ended up sitting down, and I went through the rationale. He just was not going to have the time to spend in the preparation because of his other assignments that he was totally involved in."

Reed was so upset, Pavelka felt that it led to his joining former flight director John Hodge and fifteen others who left NASA a couple of years later to move to a Department of Transportation project in Cambridge, Massachusetts. Reed told his bosses that *Apollo 13* would be his last flight, but when that mission went the way it did, he could not leave on such a note. And while *Apollo 14* was Reed's swan song in the MOCR, he insisted that not getting a spot on the first lunar landing team had nothing at all to do with his departure. "No, the reason I left was that the job had become routine and the excitement had puttered out," Reed said. "I recall sitting on the console for launch of *14* and my heart rate didn't elevate until T-minus two minutes. That was not fair to the entire operation. My edge had dulled."

That was one reason. NASA politics was another, in that it seemed to Reed that decisions were beginning to be made by committee. "Things changed," he said. "You could see this bureaucracy creep in, and it wasn't as much fun. The juices weren't going to flow in that kind of environment. We figured going up here to this brand-new place, we could start all over again. That's why we left." Toss in a divorce, and Reed concluded that "Houston just wasn't the place it had always been." Born in Nebraska and raised in Montana, Reed was deep down an adventurist seeking one challenge after another. The former FIDO eventually got shot at in Mogudishu, Somalia, while on an assignment for the Department of Defense; worked with the Drug Enforcement Administration on drug busts; traveled to Saudi Arabia following the first Gulf War; introduced advanced satellite technologies in the enforcement of sanctions in Serbia for the United Nations; and flew around the world several times on board the air force's heavily modified "Speckled Trout" KC-135.

Bob Carlton arrived early for his shift on the morning of 20 July 1969, as did virtually everyone else on the landing team. That was not necessarily anything out of the ordinary, though. Controllers *always* showed up before they took over on console to see if there were any issues they needed to know about. Carlton got off the elevator on the third floor, and almost as soon as he did, he got an ominous message that officials from Grumman—the maker of the LM—needed to speak with him. From the foreboding tone of the message and its urgency, he had a gut feeling the conversation was not going to be a pleasant one. What the builders of the LM had to say left Carlton dumbfounded.

A potential fracture mechanics problem had been detected in the propellant tanks—in essence, the metal of the high-pressure tanks was designed to expand and have some elasticity, much like a balloon. However, there was concern that the issue might cause the tank walls to get thinner and weaker as they stretched and possibly rupture in the process. The descent engine was nestled right beneath those tanks, and the hotter it got during the landing, the hotter the metal of those tanks could become. The risk was obvious.

Worse yet, there was no way to quantify the extent of the problem. There were temperature sensors on the tanks, but there were no numbers to determine when an abort should be called or even when the tanks should be watched, in Carlton's words, "super close." The only thing coming his way was that there *might* be some sort of issue, that it *could* be serious, and that the tank *might* blow up if it got too hot. How hot was *too* hot? No one could say for sure.

"Can you imagine my feelings?" he asked. "I didn't know how to handle it. They hadn't given me enough information to handle it, but I dang sure wasn't going in there and tell the flight director we weren't going to land this mission." A couple of days past the forty-fourth anniversary of the *Apollo 11* lunar landing, the moment seemed as fresh and as vivid in Carlton's mind as it was that day back in July 1969. He did not inform Kranz because, he continued, "it was a very complicated thing, and I didn't have the answers. We would've had a *long*, big discussion taking place when we ought to have had 1,001 other things in high-priority mode. I just didn't want to sidetrack us with something I did not have figured out. It was pointless to sit down and discuss it with Kranz. All I would have done is introduce a great big factor of confusion, alarm, concern. It would've focused our attention away from what we ought to have been looking at. There was a heck of a lot going on."

Carlton trudged into the MOCR "almost paralyzed," he admitted. His plan was this—he would keep an eye on the tank temperature gauges, and if they happened to spike, he would call the SPAN room and have Grumman's representatives explain the need for an abort. In his mind, it was the only solution.

Situated on the far-right end of the second row, Carlton could peer over the top of his console at Steve Bales, who was situated at the guidance console in the Trench. Bales felt like he had the weight of the world on his shoulders as well. The computer alarms that triggered the aborted sim were still fresh on his mind as he walked into the MOCR. When he did, instead of a comfortable seventy-two degrees, the air in the room felt more like ninety with humidity every bit as high. The consoles might as well have been sitting outside in the hot Houston sun.

Carlton and Bales were not the only ones in the control room who were "clutched," as Carlton would have put it. Kranz knew that, and he also knew that he wanted to say something to reassure his troops. He called for everyone in the MOCR to go to the assistant flight director's private communications loop—no one else would ever hear what he was about to say, because it was not recorded—and then began:

Okay, all flight controllers, listen up. Today is our day, and the hopes and the dreams of the entire world are with us. This is our time and our place, and we will remember this day and what we will do here always. In the next hour we will do something that has never been done before. We will land an American on the moon. The risks are high. That is the nature of our work. We worked long hours and had some tough times but we have mastered our work. Now we are going to make this work pay off. You are a hell of a good team, one that I feel privileged to lead. Whatever happens, I will stand behind every call that you will make. Good luck and God bless us today.

For Bales, the pep talk was exactly the thing he needed to hear at exactly the moment he needed to hear it. Bales would have been willing to follow Kranz through hell itself that day, and he was not alone. "I still keep [Kranz's words] with me today. That's how important it was," Bales said. "He was saying to us, 'We're going to do the best we can. If it doesn't turn out well, we all go out of here saying it didn't turn out well, not that it was that guy's fault or this guy's fault.'"

Telcom Jack Knight was not assigned to the landing phase, so he was in the SSR to follow along with the play-by-play. He heard Kranz's speech, and wished for decades afterward that it had been recorded for posterity's sake. It was so powerful that it brought Knight to a place of deep emotion even after all those years.

When Kranz finished with his remarks, he ordered the control room doors locked. It was time. The next few minutes would be some of the most tense and compelling in the lives of those who worked the flight in the MOCR and back rooms. The descent orbit initiation (DOI) began on the far side of the moon with a thirty-second burn that placed *Eagle* into an orbit that swung the LM to within fifty thousand feet of the lunar surface on the near side. As soon as the spacecraft peeked out from behind the moon, controllers around the room raced to get readings to ensure that it was safe to continue with a powered descent initiation (PDI) burn designed to bleed off the LM's orbital velocity.

Nearly sixteen minutes after coming back around to the lunar near side, the PDI braking phase commenced. It began with a short twenty-six-second burst of the descent engine at just 10 percent thrust, known as an ullage burn, to force floating propellant into the engine's intake valve. Data dropped out just then, and as Duke relayed a message through Collins in *Columbia* to have Aldrin switch antennas, PDI began in earnest by throttling up to 94 percent of the descent engine's rated thrust. Starting out in a heads-down position so Armstrong and Aldrin could get a quick visual read of their altitude and range by checking out the lunar surface, *Eagle* then swung around to heads up, where the astronauts faced the nothingness of space as the LM's landing radar locked onto the surface. As soon as it did, Bales knew something was amiss.

Eagle was descending too fast, to the tune of twenty feet per second. At thirty-five feet per second, Bales would have been forced to call an abort. He was already more than halfway there, and there were plenty of "what ifs" to consider. What if the guidance system was misaligned? What if one of the accelerometers had a bias? What if the error continued to grow?

A decision to call off the landing was staring Bales in the face, but in just thirty seconds or so, he was able to figure out that there was nothing wrong with the flight computer's navigation capability. Instead, PDI had begun and was proceeding with the LM some three miles farther down range than expected. No one would ever know for sure what caused the problem, but there were, of course, theories. Some figured that residual air in the docking tunnel somehow popped *Eagle* into the error when it undocked with

Columbia. Others felt that small inputs from the Reaction Control System (RCS) made the difference.

Whatever the cause of the issue might have been, Bales was satisfied and remembered turning to FIDO Jay Greene and remarking, "We're in great shape." He could not have known that his and Jack Garman's biggest test was yet to come.

A few moments later, Kranz went around the horn with a round of "go/ no go" calls to continue the descent. If Bales became well known in later years for anything other than serving as guidance officer for the *Apollo 11* lunar landing, it was his—what's the best way to put this?—enthusiastic "Go!" calls while doing so. Garman joked that Bales yelled because he had yelled, but each of Bales's calls that day was pronounced, and Bales would later say that was the way he almost always did it. Granted, these were probably a little more adrenaline charged than others he had made during sims. "If Don Puddy would've started talking in the tone I talked, Gene would've thought something was wrong with Don," Bales said. "But he knew each one of us, and we would just talk differently. I was cranked up, high volume, high everything. In fact, I suspect that if I'd have been quiet, he would've thought something was wrong with me."

During the go/no go poll to press on with powered descent, Bales all but bellowed his affirmation, and after he did so, there was a brief but very definite chuckle in Kranz's voice as he pressed on to other controllers. The flight director was not the only one who apparently enjoyed Bales's calls that afternoon.

The conversation with Grumman was still haunting Carlton. He had also since dealt with an erroneous thruster failure signal on *Eagle* during the descent. He had seen a similar issue during a simulation leading up to the flight, and he knew that it was merely an instrumentation issue when the thruster's gimbal numbers remained rock-solid steady.

"The sim guys saved my neck," Carlton said. "I don't know what I would've done if we hadn't come up with that little scheme, because when you saw a failed-thruster light on, I was spring-loaded to the panic position." When Kranz asked for the PDI go/no go, Carlton was "as taut as a wire" and actually gave his consent before Kranz even asked him for it.

We're going, Flight.

The very next call was to Bales, and Carlton would always appreciate the fact that his fellow flight controller was so youthfully exuberant. "He said, '*Gooooooooooooooooo!*'" Carlton remembered with an all-out laugh. "I empathized with that, because I thought, 'You know, I'm just that strung out myself. I'm glad he did that, because now I'll make a special effort to sound calm. It probably would've been me that did it, if Steve hadn't done it. It relieved the tension, though, then everybody kind of relaxed a little bit."

Bales could not relax just yet. Another computer alarm crisis was about to rear its ugly head.

From the moment the Primary Guidance Navigation and Control System computer was turned on, its resources began to be eaten away by an overload of some 10 to 15 percent. No one knew how hard the computer was working, and just five minutes into the powered descent, the first of five computer program alarms rang out.

Bales got on the loop to Garman.

1202. What's that?

Garman responded.

It's executive overflow. If it does not occur again, we're fine.

The computer was working overtime and was in the process of dropping tasks that were not absolutely essential in order to concentrate on ones that were. Moments later, Armstrong was not so much requesting an answer as demanding one.

Give us a reading on the 1202 program alarm.

Garman quickly checked the cheat sheet he had put together, and told Bales that things were good to go for the time being. Just as the last syllable slipped from Armstrong's lips, Bales assured Kranz.

We're go on that, Flight.

The alarms sent Garman's blood pressure "through the ceiling," he would one day joke. "I just reacted," Garman recalled. "I looked down, saw what it was, and told Gran Paules (who was sitting in on the guidance console during the landing) and Steve Bales that as long as it didn't reoccur—and I meant to say, 'As long as it didn't reoccur too often'—that we were fine. If the computer was really in trouble, the vehicle would've started tumbling long before we had a chance to tell them there was a problem."

The episode was a prime example of the working relationship between a controller in the front room and his back-room support staff. Bales's copy of Garman's cheat sheet was in a notebook, covered by various other sheets of paper. Even if it had been front and center, he might not have had the time to find the alarm in question. "I don't know if Jack remembered it from memory or if he had this right out in front of him, but either way, he was faster than I was, which didn't surprise me at all," Bales admitted. Russ Larsen of MIT was seated next to Garman in the SSR, and he could offer only a thumbs-up during the computer alarms. Don Eyles, who would later save the day during the flight of *Apollo 14*, remembered that his MIT colleague once said that he had been too scared to actually form words.

As soon as Bales gave his go call, Duke was on the air-to-ground loop telling Armstrong and Aldrin that they could continue. He did not even wait for confirmation from Kranz. "I was winging it," Duke said. "If you're in the cockpit and you get this computer alarm, you start thinking about an abort. I thought it was critical that they get the straight word. When Bales said, 'We're go, Flight,' I just said we're go. I didn't wait for Flight. Gene was going to say, 'We're go.' That kept happening. He never said anything about it, so I just winged it at that point."

Another 1202 alert was triggered less than a minute later and then three more alarms—one 1201 and two 1202s, signaling essentially the same issue— took place within the span of just forty seconds. After the third, Bales almost immediately called over the flight director's loop with much more confidence in his voice.

Same type. We're go, Flight.

A month after the flight, President Richard M. Nixon presented the crew with the Presidential Medal of Freedom at a grand ceremony in Los Angeles. The chief justice of the U.S. Supreme Court was there, as were forty-four of the nation's fifty governors and fifty members of the House of Representatives and Senate. It was an impressive gathering, and Bales was chosen to accept the NASA Group Achievement Award on behalf of its mission operations group. "Steve Bales," the president began, "made a critical decision just before *Eagle* landed on the Sea of Tranquility that could have made the difference between success or failure. . . . This is the young man, when the computers seemed to be confused and when he could have said, 'Stop,' or when he could have said, 'Wait,' said, 'Go.'"

Those few moments were as quiet as Jerry Bostick had ever heard the control room. Personally, he felt that Armstrong was the right man for the job. He was not one who would have taken unnecessary chances. To put it another way, Armstrong was not going to do anything stupid. He would either abort safely or land. It was that simple. Bostick had the very same sense of confidence in Bales, so much so that he bought the young man a bottle of Scotch after the flight in celebration. "I felt very proud of everybody, especially Steve," Bostick said. "I think he made the right decision at the right time. He made it without any stammering or hesitation. He performed a job that I expected all the guys in the Trench to do."

Hugh Blair-Smith, who helped develop the guidance computer while at the MIT Instrumentation Laboratory, wrote that a "myth" developed when some believed that the computer "had somehow 'failed' in a way that required human intervention or 'takeover.' The truth is exactly the opposite: the PGNS software had been deliberately designed to recover from such unexpected disturbances and persevere with the high-priority tasks that flew the vehicle. All the humans had to do was to notice that flight was proceeding correctly, and forgive the disappearance of some displays."

The final three alarms took place after *Eagle* had pitched up to a not-quite vertical position in a process known as high gate. Beginning at an altitude of approximately seven thousand feet and four and a half nautical miles from the landing site, Armstrong and Aldrin could finally peer through their small windows and visually monitor their approach to the lunar surface. The final approach started, and in less than two minutes, the spacecraft dropped to just a few hundred feet above the surface. From maybe two thousand feet on down, Kranz knew that responsibility for the landing was rapidly shifting from the MOCR to the two men doing the flying. It was, after all, their behinds that were on the line in what Kranz and fellow aviators had always called the "dead man's curve."

Dead man's curve? Absolutely. Every inch lower was new, completely uncharted territory.

As the descent continued through low gate, the point at which Armstrong could take over manual control, *Eagle* was coming down in a football-field-sized crater littered with boulders. Armstrong did just that at about six hundred feet up, and began to steer the LM clear of the treacherous rocks below. Back in the MOCR, no one could have known what Armstrong and Aldrin were seeing through their triangular-shaped windows. Duke told Kranz in a tone of marked seriousness, "I think we better be quiet, Flight."

Duke's boss in the astronaut office had triggered the request. "Deke Slay-

14. As *Eagle* drew ever closer to the lunar surface, capcom Charlie Duke asked flight director Gene Kranz for silence over the comm loops. Kranz quickly complied. Courtesy NASA.

ton was sitting next to me and he said, 'Shut up and let 'em land,' and I said, 'Yes, sir!'" Duke remembered with a chuckle. "He was right. We were giving them too much information, I thought."

Kranz answered the future moonwalker's request by telling his controllers that from that point on, the only callouts would be for fuel. Carlton knew that those levels were already low, and getting lower. It had always been his nightmare to have an LM run out of fuel while landing and not know it until too late, and this time at least, he could see it coming. A low-level sensor in the tank was uncovered in the tank as it neared empty, with maybe a couple minutes' worth remaining. Sims had taught him what kind of fuel levels to expect at various altitudes in the landing cycle, and Carlton's heart dropped.

Fuel had *never* been this low this high up, and even when the craft came back over the crater's lip and the altitude lessened suddenly, the remainder was still lower than he expected. Generally, Armstrong and Aldrin had already landed in simulations well before Carlton ever saw the low-level light flash on his console. Not this time. "Knowing that we were going to land long, I was prepared for us to go low of fuel, but I had no idea we'd run as low as we did," Carlton said. "We saw low level, and I glanced at the altitude and I thought, 'Ohhhh, crap.' I didn't know if we were going to make it or not."

Kranz and Carlton both knew what was about to happen. Kranz called, using his colleague's name instead of console position.

Okay, Bob, I'll be standing by for your callouts shortly.

Carlton noted the low-level light, and then a few seconds later, told Kranz to stand by for word that only sixty seconds' worth of fuel was left. Another call came, and nobody wanted to hear it.

Sixty.

Kranz repeated.

Sixty seconds.

Duke passed word up to the crew, just as the engine started to kick up dust. This was going to be far too close for comfort, but from the sounds of their voices, it might as well have been just another simulation.

Stand by for thirty.

Thirty.

Again, Kranz and Duke echoed the call. In the Trench, retro officer Chuck Deiterich was as cool as a cucumber. He was not sweating the landing. "I never really got too excited about it," Deiterich said. "I felt they had enough time to get down, so I wasn't concerned about an abort. Thirty seconds is a *long* time. Maybe I was being naïve, I don't know. But when you work in the control center, you worry about your job, you worry about the other people you might affect, and you worry about how they might affect you. Something like how much propellant they've got is Bob Carlton's call, so you trust him to do the right thing. It's a team effort."

Moments later, probes extending from three of the LM's four legs made contact with the surface. Aldrin called it.

Contact light.

Eagle's engine stopped, and as the astronauts raced through their procedures checklist, Carlton saw the stoppage on his console. He confirmed it to Kranz with little sign of emotion in his voice.

We've had shutdown.

By the count of the stopwatch Carlton was holding in his hand, only eighteen seconds of fuel remained before he would have been forced to call an abort. There was actually closer to forty-five seconds or so, but Carlton had intentionally left a reserve due to the amount of time an abort call would have taken to pass from him to Kranz to Duke to the crew and for action to have been taken.

It was at that point that Armstrong's voice rang back to Earth. *Houston . . . uh . . . Tranquility Base here. The* Eagle *has landed.* Armstrong told Duke beforehand not to be surprised if the landing site was so named, but most in the room, including Kranz, had no inkling what it might be called.

Even if he was expecting "Tranquility Base," the capcom momentarily fumbled his response in an excited rush of adrenaline. *Roger, Twan . . . ,* Duke began, then paused a brief second before continuing, *Tranquility. We copy you on the ground. You've got a bunch of guys about to turn blue. We're breathing again. Thanks a lot.* Minutes later, Duke would remind Kranz of the landing site's call sign. Kranz replied, apparently ribbing him for his slip:

Okay, that sounds like a good one . . . if you can say it.

Bales was sure the "guys about to turn blue" crack had been aimed squarely at him. "I was one of them who was about to turn blue," Bales laughed. "I looked over at Jay Greene. He was the opposite of me. He was always cool most of the time, and even he could hardly talk. We made it. We made it. We made it."

Kranz did not have time to react one way or the other, because his attention was immediately focused on the first polling of his control team on whether *Eagle* could remain on the surface—and it could not continue to be called go/no go. Bill Tindall was considered the architect of the techniques that took Apollo to the lunar surface. He had once wondered in one of his famous "Tindall-gram" memos, "Once we get to the Moon does Go mean 'stay' on the surface, and does No Go mean abort from the surface? I think the Go/No Go decision should be changed to Stay/No Stay or something like that. Just call me 'Aunt Emma.'" Tindall was such a respected member of the NASA community that Kranz invited him to sit next to him at his console during the landing as an honorary flight director, leader of Gray Flight. "Tindall was the guy who put all the pieces together, and all we did was execute them," Kranz said. "I saw him up in the viewing room, and I told him to come on down and sit in the console with me for the landing. He didn't want to come down, but basically I cleared everybody away and we had Bill Tindall there for landing. I think that was probably the happiest day of his life, a spectacular guy."

As a result of Tindall's memo, it did in fact become a stay/no stay call. Kranz was so intent on the job at hand that he had already told the MOCR to stand by for the T1 decision before Armstrong uttered his famous "Tranquility Base" line.

Almost from the moment it was confirmed that *Eagle* had settled into its nest in the Sea of Tranquility, background clapping could be heard over the comm loops. The viewing room erupted in cheering, clapping, stomping on the floor, and banging on the glass. Kranz would have none of it. "My immediate job was to keep my team focused on the task," Kranz said. "It was pretty tough to do. That was the one surprise. For all the training we'd done, we'd never had people in the viewing room who erupted in cheering and stomping their feet. The sound of their recognition of the landing sort of filtered into the control room, so it really was a question of keeping everybody focused because we'd really been sucking air in those last two minutes."

Finally, Kranz had enough and barked, "Okay, keep the chatter down in this room." As he brought everyone else's emotions under control, Kranz was trying to do the very same thing for himself. He was getting choked up with emotion. "It's sort of like your first landing in a high-performance jet aircraft was," Kranz said. "As soon as you touch down, you have that instant of exhilaration to say, 'I did it!' You have to stay focused upon the task, because you still have the landing rollout. You've got to lower the nose gear. You've got to make sure you don't hit the barrier. To me, it was just a period of absolute, instantaneous recognition that we'd just touched down and then turning around very quickly to get back on track."

At the exact moment Armstrong was telling the world that the *Eagle* had landed, Carlton was in the process of stopping any celebrations on the part of his SSR back room before they ever started.

Okay, fellas. Steady now. Stay with it. Keep your eye on it.

Bob Nance, who watched over the descent engine in the SSR, sounded almost incredulous moments after landing.

Looks beautiful.

Carlton answered.

Okay . . . keep your eye on it.

Nance's voice was still filled with a tone of wonder.

Everything is steady, steady as a rock.

Carlton's and Nance's eyes were still glued to their consoles fifteen or twenty minutes later, as they stood ever vigilant over their bird. Nance noticed pressure rising in a line that led from a heat exchanger to the descent engine shutoff valve, and after he and Carlton scratched their heads for several minutes as to the cause, the loop lit up.

"Bob, I'll tell you what it is!" Carlton remembered Nance announcing proudly. "It's the heat exchanger. It's froze up! It's got the fuel trapped!"

Without acknowledging Nance or even questioning him about the issue, Carlton went onto the flight's director's loop and informed Kranz what was taking place. "You work together so long, one will start a sentence to talk about a problem, and the other will finish the sentence for him with the answer," Carlton said. Carlton trusted Nance's opinion to the point where he did not question it in the least. He was *that* confident going to Kranz with the information.

During post-landing venting of the fuel and oxidizer tanks, a small amount of leftover fuel froze in the heat exchanger and that in turn caused the rising pressure in the line. "It was like a pressure cooker," Carlton continued. If the propellant line had ruptured, would it have been that big a deal? The line was located in the guts of the descent engine, and the descent engine had already done its job. That much was true, but if the line burst and sprayed fuel onto the warm engine bell, what then?

Thirty-five minutes after landing, Armstrong and Aldrin were informed of the line's increasing pressure. Both men later downplayed the risk, and it is not hard to imagine why. They had something else on their minds at that point—a moonwalk.

According to the *Apollo 11* press kit, the long-awaited moonwalk was supposed to start nearly ten hours after touching down on the surface. That allowed for an extensive check of the LM, which was all well and good, but such a delay was also to have included a two-hour nap.

After the adrenaline-charged landing, few could have reasonably expected Armstrong and Aldrin to actually get any rest during the rest period. They had not come all that way just to get there and then go to sleep. With that in mind, Bruce McCandless figured he still had some time on his hands and headed home for a bite of dinner before taking over as capcom for the EVA.

McCandless came from a long line of ultra-successful navy men—his maternal grandfather and his father were both awarded the Medal of Honor, and his paternal grandfather had risen to the rank of commodore. All four graduated from the U.S. Naval Academy in Annapolis, Maryland, and the youngest McCandless graduated second in a 1958 class of 899 midshipmen. NASA came calling eight years later, and he became a member of the 1966 class of astronauts. By the time *Apollo 11* rolled around, he was still waiting in line to fly.

A little less than two hours into the surface stay, Armstrong began to put an end to the will-they-rest-or-will-they-walk drama. "Our recommendation at this point is planning an EVA, with your concurrence, starting at about 8 o'clock this evening, Houston time," the *Apollo 11* commander told Duke, still on duty as capcom. It took Duke just twenty-six seconds to relay the ground's agreement. McCandless's home-cooked meal that night was not going to happen.

"By the time I got home, my wife came running down the driveway, saying, 'They can't sleep. Go back!' I turned around and drove right back," McCandless remembered. While returning to MSC, he looked up and spotted the moon. It did not look any different from the countless times he had seen it before, but this time at least, there was a *huge* change. He had friends and neighbors up there, and he was about to be talking to them in front of a worldwide audience.

McCandless made it back to the MOCR in time to join flight director Cliff Charlesworth's Green Team for the start of the EVA preparations. Jim Joki and Bill Peters had not taken any chances on leaving the MOCR. They were in the control room for the landing, and when the big moment arrived, Peters remembered slapping Joki on the back so hard that Joki actually cringed. "He gave me such a slap, he knocked me right out of my chair," Joki corrected with a smile. Joki was assigned to monitor Armstrong's spacesuit during the moonwalk, while Peters was to watch over Aldrin's. The fact they were there was proof enough that they suspected the EVA might very well be moved up.

"Jim Joki said, 'They're going to do it now. They're not going to go to sleep. There's no way,'" Peters said. "We manned up specifically to sit there and wait for it. We said, 'We're not going to sit at home and pretend to sleep while they get ready to do an EVA. No way.'"

The two EMU spots were separate positions in the control room through the first lunar landing, but from the flight of *Apollo 12* on, responsibility for the spacesuits was assumed by the LM's telcom console up in the second row. The slot was forevermore called telmu—or, if you happened to be Gene Kranz or Ed Fendell, "tel-uh-mu."

For *Apollo 11*, Joki and Peters were situated at what had been the booster console on the left end of the Trench, nearest the door. Pete Conrad and Alan Bean were there, just months away from their own landing on *Apollo 12*. So were their backups, Dave Scott and Jim Irwin, who would eventually make the trip during the flight of *Apollo 15*. Before the two EMU guys could go to work, they had to shoo the astronauts away from their stations. "When it came time for us to work, I said, 'Sorry, guys. This is *my* console,'" Peters said.

As Armstrong and Aldrin suited up for their stroll on the moon, Peters noticed that Aldrin was turning his suit fan on and off, on and off, on and off, cycling it five or six times for no apparent reason. Peters again jabbed Joki, this time more gently, to see if he might have a guess as to what was happening. "Jim was starting to be concerned he might burn the circuit out," Peters said. "Of course, he didn't. I asked Buzz about it at the fortieth reunion in 2009, and he wouldn't admit to a thing."

The suits were in good shape. It was time to go outside.

The conversations between McCandless, Armstrong, and Aldrin over the course of the two-hour EVA would be etched in the memories of the hundreds of millions of people around the world who were listening in.

Okay, Neil. We can see you coming down the ladder now.

I'm at the foot of the ladder. The LM footpads are only depressed in the surface out one or two inches, although the surface appears to be very, very fine grained as you get close to it. It's almost like a powder.

Then, this. Pulses everywhere quickened.

Okay. I'm going to step off the LM now.

Compared to the expeditions undertaken by later landing crews that ventured miles from the LM, Armstrong's first tentative move onto the surface was a mere baby step. That did not matter now. This was drama of the highest order.

That's one small step for man, one giant leap for mankind.

Did Armstrong actually say, "That's one small step for *a* man?" No, he did not, although he would later tell author Andrew Chaikin that he had intended to do so, and more than one apologist would later attempt to prove that the indefinite article was somehow lost in transmission. It was not, because he did not say it. McCandless could not say one way or the other. "I really cannot answer that question," McCandless responded. "Prior to launch, I had asked Neil several times what his first words would be. He was always noncommittal. I think that he did not want to tempt fate. At any rate, when the time came, the communications link was just noisy enough that I could not tell whether there was an 'a' in there or not."

McCandless said little in those first few minutes but finally broke onto the loop to remind Armstrong about scooping up a contingency sample of lunar rocks and dust. It would have been unthinkable had an emergency forced Armstrong back into the LM without at least a few examples for the rock hounds back on Earth to study, but humanity's first moonwalker initially concentrated on describing the surface and a panoramic series of photographs of the landing site. McCandless attempted to bring Armstrong back around to the chore.

Neil, we're reading you loud and clear. We see you getting some pictures and the contingency sample.

Just a few seconds later, after a prompt from Charlesworth, McCandless tried again.

Neil, this is Houston. Did you copy about the contingency sample?

Armstrong responded by telling McCandless that he would get to the sample as soon as he finished the panorama, and he did just that. That was exactly what it meant to be the only person in the world talking to men walking on the surface of another. "The job of the capcom is to help the flight crew and keep quiet, unless you *have* to say something," McCandless said. "It was their show. My job was to communicate, keep them on a timeline, and make sure they didn't forget something. It was a team effort."

Keeping Armstrong and Aldrin on task was one thing, but keeping the president of the United States at bay was something else altogether. McCandless had no idea that President Richard M. Nixon might be placing a call to the moon. "Probably the biggest surprise was shortly after the EVA started, the White House came in and said that the president would like to talk to the *Apollo 11* crew," he remembered. "It was probably an oversight, but we had never considered that as a possibility. So for about an hour, my job was stiff-arming the president."

The timeline was the timeline, and the leader of the free world would have to wait for his turn. At last, a little more than an hour into the EVA, McCandless called Armstrong and Aldrin to attention. Both were framed perfectly by the surface television camera, with *Eagle* and the American flag in the shot for good measure. McCandless called up to the crew.

Neil and Buzz, the president of the United States is in his office now and would like to say a few words to you. Over.

That would be an honor.

After a quick go-ahead from McCandless, Nixon's unmistakable gravelly voice rang out over the loop.

Hello, Neil and Buzz. I'm talking to you by telephone from the Oval Room at the White House, and this certainly has to be the most historic telephone call ever made from the White House. I just can't tell you how proud we all are of what you . . .

Audio of the call dropped out for a split second, but when it returned, Nixon was in full song:

For every American, this has to be the proudest day of our lives. And for people all over the world, I am sure that they, too, join with Americans in recognizing what an immense feat this is. Because of what you have done, the heavens have become a part of man's world. And as you talk to us from the Sea of Tranquility, it inspires us to redouble our efforts to bring peace and tranquility to Earth. For one priceless moment in the whole history of man, all the people on this Earth are truly one; one in their pride in what you have done, and one in our prayers that you will return safely to Earth.

The irony was simply too much to ignore in the coming years—Nixon made such a fawning phone call to Armstrong and Aldrin, only to kill the Apollo program not long afterward. McCandless did not have much more luck in holding off his boss, Deke Slayton, than he had with Nixon. McCandless had considered it an honor when Slayton, one of NASA's famed Mercury Seven original astronauts and the all-powerful director of Flight Crew Operations, sat down just to his left in the MOCR. "I'd only been in the program three years, so he was like God, almost," McCandless quipped.

If McCandless thought Slayton was going to give him a nice, casual pat on the back for a job well done during the moonwalk, he had another thing coming. With maybe an hour or so left in the EVA, half its planned length, Slayton insisted that McCandless have Armstrong and Aldrin start wrapping things up. "He started whispering in my ear, 'Better start bringing them in now. You don't want to take any risks. Let's wrap it up,'" McCandless said. "Of course, that was *not* in accordance with the plan and everything else we had so carefully trained on."

McCandless was in a bind. This was not a conversation that he wanted to have with Charlesworth over the flight director's loop, and he could not get up, leave the capcom console, and go speak with him directly. There was simply too much going on for that to happen. "I didn't want to get on the flight director's loop and say, 'Hey, Deke is harassing me!' or whatever," McCandless continued. "To make a long story short, I had two earpieces. I put the other earpiece in and pressed on. Deke never brought the subject up again."

Or did he?

McCandless was a member of the 1966 astronaut candidate class, and fourteen of its nineteen members flew during Apollo, Skylab, and the Apollo-Soyuz Test Project. Three—Duke, Irwin, and Edgar D. Mitchell—walked on the moon. McCandless waited eighteen long years before he flew for the first time, as a member of the crew of STS-41B on board the Space Shuttle *Challenger* in early 1984. During the flight he was the subject of one of the most famous photograph of the Space Shuttle era when he became the first person to test the untethered Manned Maneuvering Unit (MMU). The shot, taken by crewmate Robert L. "Hoot" Gibson, is a study in beautiful contrasts between the vast blackness of space, the pure white of McCandless's MMU, and the blue beauty of the earth below.

Still, McCandless had been in line to fly a very, very long time, and he could not help but wonder why. Had Slayton and/or Chris Kraft been somehow involved in keeping him on the bench? "Thirty years after the fact, somebody said that they'd heard Kraft remark the reason I didn't get a flight in Apollo was because of insubordination," McCandless admitted. "The only incident I can relate back to was that one where I basically ignored Deke. I was also sort of naïve at the time. I have no idea exactly what happened."

Eyes all around the room were all but glued to the large monitor to the right front of the room, watching as the two astronauts went about their work on the surface. Not Jim Joki, who would claim to be the only controller in the MOCR who did not peek at the television transmission even once. Not even Bill Peters, Joki said, could claim that distinction. "I *never* looked up," he continued. "They should have had a heart monitor on me. When they got back in and got out of their gear and threw the backpacks on the lunar surface, I had a heart attack. No . . . not really . . . but there went all my equipment."

The first part of President Kennedy's directive had been accomplished with the landing and moonwalk, but the job was not finished. The second part—the most important part—was to return the crew of *Apollo 11* safely to Earth.

First, though, somebody needed to figure out exactly where *Eagle* had landed. Dave Reed took over from Ed Pavelka at the FIDO console for the pre-lunar launch shift and set about trying to calculate an ignition time for *Eagle*'s ascent engine. The numbers would have to be precise in order to allow Armstrong, Aldrin, and *Eagle* to rendezvous with Collins and *Columbia*. The only problem was that with the down track error, combined with the maneuvering around that Armstrong had done to avoid the boulder field, no one was quite sure where *Eagle* had come to a rest. When he got settled in, Reed punched the comm button for the Real Time Computer Complex and asked for the landing coordinates. Reed was surprised by the answer.

Take your pick, FIDO.

Reed was in no mood for joking. No less than five different sites were possibilities—one from the Manned Spaceflight Network (MSFN) landing radar; one from the LM's primary guidance computer; and another from the backup guidance computer; the targeted landing spot; and last but not least, the geologists had added their two cents worth based on the moonwalkers' descriptions of the area. None of them were in close proximity to each other, and when combined with uncertainties over *Columbia*'s trajectory overhead, Reed said, "there were combinations of different answers, and multiple combinations thereof. The bottom line was that this was a relative problem." Later studies showed that the LM was nearly five miles from the closest guess.

Pete Williams, who worked down in the first-floor Real Time Computer Complex, came up with a solution. *Eagle* could track *Columbia* with the rendezvous radar located at the very top of the ascent stage, and combined with an accurate read on the CSM's orbital track, the process could work backward to the find the LM. Making matters all the more urgent, time was running out—*Columbia* had only two more passes overhead before the scheduled launch from the surface.

Reed unplugged from his spot in the Trench and made his way up to Milt Windler's perch at the flight director's console to explain the situation as best he knew it. "They instructed the capcom to wake up Buzz and tell him we wanted to do a rendezvous radar check," Reed said. "We figured he'd pick up the Command Module coming over the hill. I'm sitting down there watching my screens and looking for the telemetry that is going to tell me that he got it. Sure enough, over come the vectors, Pete picks them up downstairs, and we recompute where the relative position of the LM is. By using the rendezvous radar, all the relative inaccuracies were nullified. That was the beauty of what we did."

In coming years, Reed came into contact with Armstrong and asked if anyone had ever told the most famous astronaut of them all that the MOCR had not known where *Eagle* landed. "He was *so* cool," Reed said. "He said, 'No, you didn't, but I figured that'd be *your* problem to solve, anyhow.' That's all he said."

One last shift change put Lunney's Black Team on duty for the departure from the lunar surface. Lunney did not seem all that concerned. "I think the landing and all that was associated with it and then watching the EVA were the high points," he began. "When we got to the ascent back into lunar orbit, I think we felt that in some sense, the hard part was over. We knew that this had to work, but we were pretty confident it would."

Hal Loden was not quite as certain down at the control console, and in the MOCR, responsibility for the ascent engine was his. It had been tested several times both on the ground and in flight, and there were all kinds of redundancies built into the control system for igniting it. Loden was comfortable enough with that part of the equation, but what about the unknowns? What might the Attitude Control System (ACS) do? What if more RCS propellant was used than had been planned? No one had ever lifted off from the lunar surface before.

The ascent had Loden's attention. "That particular phase of the mission had never really been tested from the standpoint of real hardware, other than firing the engine and thrusters on test stands. So, yeah, I was a bit concerned as to what was going to happen." Despite his butterflies, Loden was seeing nothing concrete that might have caused him to alert Lunney. All he could do was keep whatever apprehension he had at bay and hope for the best. "When you get down to zero, you can't stand up and say, 'Flight, I don't feel good! Don't do this!'" Loden continued. "You've just got to understand that the best minds in the engineering world have put that machine together, and we had the best pilots flying it. You've just got to go on faith that everything's going to work right."

Capcom Ronald E. "Ron" Evans helped Armstrong and Aldrin through their final preparations, and finally, Aldrin could be heard counting down their final seconds on the moon.

Nine.

Eight.

Seven.

Six.

Five.

Abort stage, engine arm, ascent, proceed.

Eagle had spent 21 hours, 36 minutes, and 20.9 seconds at Tranquility Base.

Millions of people were already beginning to come to grips with the enormity of what NASA had just accomplished. There were house parties, celebrations on town squares all over the world, and quiet vigils in bunkers in war-torn Vietnam. Ironically, it was the people closest to the situation who could not reflect on the flight of *Apollo 11.*

Reflection had to wait until after the flight or maybe even decades. Then and only then could anyone in the MOCR comprehend what had taken place that magical week in July 1969.

Surprised as he might have been about the successful landing, Ed Fendell had gone off shift shortly thereafter. He went back to his Houston apartment, and when he got up on the morning following the EVA, he went to a local dive for a quick breakfast. He sat down at the counter, unfolded a newspaper—which he still has—and started reading.

Two men soon sat down right next to him. They were a little older, grimy

15. FIDO Dave Reed (light-colored jacket) gets his launch plot board signed during celebrations that followed *Apollo 11*'s splashdown. It eventually featured 139 signatures, including the crew itself after returning from quarantine. Courtesy NASA.

from work at a gas station just down the street. One of them started talking. "You know, I went all through World War II. I landed at Normandy on D-Day," the man said. The man had his way to Paris, and on into Berlin. If he did not have Fendell's full attention yet, he was about to when he continued, "Yesterday was the day that I felt the proudest to be an American."

It was at that point that Fendell "lost it." He paid as quickly as he could, grabbed his paper, and walked out to his car.

Once there, he started to cry.

Columbia splashed down at 11:50 a.m. Houston time on 24 July, almost dead center in the Pacific Ocean. The recovery carrier USS *Hornet* was thirteen nautical miles away, and as soon as Armstrong, Aldrin, and Collins were safe and sound on the carrier deck, the MOCR erupted in unabashed celebration. In the midst of it all, Dave Reed was on the hunt for autographs.

Reed secured a three-foot by three-foot plot board that had been used in the Flight Dynamics SSR during launch and planned on getting it signed as soon as the mission was over. While most everyone else was checking out the screen at the front of the room to see if they might possibly be on television, Reed focused intently on scanning the crowd to see who might be available to sign the board. Collecting souvenirs from spaceflights was as old as the business itself, and if an item had actually been used during a mission, it was all the better. When he was finished, it had been signed by flight directors, controllers, astronauts, and various others who had some sort of connection with the flight of *Apollo 11*—139 people in all. The crew signed after getting out of quarantine. As his fellow controllers signed their names, Reed listed them all on a piece of scratch paper and then did some figuring.

The average age of the people who had just landed men on the moon was just twenty-eight years and change.

The priceless piece of history hung for several years in the lobby of Building 30. Then somebody decided that it should go to the Smithsonian Institution. Reed has not seen his signed plot board since.

That was not the only treasured memento that got away. An older gentleman broke out of the crowd during *Apollo 11*'s 16 August 1969 welcome-home parade in Houston to hand Neil Armstrong a small American flag. That was no small feat, considering the fact that some 300,000 people were estimated to have attended the celebration. The man was Harry Franklin Deiterich—Chuck's father.

Later, Armstrong offered to return the souvenir to the younger Deiterich. Hindsight being perfect, the item would have held no small amount of significance because of both the original giver and the recipient. Rather than accepting it, however, the MOCR stalwart told the famous astronaut to keep the flag.

8. "Great Job, Young Man"

Some called it luck.

Some called it preparation meeting opportunity.

Some called it destiny.

Some called it arguably the greatest call ever made in the MOCR with the success or failure of a mission hanging in the balance.

The truth is that it was a combination of all these things, and it began on John Aaron's drive home from a difficult day at work a year or so earlier.

It had been a long day. The MOCR was not actually even controlling the test—Aaron, flight director Glynn Lunney, and maybe a handful of others were just listening in and evaluating whether or not the CSM's instrumentation and software were in working order. Astronauts—years later, Aaron could not remember which ones—had been flipping switches in the spacecraft all day and into the night, to the point where local test operator "astronauts" had taken over. It was around midnight, and Aaron was already exhausted when the capsule's systems experienced a complete brownout.

Rather than completely erasing data from his console monitor, the problem instead caused a random set of nonsensical numbers to appear. Aaron could hear controllers at the Cape trying to figure out what had just happened, and to make matters worse, their fix for the situation was not working. Almost immediately, Aaron went to Lunney.

Glynn, I know we're not supposed to be making inputs during this run, but they're screwing around with this while they've got the whole Command Module powered by only one battery. That battery's going to heat up and probably quit if we don't call them.

Lunney knew that when Aaron spoke in virtually any situation, much less one that he felt this strongly about, he could be trusted. Although he was tired, Aaron had the presence of mind to grab some screen shots of the data that had appeared on his monitor. Before he finally headed home for the night, he had hard copies made.

That was the way John Aaron's brain worked—it was the random numbers on his screen that intrigued him. It was not good enough that the simulation was over. It was not even sufficient that his gut feeling on the battery had been absolutely correct. He had something else on his mind as he trudged to his car in the early morning quiet for the trip home. What caused the upset in the first place, that crazy, random pattern on his readouts?

Aaron and Dick Brown, an instrumentation guru in the CSM SSR back room, spent the entire next day on the issue. The men had first worked together during Gemini, when Brown was with McDonnell Aircraft. So valued was Brown's input that NASA management convinced him to move over to North American as the company struggled to get its Command Module off the ground. Brown was the unassuming quiet type, steady and hard-working, and almost everyone knew that he was the go-to guy when they needed an in-depth analysis or no-nonsense answer.

Together, Aaron and Brown came up with an answer for the electrical brownout.

The design of the CSM instrumentation was a mixed bag when it came to telemetry. Most subsystems converted their own sensor signals into compatible signals for direct input to onboard meters and a telemetry system for downlink to displays in the MOCR. Nearly fifty others depended on a centrally located box—the Signal Conditioning Equipment (SCE)—to convert signals into usable data. A large portion of them were associated with the CSM's electrical power system. The box had redundant power supplies, and the primary supply contained a trip circuit that would shut the whole thing down if a large swing in direct-current voltage took place. The auxiliary power supply was a backup, and when selected the SCE would attempt to continue to operate even with low input voltage.

That was what had happened during the integrated test. The SCE box's primary power supply tripped off, with outputs frozen at levels that made no sense whatsoever. Other equipment in the Command Module cycled off due to the undervoltage conditions as well. "Quite a confusing mess to behold," Aaron recalled. "The test conductor seemed at a loss as to what to do." Reconnecting the ground power supplies back to the main buses cleared up most of the lights and alarms.

Aaron did not document the solution other than to go over with other EECOMs how the general test configuration had been screwed up. When it came to the odd way the SCE box reacted to the brownout, Aaron did not so much as jot down a note anywhere. He just filed the information away in the deep recesses of his mind, where it waited to be called back up on a moment's notice.

That moment came at just past 10:22 a.m. in Houston on 14 November 1969, a little more than thirty-six seconds into the flight of *Apollo 12*.

Mission Rule 1-404 stated it clearly enough, that a vehicle would not be launched when its flight path would carry it through a cumulonimbus—or thunderstorm—cloud formation. Some would later suggest that the rule was waived because President Nixon was at the Cape to watch Pete Conrad, Dick Gordon, and Alan Bean start their mission, but that was not it. The launch team on site in Florida felt comfortable with launching in the rain, dark clouds hovering just a thousand feet above the launch pad. The sky was so dark in some photos, it appeared as if the liftoff took place in the middle of the night rather than nearly noon. Raindrops splattered a motion-picture camera recording the whole thing.

As soon as the Saturn V began to move upward, chatter started back in the MOCR. Down in the front row, booster officer Frank Van Rensselaer was first up.

Thrust is go, all engines.

Gerry Griffin, working his first ascent in his debut as lead flight director, was all business.

Roger, Booster.

Next came FIDO Jay Greene, who gave a verbal thumbs-up for the roll program that set the Saturn V on its course toward orbit.

Flight, FIDO. We're go on the RP.

Conrad did not sound much bothered by the commotion. It was almost possible to imagine the gap-toothed grin spreading across his face as he reported back to capcom Jerry Carr.

Roger, cleared the tower. I've got a pitch and a roll program, and this baby is really going.

Roger, Pete.

That's a lovely liftoff. That's not bad at all.

Conrad spoke *way* too soon.

The instant retro officer Chuck Deiterich told Griffin that clocks onboard the spacecraft and in the MOCR were in synch, at 36.5 seconds in, a burst of static crackled through headsets in the MOCR. Atmospheric conditions were just right, and lightning sparked by the electrical discharges of the Saturn V and its long contrail back to the ground hammered the vehicle. Fifteen and a half seconds later, it happened again.

With the feedback still ringing in his ears, Griffin shot a glance at the large trajectory display at the front of the room. Was the vehicle spinning wildly out of control? Glynn Lunney was riding shotgun with him that day, and they exchanged a quick glance. Griffin's first call was not to Aaron, but to Jay Greene.

How you looking, FIDO?

Greene's response was immediate, and it was good news.

We're go, Flight. We're good. Right on target.

The CSM was launched with cabin pressure about a half pound above ambient atmospheric pressure of 14.7 psi. At about 12,000 feet in altitude, the difference grew to about 6 psi. The capsule had to start venting or else come apart at the seams from the inside out. Larry Sheaks, watching over the environmental control systems back in the aeromed SSR, chimed in right on time even as a thousand other thoughts raced through Aaron's mind.

Cabin relieving, EECOM.

At that moment, Conrad told the room what was already painfully clear.

Okay, we just lost the platform, gang. I don't know what happened here. We had everything in the world drop out.

Carr had nothing to offer, other than a simple acknowledgment.

Roger.

"One of the watchwords was, 'Keep your trap shut until somebody figures out what the situation is,'" said Carr, who likened the scene in the room to pandemonium in those first few seconds. "You don't send anything up there unless the flight director tells you to. I guess the important thing was to keep your trap shut, listen, and try and understand. If you can help with the problem on the mission control loop, you can do that, but you've got no business calling information up to the crew without clearance from the flight director."

Conrad commenced to reading off the longest litany of launch anomalies anybody in the MOCR had ever heard.

I got three fuel-cell lights, an AC Bus light, a fuel-cell disconnect, AC Bus overload 1 and 2, Main Bus A and B out.

Less than a minute into his first launch as flight director, Griffin knew that the possibility of an abort was all too real. At first, he had thought the problem might just be something as simple as instrumentation. When Conrad started calling off his caution and warning lights, Griffin's brief glimmer of hope was blown completely out of the water. The simulations he had been through were always tough, but even those did not seem *this* bad. "I thought, 'Good God, this can't be,'" Griffin said. "My next thought was, 'If we have to abort, let's get some more altitude and give us more time for the chutes to work.' An abort is never a good thing. At best, it's pretty dynamic. At worst, it can be catastrophic."

The pattern Aaron was seeing on his two monitors was familiar. The numbers, almost to two decimal places, looked the same, but when and where had he seen them before? Sy Liebergot had been on the EECOM console leading up to the launch, and after sticking around following his shift, he remembered Aaron staring intently at his screen not saying a word. As Griffin called out to him, a thought struck Aaron like a ton of bricks.

How's it . . . how's it looking, EECOM?

Aaron replied, but it was not to Griffin. He called back to James J. "Jim" Kelly, his electrical power systems controller in the vehicle systems SSR. Kelly was in night school when he got his start at MSC, working as a security guard. He wound up as a sergeant who oversaw the badging station, and it was there that he met the people who set him on a course that eventually led to the SSR. The two men eventually became so close that Kelly usually called Aaron by his family nickname, and "Bud" Aaron had served as the best man at Kelly's wedding to wife Brenda less than two weeks earlier.

Bud had an idea that he quickly tried to run by Kelly.

Is that the SCE?

His friend sounded unsure.

Well, I don't know, John. It sure looks like it.

Kelly had been in on monitoring the test the year before, and he called the forty-some-odd-hour grind "the stupidest thing we ever did, but let me tell you what that stupid thing did." That was where they had both seen the brownout, and he had known about the SCE fix as well. He just did not come back to it as quickly as Aaron. "I'm going to give John Aaron that one," Kelly said. "Let me tell ya . . . I knew what had happened, I saw what had happened. My mind didn't click as fast as his, okay? Once he said that, it rang a bell. There was no panic."

Aaron's SSR support was interrupted by Griffin again trying to get an answer, this time sounding more insistent.

EECOM, what do you see?

Fifty-one seconds after the first strike, Aaron gave Griffin an answer. There was no uncertainty in his voice as he gave his recommendation, although it might have spilled out of his mouth a bit faster than his Oklahoma drawl might normally have allowed.

Flight, EECOM. Try SCE to Aux.

Aaron was sure the first part of his problem was about to be solved. "When I made the call, I was a hundred percent confident that would fix the problem that I was trying to fix first, and that was to get some valid data," he said. "I was getting all these nonsensical readouts on my tube, and the crew was talking about all the lights that were on in the spacecraft and all the alarms going off. I was staring at data I knew wasn't valid."

The flight director had never heard of the switch before, and did not so much as have a clue as to where it was located.

Say again? SCE to Aux?

Aux.

Griffin repeated the request, almost as if to himself, mulling it over for a split second, trying to figure where the switch was and what it might do to help.

SCE to Aux.

Auxiliary, Flight.

That was enough for Griffin, and he passed Aaron's call along to Carr to relay to the crew. "It was just a switch we never fiddled with," said Griffin, the former GNC. "I had worked with John for a long time. I worked side by side with him in Gemini. John had a way of saying and doing things that when he said to do so and so, you could take it to the bank."

Achieving that kind of faith in his abilities on the part of the flight director was a trait that Aaron had worked on since joining NASA. Carr likened it to the implicit trust marines had in each other while in the field. "Every flight director yearns to have that trust in all the flight controllers, because it's needed in the heat of battle," Aaron said. "I will tell you that there could have been other people sitting at that console reporting to Gerry on that flight that might not have been that crisp. Gerry as well as the other flight directors and I had a tremendous rapport, and there was tremendous trust there. I was fortunate enough that when things got in trouble, I was kind of the go-to guy. That's why I found myself on the launch phase."

Once he got the go-ahead from Griffin, Carr did not hesitate.

Apollo 12, Houston. Try SCE to Auxiliary. Over.

Conrad was every bit as perplexed about the switch's location and purpose as were Griffin and Carr.

NCE to Auxiliary?

Carr quickly corrected him, emphasizing the abbreviation as clearly as he could.

SCE. . . SCE to Auxiliary.

"That crew was more fun than a barrel of monkeys to work with," Carr said. "Pete was the kind of a guy who could lead beautifully. He would let you know what he needed to have done, and if he thought you needed more instruction, he would tell you how he thought you ought to do it, but then he left you alone and you got the work done. The whole team got to the point where we'd rather die than fail Pete. He was that kind of a leader. I've always thought of Pete as my mentor, and I'm sure a lot of other people felt the same way as well."

Legend would hold that the rookie Bean was the only one of the three crewmen who knew where the SCE switch was located, but that was not actually the case. As a CMP who had helped design controls and displays for the spacecraft, Gordon was familiar with virtually every square inch of the Command Module. He knew not only where to find the switch, but what it did as well. The switch was on the bottom row of Panel C, at the lower-most part of a section extending outward from the right side of the main wall of gauges and switches, within easy reach of Bean's right hand. While Conrad wondered out loud to the rest of the crew what the hell the SCE was, Bean flipped the switch.

The fix worked, and good data instantly flashed up on monitors in the MOCR and SSR. Before Carr finished repeating the name of the switch to Conrad, Kelly came on the loop to Aaron and uttered some of the most beautiful words either of them had probably ever heard in the MOCR.

Okay, we got it back, EECOM. Looks good.

As he did, Griffin asked once again about the panel. It did not matter, as Aaron echoed his friend's call almost word for word.

We got it back, Flight. Looks good.

Another few seconds and Kelly was back in Aaron's ear.

Staging's set. You want to try and reconnect the fuel cells?

Yeah, let's do that.

Flight, EECOM.

Go.

Try to put the fuel cells back on the line, and if not, try Batt Charlie to Main A and B.

That got results. The crew began resetting the fuel cells one by one. As soon as the first was reconnected to its bus, voltage increased to the low end of the normal operating range. A large number of caution and warning lights on Aaron's console blinked off, and once they were all up and running again, most of the spacecraft's electrical readouts returned to normal.

The flight was not out of the woods just yet. The Inertial Measurement Unit (IMU) "eight ball" attitude indicators situated in front of Conrad and Gordon were still spinning wildly, and once the crew had a chance to finally catch its breath, the CMP wanted Buck Willoughby and his back room to get started coming up with some sort of solution.

We'd like to have the GNC guys think about how we're going to catch that thing, because it's just drifting, just floating.

Seated to Aaron's right, Willoughby pulled out a set of schematics and went to work finding the right circuit breakers to pull. Griffin called to see how the work was going.

What do you want to do with the platform now?

We'll get you an answer in just a second, Flight.

Best hurry.

Down on the capcom console, Carr had a suggestion of his own.

Want to tell him how his IU's doing? That might make him feel better.

Yeah, tell him he's right on the trajectory. No problems there.

Carr passed it along, a light tone in his voice.

Apollo 12, Houston. *You're right smack dab on the trajectory. Your IU's doing a beautiful job.*

If Conrad was concerned about anything at that point, it was not possible to tell over the air-to-ground loop. He came back to Carr with almost an all-out giggle in his voice.

Okay. We're all chuckling up here over the lights. We all said there were so many on we couldn't read them.

Willoughby called to Griffin with his solution.

Have them take the IMU power to Standby and then back to On.

IMU power to Standby and then to On. You expect that'll stop it?

Well, it should start the ninety-second cage cycle.

Griffin interrupted him.

Okay, capcom, IMU power to Standby, then to On.

Carr complied, and while Conrad wanted to wait until after getting to orbit, the veteran astronaut came back to the solution a few moments later to clarify.

You want the LMP to turn off the G&N power and then bring it back on, and you want me to use my IMU cage switch, is that right?

Griffin told Carr to have him stand by, and asked Willoughby to confirm. The GNC told the flight director that if the switch did not work, pulling the IMU's circuit breakers and leaving them off for a while might. They had a running discussion over the course of the next minute or so, Griffin asking if it might be possible to feed a course alignment into the guidance computer's display and keyboard, otherwise known as a DSKY—pronounced "disc-key." That was the problem, Willoughby told him. The computer already thought it was aligned, but was missing some key bit of information.

An idea came to Willoughby.

Flight, can they reach Panel 5 circuit breakers?

Should be able to.

That was it.

Flight, GNC.

There was no answer from Griffin, who had his attention on the burn of the S-IVB's engine, so Willoughby tried again.

Flight, GNC.

Go.

They should be able to pull the Main A, Main B circuit breakers on Panel 5.

Okay.

When Griffin told Carr to have the crew do just that, the capcom protested.

Flight, you really want to do that? We're almost to a point where they can use the switch now.

Griffin made a snap decision.

They're probably going to be a little while getting to it, though, while they're cleaning up the cockpit. Yeah, let's go ahead and have him pull the circuit breakers.

And so it was that the flight of *Apollo 12* got its electrical power and IMU back online. "Buck's call was a major contributor to the mission's ultimate success," said Aaron of Willoughby, a former marine fighter pilot who passed away on 8 September 2009 after a battle with Alzheimer's. "Had the platform continued in the mode of max rate of tumble, it is doubtful that the platform could have survived. With the IMU platform failed, the mission would have been aborted after a couple of revolutions in low-Earth orbit. Although not well recognized, Buck likely also saved the mission to the moon that day."

In the Trench, everyone except for Van Rensselaer was having troubles. Booster was good to go throughout the incident. "The ol' Saturn V just chugged along," Van Rensselaer said. "It was independently grounded from the Command Module, so the lightning strike did a number on the Command Module, but we didn't even lose a piece of data on the Saturn V. I just kept telling the flight director, 'We're go, Flight. We're go.' That was exciting, but for me, it was like just a nominal flight."

Greene, Deiterich, and guidance officer Gary Renick had not been quite as fortunate. The guidance system had been knocked out, and while the vehicle's trajectory looked perfect, Renick was responsible for computing the angles between the CSM and the rest of the booster and making sure that both were on the same track. For a few heart-stopping seconds, that appeared not to be the case. "All of a sudden, we got this wild difference when the lightning struck," Renick remembered. "It was kind of scary for a few seconds there, trying to figure out what the hell happened. Fortunately, the booster just kept right on trucking along. That was probably the scariest time I ever had on console."

After everything else had been sorted out, the Carnarvon tracking station acquired telemetry from the vehicle nearly five minutes earlier than expected. Greene and Deiterich looked at each other, and they had virtually the same thought. Had the mission's problems not been solved after all? "The only way we'd acquisition early is if you get there sooner, and if you get there sooner, it means you're in a lower orbit," Deiterich said. "We were kind of concerned about that."

Concerned? That was one way to put it, and Greene had another. "There's only one way we can get here five minutes early," he remembered telling Deiterich, "and that's if we're reentering and we don't know where we are."

The issue turned out to be the result of a multipath error, a phenomenon in which analog waves between the spacecraft and the ground-based radar travel in two or more paths caused by atmospheric reflection and/or refraction. The multipath waves create a "ghost" target, and that was what showed up early. "Scared the hell out of me, but we never told anybody," Greene concluded.

Author Andrew L. "Andy" Chaikin wrote in his marvelous book *A Man on the Moon* that the lightning strike would become a war story that Conrad, Gordon, and Bean would enjoy telling for the rest of their lives. It was no different for the men who had lived through it in the MOCR and SSR.

If the blockbuster movie *Apollo 13* made men like Gene Kranz and Sy Liebergot famous to the outside world, it was the launch of the flight before it that first made John Aaron a legend. The episode was captured in the HBO miniseries *From the Earth to the Moon*, and a space enthusiast once sent Aaron his expired license tag. Its personalized inscription was a familiar one.

SCE to Aux.

Such respect was not limited to Hollywood or space fandom. Much more important to Aaron, he had the respect of his peers. Liebergot remembered once marveling to Rod Loe about his fellow EECOM's uncanny ability, and Loe's response was a simple one.

Sy, let me tell you something. You won't be the first guy that has an inferiority complex about John Aaron, so get over it.

After filing away the brownout during the test the year before, Aaron was in the right place at the right time. "I was the one who happened to be on the console, out of four or five EECOMs that could have been there," Aaron began. "They would have never seen it and never knew about it. We'd never practiced it. We'd never had even thought about being struck by lightning, which was kind of odd when you think about it. Florida, that's the lightning capital of the world. It was almost a God-given destiny. We were just very lucky. We were prepared, but I'm telling you, there was a hell of a lot of luck in the Apollo program. It just was meant to be."

What if Aaron had not seen the very same kind of data dropout during the test the year before? Would he have known what to do when it again took place in real time, with a mission to the moon on the line? Had another EECOM been on duty during the fateful ascent, would he have been familiar with the problem?

In the end, the question of all questions was this.

What if John Aaron had not made the SCE to Aux call when and where he did?

Gerry Griffin had thought about that very question. While he could not say for sure one way or the other, something told him that if the Saturn V had remained on a satisfactory trajectory, he would have continued to ride it to Earth orbit and not called an abort. At that point, surely *somebody* would have come up with a fix—somebody in the MOCR, the SSR, or any of a number of contractors around the country. If not, Griffin figured that the Trench could have given the crew the correct de-orbit parameters and they could have come home. An abort threw so many uncertainties into the mix, and at the very best, they revolved around where the spacecraft would come down and how far away the closest recovery forces were.

Once *Apollo 12* made it to orbit, the question of whether it would be able to continue on to the moon remained. What, if any, damage had the lightning done to the Command and Service Module's systems? What about the spindly LM housed inside the S-IVB third stage? Had the lightning triggered the pyrotechnics that would release the parachutes after reentry and just before splashdown? Was the heat shield somehow damaged?

Very quietly, Chris Kraft made his rounds through the room. He told Griffin and Aaron separately not to worry about it, that they did not have to go to the moon that day. The decision was Griffin's, Kraft told the young flight director, and he would stand behind him regardless of which way the call went. "That's the indicator of a leader, instead of a manager," Griffin said. "That was his strong suit. We wanted to do things right for him." By then, Aaron was in a cold sweat after coming through in the clutch the way he had. He felt a hand on his shoulder, and it was Kraft.

That was a great job, young man.

Kraft then asked him to take a couple of orbits and come up with a quick checklist and test sequence to make sure the spacecraft was good to go. "He said, 'I just came down here to tell you that if you don't think so, we don't have to go to the moon today, young man,'" Aaron remembered.

He was not the first person Kraft ever called "young man" and he was certainly not the last, but with so many others, it was followed by an admonishment. A few very simple words, but coming from Kraft, it simply was not possible to underestimate what they meant to the flight controller. *Apollo 12* proceeded to the moon because, as far as anybody could tell, there had been no real damage to the *Yankee Clipper* CSM or the LM *Intrepid*. If the chutes were bad, reentering immediately was no better an option than in ten days, after Conrad and Bean had their time on the lunar surface. If anything *had* gone wrong and the crew was lost, Glynn Lunney felt sure it was still the right call to make.

Aaron retired from NASA in the year 2000, and Kraft's compliment had stuck with him all those years. Kraft showed up at his retirement party, which included both sincere praise and a good-natured roasting. Several speakers were lined up beforehand, but when the master of ceremonies asked if anybody else would like to say anything, Kraft raised his hand. He did not want to speak, but instead had a question for Aaron. The room got quiet, and surely, the steely eyed missile man's heart skipped a beat. What could Kraft possibly be about to ask?

I want to know on Apollo 12 *how you knew that it was okay to go to the moon.*

The room got *really* quiet. Everybody had heard the stories before secondhand, but to hear Aaron explain it to Kraft would surely be priceless. Aaron was twenty-six years old when he made the SCE to Aux call—think about that one for a second—and he had never really contemplated whether or not going to the moon had been the right decision. He was stunned by the question in that setting, in front of all those people.

Aaron started by telling the "young man" story, about how Kraft had come down to his console to tell him that he had done a great job and not to worry about whether or not to make the trip to the moon. The audience, Aaron said, had never heard the story and as far as he was concerned, that was the end of it. It was not. Kraft spoke up again.

Well, young man. I'm still looking for the answer to my question.

Young Man tried again, this time explaining that everything that *could* be checked had been. There was nothing anybody could do about the chutes or the heat shield, but he felt comfortable with the risk versus reward.

That was good enough for Kraft.

The landing of *Apollo 11* bothered Dave Reed.

Yes, it was the first time human beings had set down on another world and, yes, it was historic and momentous and all that. What it had not been was perfect, and Reed was a perfectionist.

Not knowing exactly where the LM came down was not a minor detail, either. Targets were targets, and on *Apollo 12*, the landing objective was very specific'. The unmanned *Surveyor 3* landed in the Ocean of Storms nearly thirty-one months before Conrad and Bean visited, and if there was time, planners wanted to study long-term effects of the lunar environment on its equipment by actually bringing a piece of it back. As a result, *Intrepid* would have to settle into the Ocean of Storms within easy walking distance.

But how?

Concentrations of mass, known in NASA-speak as "mascons," tended to wreak havoc on a flight's lunar orbit. As a flight passed over a mascon, it was pulled ever so slightly toward the moon and then released. The ground tried its best to keep up with it all via tracking, but when time came to separate the LM from the CSM for its descent orbit initiation burn, the Trench had to rely on a track that was one or two revolutions old. The problem was that nobody knew how much the mascons impacted the current orbit or the one that was about to begin.

Emil R. Scheisser was the chief of MPAD's Orbit Determination Section, Mathematical Physics Branch, and it was up to him to come up with a solution. It was in good hands—Neil Armstrong was once asked about people he had worked with at NASA who stood out in terms of talent and ability, and without hesitation, he replied, "Emil Scheisser! I'd vote for Emil every time."

What Scheisser came up with was a relatively simple fix. The best Reed could hope to do in the Trench was predict the orbit as if there were no mascons present, and what Scheisser proposed was to compare that with the actual track in order to come up with the difference, known as a down-range error. The error was measured in feet—on *Apollo 12*, it was 4,200 feet off—and given by trajectory support in the SSR to Reed. The flight's prime FIDO had it passed up to the crew for entry into the LM's guidance system with a Noun 69 program update, approximately ninety seconds after the descent burn began.

The answer was not Reed's, but it was up to him to help put it into practice. He and Conrad had discussed the pinpoint landing at Snowman, a series of five craters that very loosely resembled just that, and the veteran astronaut was unsure if the Trench or anybody else could pull it off. Conrad picked one target, then another, and Reed went right back to work, none the worse for wear. That got Conrad right where it counted.

You can't hit it anyhow! Target me for the center of the Surveyor *crater.*

If Conrad thought that he was going to get under Reed's skin with the new demand, even if it was in jest, he missed the mark.

You got it, babe.

Jerry Bostick remembered Reed being even more specific with Conrad about *Surveyor.*

I'm going to bring you down on top of it.

When Neil Armstrong and Buzz Aldrin made their descent to the lunar surface that summer, they had been all business, all the time. Conrad, on the other hand, sounded like an excited sailor coming in for shore leave as he and Bean glided below seven thousand feet in altitude. He all but shouted when he got his first glimpse of Snowman.

Hey, there it is! There it is! Son of a gun! Right down the middle of the road!

Bean was trying his best to stay on task.

Outstanding. Forty-two degrees, Pete. Forty-two. Look out there.

Conrad continued his commentary.

I can't believe it! Amazing! Fantastic! Forty-two degrees, babe. Just keep talking.

Jerry Carr was back at the capcom console, and when he broke onto the loop to give the go-ahead for landing, there was no reply from the lunar-surface-bound crew. Conrad was having far too good a time.

That's so fantastic, I can't believe it.

The boys on the ground do okay.

Bean glanced out the window on the right side of the LM cabin.

Oh! Look at that crater, right where it's supposed to be.

Reed had done an excellent job, to the point where *Intrepid* did, in fact, appear to be coming down into the center of *Surveyor 3*'s nearby large crater. Conrad punched a couple of updates into the guidance computer and then took manual control at about four hundred feet. The last few moments were mostly a steady stream of altitude and descent rate updates from Bean, and Carr gave the same dramatic thirty-second call that Armstrong and Aldrin had heard a few months before. This time, however, it seemed a mere formality.

As they went through their post-landing checklist, Bean was exultant. *Good landing, Pete! Outstanding, man! Beau-TEE-ful!*

The target was 170 feet south and 380 feet west of *Surveyor 3*, so as not to contaminate it with exhaust from the LM or any dust that its descent engine might kick up. Although Conrad and Bean could not see it through either of their windows, *Surveyor 3* was just 535 feet away. "Pete Conrad and Al Bean had a few American flags with them on that flight and they gave me one when they returned," Reed said. "From that mission on, pinpoint landing was assured. Without it, we never could have done the exploration that we needed to accomplish on subsequent flights."

Within a minute or so of stepping foot on the surface, Conrad spotted it and laughed with Bean.

Boy, you'll never believe it. Guess what I see sitting on the side of the crater!
The old Surveyor, *huh?*
The old Surveyor, *yes sir. Does that look neat! It can't be any further than 600 feet from here. How about that?*

That was music to Dave Reed's ears.

As Conrad bounced across the Ocean of Storms alone, Bean stayed behind in the LM to watch over, photograph, and pass equipment back and forth with his cohort. Bean moved from one side of the cabin to the other, and in the process nearly closed the hatch.

The sublimator on their backpacks acted basically as the radiator on a car would, and the outgassing on Bean's took care of shutting the door the rest of the way. When it shut, cabin pressure in *Intrepid* rose slightly and that in turn caused Bean's sublimator to break through and leak out 1.2 pounds of water.

Six minutes into Conrad's first solo EVA, the issue sounded an alarm. As problems go, it was an easy one to overcome. Once Bean noticed the hatch closed, he opened it back up and returned the cabin to full vacuum. Not surprisingly, he and Conrad were able to joke about it all.

Ahhhh!
What did . . . what did you just do, Al?
Man, I just figured it out.

You sure did. You just blew water out the front of the cabin.

That's what happened to the PLSS.

What's that?

Oh, the door had flown shut, like it did before, and it probably bothered the sublimator because it wasn't in a good vacuum anymore. So the door is probably going to start working in a minute.

I should hope so. When you opened the door, that thing shot iceballs straight out the hatch.

Jim Joki was responsible for the PLSS and he heard the episode unfolding from nearly a quarter of a million miles away. "They were giggling and having a good time," he remembered. "Those two guys were just the opposite of Neil and Buzz. Neil and Buzz were so technical." For Joki, the disappointment was that he heard it from the SSR. Responsibility for the EMU had been absorbed by the LM's telcom console following the flight of *Apollo 11*, and the position was renamed telmu. Joki had been immersed in the development and testing of the PLSS backpack and considered himself a leading expert, so getting bumped to the back room was hard to swallow. "It was . . . it was," Joki began. "I felt like sort of a failure." Jack Knight told him to take heart, that he had been the only person who ever worked the LM EMU console in the front room during a flight. It was consolation, but only a little.

After the flight of *Apollo 13*, Joki went to work on a master's degree in physiology. He liked the field so much that he eventually left NASA to go to medical school, and after moving to Seattle, he specialized in obstetrics and gynecology. "We had a parting of the ways," Joki continued. "Every time I see Kranz, he always says, 'Joki, you're the guy that quit on us . . . how ya doin'?' We're all buddies now, but I think I probably pissed him off by continuing school." The role Joki played during the Apollo years continued to be a part of his life, and former flight controllers who visited him in Seattle would marvel at his collection of autographed photos and flown flags.

He heard baby monitors in a hospital once, and was told that they were watching over individuals in a mothership during a nine-month mission. His two careers, he concluded, had not been all that different after all. "I'm doing the same thing as I was in mission control, I treat my patients the same way," Joki said. "We're going by mission rules, we have guidelines.

I have to take care of all contingencies to get you to a successful completion of that mission."

Once Bean made it to the surface and inadvertently pointed the lens of the new color television camera at the sun, Joki was not the only one who was just listening in on the EVA. It was fried beyond repair, and there was nothing Ed Fendell or any of his fellow INCOS could do about it. There was no fix to be made.

The world had to listen in on The Pete and Al Show, rather than watch it in living color. The problem was a minor, if somewhat inconvenient, one. The rest of their spacewalks went off almost like clockwork, right up to and including their visit to *Surveyor 3* during the second and final EVA. Although he played no particular part in what took place on the lunar surface, Dave Reed was still amazed at how things sometimes unfolded in those days.

Two weeks out from launch, Reed was in a review meeting up on the top floor of Building 1 when the subject of *Surveyor 3* came up. It was not a primary objective—just icing on the cake—but scientists wanted its digger arm and camera. The timeline gave Conrad and Bean twenty minutes to get the work done, and Conrad knew it was not going to happen in that short an amount of time using the kind of bulky gloves they would be wearing. George Low had an idea—what they needed was a pair of bolt cutters.

Somebody jumped up and said that, yes, it could be done. All he needed was to line up a rapid-fire procurement team to get specs written up and to solicit bids from contractors. From start to finish, the whole process would take maybe a month. There was only one problem with the plan, Low said.

We're launching in two weeks.

What happened next was what truly amazed Reed. If the proposed procurement process seemed to be fast at just a month long, Low's was even quicker. He had the doors closed to the meeting room before giving that same bright, young, energetic engineer his marching orders.

I want you to go to Sears and get two bolt cutters. Bring them back, sand off the Sears label, and stamp them flight qualified. What's the next item on the agenda?

Simple as that.

Yankee Clipper splashed down into the rough Pacific Ocean just four and a half miles from the recovery ship USS *Hornet*. The landing was so hard, at some 15 Gs, it not only knocked part of the heat shield loose but also freed a camera from its mount in the cockpit that then whacked Bean just above his right eye. It was a hard landing to be sure, but not nearly as hard as it would have been without parachutes. They had not been damaged in the lightning strike after all, and worked flawlessly.

While one disaster had been averted, the MOCR had not seen anything yet.

9. "We've Got More Than a Problem"

Apollo 8 showed that human beings could journey to the moon and back.

Apollo 11 and *Apollo 12* showed that astronauts could land and walk on its surface.

Apollo 13 proved mission control could bring those space voyagers back home again when their lives were on the line.

There was no lunar landing during the flight of *Apollo 13*, no momentous words to be spoken from the surface, no rocks to be returned to Earth. What the mission did instead was unleash heroics of a different sort. "It was almost as if the whole reason we were there was culminated in that moment," John Aaron began. "The ground controllers worked so well as a team, we were able to successfully salvage that mission and get the crew home safely. *Apollo 8* is a highlight in terms of what a country can do and what makes us feel good. *Apollo 13* was the final proof of just what flight controllers could do."

Aaron was on to something. The miraculous recovery of the *Apollo 13* crew of Jim Lovell, Fred Haise, and Jack Swigert was perhaps the finest example of teamwork in NASA's history. No one person was most responsible for their safe return—not Aaron, nor Arnie Aldrich, nor Bill Peters, each of whom oversaw crucial procedures and checklists in the days after the accident.

Nor was Milt Windler, the mission's lead flight director. Nor Glynn Lunney, whose calm, measured leadership style impressed more than one of his charges that week. Nor Sy Liebergot, the EECOM on duty at the time of the mishap.

Gerry Griffin, Jerry Bostick, Dave Reed, Jack Knight, Chuck Deiterich, Merlin Merritt, Bill Stoval, Bill Boone, and Bob Heselmeyer all made significant contributions. The SPAN rooms, MER, and contractors across the country ran around the clock. Gene Kranz could not have done it on his own. Instead, each of these men and many, many more people banded together to bring Lovell, Haise, and Swigert home safe and relatively sound.

The Trench's trajectory calculations would not have meant a thing had the systems guys up on the second row not been able to stretch their consumables. The same was true in reverse. It would not have mattered in the least how much water and oxygen remained if the trajectory of the Command Module *Odyssey* caused it to either bounce off the earth's atmosphere or burn up during reentry.

American astronauts were some of the most famous people on the planet, and they were viewed by millions around the world as virtual superheroes. It was indeed the lives of the *Apollo 13* crew that were on the line. They were the ones who felt the shudder of the explosion, who saw oxygen bleeding from their spacecraft, who endured miserable freezing temperatures, and who were in danger of carbon dioxide poisoning. All the while, they had to somehow remain coherent enough to manage midcourse corrections, power-up procedures, and reentry checklists.

But first, somebody back on the ground had to figure out how to do it all. If ever there was an all-for-one-and-one-for-all moment in the history of the MOCR, this was it.

The high-activity phases of a flight—launch, lunar descent, and lunar ascent and rendezvous—were like a feather in the cap of a NASA flight controller. The assignments were not handed out to stroke somebody's ego or because the line looked good on a resume. Instead, standing vigil at those times was recognition that they could do their jobs and do them very well under pressure. Of the nine FIDOs who worked in the front room during the Apollo era, only two worked a lunar descent; three handled all of the lunar ascents and rendezvous; and four took care of the launches.

Before the manning lists for the flight of *Apollo 13* came out, Bill Boone and Bill Stoval felt sure they might land one of those coveted spots. Stoval was pumped, thinking he might have a shot at launch, while Boone would have been happy with launch . . . lunar descent . . . blast-off from the moon and rendezvous between the LM and CSM . . . whatever might come his way. The two men came away disappointed—Stoval was on Gene Kranz's White Team and Boone on Glynn Lunney's Black, and both groups were slated to handle the much-less dynamic coasts to and from the moon.

Stoval was a freshman at the University of Wyoming at the same time as Dave Reed was a senior, and it was Reed who hooked Stoval up with his job at NASA. Although Jerry Bostick penciled Stoval in as FIDO for the launch of *Apollo 13*, Reed felt that his younger counterpart was not yet quite ready. "That really sort of pissed me off," admitted Stoval, who arrived in Houston to start work at NASA on the Fourth of July weekend in 1967. "It hurt my feelings, and created sort of a rift between me and Dave for a while." Stoval, though, had the ability to get past the episode and see it for what it was. "In the grand scheme of things, he might have been right," Stoval continued. "He probably *was* right." When Stoval was inducted into the University of Wyoming Engineering Hall of Fame in 2007, Reed and Bostick both wrote letters of recommendation for him.

Boone, on the other hand, had already been a witness to history long before he started work at NASA. After growing up in Leland, Mississippi, Boone became a page for U.S. senator John C. Stennis and helped escort dignitaries like Herbert C. Hoover, Lyndon B. Johnson, and Richard M. Nixon to their seats on the rostrum prior to John F. Kennedy's presidential inauguration. When the man who would soon send the country on its way to the moon gave his famous "ask not what your country can do for you, ask what you can do for your country" inaugural address, Bill Boone was standing maybe twenty yards away.

While a student at Mississippi State University, he was not an engineering but a math major. That made Boone "a different cat" in the MOCR, and it took him a long time to feel comfortable there. By *Apollo 13*, he felt he was up to speed and wanted nothing more than to be on duty for a high-activity phase. When he did not get one, he was as spun out as Stoval had been. "We all wanted the activity phases, because that was where the fun was," Boone said. "I was really torqued off. I remember going up to Bostick and having a heated discussion with him. I basically just threw my badge on the table and said, 'I'm out of here. I'm not going to do the sleep shift. That's not what I came here to do.'" Boone was coaxed back into the fold, and *Apollo 13* turned out to be what he called his "fifteen minutes of fame."

Boone and Stoval were not the only ones disappointed as launch approached, but Ken Mattingly had a far different reason for being down in the dumps. Before joining the astronaut office in 1966, Mattingly had launched and landed jet fighters on the decks of the uss *Saratoga* and the uss *Franklin D. Roosevelt*. He forged bonds with his fellow naval aviators, and he left it behind only for the possibility of one day venturing into space. Being named as an astronaut was obviously a fine achievement, but actually flying on an Apollo crew? *That* was the question. He and his eighteen 1966 classmates took to calling themselves the "Excess Nineteen," not knowing when, or even if, any of them would ever journey to the moon. The wait was difficult, especially for a hotshot jet jockey like Mattingly.

The friends he had known in the navy were starting to get shot down in the skies over Vietnam, and some were dying. In what he felt was a stark contrast, Mattingly was leading what he called "The Life of Riley" while his buddies were at war. Such a contrast was stark. The conflict in Vietnam was the flashpoint around which much of the turmoil of the 1960s was centered, although it tore at Mattingly for a far different reason. Protesters wanted to know why the country was in Vietnam, and Mattingly wondered why he was not. It was the letters from wives of some of his friends who had not made it that truly bothered him. "I had very serious reservations," Mattingly remembered. "I got to the point where I thought, 'I can't sit here and do this while they're getting taken to the cleaners.'"

Mattingly went to Alan Shepard, his boss in the astronaut office, and told him that he wanted to leave the astronaut corps and start flying again in the navy. Surely, "Big Al" would understand as a fellow naval aviator. Rather than accept the resignation then and there, however, Shepard asked Mattingly to wait a week and think about his decision. After that, if he still wanted to leave NASA, Shepard would help make it happen.

Within that very same week, on 6 August 1969, it was announced that Mattingly would join the crew of *Apollo 13* and fly with Lovell and Haise as the mission's CMP. "Al just looked at me, smiled, and never said another word," Mattingly said. Shepard had good reason to grin, for it was the very same press release that told of his assignment as the commander of *Apollo 14*.

Charlie Duke came down with a case of rubella—better known as German measles. Duke was on the backup crew, and that meant that Lovell, Haise, and Mattingly had all been exposed. Tests determined that Lovell and Haise were most likely immune, but their CMP probably was not.

Swigert started getting time in the simulators, and with just a handful of days remaining before launch, Mattingly turned his car radio on to hear the news that he had officially been replaced. He obviously knew getting bumped was a possibility, but to get the news like that must have seemed unspeakably cruel.

It was an understandably dejected Mattingly who took a T-33 from the Cape back to Ellington Field in Houston, and the very next day, he found himself in the MOCR for liftoff. He had no assignment, no real reason to be there. The viewing room was packed, so he simply took a seat on the aisle steps near capcom Joseph P. Kerwin's console. "Let me put it to you this way. I think Gary Sinise is a good actor, but when it comes to feeling sorry for yourself, he's a pure amateur," deadpanned Mattingly, referring to the actor who portrayed him in Ron Howard's 1995 film. "There are no words that can describe it. I told myself, 'There will be something Joe doesn't know that I know, and I'll have to help him. Well, it didn't take very long to find out that wasn't true."

The Saturn V rumbled off KSC's Pad 39A at 2:13 p.m. Eastern on Saturday, 11 April 1970. It was an hour behind in Houston—or, in military time, 13:13. The first-stage S-IC engines pushed the 6.5-million-pound vehicle skyward by producing 7.6 million pounds of thrust and consuming 4.8 million pounds of kerosene and liquid oxygen propellant in a little more than two minutes and forty-three seconds.

At eighty-one feet, seven inches tall, the S-II second stage took over at that point. The flight's first anomaly was just ahead, when the center of the S-II's five clustered engines shut down five and a half minutes into the flight due to substantial oscillations. The issue was no big deal according to Frank Van Rensselaer, the Marshall Space Flight Center employee on duty at the booster console down on the far left of the Trench. "The second stage had to burn longer to get to where it needed to go, since it was only four engines burning instead of five," Van Rensselaer explained. "We had practiced that, and we knew how much longer it was going to take as a function of when the engine went out."

Apollo 13 was Milt Windler's first mission as lead flight director. He tossed Van Rensselaer a quick query to see if they had a real problem on their hands, and Van Rensselaer said there was not.

Negative, not right now, Flight. All the other engines are go.

Forty seconds after the shutdown, Lovell was on the air-to-ground loop asking about the issue. Kerwin calmly responded.

Jim, Houston. We don't have the story on why the inboard out was early, but the other engines are go and you are go.

If there was a tendency to downplay the center-engine cutoff in light of what was to come, Windler hinted that it should not have been the case. "I got assigned to be the lead flight director on *13*, which nobody remembers very much," he quipped, tongue firmly in cheek. "It lost an engine [during the launch phase], which was probably the most dangerous part of the flight, but nobody knows that." This was Windler's concern. If the engine continued to vibrate the way it had been, "it would've blown up, probably. A few more oscillations, which wouldn't have taken very many seconds, and it would've probably been a catastrophic failure. But, presumably, we would've aborted the spacecraft and we would've survived that. It wouldn't have been like *Challenger*."

Before Windler had the chance to consider an abort, the engine shut down on its own. Down in the Trench, lead FIDO Dave Reed was very carefully watching the events unfold. When the center engine went out, the launch vehicle's altitude was 10.7 nautical miles lower and its velocity was 5,685.3 feet per second slower than expected. The s-11 finally shut down, then separated from the s-1VB third stage. Second-stage shutdown and third-stage ignition both took place thirty-four seconds late, in order to keep boosting uphill. After a forty-four-second delay in shutting down the third stage, the vehicle was just 1.9 feet per second slower and 0.2 nautical miles lower in altitude than planned when it at last reached orbit.

"I would have had to wait until the loss of the engine affected the trajectory to the point of violating a limit line," Reed recalled. "We'd seen early engine out before and nominally what happens as a result is that the trajectory depresses as the other four engines burn longer—thrust drops from 1 million to 800,000 pounds—and then the s-1VB has to make up any shortfall. Any depression of the flight path would have to have been quite severe before I would have invoked action."

The sadness that enveloped Mattingly was almost palpable in the control center. His place on the steps put him just behind and just a few feet or so from Reed. After *Apollo 13* was inserted into its orbit, Reed spun around in his chair to confirm for Mattingly that all was well. And when Reed was

16. Ken Mattingly had nowhere else to go after being bumped from the crew of *Apollo 13*, so he headed into the MOCR during the flight's launch. FIDO Dave Reed would later say he saw tears in Mattingly's eyes as the flight got under way. Courtesy NASA.

sure that he saw tears in the grounded astronaut's eyes, he spun right back around without saying a word.

The gloomy black rain cloud hanging over Mattingly was nothing compared to the brutal force of an F5 tornado that was about to hit the MOCR.

Gerry Griffin's Gold Team was on duty during the translunar coast, and he would joke years later that the spacecraft was in perfect shape before he turned it over to Kranz on Monday, 13 April 1970. Every flight director on every shift during every flight dealt with glitches, and Kranz had already seen two after taking over for Griffin that day. The High Gain Antenna on *Odyssey* seemed to have a mind of its own, not working in its automatic modes and then shutting off and coming back on again unexpectedly. Heading into a sleep period, there was not enough time to work the issue with the crew, so Kranz left it as an open action item. Then, forty-six hours and forty seconds into the flight, a short circuit in its quantity gauge caused Oxygen Tank 2 to cycle high and low four separate times before finally landing at off-scale high. Sy Liebergot was working the issue when a planned television transmission from the linked spacecraft—The

17. The last calm moments the MOCR team would have during the flight of *Apollo 13* took place during a television broadcast on the night of Monday, 13 April 1970. Courtesy NASA.

Jim, Freddo, and Jack Show—began fifty-five hours, fourteen minutes after launch at approximately 8:26 p.m. in Houston.

None of the networks were carrying the feed. It was the irony of all ironies that going to the moon had become what the general public considered to be routine.

Sy Liebergot might have been headed back home, or maybe out to get a beer after the shift ended. That was Ken Mattingly's plan, to grab a brew or maybe even something a little stiffer after a chance encounter in the VIP room with George W. S. Abbey, who was at the time a technical assistant to MSC director Robert R. "Bob" Gilruth. Abbey told Mattingly he looked like he needed a drink, and suggested that the two of them make their way to the Singin' Wheel. That sounded good enough to the still-blue Mattingly, so Abbey left to get his briefcase.

Mattingly and Abbey never made it to the bar, because it was at that point when all hell broke loose in the control room.

Still keeping watch over the off-scale-high issue on Oxygen Tank 2, Liebergot asked Kranz to have the two liquid oxygen and the two liquid hydrogen tanks stirred shortly after the end of the television transmission. Kranz described the cryogenic mixture of the tanks as a "thick soupy vapor," while Liebergot said it was a "very dense fog." Whatever the case might have been, it tended to stratify in zero gravity and it needed to be stirred in order to get a good read on its quantity levels.

No one knew that a line of dominoes dating back nearly two years was about to be set into disastrous motion. The tank had been dropped a mere two inches back in October 1968, but just enough to jar loose a fill and drain tube. Then, during a countdown demonstration test three weeks before launch, the tank failed to drain properly. The solution was basically to boil off the remaining oxygen using internal tank heaters. Rather than staying at a design limit of no more than 85 degrees, however, the tank heater element and wiring baked for eight hours at temperatures reaching a peak of 1,000 degrees due to a failed safety switch. Teflon wiring on the heater circuit was left charred and frayed.

All that was left in the recipe for disaster was a spark to ignite the whole thing. After telling Liebergot to allow the crew some time to settle down after closing out the broadcast, Kranz gave capcom Jack R. Lousma the go-ahead to have the tanks stirred.

Thirteen, we've got one more item for you, when you get a chance. We'd like you to stir up your cryo tanks.

Swigert's reply drifted down from the spacecraft.

Okay. Stand by.

Nothing more, nothing less. The flight was about to dominate world headlines and the attention of the MOCR for the rest of the week, and the start of it all was as simple as that.

The accident did not take place at the instant Swigert threw the four switches on *Odyssey*'s control panel, although that was certainly the trigger point from which there was no turning back. Three of the stirs worked perfectly. One did not. Ninety-five seconds later, telemetry between the ground and the spacecraft was lost for 1.8 seconds. It was during that brief down time that a master caution and warning was triggered in the Command Module. Lovell was in the lower equipment bay, stowing the television camera; Haise was in the docking tunnel between *Odyssey* and *Aquarius*; and Swigert was in the left-hand couch. An explosion of the basketball-shaped Oxygen Tank 2 estimated to have a force of seven pounds of dynamite rocked the spacecraft, completely ripping off the panel covering Bay 4 on the side of the Service Module.

Just before the loss of telemetry, the pressure in Oxygen Tank 2 reached 995.7 pounds per square inch. And *that* was down from a high of 1,008.3 psi just a few seconds before. The vacuum of space almost immediately contained the explosion, which might very well have saved the spacecraft from being torn to shreds then and there.

Liebergot and his SSR staff of Dick Brown, his electrical power system officer; George Bliss; and Larry Sheaks on environmental control systems were still watching the other oxygen tank after the stir. Their attention elsewhere, it caused them to miss the flickering data that signaled the ruptured tank.

It was 9:08 p.m. in Houston, and Swigert's voice sent a jolt through the MOCR.

Okay, Houston. We've had a problem here.

At almost the same instant, guidance officer Will Fenner became the first controller to report an accident-related issue to Kranz over the flight director's loop. Fenner, who passed away in March 2000, was remembered by Jerry Bostick as sort of a "Fox Jr." because, like Charley Parker, he was always so calm and collected. The only accolades he ever wanted—forget the fact that he was the first to tell Kranz something out of the ordinary had just taken place—was to be recognized by his peers as a trustworthy guy. "He was a slow talker but had a brain as fast as anyone I've ever known," Bostick said. Fenner never seemed to get excited, and his slow Texas drawl did not betray any panic over the flight director's loop to Kranz.

We've had a hardware restart. I don't know what it was.

It was at that point that Liebergot's comm loop came alive with activity.

What's the matter with the data, EECOM?

We've got more than a problem.

Liebergot reached out to his back room.

Okay, listen, you guys. We've lost Fuel Cell 1 and 2 pressure.

Lousma had been turned around in his chair, talking to Kranz offline when Swigert turned the world upside down. He heard one of the crew say something but was not quite certain who it had been or what they had said.

This is Houston. Say again, please.

This time, it was Lovell who called down from *Odyssey*.

Houston, we've had a problem. We've had a Main Bus B undervolt.

Liebergot looked at his screens and everything appeared to have gone haywire. His data showed that Oxygen Tank 2's pressure had just disappeared. At the same time, he saw that Oxygen Tank 1's pressure was dropping like a rock and that Fuel Cells 1 and 3 both indicated the presence of an unrecoverable shutdown. That rendered them useless for the remainder of the mission.

The situation was getting worse by the second. Without a power source, Main Bus B went down. That silenced all electrical equipment connected to that power distribution point. With pressure still dropping in Oxygen Tank 1, Fuel Cell 2 would soon be toast as well due to the loss of oxygen supply it needed to generate electrical power.

Liebergot wondered if what he was seeing was real. If so, *Odyssey* would soon be dark and quiet because its remaining systems would simply shut down and experience a total blackout. It would be a first for a manned spacecraft, but certainly not the good kind of first NASA and the nation celebrated. The fuel cell systems were the main source of power and drinking water for *Odyssey*, and the oxygen tanks were the sole supply of breathable oxygen for the crew. There was no other way to put it. The situation at hand was bleak and getting bleaker.

Such massive simultaneous failures were not supposed to happen. Was this just an illusion caused by a failure of the telemetry data system? Liebergot fell back on countless hours of simulations training that emphasized getting a jump on the problem by checking known potential single-point failures in the telemetry system. Instrumentation failure could often be the real source of the numerous anomalous and seemingly unrelated readouts he was seeing—but not this time. To continue troubleshooting required maintaining power to the systems, and even though it would mean consuming stored power reserved for *Odyssey*'s earth entry and post-landing phase, Liebergot made the decision to connect one of the reserve batteries to the main bus.

Veteran telmu Bill Peters had been sitting with Bob Heselmeyer, the new kid on the block who was working just the second or third shift of his very first flight at the console. Peters unplugged his headset to leave for the night—after all, there was not much to do since the LM was not yet scheduled to be powered up—and took just a couple of steps before he caught something out of the corner of his eye.

Liebergot's status lights were lit up like a Fourth of July fireworks display, and the EECOM had what Peters called a two-handed death grip on the handles framing both sides of his monitor. Although Peters was *this* close to leaving for the night, he could not recall years later when he actually made it home. He tried sleeping in the dorm, but he found it to be small and uncomfortable, and besides that, the other guys who sacked out there snored too much.

This is what the next few days were to be like for those who worked the flight of *Apollo 13*. "Rest is defined as when you can't stay awake any longer no matter how hard you try," Peters said. "At some time or another, I laid down on the floor under the console and went to sleep with my headset on." Incredible.

Heselmeyer quickly called Peters back. "From where I was sitting, right there next to Sy's console, I looked over and saw his console just abuzz with light," Heselmeyer recalled. "Essentially, my first thought was, 'If that's *not* an instrumentation problem, then something really serious is happening.' Shazam, there it all was. My second thought was that Sy had a problem, because it all happened so fast, there wasn't a starting place to troubleshoot."

Just six seconds after Lovell's soon-to-be-famous pronouncement, Kranz asked Liebergot if he was seeing the undervolt on Main Bus B. The issues were piling up, and Liebergot told his flight director that he did not. When Kranz replied that the crew had reported it, the EECOM tried to staunch the flow.

Okay, Flight. We've got some instrumentation funnies. Let me add 'em up.
Kranz's reply was crisp.
Rog.

Liebergot went through a litany of issues with Dick Brown back in the SSR. "To me, I thought it was an instrumentation problem, because I was hoping and praying that it was going to be *Apollo 12*, where just a switch would make it all come back," said Liebergot, referring to the preceding flight's lightning strike during launch. "It wasn't my luck. I tried to put Gene Kranz off for a couple minutes." As Liebergot and Brown went through their paces, Haise dropped another bombshell from more than 200,000 miles away.

We had a pretty large bang associated with the caution and warning there.

Eighty seconds had passed since the tank ruptured, and this was the first hint received by the MOCR that this was not just an event taking place on some instrument panel. The crew felt the explosion, because their ship felt it. Sudden accelerometer activity on the roll, pitch, and yaw axes gyros was detected. Instrumentation issues do not generally cause large bangs or thumps, as described by the crew in post-mission debriefs. Two minutes after Haise's observation, Kranz sounded like he was still holding out some hope.

EECOM, you seeing any AC problems? It looks like we might have a lot of instrumentation problems.

Liebergot confirmed that the power distribution point was, in fact, still in trouble. Kranz's response was quick.

Well, let's get some recommendations here, Sy, if you've got any better ideas.

Kranz waited for a few moments, then pressed again.

Sy, what do you want to do? Hold your own?

Another brief pause, then another query.

Sy, have you got a sick sensor-type problem there or what?

Fuel Cell 1 and Fuel Cell 3 were offline, and Liebergot wanted the crew to attempt to reconnect them to the buses. Once more, Kranz asked if there were instrumentation problems and Liebergot said that AC Bus 2 was reading just four volts. That meant, in effect, that it was dead. Although Kranz was either actively or passively monitoring seventeen different comm loops at the time of the accident, he was soon listening to only two—his own flight director loop and the air-to-ground transmissions. "The training process really allows you to remain focused on one or two loops, and you're listening for key words," Kranz said. "The training process alerts you to the tone of the crew's voices and the tone of the controllers' voices. In addition to that, you've got key words that you've used throughout the training process that will get additional attention. This is unique to every controller in the room. They have a way of phrasing things that immediately alerts you to listen up."

Lousma continued his conversations with the crew and he knew they needed some answers pronto. Lousma had already asked once when he came on the loop to Kranz with similar, if not somewhat more insistent, questions.

Is there any kind of leads we can give them? Are we looking at instrumentation? We got real problems or what?

That was just the problem. No one knew for sure exactly what had happened. If it was indeed instrumentation, nothing of any real significance had actually taken place. There had been a big bang, yes, but nothing was tagging up. What could Lousma tell the crew? Nothing at this point. "My job was not to protect the control center, but to act as if I were on board the spacecraft and get the information to them," Lousma said. "Whatever frustration I might have had would've been from that point of view. One of the difficulties, of course, was that much of the telemetry was blown out, so a lot of the information that we would've used to understand the health of the spacecraft came up missing. So the frustration was rampant within the control center, I think. We went down a few dark alleys, realizing all the time this was something different than we'd ever seen before."

A former air force jet fighter pilot, Kranz had no qualms whatsoever with describing his own sense of vexation.

It took a while to catch on. During that period of time, it was very frustrating because the crew was trying to solve a lot of these problems on their own and they kept changing configurations. About the time we were ready to give some recommendations, the crew would've changed configurations. So we had to regroup and come up with another set of directions for them. During those initial few minutes, there was an awful lot of confusion and a lot of communication, air-to-ground wise. We were behind the power curve, and the crew was trying to solve the problem on their own because we weren't providing them as much assistance as we needed. Jack Lousma was my capcom, and basically he kept saying, "Is there anything we can do to help them? Anything we can do to help them?" But by that time, the crew would've changed configurations, so then we were back to square one.

Arnie Aldrich, the chief of the CSM Systems branch, was in the SPAN room when the accident took place. There were no answers, and the folks in the MOCR seemed to be "all over the place" as to what the problem might have been. Aldrich also understood that John Aaron was the best EECOM he had. "I just knew we needed to have John," Aldrich said. "I knew John would get the answer immediately, and he did." Aldrich called Aaron, who was at home shaving, and told him as best he could what was taking place. They were in this thing deep and needed to start getting things straightened out now. The memory of Aldrich's phone call remained vivid in Aaron's mind more than four decades later.

"I was standing in front of the mirror, shaving," Aaron began. "My wife handed me the telephone and she said, 'It's Arnie.' He said, 'John, I want to tell you we've got a problem out here, and the guys are chasing it like it's an instrumentation problem.'" Incredibly, Aaron had all but memorized all the circuits that were common in instrumentation systems and the way they worked to provide information back to the ground. If a circuit or junction failed, he knew which parameters it would affect.

Aaron had Aldrich go to the consoles and read him off some numbers here and there. "He did that a couple of times on two or three aggregation points within the electronics," Aaron said. "That's when I said, 'Arnie, I don't know what the problem is. The kinds of things you're telling me are *not* single-point failures. They're some combination of lots of failures. I will be right there, but in the meantime, you tell those guys to treat this as a real problem. It's *not* an instrumentation problem.'"

There were problems aplenty in the MOCR, not just at the EECOM console. INCO Gary Scott was working problems with the High Gain Antenna, which had been struck and damaged by the blown-off panel. Seated to Liebergot's immediate right, GNC Buck Willoughby dealt with random thruster firings. Will Fenner saw that the linked spacecraft was moving around unexpectedly. The reason why was about to become painfully clear.

A little more than fourteen minutes after the mishap, Lovell's voice again got the attention of the MOCR. This time, it was even more chilling.

It looks to me, looking out the hatch, that we are venting something.

The instant Lovell finished speaking, Kranz repeated the report, drawing out the last syllable almost as if he was speaking to himself.

The crew thinks they're venting something . . .

Liebergot chimed in.

I heard that, Flight.

Lousma was concerned by the news of the venting, but he was also a good marine, and good marines do not fly off the handle at the first sign of trouble. "I never felt threatened or rattled or confused or excited," he said. "This was not the first emergency I'd ever been in. I'd also learned through some flying experiences that to get rattled is not the thing to do. You solve the problem as it comes along."

By this time, Glynn Lunney had made his way into the control room. Others were on their way. Gerry Griffin and Ed Fendell had played softball that night and were having a postgame beer when they learned of the accident. Griffin eventually showed up, still in his sweats. He stayed for maybe half an hour, listened for a while, knowing that a landing was off, and then went home to try to get some sleep. Fendell made it to the space center only to find the parking lot full, so what the heck? He found the first available space, jumped out, and promptly locked his keys in the car. It sat there for five days—in a space reserved for none other than director of Flight Operations Sigurd A. "Sig" Sjoberg.

Ken Mattingly was there, too, his drink with George Abbey now forgotten. "Sy said something to Gene about, 'We're still trying to see where we can have this instrumentation flaw,'" Mattingly remembered. "Gene looked at him and said, 'Sy, when was the last time instrumentation blew gas out the side?' And Sy's face just went . . . clunk. Everybody was in that scramble mode, being that there were totally unintelligible signatures, trying to make sense of it and at the same time recognizing that whatever is going on, that spacecraft is coming apart."

Less than a minute after it became clear that the spacecraft was bleeding, Liebergot was scanning his monitors to see if he could somehow figure out where it was coming from. The flight director was seated almost directly behind the EECOM console, and he knew that Liebergot would need all the help he could get.

I assume you've called in your backup EECOMs.

There was no reply.

EECOM?

Flight, say again.

Have you called in your backup EECOMs now? See if we can get some more brainpower on this thing.

Most if not all of Lunney's Black Team was also in the room, trying to help work the issues. Each console had four plug-ins for headset jacks, and almost every single one was in use. Lousma, too, had plenty of company from his fellow astronauts at the capcom console. "They had access to the control center, and they wanted to see for their own eyes exactly what was going on," Lousma said. "You wouldn't get that from the room in back, nor would they get it from sitting by their televisions. The way to do it was to come down to the control center, and they basically felt they had access to my console, because that's where they would've sat if they were in there doing my job." Although they were there watching over his shoulder, Lousma insisted that they were never a distraction.

That might not have been the case for others in the room at the time. Listen closely to the comm loops from that night, and a marked increase in background buzz is clearly evident when someone is speaking. At one point, Kranz recalled standing up and yelling over the consoles, "Okay, all flight controllers, cut the chatter. I want every member of the White Team to settle down and get back on the voice loops. The rest of you shut up!" Kranz then took to his own flight director's loop, and this time, he was rallying the troops and at the same time getting across the seriousness of the situation.

Okay, now, let's everybody keep cool. We've got a LM *still attached. The* LM *spacecraft's good, so if we need to get back home, we've got a* LM *to do a good portion of it with.*

That was the first time *Aquarius* had been mentioned by Kranz over the loop as a potential solution to the problem. It would certainly not be the last.

Okay, let's make sure we don't do anything that's going to blow our CSM *electrical power with the batteries or that will cause us to lose . . . Fuel Cell Number 2. We want to keep the* O2 *on that kind of stuff working. We'd like to have* RCS, *but we've got the Command Module system, so we're in good shape if we need to get home.*

It is likely that Kranz meant to say Lunar Module in that last sentence. He concluded the message with a line that would become one of the flight's most well known, if for no other reason than his distinct emphasis on the last word.

Let's solve the problem, but let's not make it any worse by guessin'.

Kranz had gone from thinking this was just another relatively quick-fix glitch to Buck Willoughby's report that several of the thruster jet valves had closed. This was a whole new phase of his thought process, which he years later described as, "Tread lightly, lest ye step in crap." It was the venting that brought Kranz around to the full seriousness of what was happening with his spacecraft.

It was at that point, Kranz said, that the situation entered survival mode in his mind. "Over about a ten- to twelve-minute period of time, I went through three stages," Kranz explained. "I called them downmoding. It's the same thing you do when you have an aircraft that's got a problem. Basically, you now get totally focused upon this one problem we got, which is one of survival."

Despite the back-and-forth conversations he was having with Kranz and his back room, or maybe because of them, Liebergot felt a deepening sense of isolation as the crisis continued to unfold. This was his problem to handle, and he had his hands full getting it squared away. John Aaron had known what to do during the launch of *Apollo 12* just like that, but that was not happening for Liebergot. "It was an incredibly tense time," Liebergot wrote in his book, *Apollo EECOM: Journey of a Lifetime.* "A monster CSM failure had occurred and I had no quick answers. As EECOM, I felt very much on the spot. I could feel the chill of panic begin to well up. There was no one to whom I could turn, and I will admit that a fleeting thought of getting up and going home *did* cross my mind. Of course, that was not an option! I firmed my grip on the security handles of my console, and brought my emotions under control."

Lovell's observation about the venting was, for lack of a better way to put it, the "oh, shit" moment for Jerry Bostick. He was not actually on the manning list for that shift, but he was there. Kranz remembered Bostick almost always being in the MOCR, almost like part of the decor. Less than five minutes after "Houston, we've had a problem," Bobby T. Spencer rechecked his numbers for a direct-return abort at the retro console. That would have amounted to stopping a speeding bullet in midflight and redirecting its course in the exact opposite direction.

Such an intention was noble enough—get home now, or at the very least, as soon as possible. A direct abort could have been done at that point in theory, but it would have required a huge burn of some six thousand feet per second from the SPS. That would have wrung out almost the very last drop of fuel and then what? Lovell, Haise, and Swigert would have been up a creek without an SPS. There was more. The SPS was the big engine at the back of the Service Module, and nobody knew if it had been damaged in the explosion. Moreover, a powered maneuver by the SPS would have required maybe 50 amp-hours of power out of the CSM entry batteries, and there was not enough to spare.

Dave Reed, like many others, had all kinds of reservations over the extent of the damage that had been done to the spacecraft. "Chuck Deiterich and I made our case for why we did not want to do a direct abort, and we strongly recommended that we go around," Reed added. "I gave them lots of arguments. One of the ones I remember giving them was, 'Guys, theoretically, you blew a hole in the side of that thing, but do you know what it looks like? You really don't know, do you?' Chuck and I were pretty adamant that the way to go was around the moon."

Within just twenty minutes of the accident, members of the Trench decided among themselves that the best course of action was to perform a burn using the LM's Descent Propulsion System (DPS, pronounced "dips") to get on a free-return trajectory. *Apollo 13* would continue its outbound journey and then use the moon's gravitational force to slingshot the spacecraft back to Earth. The SSR started work on the burn, and IBM was helping put together software to do it down in the RTCC. It was not exactly the way he had planned it, but FIDO Bill Stoval had gotten his high-activity phase. He began to compute the minimum delta-v—the force needed to move a spacecraft from one trajectory to another—that would be needed for the free return.

Also weighing in on free return's favor was the fact that the Trench had at least a couple of options for which they had already simmed. Once on a free-return trajectory, the nonstop fly-by maneuver without going into lunar orbit was one of them. Another was known as a pericynthion (PC)–plus 2 burn, in which the DPS engine would be ignited two hours after the point at which the spacecraft came closest to the moon's surface in order to speed up the return. A midcourse correction here and there would be tossed in for good measure to stay in the reentry corridor. "It was a no-brainer, frankly," Lunney said. "When the guys went through the analysis, it was not like you've got to make a real big judgment call. It was like, 'This is what the math tells you and it's unmistakably clear what you have to do.' Once that got explained out loud, everybody was okay with that."

Free return was the way to go, but would there be enough life-sustaining juice left in the spacecraft? Nearly twenty minutes after the accident, Liebergot cleared his throat and told Kranz that the best option at that point was to start a 10-amp power-down. After a brief exchange over how far to go on their emergency checklist, Kranz added an emphatic note to the proceedings.

Let's make sure we don't blow the whole mission.

The whole mission, as it existed in the official flight plan, had already been blown. Five minutes later, the full extent of the problem seemed to bore down on Liebergot like a sledge hammer.

Flight, I've got a feeling we've lost two fuel cells. I hate to put it that way, but I don't know why we've lost them. It doesn't all tag up, and it's not an instrumentation problem.

When John Aaron made it to the MOCR about forty minutes after the accident, he did not bother to put on a headset but instead spent another fifteen minutes or so walking behind the systems consoles on the second row of the MOCR and looking over the data that was streaming down from *Odyssey*. Aaron approached Liebergot. "I said, 'Sy, this is fruitless. You have brought the emergency batteries on to power the spacecraft while you troubleshoot this problem. We're not going to be able to fix it, so you need to turn the Command and Service Module *off*,'" Aaron remembered. "That had never been done before. I said, 'You've got to turn it *off*. You've got to save the batteries. I don't know what's happened, but you save those batteries and you turn it off.'"

What Aaron was suggesting—make that *insisting*—was the most traumatic thing anyone in the room had ever done in support of a spaceflight. There had never been an emergency like this, in which the CSM mother ship had to be completely shut down three-fourths of the way to the moon. Such a notion was so inconceivable, there were no procedures whatsoever in place to turn the whole thing back on. It would not be long before working on those procedures became Aaron's life.

Liebergot, in turn, requested a still more stringent power-down and this time told Kranz that he should start thinking about getting into the LM and using its systems. Kranz ordered Heselmeyer to have his back room start figuring out the minimum power in the LM to sustain life. Going into the flight, Heselmeyer was sure he had been placed on Kranz's team so the veteran could keep an eye on the new guy. This was his baptism by fire. It was everybody's baptism by fire, for that matter. "All the chatter was trying to figure out what was going on," Heselmeyer said. "It was becoming more and more obvious that it was likely that the LM was going to be where they were going to need to get to." Still, *Aquarius* would not be powered up and fully used as a lifeboat until after Lunney's team came on shift about twenty minutes later.

Nearly an hour had passed since the end of the television transmission. Swigert reported that the number of particles surrounding the spacecraft had decreased greatly, and that whatever it was that was venting had almost stopped. That might have been a good thing under ordinary circumstances, but this was not just another hum-drum night on console, and Liebergot knew it. Finally, he reported to Kranz that Oxygen Tank 1 would hit 100 psi—the point at which there would be too little oxygen to be forced into the pickups—in one hour, fifty-four minutes. He added an ominous postscript.

That's the end right there.

Kranz's attention was focused on the LM, and he told FIDO Bill Stoval that unless the MOCR got a heck of a lot smarter, they were wasting their time planning to use the SPS. From there on out, he added, planning should involve the use of the LM DPS and RCS systems, and only as a third option, *Odyssey's* RCS. Stoval responded, asking if Kranz wanted to get back to Earth as soon as possible. Absolutely. At the very same time as Kranz and Stoval were having that conversation, Liebergot and his back room were finally coming to grips with the source of all that ailed the spacecraft—and the MOCR by proxy.

Scott H. Simpkinson started work for the National Advisory Committee for Aeronautics—NASA's forerunner—in 1943. He was on duty in the SPAN room during the *Apollo 13* crisis, and he thought that the thing to do might be to close the reactant valves on the two balky fuel cells. Might that be where the leaks were located? Liebergot once again touched base with Dick Brown in the SSR.

Brown did not seem to care for the idea of shutting the oxygen source down, at least initially. Closing the reactant valves meant that the fuel cells were lost, and Brown added that he was not sure if the problem was not somewhere in the tank itself. The more they talked, the more the fog seemed to clear.

It would have to be in the cryo tanks for them both to go.

Yes. That was it, Liebergot figured at last. Something had happened that impacted both oxygen tanks, and whatever took place had also hampered the manifold connection to the three fuel cells. That it was not a single or double failure, but what Liebergot later called a quadruple failure, seemed unfathomable. If anything like it had ever been thrown at the MOCR during a simulation, the guilty party in the curtained room to the front right of the control room almost certainly would have drawn more than a few angry stares. Stuff like that just did not happen—but it had this time.

Less than fifteen minutes later, Kranz was telling his team to get ready for the handover to the Black Team. A fresh team would be thinking clearer, and the White Team could continue to work in support. It was 10:17 p.m. in Houston, barely an hour after the accident.

Never before had a shift change taken place with a spacecraft in quite so dire a predicament. The issues facing Lunney were numerous, and he listed at least some of them in a paper he wrote for NASA's Oral History project.

A loud bang had been reported, and the crew was seeing particles of some variety venting out of the spacecraft.

The pressure on Oxygen Tank 2 was reading zero, and Sy Liebergot had predicted that Oxygen Tank 1 would last less than a couple of hours.

Fuel Cells 1 and 3 were not supplying power, and the reactant valve had already been closed on Fuel Cell 3. Because both fed off Fuel Cell 3, Main Bus B and AC Bus 2 were also at zilch.

Considerable reconfiguration had been performed to get enough thrusters powered by Main Bus A. The still-outbound LM and CSM stack was not yet on a free-return trajectory. That burn would take place on Lunney's watch, and so would an emergency power-up of the LM so that it could be used as a lifeboat. Last, but certainly not least, was the fact that the crippled Command Module had to be shut down.

Other than that Everest-sized mountain of responsibilities, it was going to be a nice, quiet evening for Lunney and the Black Team. "There were a number of things that had to be done fairly quickly," Lunney conceded. In the back of his mind the whole time was the cardinal rule, "We don't want to do anything to screw it up more than it's already screwed up." Ken Mattingly was truly impressed by Lunney's show of leadership over the next few hours. "Glynn went around the room and methodically went to every console and gave them a specific question to get an answer to," Mattingly remembered. "They were things he knew he would need to know in the next thirty minutes, which gave everybody an assignment." There was more, Mattingly said.

If there was a hero, Glynn Lunney was, by himself, a hero, because when he walked in the room, I guarantee you, nobody knew what the hell was going on. Glynn walked in, took over this mess, and he just brought calm to the situation. I've never seen such an extraordinary example of leadership in my entire career. Absolutely magnificent. No general or admiral in wartime could ever be more magnificent than Glynn was that night. He and he alone brought all of the scared people together. And you've got to remember that the flight controllers in those days were—they were kids in their thirties. They were good, but very few of them had ever run into these kinds of choices in life, and they weren't used to that. All of a sudden, their confidence had been shaken. They were faced with things that they didn't understand, and Glynn walked in there, and he just kind of took charge.

While Lunney took charge in the control room, Kranz presided over a meeting one floor down from the MOCR in Room 210 that began at about 10:30 p.m. in Houston. Aaron joined the meeting late, having stayed in the MOCR to oversee the orderly turn-off of the CSM. Aaron would vividly remember an exchange that took place near the end of that process, when it came time to pull one of the last circuit breakers that removed power from the heater that kept the IMU platform within temperature limits. GNC Gary Coen pleaded his case to Aaron.

John, it only takes less than half an amp of current. Without it, the platform may never work again.

Aaron responded the only way he could, with reason. Half an amp times the estimated 100 hours it would take to get back to Earth was 50 amp-hours. That was more energy than what remained in one of the batteries that *Odyssey* had left. Coen, realizing the magnitude of the power crunch, responded simply.

Okay, John.

Aaron remembered, "It's amazing that we were struggling with an item that was the power drain equivalent of a twelve-watt light bulb, but managing to such small levels meant the difference between success and failure relative to having a shot at a successful reentry."

That was the kind of agonizing number-crunching Kranz and his team would work on from that point forward, while the teams led by Lunney, Milt Windler, and Gerry Griffin sat the consoles in the front room. Before taking over for reentry, the White Team worked just one more shift in the front room the rest of the week—Kranz's crew was in place for the all-important "PC–plus 2 burn" Tuesday night.

Aaron hopped out of the frying pan and into the fire by going to Kranz's meeting. For the rest of the flight, he would oversee the power-up checklist for the CSM; Bill Peters would be in charge of the LM's systems; and Arnie Aldrich held on to a procedures checklist for reentry. "I had worked with all of these guys," Kranz said. "I knew them intimately. John Aaron was one guy I used, from a standpoint of resources. Arnie Aldrich was Aaron's boss as the branch chief, and he did the reentry checklist work. Bill Peters basically looked over everybody's shoulders to see if there was anything we were missing on the LM."

The flight director had started the meeting with what Aaron called a "pep talk"—the situation was stabilized, the LM was in control, and the spacecraft would soon be on a free-return trajectory around the moon and headed back to Earth. Then, once back in the vicinity of Earth, the CSM would go through a normal power-up procedure. Aaron was not sure how the CSM would be powered up, or even if it could be once it had been shut down so definitively. That's when Aaron stood up.

Gene, you can't do that.

Why's that, John?

Because you don't have enough power.

It was at that point when Kranz made one of the quickest decisions of his life.

Okay, EECOM. *You're in charge of power. Anyone needing power, talk to Aaron.*

Just that fast, Aaron was put in charge of everything that needed electrical power for the rest of the mission.

Even then, Aaron had a sinking feeling in the pit of his stomach. "Me, initially, I had doubts that we could do it," he admitted. "After the meeting in Room 210, I thought it looked nearly impossible. Realizing my state, I remember I forced myself to look at the problem from a different perspective. Rather than focusing on thinking that it was impossible, I forced myself to start working with the mindset of 'What will it take to *make* this possible?' Such a switch in thinking got me on the road to a workable solution."

If anybody needed power for the rest of the week, they talked to Aaron. They pleaded with Aaron. They argued with Aaron.

Really, they were up against the formidable duo of Aaron and his SSR back-room counterpart Jim Kelly, whom Aaron called "absolutely instrumental" in putting the power profile together. There was already a deep trust between them when *Apollo 13* flew, but Kelly was not in place just because he was Aaron's buddy. He knew his stuff, and he was the sort who had already contemplated what might happen if two fuel cells were lost on the way to the moon. "We had access directly back to the Rockwell and North American plant," Kelly said. "If NASA needed something, they didn't have to go through all this damn formality. We just hopped on an airplane if necessary, put a Rockwell badge on, walked in the plant, and started asking questions." Prior to *Apollo 11*, one of the questions Kelly asked was how many watts each circuit breaker on the spacecraft drew and if there were any backdoors to that circuit breaker. When he met some initial resistance, he went to the Rockwell boss and got the information he wanted.

Aaron and Kelly had their hands full. "People were howling and screaming—not really howling and screaming—they were trying to figure out what was going on and trying to voice a solution," Kelly continued. "John and I kind of looked at each other, and John knew I had some ideas. He just asked everybody to leave the room and come back later. When they came back, we had a rough sketch on the board of a power-up sequence. We had no idea at that point what we even had to work with."

What Kelly initially described as howling and screaming, Aaron called "a tussle between those who wanted power and the guy who didn't have it." Aaron knew systems throughout the spacecraft, and knew how they interacted with each other. What he also accepted was the fact that there was sometimes a huge difference between the power a controller wanted and what was actually needed. "I got up to the blackboard and started sketching out when we could turn on what, and of course that started people saying, 'Oh, no, no, EECOM. I've gotta have this on and not only that, I've gotta have it on longer than you want it on.' We weren't getting anywhere right away. I did that for about ten minutes and I said, 'Hold on. Why don't you guys go get some coffee and come back here in forty-five minutes, and we'll have something that's more refined for you.'"

Peters and Aldrich were also busy getting up to speed. Using the LM to ferry the crew back home was doable, Peters thought, but he was not quite sure. The LM had been designed to support two people—Lovell and Haise—for up to forty-five hours. Not only was Swigert a third person to consider, but the return could take anywhere from seventy-seven to one hundred hours depending on the burns to come.

The math was not working out, and the uncertainty weighed on Peters in a huge way. "To be honest, for the next three days, I had butterflies in my stomach," he admitted. "It was that sickening feeling that, 'Oh, crap. I can't do anything about this.'" It was not until later, after the stack had swung around the moon, performed the PC–plus 2 maneuver, and the LM itself was powered down, that Peters's case of the nerves finally eased. "It was a very tense time in my life," he added.

Arnie Aldrich's job put him in contact with the MOCR, the SPAN room, and the MER. Once he was put in charge of the reentry checklist, his task was not only to put it together, but also to get it blessed by North American—and if not blessed, then at the very least to make the makers of the CSM aware of what was going to take place. Every day, he tagged up with Aaron and Kelly, to see where they were with the power-up procedures. He reviewed what was going on in the simulators. Analyses were conducted on equipment, to see if it could withstand the kind of cold to which it was going to be subjected in an unpowered CSM. The sequencing was crucial.

To avoid any confusion over which version might contain the latest updates, there was one copy of the reentry checklist and one copy only. Aldrich guarded it with his life. "The changes to be made over the three days were all penciled in and initialed," Aldrich said. "In the end, I had to go and meet with Kranz and Rocco (A.) Petrone (the Apollo program director) and tell them what I'd done. I said, 'This is *the* checklist. Here it is.' Then I turned it back to John, and he executed it. He and Jim Kelly had done the bulk of the analysis and the work on the pieces that kept feeding into this thing until it got put all together."

Many would later claim that they never doubted the crew's survival. "There was a feeling of faith," telmu officer Merlin Merritt remembered. "There was a feeling of, 'I don't know how it's going to happen. There was certainly a question of not knowing. You can only do so much. You pray, you do what you can do, which is what we did, and leave the rest up to

God. I sort of felt all along that they would get back, that God would work it out. I never had a feeling of hopelessness or depression."

Kranz also believed that the crew would make it back alive, and he said he moved from belief to certainty after the PC–plus 2 "get home fast" burn. Dave Reed insisted he had not the first worry about Lovell, Haise, and Swigert making it back. Gerry Griffin had been trained to never give up hope. Bill Stoval, however, was not among the optimists. "Once we lost the landing, then clearly all emphasis shifted to saving the crew," Stoval said. "That wasn't clear. When I got home that night, I told my wife, Ruth, I thought they were dead. I thought we were going to run out of consumables. It wasn't a trajectory problem. It was going to be an air or electricity problem."

Less than forty minutes had passed since Sy Liebergot announced that the quantity in Oxygen Tank 1 would last only another two hours or so, but the news from his counterpart EECOM Clint Burton got progressively worse almost from the very beginning of the Black Team's shift. Just forty minutes remained. Four minutes after that call, eighteen remained. Fifteen. "It hurts to be the bearer of bad news time after time after time," said Burton, who died on 17 September 2006. "Nonetheless, it fell my duty to be that bearer of bad news time after time after time."

Lunney and the controllers under him that night must have felt like an embattled company of soldiers, hunkered down in their foxhole and facing one bombardment after another. No sooner had Lunney dealt with one critical issue than another was needing his immediate attention.

Gary Renick, working the guidance slot in the Trench, wondered if the IMU would survive the cold of a complete power-down of *Odyssey*. He was not the only one. Extraordinary measures had always been taken to limit the temperature range on the vital instrument back on the ground. The problem was that no official data existed on what might happen if and when it was subjected to subfreezing temperatures—which was exactly what was about to happen following the power-down of the Command Module.

No official data existed, but legend holds that a technician heard the worried discussion about whether or not an IMU would survive in the cold. Turns out, the guy once had one in the backseat of his car when he was sent home due to an ice storm. The expensive and delicate piece of space equipment was left in the car overnight and then taken back to work, nobody any the wiser. It evidently worked perfectly afterward. "We said, 'That's good enough for us,'" Ken Mattingly admitted.

Astronaut Tom Stafford helped Lunney understand the importance of transferring the Command Module's inertial guidance alignment to the Lunar Module. "Tom said, 'Keep the platform up if you at all can,'" Lunney said. "He wasn't on duty for the flight. He wasn't on the manning list, but he was there. We all knew each other. We had been through all this stuff together in simulations. It was a comforting kind of thing." Lunney opted to take the time and utilize electrical power from both vehicles to make the transfer.

A little more than thirty minutes into the Black Team's shift, Renick wanted to run a P52 automatic star pointing program. It was one in which the IMU required realignment from a known orientation, but it was doubtful any of the three *Apollo 13* crewmen could align the sextant on any two actual stars, for the very same reason Stafford was so insistent on maintaining alignment in the LM for as long as possible. With so many particles of debris and venting still surrounding the spacecraft, they *all* looked like stars.

For the first time, Lunney sounded just short of perturbed. He shot back.

That's what I'm asking you. Do you have one now? *We don't have much time. Do you have a good one now, as far as you know?*

Renick answered Lunney's question with a question of his own.

A good alignment?

Lunney spoke again, still sounding somewhat aggrieved.

Yeah, that's what I'm asking you. Do you have a good alignment? I'm not worried about tenths of a degree, either.

It ought to be that good, Flight.

Yeah, okay.

Information was flying at the flight director. During the lightning-quick exchange between Lunney and Renick, both GNC Jack Kamman and then Burton attempted to break in. Burton won out.

Okay, we need to open up the surge tank. The manifold pressure's dropping.

There was a pause, as if Lunney was trying to decide what to do next. The surge tank contained a small amount of reserve oxygen, and Burton was telling him that it was all that was left. Forget power. The astronauts needed to breathe. It was the very last line of defense in *Odyssey*, and Lunney knew it.

Uhhhhhh . . .

Lunney then let out a short breath, audible on the flight director's loop, before he continued.

Okay, wouldn't you rather power it up from the LM *. . . or pump that up in the* LM?

Burton momentarily stammered.

Well . . . we . . . we . . . w . . .

He got it out.

We got to get into the LM *first, Flight.*

Other orders in NASA's history might have been given as quickly as the one Lunney was about to issue to Lousma, who was still on duty, but *none* were ever quicker or more decisive.

Capcom, get 'em going in the LM. *We've gotta get the oxygen on the* LM.

Lovell and Haise were already there.

If the exchange with Renick had Lunney on the verge of frustration, Burton had just kicked him where the sun did not shine. Control officer Hal Loden and telmu Merlin Merritt raced to shorten LM power-up procedures that in normal circumstances took at least two hours to complete. They needed to get the job done fast, because Lunney intended to keep power trickling in the CSM only for as long as it took to get its guidance platform transferred to the LM. Loden's gut feeling had shifted from one of disappointment at not making the lunar landing to, once it became apparent just how serious a turn that mission had taken, one of uncertainty. The crew, he had to admit to himself, was in "deep yogurt."

"Their whole survival was going to depend on whatever we could do to help them on the ground," Loden said. In simulations, situations had been imagined in which the LM would be used as a lifeboat. The procedures that came about, however, met with mixed results. That was the kindest way Loden could describe it. "We had some thoughts down on paper about what we needed to do, but it wasn't nearly to the extent of what we wound up having to do," he added. "So, yeah, I was concerned. Everybody in the control room had to be concerned. If they weren't, they probably didn't understand the situation."

Swigert was getting *Odyssey* powered down at the same time Lovell and

Haise were in *Aquarius*, getting it powered up. As quickly as they were trying to get things done, something was almost bound to get lost in the shuffle. More than an hour into the Black Team's turn on console, Lousma had to remind the astronauts not to speak at once. Then, the CSM's thrusters wound up disabled before the LM's were brought on line. Lunney nor Lousma could hardly believe it. Lunney began.

I want to be sure we got control somewhere. I'm not satisfied we do yet.

The disbelief in Lousma's voice was thick.

Okay. We haven't got ourselves in a position here where we have no attitude control in either vehicle, have we?

I'm . . . I'm waiting to see when we get attitude control in the LM. Would they . . . would you ask them to call us when they have attitude control in the LM? And then we'll power the inverters et cetera down in the CSM.

Loden broke in and said that once control was established in the LM, some cleanup work needed to be done in the power-up procedures. As Loden and Lunney talked, Lousma got word from Haise in the LM that he and Lovell were still working on pressurizing the Attitude Control System. In other words—no joy. Lousma got back on the loop to Lunney, and for a brief moment, stumbled over his words.

Hey, Flight. They don't have attitude control and we don't have it in the CM. . . CMS. . . CM. . .

Okay. Well, we're trying to get it up, right?

Lousma's reply was matter of fact.

Yeah, they are.

Lunney was not pleased with the slip-up. "It turned out to be not a real problem, but I was really pissed at myself because it was—well, it was kind of the only mistake we made that night," Lunney admitted. Lousma, on the other hand, would not remember the episode. It had not caused any sort of real, pressing issue—there were plenty of those to go around already—so why sweat it? "Frankly, I don't recall this lapse in the transfer of attitude control, probably because the time period of no control was so short that it had not yet caused a problem," Lousma said. "With so many identified problems already presenting themselves in need of immediate attention, a no-control configuration not yet causing a noticeable problem would be easy to overlook until some no-control behavior was noticed. It appears Glynn directed transfer of attitude control before the symptoms of no control showed up, thus making the situation a non-event."

One hour, thirty-five minutes after the start of the Black Team's shift, *Odyssey* was finally powered down. About 20 amp-hours of the entry battery's power—as much as 15 percent—had been used before the CSM was finally put to sleep. As the steps to do so wound down, Lunney experienced the sensation of the bottom falling out from under him for the first and only time in his ten-year career on consoles during flights and training.

We were abandoning ship in the middle of the North Atlantic, at night, in the storm, and we were in this little life raft. It really struck home, like a big, hollow feeling in my stomach. It was something like, "Holy shit. I can't believe this is really happening." It was a sinking feeling, but it didn't last very long, probably measured in a few seconds. It was pronounced on me, because of the sense of a black hole abyss just sucking us all into it. The training took over. There's no Superman tale about this, because probably everybody in one way or another at some kind of moment were approaching the dead-serious realization of how much trouble we were really in. If you didn't get the feeling of looking into the abyss, you weren't paying attention.

Odyssey was now lifeless, but critical work remained. An attempt to come up with a passive thermal control barbeque mode was made, to keep the stack from burning to a crisp on one side and freezing on the other. Someone realized that there were not enough carbon-dioxide scrubbers in the LM. It was not a problem at the moment, but it was going to be in the not-too-distant future. There was more than enough oxygen in the LM for the crew's return, but water was another matter. The astronauts themselves needed water to survive, of course, but water was also used as coolant for equipment inside the spacecraft. Some early estimates figured that the supply would run out at ninety-four hours into the mission, and that was going to be more than two full days short. However, that was based on the assumption that the LM would run on about 35 amps for the rest of the flight.

Merlin Merritt wanted that number down, and he wanted it down as soon as possible. If that meant turning the LM's guidance system off in the process, then so be it. He told Lunney so in as forceful a manner as MOCR decorum would allow. "I finally just unplugged my headset, which was kind of a no-no, and went up to him on his row there, and sort of got in his face," Merritt said. "I said, 'Glynn, if we don't power down this thing, we're not going to make it.' He said, 'Okay, well, let me see your data.'" Lunney remembered the exchange well. "That was really the closest thing to a difference of opinion, but it really never even manifested itself as such," Lunney said with a laugh. "Occasionally, they would remind me that they would like to get powered down as soon as possible. I was in the position of saying, 'Yes, I know. I agree with you. I agree with you. *But* . . . our real job is to get them back home, not to save power.'"

What Merritt got was a compromise of sorts. A few items here and there were turned off in the LM, dropping its power usage from 32 to 25 amps after the free-return maneuver and before the PC–plus 2 burn. The guidance system remained online until after the "get home fast" maneuver, at which time virtually everything was shut down. Kranz was adamant that the platform remain on until then. "There was never any question in my mind," Kranz said. "I would've fought to the death to prevent anyone from trying to turn that platform down. That was as essential to survival as water and air and electrical power."

While Merritt concerned himself with power usage in the LM, FIDO Bill Boone worried about urine dumps. Venting from the damaged spacecraft was moving its trajectory "all over the map," according to Boone. On previous flights, it had been possible to actually see overboard urine dumps cause a small change in trajectory. "There were so many things that were happening," Boone said. "We were trying to minimize any effect it had on the Doppler, so we could figure out where we were. That's when I made the call." Boone asked Lunney to halt the urine dumps, and Lousma passed the word up to the crew less than half an hour after the free-return burn.

Two words were not added to the request when it was passed up to the crew.

For now.

Boone was unable to remember if it had been his intention to call a permanent or just a temporary halt to the dumps, but the fact was, there were no more during the flight of *Apollo 13*. For the remainder of the mission, Boone's call forced the crew to search the two cabins for any possible storage containers. "If somebody would've asked later, I probably would've said, 'Let's don't,'" Boone said. "We really did not have a good handle on the trajectory until we got close to reentry. Fred Haise still gives me a ration about that."

A little more than five and a half hours after the accident, at about 2:43 a.m. on Tuesday, 14 April in Houston, the LM's descent engine burned for 34.23 seconds to get the docked vehicles on a free-return trajectory. The burn was projected to drop *Odyssey* into the Indian Ocean early on Saturday, 18 April. "When we did that midcourse and the Lunar Module engine and the Lunar Module guidance system all worked the way we planned it, that was another boost in the fact that we were now back on a free-return trajectory," Lunney said. "It was a psychological boost for people. The crew never said much about it, but I suspect it put them in a better frame of mind than they might otherwise have been."

The Black Team left their consoles four and a half hours after the burn, and when Lunney gave way to Gerry Griffin, he felt that his consumables projections were "solid." The power-down of both vehicles dramatically decreased water usage, easing that particular crisis. "For me, I felt that the Black Team shift immediately after the explosion and for the next fourteen hours was the best piece of operations work I ever did or could hope to do," Lunney said. "It posed a continuous demand for the best decisions often without hard data and mostly on the basis of judgment, in the face of the most severe in-flight emergency faced thus far in manned spaceflight. There might have been a better solution, but it still is not apparent what it would be. Perhaps we could have been a little quicker at times, but we were consciously deliberate." In short, Lunney concluded that he and his team had delivered their best when it counted the most.

For almost exactly nine hours, Merlin Merritt had been at the center of the most prolonged in-flight emergency NASA had ever faced at that point. After the busiest shift he and most everyone else had ever experienced at NASA, Merritt and an acquaintance found an empty room and prayed. "We didn't want to make any mistakes, and asked that the Lord would guide us," Merritt recalled.

Despite all that had happened, the spacecraft still would not disappear behind the far side of the moon for another eleven hours.

After Gerry Griffin's Gold Team took over in the MOCR, the big items up for debate were how big a PC–plus 2 burn to make and figuring out how to ensure its alignment with the LM's Alignment Optical Telescope (AOT). The normal process was to fix the AOT on a particular star, but with so many particles and debris still hovering about the spacecraft, there was no way to tell which was which.

Guidance officer Ken Russell came up with an alternative. Why not use the biggest star around—the sun—for the check? There were all kinds of problems with Russell's suggestion. With a target as big as the sun, the alignment would not be as precise as one performed on a much-further-distant star. The AOT was fixed in the LM, so it could not be swiveled to get the star in its sights. Instead, Lovell would have to maneuver *Aquarius* into just the right position. Still, there was no better option.

When Griffin's Trench team—Russell, Dave Reed, and Chuck Deiterich—approached Griffin at his console, they had his attention. They explained the AOT sun check and told him it was their best if not only option, and Griffin had it passed on to John Young and Charlie Duke in the simulators to see if it was feasible.

Lovell had his doubts while discussing it with Haise onboard the spacecraft.

I don't have all the confidence in the world in this Earth-Sun P52. You know how many times I screwed up on my arithmetic.

Yes. Don't count your chickens before they hatch.

Listen, I'm not.

The sun check did not work as well as a star sighting would have, but it worked well enough. That was the best anybody could have hoped for.

There had been some talk of doing a burn while the spacecraft was behind the moon, but the Trench pushed to wait for another couple of hours. The morning after the accident, Deiterich and Reed represented the Trench and presented five different options during a meeting in the VIP room overlooking the MOCR. It was a gathering of Who's Who in Spaceflight, because it included executive management from NASA headquarters and centers around the country; major NASA and contractor executives at MSC; and the head of the Department of Defense's recovery forces. Glynn Lunney, Gerry Griffin, Jerry Bostick, Deke Slayton, Chris Kraft, and Bob Gilruth were there, and so was Thomas O. Paine, the NASA administrator.

Option 1 required doing nothing and staying on the present course charted by the free-return burn.

Option 2 was a burn of 850 feet per second, with landing in the mid-

Pacific at 143 hours into the flight. This was Deiterich and Reed's preferred method. Deiterich had computed many different configurations for a PC–plus 2 burn, and Reed reviewed each and checked them all in his processors. "Had we done a bigger PC–plus 2 burn and lost an engine, we could've been pretty far out of the corridor," he remembered. "If we lost an engine any time during the smaller burn, we were never far from the corridor. It wouldn't take much RCS to take us back in the corridor. We wouldn't necessarily have made it to the Pacific Ocean for splashdown, but we would've been on a reasonable trajectory. We would've been in water somewhere." Lunney was on board as well and noted in his *Apollo 13* paper, "Option #2 was conservative on fuel, leaving a large reserve for midcourses, best recovery posture, solid plan for consumables."

Option 3 would have brought a burn of 2,000 feet per second and landing in the South Atlantic Ocean at 133 hours into the flight.

Options 4 and 5 were similar, in that both would have required a huge burn of nearly 4,800 feet per second and landing at 118 hours. However, the damaged Service Module would have been jettisoned in option 4 and in 5, it would have remained. "We could have gotten back a day earlier by jetting the SM, but early shutdowns of this burn had a significant problem with the entry conditions," Deiterich noted. "We also did not like the exposure of the heat shield for a long time. As it turns out, we—the whole MCC—needed the extra day to get our act together for the entry day procedures."

The case boiled down to this.

This is the data. This is what we recommend. We do not want to jettison the Service Module. We think we can get back to the Pacific Ocean at 142 hours, and we will not get on any sort of trajectory that would present a problem later.

"They bought it," Deiterich concluded.

Lunney would never forget the response from the rest of the room. "Gerry [Griffin] and I were still bracing for a prolonged discussion," Lunney wrote. "The senior NASA official was Dr. Thomas Paine, the NASA administrator. He did not know us, but of course George Low, his deputy, did. After one question from Deke Slayton, Dr. Paine took over and thanked me for the discussion and the clarity of the situation report and then he said, 'I only have one question. What can we do to help you men?' WOW." It was, to Lunney, a sign of how NASA worked in those days. Low, he was sure, must have sold Paine on the MOCR team on the flight to Houston.

He called it a "delegation of trust" that prevented what could have been a much testier meeting.

Beginning at 8:40 p.m. on Tuesday in Houston, the PC–plus 2 burn of the LM's descent engine lasted for 263.82 seconds and speeded the stack up by 860.5 feet per second. Seventeen precious hours were cut from the projected landing time—seventeen hours that would not have to be accounted for when it came to consumables—with expected splashdown now targeted for the Pacific rather than Indian Ocean. "The Gold Team worked on the details of all the options for the PC–plus 2 burn," said Griffin, who handed the flight director console back over to Gene Kranz a few hours before the maneuver. "Lunney and I both favored the choice of getting back to the Pacific, where we had recovery forces at 143 hours with some reserve in propellant. A faster return would mean the systems wouldn't have to perform as long, and there was some concern expressed about the CM thrusters staying dormant so long. But at the end of the day, the consensus favored the 143-hour elapsed time landing in the Pacific and senior NASA management concurred. So, like most decisions made in the MOCR, everyone endorsed the outcome and set out to make it happen."

The next two and a half days were similar in a lot of ways to a normal flight to the moon. "Any time you're in a coast phase, whether you're going to the moon or coming back, you don't have a lot of dynamic stuff going on," Griffin admitted. The difference was a constant talk of consumables. How much power was being used? How much water? How long would it be before carbon dioxide poisoning became an issue? "That's what made it different," Griffin continued. "It wasn't hectic. There wasn't something that had to be done in an hour. We never got to a shortage of something, where if we didn't do something quick, we were going to lose them. It was constantly trying to figure out how to squeeze a little more out of this or squeeze a little more out of that."

After the PC–plus 2 burn, the three astronauts closed up shop in *Aquarius* as well as *Odyssey*. Ordinarily, the LM operated on about 55 amps of power. Now, however, that number was down to 15 to 18 amps. That was not belt tightening. It was noose strangling, and it left guys like Bob Heselmeyer, Merlin Merritt, and Jack Knight at the telmu console without a lot to monitor. "There wasn't that much powered up, but what was powered up, I can guarantee you was watched very closely," Heselmeyer said with a chuckle.

That did not mean that they could kick back and relax. There was not a single person who worked in and around mission control that week who was not fully aware of exactly what was on the line. Heselmeyer was on duty at the time of the accident, and after attending Kranz's meeting down in Room 210, had wearily trudged into the dorm to try to get some sleep. He woke up at some point, the clothes he had worn into work the day before completely soaked in sweat. Stress had hit him with full force. The next morning, he was back on duty, this time on Griffin's Gold Team.

Heselmeyer was still in his same sweat-soaked clothes. "[I] had to go back down and sit on the console for another whole shift, not having changed or washed or anything," Heselmeyer remembered. "I was probably not the most popular guy. But I have a distinct memory of having tried to get myself cleaned up and then going back and sitting on the console, and watching those now very critical LM systems and making sure that vehicle was still doing its job."

In fact, the rookie flight controller was *not* alone. INCO Ed Fendell remembered the "human" aspect of the crisis, and it had nothing to do with crunching consumables or keeping track of trajectory. "Think about it a second . . . no, I mean it," Fendell began. "People were sitting in the control center and this thing occurred, right? With that, everybody called all their people in, right? Do you think everybody was ready to go to work? Some guys had been working in the garage. Some guys had just finished playing softball and were drinking beer, okay? And off you went to the control center and you stayed there for three days. You ate and you drank there. You spilled coffee. You spilled pizza. You spilled hamburger. You never bathed. What do you think it smelled like? We all smoked about three packs a day."

Within hours of the accident, it became apparent that the LM's two primary and three secondary carbon dioxide scrubbers would not be enough to handle the poison that the three astronauts would be exhaling with every breath. Other issues took priority early on—like powering down *Odyssey* and *Aquarius*, as well as the free-return and PC–plus 2 burns. Yet as time wore on—and the carbon dioxide got thicker in the LM—the issue of fitting the CM's square cartridges into the LM's round hole became more pressing.

"There was enough water and enough oxygen. That was not a problem," said Jack Knight, the telmu officer on the Maroon Team led by Milt

Windler. "But the ability to take out carbon dioxide was, in my mind and for my systems, *the* immediate problem—or it was going to be a problem."

Over in Building 45, R. Edward "Ed" Smylie presided over an impromptu meeting of MSC's Crew Systems Division that began at about 1 a.m. on Tuesday. Maybe, just maybe, the crew could gather up a Liquid Cooling Garment stowage bag, an outlet suit hose, and gray duct tape and rig up a solution. Toss in a cardboard arch—say a trimmed EVA cue card from the flight plan, to prevent the bag from collapsing—and voilà. The problem was on the way to being solved.

By 2:30 a.m., a mockup was being shown to Ken Mattingly over in the Mission Control Center. A plane was commandeered to bring test canisters in from the Cape. Astronaut Anthony W. "Tony" England helped with extensive testing. At 7:22 a.m. on Wednesday, capcom Joe Kerwin began reading up instructions for construction of the device.

I think the equipment you'll need will be two Command Module lithium hydroxide canisters, a roll of the gray tape, the two LCGs, because we're going to use the bags from the LCGs, and one . . . one LM cue card. One of those cardboard cue cards which you will cut off about an inch and a half out from the ring. Now, I think that's all we'll need.

While the crew collected the items, Kerwin took the time to ease Swigert's fears about something he had mentioned before the accident.

Okay, Jack. Did anybody tell you that you got a sixty-day extension on your income tax?

Forty-five minutes later, the contraption was finished. When it was put into place, the LM cabin's carbon dioxide reading stood at about 7.5 mm Hg. Thirty minutes later, it was reading just 0.3 mm Hg. The fix had worked. An identical boxy scrubber was put together, and when each was depleted, an additional canister could be taped to it to continue working unimpeded. Smylie had been the point person, but nearly a hundred people had a hand in the solution in some way or another. "It was pretty straightforward, even though we got a lot of publicity for it and Nixon even mentioned our names," Smylie said. "I always argued that was because that was one you could understand. Nobody really understood the hard things they were doing. Everybody could understand a filter. I said a mechanical engineering sophomore in college could have come up with it. It was pretty straightforward, but it was important."

The *Apollo 13* rescue was personal in many ways for many people, and Smylie was certainly no different. He lived just three doors down from Fred Haise and his family, and their sons were good friends. To avoid the press that was camped out at the astronaut's home, Fred Haise Jr. made his way through some woods behind the home and stayed for the next three days with the Smylies.

There were more scares to come. At 2:26 p.m. on Wednesday, an LM battery failed to the tune of another thump felt in the spacecraft and the venting of what appeared to the crew as "snowflakes." This time, however, it was not a substantial issue. "The LM battery that exploded continued to supply electrical power and did not prove an issue to battery amp-hour management or current load sharing by all the batteries," Bill Peters explained. "I had maintained enough reserve electrical power to cover instrumentation errors in each of the other batteries to cover a contingency, so even if the battery had completely failed, there was enough power to complete the mission."

Each of the two LM batteries was sealed in a metal box, and tests after the flight showed that a similar "explosion" in the container resulted only in a very slight lifting of its lid. That pushed out the sealing O-ring just enough to allow electrolytes to escape, which was more than likely the "snowflakes" reported by the crew.

A fourth midcourse correction was performed at 10:31 p.m. on Wednesday, and while it was a short fourteen-second burst of *Aquarius*'s descent engine at 7.8 feet per second, planning for it had cost FIDO Bill Stoval almost an entire eight-hour shift of back-and-forth conversations with those who handled the LM propulsion systems. The LM's guidance system was now turned off, so Lovell and Haise would have to fly it by the seat of their pants, with Swigert hovering on the engine-bell cover timing the burn with a stopwatch. How would the engine perform? Would the Abort Guidance System be an acceptable monitoring device for the burn? Stoval did not know if the thrust profile in the RTCC would match the thrust profile when the engine started, because he did not know if the ullage burn would be enough to push propellant into the pump.

It resulted in what he called the most frustrating day of his life in mission control. "I basically had to do the entire maneuver by myself," said Stoval, who moved over to Gerry Griffin's Gold Team after the accident.

"I couldn't get the guys on the AGS to tell me if the AGS would work. I couldn't get the guys on the engine to tell me how the engine was going to work in terms of propulsion. It was just unbelievable how little help I could get, because they were in worlds they'd never been before."

The next-to-last midcourse correction of the flight went off perfectly.

In the meantime, *Odyssey* had all but depleted one of its three entry batteries. While there was a system on board that could recharge the entry batteries off the fuel cells, that was obviously not an option because they were dead. It was Dick Brown who remembered the heater circuitry that Bill Peters had modified back in 1967.

That was the year that Peters had been assigned to meet with Grumman officials for an LM engineering design review in a large hangar in Bethpage, New York. Several folding tables were arranged in a horseshoe, and there were microphones at each spot so everyone could hear. The meeting was chaired by U.S. Air Force brigadier general Carroll H. Bolender, who had commanded more than a hundred World War II combat missions in southern France and Italy. Bolender's nickname was "Rip," and rumor was, it was very easy to find out why if and when anyone crossed him.

Peters nervously began his presentation. His team had noticed two sets of heater wiring between the Lunar and Command Modules while preparing for the meeting, and came up with a procedure in which they could be rerouted so that the CM could be used to maintain heat in the unpowered LM and its essential equipment during the trans-lunar coast. One set of wiring would be considered primary, and the other as a backup. This was no small task, with two incredibly complicated spacecraft being built by two different contractors on opposite sides of the country.

Bolender accepted the changes Peters had suggested and directed that they be implemented by Grumman and North American. Brown remembered the exchange, and eventually, the team came to the conclusion that the circuits could be used in reverse so that the CM's entry batteries could be charged by the LM. It was not the most efficient way of transferring electrical power, but it worked well enough. *Odyssey's* reentry batteries were topped off with an extra 15 percent or so Wednesday and Thursday.

Peters figured that it was just another in a long line of game changers that week. "This demonstrates that the preparation our leadership required of us provided the team with the capabilities to successfully solve one of the most complex engineering challenges of our time," Peters said. "Our analysis for years prior to the mission enabled us to understand the systems better than the designers did. We wrote procedures to use those systems in ways that the designers never anticipated. We developed troubleshooting procedures in advance of any problems that actually occurred, and we fine-tuned the capability to work together as a team through extensive simulations."

John Aaron had a deadline that he could not miss. As the earth continued to get bigger in the windows of the spacecraft, Lovell got more and more insistent concerning the power-up procedures on which Aaron and Jim Kelly were so diligently working. When the pressing deadline was mentioned to Aaron, he laughed and called it his "hour of destiny." What was once a collection of conceptual ideas had become more refined, more detailed in terms of what circuit breakers and switches to actually cycle. Controllers and contractors came back with all their tweaks, all of which had to be resolved. The ground was happy, but could the crew actually handle each and every item on the lengthy document in a short amount of time? The checklist was farmed out to astronauts in the simulators. "They would come out of there and say, 'No, no, EECOM. You've got to give me a little more time here.' Well, that meant more power," Aaron said. "I'd have to go find something else to turn off."

Finally, late Thursday afternoon, Arnie Aldrich escorted Aaron into the control room. In Aaron's hands was a single, marked copy of the power-up checklist. At some thirty-nine pages and more than four hundred entries, it was something to behold. Capcom Vance D. Brand told Lovell that he was ready to start reading up the first installment, and Lovell responded by getting Swigert on the line. Even then, Brand's first message to Swigert was to hold on for a minute and after that, for a little bit longer. Copies of the checklist needed to be made.

Okay, Jack. Going to hold up one. All the hordes of people that devised this procedure are going to be coming into the room in a minute, and they'd like to hold up until everybody can listen in.

Swigert sounded somewhat less than thrilled with the delay.

Okay, Vance. We're ready to go.

Temperatures had dropped to a low of around thirty-eight degrees in the cabin. That, along with a body- and mind-numbing array of other factors, combined to give Fred Haise a urinary tract infection. The crew was, to put it mildly, exhausted. "They never complained," said Gerry Griffin, the Gold Team flight director on duty when the procedures were read up. "A lot of that, we didn't even hear about until they got home. They never said, 'We're freezing to death,' or anything like that." While an old-school copier furiously cranked out duplicates, Deke Slayton brought to bear every ounce of his calm and collected persona when he began to chat with Swigert.

How's the temperature up there, Jack? You guys chopping wood to keep warm?

It was not unprecedented for someone other than the capcom to be speaking directly with an in-flight crew, but it was something very close to it. Swigert responded.

Deke, it's about fifty-one, I think, or fifty in the LM *and it's about—I don't know—forty-five or a little bit less in the Command Module.*

Oh, it's a nice fall day, huh?

Yes, I tell you, we don't have to worry about chilldown.

Some fifteen minutes passed before Brand was finally able to begin the lengthy process of reading the power-up procedures to Swigert. It lasted so long, Mattingly took over the capcom console midstream. The process took maybe two hours, followed by another hour of LM procedures.

"The first question they asked me was, 'Where's *my* copy?'" Aaron said. "These were the days when we didn't have high-speed Xerox machines. It was pretty slow to copy things. It was a pretty thick little package, so the flight director said, 'Standby. You go run thirty copies of this and come back.'" Aaron called the delay, at least for him if not for the crew, a blessing in disguise. "All the other console operators and then everybody in that building had access to a copy, and so they were able to follow each step as it was read up to the flight crew. Everybody got a common understanding of it at once."

Getting *Odyssey*'s power-up checklist read up to the crew was a major hurdle, but there were still plenty more to clear. The LM power margins were good to go, which allowed for an early power-up late Thursday night. It afterward operated on a fairly healthy 42 amps for the final nine hours of its lifespan. "In retrospect, the LM power was managed conservatively and that was understandable," Lunney said. "But we had not been sufficiently sensitive to the crew condition in the cold, cramped spacecraft and the difficult sleeping environment. A fully informed assessment would likely have led us to release more LM power earlier to ease the checklist planning bind and to warm the cabin. We could have provided some improvement on both those counts. Even so, the crew never complained and performed heroically."

The trajectory continued to shallow, and a fifth midcourse correction was performed at 6:52 a.m. on Friday, a little less than five hours before reentry. Gene Kranz's team returned to the MOCR, taking their places alongside the one led by Gerry Griffin. Like Bill Stoval on the one before it, the flight's last trajectory adjustment caused FIDO Dave Reed and retro officer Chuck Deiterich all kinds of headaches. They were fat—they had lots of thrust, lots of fuel, and lots of options to use either the LM's ascent or its descent engine. They could not use any power to set up the platform in the LM, but they worked around that problem by orienting the stack at the horns of the earth. To the crew, the terminator of their home planet made it look like a crescent moon and the object was to place the crosshairs of the AOT on one of its "horns" for the check.

Dave Reed insisted on running one last simulation in the RTCC before the crucial burn of the LM's RCS, and it was a good thing they did. The wrong attitude had been entered into the computer, using *Aquarius*'s orientation instead of *Odyssey*'s. "Now you're getting down to the short strokes where Chuck and I realized it's all on our backs," Reed said. "We would've killed them right then and there if we hadn't found that. Now, what possessed me to do that one last sim beats the crap out of me." Reed would later call his friend and Trenchmate Deiterich one of three heroes in the flight, along with John Aaron and Glynn Lunney. "The numbers were all scrambled. They didn't make any sense at all," Deiterich added. "So what we did was put in a Command Module maneuver in the mission plan table of zero delta-*v*, and when we did that and then computed the entry attitude, it came up correctly. I don't know if it was luck or being thorough, but had we not done that, we would've really been confused the next day when we got to the real entry time. We sorted that one out. It was an easy workaround."

Twenty-one minutes after the burn, it was time to cast off the damaged Service Module. At 7:14 a.m. on Friday in Houston, Jim Lovell's description sent yet another chill through the control room.

And there's one whole side of that spacecraft missing.

Joe Kerwin responded, similarly amazed.

Is that right?

Right by the . . . look out there, will you? Right by the High Gain Antenna, the whole panel is blown out, almost from the base to the engine.

The base? The base of the Service Module was very near the heat shield, and if it was damaged, that meant game over. The last three and a half days had been for naught. "We were still trying to figure out exactly what had happened," Gerry Griffin said. "We didn't know how bad the damage was. We were playing a little bit of 'what if' games. What if it got the chutes? That was not so likely, but what if it got the heat shield, which was where the Service Module was plugged in back there? We figured there had been damage of some kind, but we didn't know how extensive. But there wasn't a lot we could do about it."

Press on. That was all anyone could do from that point forward. While preparations to cast off the LM were underway, Glynn Lunney came to Jerry Bostick with yet another problem. The Atomic Energy Commission was bent out of shape over the Radioisotope Thermoelectric Generator (RTG) on board the LM, which would have been used to power experiments on the lunar surface. The powers that be wanted to make doubly sure that since the nuclear device was not going to be left behind on the moon, it *must* be safely deposited somewhere in the ocean. Bostick's response was quick—you've got to be kidding, right? "Glynn said, 'I know, but just double check and give me something I can tell them to make them happy,'" Bostick said. Reluctantly, Bostick told Chuck Deiterich and Dave Reed about the request and their response was pretty much the same as his had been. The two men checked and made a tiny adjustment to the LM's separation attitude to ensure that the remains of the LM that did not burn up during reentry—the RTG included—would impact the Tonga Trench and one of the deepest spots in the south Pacific.

At 9:10 a.m. in Houston, the Command Module's comm system was activated. Aaron quickly checked every possible piece of status and configuration information. "I was relieved and delighted to find the CM systems functioning properly and that the power-up procedure had worked as envisioned—and just as impressive, Jack had executed the procedures perfectly," Aaron concluded.

The CM platform was course aligned based on the LM's alignment, using the same technique used much earlier to transfer alignments from the CSM to the LM. Swigert had some difficulty with sunlight reflecting off the LM, but he was finally able to refine the alignment using star sightings.

Next came the attitude change for jettison of *Aquarius*.

Setting it up required Lovell to yaw the docked vehicles to an out-of-plane attitude, in order to minimize the possibility of making contact. Miraculously, everything had gone according to plan, when suddenly guidance officers Ken Russell and Will Presley noticed the CM's platform was headed toward gimbal lock.

The crew was quickly alerted of the problem. Lovell was using the LM platform reference to effect the attitude change, and due to the two platforms being aligned in different physical orientations, he was not aware of the impending gimbal lock. "We all held our breath," Aaron remembered. "We watched and waited as Jack, in the CM, coordinated with Jim in the LM to avoid gimbal lock. We all breathed a sigh of relief when the attitude maneuver was successfully finished."

The new procedure had not been checked for this condition prior to sending it to the crew. It had very nearly been a costly oversight, because a gimbal lock would have destroyed the alignment with very little time remaining to recover. Aaron remembered thinking that all that work and planning for reentry was almost for naught. It was just one more near-disaster on a flight that already had a long, long list of them.

Aquarius was sent on its way at 10:43 a.m. Friday. It was a spacecraft that could never have flown in the earth's atmosphere, yet it had just done its part to save the lives of three astronauts. "I think our whole telmu team was on shift for the jettison," said Merlin Merritt. "It was sort of an excited, happy time—a time of elation as we felt our telmu team had done our part to save the mission as well as the lives of the astronauts. However, as with life itself, we were excited and ready to move on to the next stage to see if the Command Module could withstand the stress of reentry. It was sort of a feeling of mission well done, but we couldn't celebrate yet."

With just a handful of minutes to go, there was not much left to say between the astronauts in the spacecraft and the controllers in the MOCR. What Kerwin and Swigert did have time for was a bit of good-natured chit-chat. Swigert began.

You have a good bedside manner.

Kerwin laughed.

That's the nicest thing anybody's ever said! How about that?

Next, it was Swigert's turn to perk up the ears of those in the Trench.

Sure wish I could go to the FIDO party tonight.

That prompted more laughter from Kerwin, who got in a dig on the bachelor Swigert's reputation as a ladies' man.

Yes, it's going to be a wild one. Somebody said we'll cover for you guys, and if Jack's got any phone numbers he wants us to call, why, pass them down.

Moments later, static. At last, 142 hours, 40 minutes, and 45.7 seconds into the flight, at 1:53 p.m. on Friday, 17 April 1970, *Odyssey* began digging back into the earth's atmosphere over Australia. Communications were lost due to the ionization of the atmosphere around the spacecraft—a period known in the MOCR as blackout—some fifteen to twenty seconds later. A hush fell over the room, quite unlike anything it had ever experienced. All eyes were on the clocks, and at the moment blackout was expected to end—nothing. Only more silence. A minute passed. Still no word from the spacecraft. Kranz asked Deiterich a question, hoping there had been some sort of mistake.

Chuck, were the clocks good?

It was almost in a whisper that the veteran retro officer answered.

They're good, Flight.

The delay meant different things to different people in the room. "They were probably the longest moments of the entire mission," Kranz said. "There's a very graphic photograph of all the flight directors standing at the console, and basically, you can just see the guys staring at the clocks. That picture was taken just about the time we were expecting acquisition of signal and we didn't get a response from the crew. The expression on the faces was looking and wondering what in the hell went wrong." Griffin was standing next to Kranz, and he was wondering the very same thing. "We couldn't raise them and we couldn't get voice comm with them," Griffin added. "Nobody said anything. We didn't even look at each other. We were all kind of looking straight ahead. I know I thought, 'Good God. We've come all this way and got them all the way back here and that dang heat shield had been damaged and they didn't make it back in.'"

An outright despair was closing in on the Trench. "In the back of our minds, Chuck and I knew we had kept having a problem with the spacecraft drifting and altering the reentry angle," Reed concluded. "It obviously was coming in shallow and instead of being three minutes like it was supposed to be, we didn't hear from them. Whose head does this fall on? Chuck and Dave. That's it. Nobody else involved. We were the ones who had to pick the vectors. We were the ones who computed the midcourses. We were the ones who decided to tweak that midcourse. My God, think about it. A minute goes by, and you still don't hear them? I'm sure there was enough gravity around me, I probably crushed the floor."

Jerry Bostick, the branch chief, went through one of the biggest mood swings of his career, if not his life. "Before we went into blackout, it was a great feeling of relief and accomplishment," he said. "We have done the impossible here. We're going to get these guys back. Then we went into blackout and it lasted about a minute longer than we were expecting. We'd never had that before. Everybody was thinking, 'There was some damage to the heat shield and we've lost them.' Personally, I went to one of the biggest letdowns I've ever had. That last minute of blackout was not a good time."

An agonizing one minute, twenty-eight seconds passed between the expected end of blackout and S-band contact finally being established with recovery aircraft. A minute later, helicopters in the area had *Odyssey* in sight. Finally, voice contact came at 2:03 p.m.

Kerwin tried to establish the connection to Houston.

Odyssey, *Houston standing by. Over.*

Five more seconds passed before Swigert's voice was heard.

Okay, Joe!

Minutes later, the drogue parachutes were out, followed by three large, billowing orange-and-white parachutes. The control room erupted in a frenzy of unabashed relief.

Odyssey, *Houston. We show you on the mains. It really looks great. Got you on television, babe.*

When the crew was on the deck of the uss *Iwo Jima*, the celebration was on in full force. They had accomplished the near impossible. Kranz described the moment in *Apollo 13: To the Edge and Back*, a 1995 documentary on the flight. "About the time that you see chutes, you'll see the cheering and the American flags come out," he said. "And then it's again tradition that you wait until the crew gets on the carrier deck." It was at that point that emotion welled up within Kranz. "At which time cigars and

18. It had been a close call, but Glynn Lunney (foreground), Gene Kranz, and the rest of the MOCR are able to celebrate moments after the *Apollo 13* Command Module *Odyssey* splashed down. Courtesy NASA.

the world map lights up and . . ." This time, Kranz stopped. "Ah, shit," he added, looking away from the camera for a second in an attempt to collect himself. "It was neat."

It had been close, but Jim, Freddo, and Jack were home. "We knew what was at stake, and we knew how deep the hole was that we were in," said Lunney, who along with Kranz, Griffin, Windler, and Sjoberg accepted the Presidential Medal of Freedom on behalf of the entire Flight Operations team during a ceremony at MSC the day after the landing. "Seeing the spacecraft on three chutes, short of landing, was a big indication that we got it figured out and figured out right." There was satisfaction and accomplishment, and no small amount of humility to boot. "If things had gone just a little bit differently, we would *not* have been able to get them back," Lunney continued. "Things could have happened in different sequence, different order, different place in the mission and it could've been impossible to recover them. Watching the parachutes, I don't know how much of that went through my head, but we were *well* aware of how close we came to losing this crew."

The splashdown party was indeed a good one that night, if not rather subdued. Most had not slept much in the last few days, so it did not quite go into the wee hours of the morning as it usually did. "Jack Swigert and Jack Schmitt were regular attendees, so Swigert knew what he was talking about," said Jerry Bostick, referring to Swigert's crack about the party. "We usually spent most of the time at the parties cutting each other down for mistakes we had made, but this one was tame in that respect. We spent most of the time congratulating each other on a job well done."

Sy Liebergot went home that day, yet he was not overly exultant. He had the nagging feeling that he had not performed like some sort of "super EECOM." He wound up with nightmares in which he relived in great detail the experience of being on console as the accident unfolded. Awakened every morning for two full weeks, Liebergot doubted himself and his performance. During yet another dream one night, he was finally able to come up with perfect answers for every problem caused by the explosion. Still, Liebergot's calls made no difference to the final outcome of the flight. Relieved, he never had another nightmarish, nighttime vision.

His subconscious, he joked, had let him off the hook.

10. Living on the Moon

It is a little less than five hundred miles from Boyle, Mississippi, to Houston, but for EECOM Bill Moon, the towns might as well have been on opposite sides of the universe.

In a room full of people who had taken a multitude of paths to work in the space program, Moon's was one of the most remarkable. Moon's father, Jew Or Ning, arrived in the United States from China on 3 September 1908 in search of the *gam sahn*—in English, the golden mountain—that he hoped life in the country would afford them. Although he was refused entry and returned to China due to an eye infection, Jew Or Ning tried again a little more than two years later.

This time, he was able to settle near Sacramento and found work on farms, ranches, sawmills, and as a camp cook for 20 Mule Team Borax Smith's Tonapah and Tidewater Railroad. He returned to his home country a handful of times, married, and was widowed before he could bring his wife or their children back to the States. He went into business and moved to the Mississippi Delta in 1925. Fourteen years later, a twenty-year-old woman named Wong She moved to America to be his wife. Jew Or Ning had eight children—one of them Jew Yui Wie, or William Joe "Bill" Moon—and the family all lived in the back of a grocery store they ran in Boyle. By age six, young Bill was working, waiting on customers and making change for their purchases.

His parents had a built-in abundance of help with that many kids running around, so they would often "loan" him to a nearby grocery store, where his real-life education continued. At ten years old, he was making five dollars a day, learning to butcher steak and chicken, and was eventually trusted enough to run the store with the help of only one other fifteen-year-old employee. Moon attended Boyle High School through the ninth grade, and after that district was consolidated with another, he moved to nearby Cleveland High School. He found acceptance, both at Cleveland High School and at Mississippi State University, where in 1960 he became a charter member of the Acacia social fraternity.

The fact that he was a minority . . . in a social fraternity . . . in the Mississippi Delta, in the heart of the Jim Crow Deep South . . . in the early 1960s . . . seems as extraordinary an accomplishment as being an integral member of a team that landed men on the surface of the moon.

After graduating from Mississippi State in 1964 with a degree in electrical engineering, Moon had a NASA job offer at the Cape but chose instead to go to work in St. Louis for McDonnell Aircraft on the electrical design for its *Phantom* F4D jet fighter. While visiting his brother in Houston, he swung by MSC to fill out yet another application. A month later he had another offer, and this time he took it. From that point on, Moon's was a fairly typical route to the MOCR. He worked the remote sites late in Gemini and during an unmanned Saturn flight, before moving into the vehicle systems SSR for the CSM—that was where the brains were, he joked.

Once in the back room, his goal was clear. Moon wanted a shot at proving himself in the MOCR. When his daughter was born around the time of *Apollo 9*, Moon turned his SSR console over to a coworker just long enough for him to make the trip to the hospital and back. "I found how to sell myself was to take responsibility for everything that I did," Moon said. "Every assignment, you made it like you owned it and you did it to the best of your ability. I liked being in a leadership position, and that's how you proved yourself on all the assignments you were given."

Although Moon was the first minority to work a console in the MOCR, it was not a fact upon which he dwelled. "I achieved my promotions based on how well I did my actions," he said. "I don't feel like I got anything given to me because I was Asian. As a matter of fact, I didn't even feel like an Asian. Among the guys, I was treated like normal. Some people may have perceived it different, but I'm always crossing the lines."

He never worked an Apollo launch—after the *Apollo 12* lightning strike, that was John Aaron's domain—but on *Apollo 16* and *17*, Aaron slid to the side for Moon to take over at the console. He took part in making history. He was just twenty-nine years old when *Apollo 14* flew, and he dressed the

19. Bill Moon (shown here with Sy Liebergot on the left) had an extraordinary journey to the MOCR. The son of Chinese immigrants, Moon grew up in rural Jim Crow Mississippi and eventually joined a social fraternity in college. Courtesy NASA.

part of the MOCR flight controller—white shirt, skinny tie, pocket protector, and horned-rim glasses. He traveled the world and the country, far, far away from his childhood home in rural Mississippi. He and his brothers and sisters were taught by their parents to strive toward their goals, and seven of the eight Moon children got college degrees.

As much as Jew Guie and Wong She hoped and dreamed their children might one day accomplish, they could never have imagined that one of them would one day take part in something like Apollo.

Nine and a half months passed between the splashdown of *Apollo 13* and the launch of *Apollo 14*, and significant changes were made to the CSM— construction of its oxygen tanks was modified, and a third oxygen tank and an auxiliary battery were added.

Although that solved the problems that plagued *Apollo 13*, it appeared that the following flight would again fall short of the moon. It was not the life-and-death struggle that faced the MOCR just a few shorts months before, but it was frustrating nevertheless. Just shy of three hours and fourteen minutes after CDR Alan Shepard, CMP Stu Roosa, and LMP Edgar D. Mitchell left the pad in Florida, and early in the coast on the way out to the moon, Roosa brought the *Kitty Hawk* Command and Service Module in for a docking with the *Antares* Lunar Module housed in the S-IVB third stage.

It had become a routine maneuver on a lunar flight, but this time, the CSM's conical-shaped probe bounced in and out of its drogue target at the top of the LM four separate times in just sixteen seconds. No joy. The contact left faint scratches in the drogue that the crew would later examine to begin figuring out what went wrong.

Roosa's voice was calm as he reported back to capcom C. Gordon Fullerton.

Okay, Houston. We hit it twice and sure looks like we're closing fast enough. I'm going to back out here and try it again.

He tried twice more in the next couple of minutes, and still, the latches would not catch. The time had not yet come to get nervous, but it was getting close as Roosa got back on the loop.

Man, we'd better back off here and think about this one, Houston.

Seven minutes later, another unsuccessful try came and went. Nearly an hour and a half later, the same thing. The implications were obvious. If Shepard and Mitchell could not get into the LM, the moon landing was off for the second flight in a row. What might that mean to the program? "*Apollo 14*, I guess, was the first time I really had a problem that could have been very critical occur, and that was when we were trying to dock up with the Lunar Module," said Pete Frank, the mission's lead flight director. "Like all those problems, you're never expecting something to happen. You've got a very routine operation going on at the dock, and it didn't capture. Well, let's back off and do it again. It didn't capture. Uh-oh. This is—wait a minute now."

In the CSM vehicle systems SSR, Jim Kelly was considered an expert on the probe. John Aaron called him to the front room, and they went off the loop so they could talk and mull things over. What could possibly be the problem, and more important, what could they do about it? The probe was purely a mechanical device, so it had no instrumentation to check and diagnose what might be keeping it from latching.

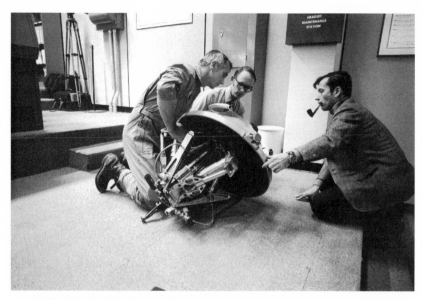

20. A balky docking probe during the flight of *Apollo 14* was not the life-or-death crisis of *Apollo 13*, but it could very well have derailed the mission nonetheless. Here, Charlie Harlan discusses a probe mockup with astronauts Gene Cernan (left) and John Young (right). Courtesy NASA.

From the outside looking in, the easiest way to bring the two spacecraft together might have been to back *Kitty Hawk* up, come at *Antares* with a full head of steam, and then slam the drogue home. If the theory sounded simple enough, in practice, it would not have worked. "The most fragile part of all this was not the Command Module," Kelly said. "It was not the probe. The fragile part was a piece of aluminum foil hanging off the end of the drogue called the LM. We were concerned about coming in too fast, at the wrong angles, in shear motions. The LM was our concern."

Another idea was taking shape, but it was a last resort. Why not have the crew put their suits and helmets back on, depressurize the cabin, and either bring the probe inside to see what might be wrong with it or reach through the tunnel and bring the CSM and LM together by hand? The first American in space seemed willing to give it a shot.

Houston, 14. I'm sure you're thinking about the possibility of going hard suit and bringing the probe inside to look at it, as we are.

Fullerton told him to stand by, that he might just have one more procedure for the crew to try. Less than five minutes later, *Apollo 14* backup commander Gene Cernan had momentarily replaced Fullerton at the capcom console.

Hey Stu, this is Geno. Do you read?

Yes, loud and clear.

Okay. We . . . we got one more idea down here before doing any hard suit work, and let me throw it out at you, and you come back with your impressions.

Roosa would very slowly close on *Antares*, and when he made contact, he would fire his thrusters to hold the CSM in place while flipping a switch to retract the probe. After discussing it at length to make sure the crew understood exactly what to do and when to do it, *Apollo 14* tried docking for a sixth time one hour and forty-three minutes after the first.

At first, there was no response in the cabin, but then, barber pole. The word came down from Roosa.

We got a hard dock, Houston.

There was a sigh of relief in the MOCR, but now the concern was about having to go through all that headache the next time the CSM and LM had to dock, after Shepard and Mitchell returned from their explorations of the lunar surface. The docking had finally been successful *this* time, but what about the next, while the crew was in lunar orbit? They might not be so lucky.

After docking, the probe was brought inside the Command Module and inspected by the crew. They could see nothing wrong with it. "We were comfortable that it was working okay," Kelly said. "When you find something that's busted, and it kind of fixes itself, there's always an uncomfortable feeling of 'What did we fix?' That rattlesnake is still there under the rock." Later, the post-lunar landing docking went perfectly. The best anybody could figure was that some sort of contamination or debris caused the failures, and a covering was afterward added to protect the probe tip from foreign material.

The rest of the coast to the moon was relatively uneventful, leaving time for the MOCR's version of the "gotcha" game. Wally Schirra was notorious for his love of practical jokes, but that was not the kind of thing that was limited just to the astronaut corps. Oh, no. Not by a long shot.

Sy Liebergot had arrived for an *Apollo 14* simulation and noticed a bright-yellow stamped label on a nearby locker that read "Capcom Locker." He felt sure it was Bruce McCandless, and then and there, a plan was hatched. Liebergot made sure he got to work for their first shift of the flight before McCandless, and proceeded to place similar stickers on each and every one of the forty-seven others in the room. He did not stop there, either, as he provided helpful directions to McCandless's work station.

This way to the capcom console.

You're getting nearer to the capcom console.

Here's the capcom console.

You're here.

The finishing touches were to the console itself. The armrests of McCandless's chair featured "Left" and "Right" stickers, and Liebergot had also helpfully pointed out its "Front" and "Back." Last but not least, he placed a "Capcom TV Monitor" sticker over the console tubes. "Bruce was not amused," Liebergot wrote in his autobiography. "He was fuming as he took his seat at his console which was only a couple of feet to my left." The best was yet to come.

Barely nine hours into the flight, Shepard's voice drifted down from the spacecraft.

Bruce, we've been wondering if you found your headset all right when you got back to the MOCR.

There was laughter as McCandless replied.

Yes, I've got it on. I didn't notice anything wrong with it. You may be a little subtle for me, but go ahead.

It was Roosa's turn to gig McCandless.

You obviously found it. It is working.

The joke was all but forgotten when another piece of debris, this time a tiny bit of solder, caused another round of headaches in the MOCR as Shepard and Mitchell prepared for their descent to the surface. A light blinked on in the LM cabin, and it was not a good one—the PGNS computer was receiving an errant signal.

Abort.

If Shepard and Mitchell had been on their way down to the surface in *Antares*, the computer would have started its procedures to head back uphill and find Roosa and *Kitty Hawk*. Jack Knight was on duty at the telmu console, and his reaction was easy enough to understand.

This is not good.

If that was easy to understand, so was the first attempt at a fix. If it was something like a piece of lint, a solder ball, something small and metallic that was not supposed to be inside the electrical component, that might be causing a false electrical contact. "At that point, I seem to remember Bob Carlton said to have them tap the panel," Knight said. Haise passed the suggestion up to the crew, the panel was tapped and the light went off, but not for long.

Abort.

Tap the panel.

Abort.

Tap the panel.

Abort.

Tap the panel.

Another abort situation was facing Gerry Griffin, who would work three of the last four descents to the lunar surface as flight director for the Gold Team. He was the only person who handled more than one. "My team was attuned to landings," Griffin said proudly. "We kind of got a feel for it, kind of like driving your own car or flying your own airplane. We knew those vehicles in and out, for that phase of the mission, exactly what they had to do." By *Apollo 8* or *9*, he would have taken anybody to work on his team and felt comfortable with it. By that time, he said, the MOCR had gotten down to the "hard core" controllers who thrived on the business of flying human beings to the moon and back. There were probably personality differences, but he did not seem to notice.

He was having too much fun.

This abort-switch problem was no laughing matter. Griffin waved off the descent for an orbit, and if Shepard and Mitchell were going to land, something had to be done as soon as possible. "Some kid at MIT," Griffin said, reworked the computer program to bypass the switch. The "kid" was Don Eyles, and the sixty-one DSKY key strokes needed for the change were read up to the crew by Haise. "I had written the code that monitored this discrete," Eyles said. "The workaround simply changed a few registers, first to fool the abort monitor into thinking that an abort was already in progress, and then to clean up afterward so that the landing could continue unaffected." The landing was on for the time being.

The next time, it was not the abort switch that went haywire, but the landing radar. Still a little more than six miles up, Mitchell knew that the radar should be about to lock onto the surface. It did not, and he radioed down to Haise.

Can't get the radar in.

Rules were rules, and the rules said that if the radar was not working at ten thousand feet, the landing would be a no go. Griffin was not worried about the problem. He knew that Shepard and Mitchell had to have a radar to land, but with so many other things going on at once, Griffin had compartmentalized the radar as a "to do" item. He knew the Trench and systems guys were working the issue, and for Griffin, that was good enough. It took just a couple of minutes before Haise transmitted a potential fix up to the crew.

Antares, Houston. We'd like you to cycle the landing radar circuit breaker.

It was a reboot before there was such a word, and it had worked. "If you were going to call an abort based on no landing radar, you wouldn't want to call it until you had to," Griffin said. "We still had time, we got the problem fixed, so I didn't dwell on it. We had to get on with the landing."

Seven minutes later, *Antares* was on the surface, and legend would later hold that Shepard would have played the gung-ho, bulletproof, indestructible hero card and landed even without the radar. No way, said Griffin. "Others may disagree with me, but in spite of everything said or supposedly said after the mission was over, there is no doubt in my mind that if we had called an abort, Al would have aborted the landing. He was too good not to."

Touchdown in Fra Mauro was the most bittersweet of moments for Haise, who had been hit with a double whammy by fate. The world saw what happened to *Apollo 13*, but he had seen another chance at a moon landing drift sadly by after serving as backup commander for *Apollo 16*. That put Haise, LMP Jerry Carr, and CMP William R. "Bill" Pogue in line to fly *Apollo 19*, but both that mission and *Apollo 18* were canceled on 2 September 1970.

When Haise sat down at the capcom console during the flight of *Apollo 14*, he knew that unless something happened to John Young, he would never walk on the moon. Shepard and Mitchell had taken *Apollo 13*'s landing target in the Frau Mauro highlands as their own, and so Haise volunteered for the capcom gig because he had trained for so long to explore there himself. "I'd been disappointed long before *Apollo 14*," he admitted. "That was over. It was past history. My disappointment was obviously during *13* itself, when we knew we couldn't make the landing, and the second time was when they canceled *18* and *19*."

The moonwalkers encountered a few minor hiccups during their first EVA, during deployment of the Apollo Lunar Surface Experiment Package (ALSEP) and with a gradual degradation of the resolution of the television picture. On the second, their primary objective was Cone Crater, but getting there proved difficult almost from the outset of their journey. Landmarks were not where they expected, and lugging the Modular Equipment Transporter (MET) proved to be such a bear that their backup crew of Gene Cernan and Joseph H. "Joe" Engle bet them a case of Scotch that they would not make it to Cone's rim because of it. Haise could not resist reminding them of the wager.

There's two guys here that figured you'd carry it up.

Mitchell did not understand at first, and asked Haise to repeat himself.

Said there's two guys sitting next to me here that kind of figured you'd end up carrying it up.

Cernan and Engle won the bet. The fact of the matter was that the two astronauts were not quite sure where they happened to be. Shepard picked a turnaround point, and at first Mitchell put up a mild protest.

Oh, let's give it a whirl. Gee whiz. We can't stop without looking into Cone Crater. We've lost everything if we don't get there.

Moments later, Haise added the grounds' two cents.

Okay, Al and Ed. In view of . . . where your location is and how long it's going to take to get to Cone, the word from the backrooms is they'd like you to consider where you are the edge of Cone Crater.

The response was not the one for which Mitchell was hoping.

Think you're finks.

Haise tried to explain the rationale.

Okay. That decision, I guess, was based on Al's estimate of another at least thirty minutes and, of course, we cannot see that from here. It's kind of your judgment on that.

Mitchell was not going down easily.

Well, we're three-quarters there. Why don't we lose our bet, Al, and leave the MET and get on up there? We could make it a lot faster without it.

Shepard told him that the rocks around them had been ejected from Cone during that eons-ago meteorite strike, but that was not good enough for the LMP.

But not the lowest part, which is what we're interested in.

Shepard relented, and they pressed on. Haise relayed a message from their boss.

And, Al and Ed, Deke says he'll cover the bet if you'll drop the MET.

Nope. Mitchell would not hear of it. He was a gamer.

It's not that hard with the MET. *We need those tools. No, the* MET'*s not slowing us down, Houston. It's just a question of time. We'll get there.*

As optimistic as Mitchell was trying to be, their thirty-minute extension evaporated in the blink of an eye. They had to stop, start sampling, and then start the return trek to *Antares*.

Al and Ed, do you have the rim in sight at this time?

Shepard misunderstood the question, and Haise repeated it.

Oh, the rim, the veteran astronaut replied. *That is negative. We . . . haven't found that yet.*

It was at that point when Haise had to give them the bad news.

Ed and Al, we've already eaten into our thirty-minute extension and we're past that now. I think we'd better proceed with the sampling and continue with the EVA.

The search for Cone was over, and they had come up short. Although he trained for Fra Mauro, Haise did not feel that he had been much of a help when it came to finding their way around. "Unfortunately, the main role I played was encouraging them to come back and stop trying to climb the side of Cone Crater," Haise remarked. "They didn't quite get to the edge. They were very, very close, but to get up there, they were going away from the LM. There was a lot of pressure to get them to call off the quest because of the time, and come back to the LM."

Shepard had one more surprise in store when he and Mitchell got back to the LM. An avid golfer, he dropped two balls into the dust of the landing site.

Houston, while you're looking that up, you might recognize what I have in my hand as the handle for the contingency sample return. It just so happens to have a genuine six iron on the bottom of it. In my left hand, I have a little white pellet that's familiar to millions of Americans. I drop it down. Unfortunately, the suit is so stiff, I can't do this with two hands, but I'm going to try an old sand trap shot here.

He swung and brought up the most valuable divot in the history of the game. Mitchell, then Haise commented, just the way they would have had this been an ordinary round back on Earth.

Hey, you got more dirt than ball that time.

That looked like a slice to me, Al.

The first lunar golfer was not about to be undone by a couple of good-natured smart remarks about his game. He dropped another ball onto the ground.

Got more dirt than ball. Here we go again. Here we go, straight as a die, one more.

He swung, and the ball disappeared out of frame of the television camera.

Miles and miles and miles!

Haise had not known of Shepard's stunt, and supposed that he had cleared it with Slayton beforehand. "He got a good whack at the second one," Haise said with a chuckle. "The mission at this point had been, obviously, declared successful for most of the primary objectives. They were just getting things cleaned up there at the LM. It was a nice little lighthearted amusement there at the end. To me, it was nothing that was super risky. It was not off color. It wasn't eating into the work timeline. So I don't see any rational reason why anybody would be against it."

A day before landing back on Earth, Liebergot and McCandless had another brief encounter. The EECOM had just called for a quantity balancing procedure on the three oxygen tanks, and when he did, the capcom brought up one of Liebergot's screens on his console in order to follow along as he read the instructions up to the crew.

Apollo 14, this is Houston. We'd like to get Oxygen Tank 3 heaters to Off now. 1 and 2, Auto. Over.

Shepard confirmed.

3, Off. 1 and 2, Auto. Okay.

Roger. That's 1 and 2, Auto. Over.

Nearly a minute passed, and McCandless apparently noticed the tank temperature rising a few degrees past the 325-degree limit that Liebergot had imposed for the procedure. He got back on the loop to Shepard.

14, Houston. Confirm Oxygen Tank 3 heaters Off. Over.

Shepard's reply was pure "Icy Commander," his well-earned nickname from a long way back. In his book, Liebergot remembered it as "dripping with acid."

Okay, we've got Oxygen Tank heater number 3, off. O-F-F. We have Oxygen Tank heaters number 1 and number 2, Auto. A-U-T-O.

"Shepard came back, and he played that military game," Liebergot said.

"The less familiar you were with him, the more you feared him. He played that to the hilt. He radioed back down, dripping with sarcasm. He was pissed. I'm screaming at McCandless, 'No, don't! Everything's cool!' I finally had to bury my head on the console, because I was going to get blamed by Shepard for that, not McCandless."

Laughing, McCandless did not have much to offer other than a simple acknowledgment.

Roger, 14.

Apollo 15 was Glynn Lunney's last mission at the flight director's console, and that was not the only place in the MOCR where a changing of the guard was taking place.

Rod Loe had not been on the manning lists for several flights, and Bob Carlton had not worked the front room since *Apollo 11*. John Hodge, Dave Reed, and several others moved en masse to the Department of Transportation. In their place came new controllers like Bill Moon, young and eager to get in on the exploits of Apollo. Lunney had already been to the Soviet Union in late November/early December of 1971 to help begin laying the groundwork for the Apollo-Soyuz Test Project, and he had been made manager for both it and the Apollo Experiments branch of the Apollo Spacecraft Program.

Ever so slowly, management was beckoning Lunney. Operations had been a part of his life since 1959, and he had worked in every American manned program since. He had for years been helping to build a highway to the moon, and while Lunney was not necessarily looking for an off-ramp, it eventually found him. It was time to move on and give the younger guys a chance. "I never thought of it as bittersweet, but in a way it was," said Lunney, who worked his first and only descent to the lunar surface on *Apollo 15*. "It wasn't like I was just leaving. It was time to move on from the work I was doing in operations, and it was time to move to a brand-new world that I really had never operated in before, which was program management. Things were changing all around me, and I was being asked to do some things that went beyond what I'd done before. All that just sort of tumbled out and was on top of me before I even realized that it was."

Lunney was not the only flight director in the process of moving onward and upward. That was the way Gene Kranz and Cliff Charlesworth were headed, and Gerry Griffin gladly took the handoff and ran with it. *Apollo 15* was to be the first of NASA's "J" missions, which were extended explorations of the moon complete with an upgraded LM and PLSS backpack, which were good for EVAs of up to seven hours, and a high-tech dune buggy called the Lunar Roving Vehicle, or Rover for short. The entire crew—CDR Dave Scott and rookies LMP Jim Irwin and CMP Alfred M. "Al" Worden—had taken to geology with great gusto. Once Griffin joined them on a number of field trips, he understood why.

Before, focus had been on transportation—getting a crew to the moon and then getting it back safe and sound. Science was a part of each flight, but that did not take priority. Just pick up a few rocks here and there, make it to the rim of Cone Crater or not, then be done with it and get the heck out of Dodge for a safe trip back to Mother Earth. It was not necessarily us against them when it came to NASA and the science community, but they were not exactly one big happy family, either.

There seemed to be a breakthrough on *Apollo 15*, and not just because it was to be the first three-day stay on the moon. A big reason for that was Scott, who invited Griffin to tag along out to New Mexico for a geology field trip. The site was similar to what Scott and Irwin would find at their landing site near Hadley Rille, and it was there that the mission's lead flight director began to take an interest in geology as well. "The bug kind of bit me, too," Griffin said. "It was *really* fascinating. We all got kind of a turn-on to the science, the real purpose for why we were going, rather than just the transportation." Griffin, in fact, wound up spending time in the field before each of the last three lunar landings.

Planning for the J missions was intense. The LM had to be upgraded to last three days on the surface. The Rover had to be developed, and a way figured out to fit it on the side of the LM. Astronauts had to learn how to become geologists, and later, a geologist would have to learn how to become an astronaut. Ed Fendell, though, was not concerned about any of that. A young NASA engineer by the name of William E. "Bill" Perry had come up with the idea for a camera that could pan, tilt, zoom in, and zoom out. Chris Kraft, who by then had been made deputy director at MSC, was in favor of the camera and putting into place a way to control it from the MOCR. That way, there would be a way to follow the crew without them actually having to continually move it here and there.

Responsibility for the camera fell to Fendell's INCO group. Yet as he went through the chain of command, he met a certain amount of resistance. It meant selling it to the program office, building the system, spending the money, hiring a contractor, the whole spiel. A meeting was scheduled, and Fendell had one slide to present, and it read simply, "FOD [Flight Operations Directorate] has no requirement for a controllable television." As he entered the room, Fendell handed over the slide and then sat down to wait. First, Anthony J. "Tony" Calio, the head of the Science and Applications Directorate (S&AD), made his case and his slide was basically the same as Fendell's.

S&AD has no requirement for controllable television.

"Kraft starts to eat his ass out," Fendell began. "I mean, he is cutting him a new ass. He is chewing him out for being stupid, near-sighted, et cetera, da-da, da-da. The whole room is just sitting there cringing, and I'm saying, 'Oh, God. I'm gonna get it bad. I've got this requirement and my ex-boss is going to chew me a new asshole.'"

Mel Brooks knew what was coming, and told Fendell to have his slide pulled as soon as humanly possible. There was no time.

I can't pull my slide. The slide's in there.

Brooks did not help Fendell's morale.

Oh, shit. You're going to get killed.

When Fendell's turn finally came, he meekly—as if Ed Fendell *ever* did anything meekly—went to the front of the room to face the music or the firing squad, whichever the case might have been.

Can I have the first slide please?

When it came up, the room broke into laughter. Kraft looked at him, shook his head, and gave him an order.

Sit down.

Chris Kraft got his camera.

Launch went smoothly enough on 26 July 1971, but on at least a couple of different occasions on the coast out to the moon, a definite sense of disconnect developed between flight director Milt Windler and EECOM Sy Liebergot.

The first of those took place nearly a day and a half into the mission, when telmu Merlin Merritt reminded Liebergot that an hour had passed since the crew was to have performed an "LM enrichment" procedure in which its cabin pressure was equalized with that of the CSM. Scott and Irwin would

21. After a rather interesting meeting, Chris Kraft got the controllable camera he wanted for the later Apollo moon landings. Ed Fendell had just a two-year associate's degree in merchandising but was placed in control of the camera and all things having to do with Apollo communications. Courtesy NASA.

lower the pressure in their suits for their descent to the lunar surface, but before doing so, the concentrated oxygen in both vehicles allowed them to do a pre-breathing exercise in order to purge their bodies of nitrogen and avoid a malady known as the bends. The MOCR didn't have the telemetry for the pressure gauge located in the docking tunnel between the two spacecraft, so there was no way to tell other than asking the crew. Over the comm loop, Windler pressed for details.

Why is it important to do that?

Liebergot came back to Windler with a quick response.

Because, Flight, it's going to be an hour from that point before we can equalize pressure with the LM, okay? And you're nailed to that hour if what we suspect is true, that you're going to have to drop the LM 2 psi. So why don't we just go ahead and ask them? It's no big deal either way. It'll tell us a lot more than we know right now, relative to the flight plan.

Not only was Liebergot pitching in his two cents' worth, so did Merritt and astronaut Dick Gordon, who was working alongside Karl G. Henize at the capcom console. Some time passed before Windler had Henize ask the crew about the procedure, and with Scott's reply, Liebergot had just about reached his boiling point.

Not yet, Karl. We will, though.

Liebergot was "so pissed" at Windler, he would later recall how he turned around to confront the flight director.

Windler, someday you're going to hurt somebody.

Rarely, if ever, had a flight director been spoken to so bluntly and brusquely in the MOCR. There had been many a heated debate between flight directors and their controllers, but that was the kind of thing that took place somewhere else, not in the control room and not with a crew on its way to the moon.

According to Liebergot, Windler responded by lunging at him over the console. "If I needed to know something, I needed to know it and don't give me this crap about, 'Let's not bother the crew right now,'" the former EECOM said. "They're probably sitting there, picking their nose. After about an hour of Windler picking and picking and gaining the necessary knowledge and tying up the flight director loop for an hour so he could thoroughly understand what LM enrichment was, he said, 'You should've had it on telemetry if you really needed to know it.'"

Neither Windler, nor Merritt, nor Gordon had any memory of any kind of physical confrontation between the two men. Cynics might suggest Windler had good reason not to remember it, but with Merritt and Gordon also in separate agreement, it would seem to confirm that whatever might have happened between the two was very brief and that cooler heads prevailed.

Helping matters not in the least was yet another issue the very next day, when a leak developed around a water chlorination port. The port had leaked during preflight checks on the pad, and as Liebergot and George W. Conway in the SSR worked to find the fix, Windler got on the loop to ask about the excess water that was building up.

Why don't we just pump all that overboard, then?

Conway answered the question almost before Windler was finished asking it.

Negative.

Liebergot demurred, saying that he didn't want to chance busting the

CSM's passive thermal control barbeque roll that the overboard vent might cause. That did not satisfy the flight director.

I guess I'm not too concerned about the PTC. We can reestablish PTC, EECOM, a lot quicker than we can dry out the cabin.

The frustration in Liebergot's voice was clearly evident.

Flight, it's not an emergency right now. Just let me read this procedure. Leakage was noted pre-launch, and I think we may be able to cure it with this little procedure I've been trying to read.

And so it went.

Okay, look, Liebergot began a few minutes later. *Let's read the procedure up to them and get it done with. We're wasting time here.*

Interrupting Liebergot, Windler had a thought.

We got anything to lose by taking the water gun and squirting that . . .

It was the EECOM's turn to break in.

Yeah, we could have this procedure accomplished already.

Recordings of the episodes from Liebergot's comm loop were included on a CD that came with his book years later. He kept them, just in case. "I thought he was going to come after me after the mission, but he didn't," Liebergot admitted. "I don't think he's ever read my book, because I've seen him since and he hasn't said anything."

After a smooth landing on 30 July 1971, Scott did the first and only stand-up EVA through the upper hatch of the LM to survey the site. He and Irwin then rested, and nearly fifteen hours after touchdown, they at last headed outside.

When they tried to deploy the Rover, they met with resistance. The saddle that connected the Rover to the LM *Falcon* during the descent had very close tolerances, so much so that it had to be almost completely free of stress to easily separate. *Falcon* was tilted slightly to the rear and sideways, and that made for an even tougher separation. Bill Peters was prime telmu for the flight, and he had one suggestion from Harry Smith in the SSR on how to remedy the situation, another from Marshall Space Flight Center officials in SPAN.

Peters had to make a decision and could almost feel the eyes of Scott, Irwin, flight director Pete Frank, and the rest of the world watching in on live television. Smith had worked on deployment tests of the Rover at the Boeing plant in Kent, Washington, in which it had hung up in the same way. When it was relieved of as much stress as possible, it was freed. Peters opted to go with that instead of SPAN. "I had faith and confidence in my guy that had been there and he said, 'We saw exactly that before and this is exactly what you do to release it,'" Peters said.

Capcom Joseph P. "Joe" Allen called to Scott and Irwin.

Dave and Jim, pull the Rover as far out as you can away from the LM, *and then pull on the front end, if you could. And by that we mean lift up on the front end.*

It worked, but that might not have been the end of the story. Marshall was responsible for the Rover, and Peters later heard that Huntsville had filed an official complaint that Peters had not gone with their suggestion. "In retrospect, I know I made the right decision," Peters said. "I certainly didn't pacify the managers. They got a little aggravated at me. It wasn't what they wanted, simple as that. They wanted to go through some other procedure. It was one of the spur-of-the-moment things, like when you're driving an automobile and you jerk the wheel one way instead of the other. You have to make a decision, and you have to make it now." That kind of confidence in his abilities and those of his support team was a strength of Flight Operations, he continued. Make a decision and then fly through whatever flak might come. "I think it was Chris Kraft who called that 'intellectual arrogance,'" Peters said. "I guess we all had it. I think I still have it, but it doesn't fly well with politicians."

A packed flight plan combined with their own enthusiasm for lunar geology caused Scott and Irwin to go after their duties like no other crew ever had. Scott developed hemorrhages under fingernails of both hands because the sleeves of his suit were too short, forcing his fingers too far into the tips of his gloves. Irwin was unable to work the drink valve in his helmet during the first and second moonwalks; Scott's drink mouthpiece became dislodged during the second; and neither of them even attempted to use their in-suit drinking devices during the third and final EVA. Scott pulled a shoulder muscle while trying to pull a balky drill stem loose from the surface during the last of their three EVAs, and the pain kept him from getting a good night's sleep afterward. A total of nineteen hours, seven minutes, and fifty-three seconds spent outside left both men standing on the brink of exhaustion.

There was little time for rest once they rejoined Worden in the CSM

Endeavour in lunar orbit. They had to transfer rock samples from the LM to the CSM, again put on their spacesuits for a pressure check, and then close out the tunnel between the two spacecraft before cutting *Falcon* loose. The pressure checks and tunnel closeout did not go well and Glynn Lunney ended up having each step read up to the crew, one by one, in an attempt to get the process back on track. Gene Kranz, who had sat with Lunney for the last couple of hours, wrote in his autobiography that he "was spooked just listening. Even in the most bloodcurdling simulation I had never seen the crew and ground so out of phase."

"I think several things were going on," Lunney added. "The crew had been through a straining day, long day, demanding day, et cetera, et cetera. Then they had this other physical problem that we didn't really know about very easily. We didn't have any reason to try to find a way to make the day easier for them. We were trying to find a way to make the day *right* for them."

The physical problem to which Lunney referred was a series of heart irregularities that Irwin and, to a much lesser extent, Scott both had exhibited during the flight. Forty-one minutes before launch, Irwin had experienced "an isolated premature ventricular contraction"—in essence, what would commonly be called a heart flutter. They remained at the rate of about one or two an hour on the way to the moon, during each of the three EVAS, *Falcon's* ascent from the moon, and docking with *Endeavour*. They were not considered significant, because the doctors had seen similar issues with Irwin during training and he had come away none the worse for wear.

Shortly after the two spacecraft rejoined, however, Irwin also experienced a bigeminal rhythm in which his heart alternated between normal and premature beats for ten to twenty beats. That was followed by a series of premature ventricular and atrial beats, interspersed with normal ones. Scott had also experienced some arrhythmias, but nothing quite like this.

Irwin did not experience any kind of pressure or pain in his chest, and he was reportedly unaware that anything usual had happened. Still, the book *Biomedical Results of Apollo* added rather ominously, "Astronaut Irwin reported later that he had experienced a feeling of a brief loss of contact as though he had momentarily gone to sleep. In retrospect, this episode could have been a momentary loss of consciousness at the precise time the arrhythmia was noted." The report did not confirm that Irwin actually lost consciousness, just that he *could* have.

Later tests confirmed that Irwin had an undetected coronary artery disease that existed before the mission. Had doctors known anything about it, Irwin would likely not have been on the crew—it was, after all, a heart murmur that had led to Deke Slayton's grounding.

Irwin had an acute heart attack about two years after returning from the moon, and he became the first moonwalker to pass away on 8 August 1991 after suffering yet another.

Flight surgeon Chuck Berry was in the room and beginning to tell Chris Kraft what was taking place with Irwin. He was sure it was the result of a potassium deficiency made worse by their exhaustive work on the moon, and he also laid out the issues both he and Scott had experienced earlier. The three flight directors—Griffin, Lunney, and Kranz—all intently listened in. "I must admit that I felt like privacy was dominating safety," Lunney said. "When you have to be so careful about what you talk about that you're not communicating to people the real circumstances that are at hand, the balance is wrong."

Griffin saw it as a concern, but also as a transitory event that came and went with no impact on the flight. He remained friends with both Scott and Irwin long after the flight, and in all those years, they never discussed the heart irregularities of the *Apollo 15* astronauts. "Must not have been a topic too high on Dave's or Jim's agenda," Griffin concluded. "Remember how long ago this happened. It was 1971 and [Irwin's preexisting heart disease] went undetected. He made it to the moon, and did a superb job. I say, 'Good for Jim!' He lived another active twenty years, and even went on several expeditions to Mount Ararat looking for Noah's Ark. Not bad!"

This was a new one, a "deputy" flight director.

The 23 November 1971 press release announced the hiring of four such positions—Don Puddy and Phil Shaffer, who would work the upcoming flight of *Apollo 16*, and Chuck Lewis and Neil Hutchinson, who took over for *Apollo 17*. Each would get a trial run on console, in preparation for Skylab, the Apollo-Soyuz Test Project, and the Space Shuttle program that was still a decade in the future.

Shaffer started out in the MOCR as a FIDO in the Trench. His career progressed to the point where he was working as chief of data priority for both Apollo and Skylab, and now that he was Purple Flight as well, Chuck

Deiterich and Bill Stoval would come to him with a question but first ask what hat he was wearing at the moment. Was he Jolly Red, the giant of a man who was a kindred spirit in the Trench, assistant chief of the branch? Was he a data priority guy, or maybe Purple Flight? When they asked, they were probably only half joking. "Those guys in the Trench were a real pain," Shaffer once said. "They really were. They were the worst of the worst when it came to the prima donnas. They thought they were something special." If they thought they were hot stuff, however, he probably did, too, because at the end of the day, he was still one of them.

The new deputy flight directors were thrown to the wolves, but only in training. That was the way it worked for everybody who worked in the MOCR, not just them. When it came time for shifts on their first flights, they got the relatively easy ones—coasts to and from the moon and so forth. Shaffer got his baptism on the way out to the moon on *Apollo 16*, a little more than thirty-eight hours into the flight that launched on 16 April 1972. Gene Kranz came into the MOCR to sit with Shaffer for an hour or two, but after that, Jolly Red was on his own.

Almost as soon as Kranz left, the Inertial Measurement Unit went on the blink, leaving the crew of John Young, Ken Mattingly, and Charlie Duke without an attitude reference. "I wasn't particularly concerned about that, because it happens, except that the guidance officer was also new," Shaffer said. Jerry Mill was working his first solo shift as well, and when the problem took place, "he stood straight up and said, 'Oh!'" Shaffer remembered. "I knew I was in trouble." Before an erasable software program was uplinked to the crew to remedy the malady and because there were still tiny pieces of debris from the LM bay panels on the S-IVB trailing the vehicles, Mattingly used the sun and moon as references to realign his platform.

Those were the kinds of shifts that Mill sometimes pulled in the MOCR, the ones where he might have lunch at 3 a.m. The cafeteria was located just on the other side of the simulation room to the right front of the room, just down the hallway. It was low rent, not fancy, typical government chairs, trays, plates, everything. For some reason, Mill would always remember that the worst thing he could possibly order was the scrambled eggs.

"If you're working the night shift, the graveyard, the crew's asleep and all the important people are long gone," Mill said. "It's just the people who have to maintain the vehicle being the observers, ready to call the prime team in if a disaster happens. You try to stay awake by drinking lots of coffee, by BSing." He and Bill Stoval would sometimes pass the hours by running numbers through the RTCC, to see, for instance, what the velocity of a spacecraft might be if it simply stopped on its way to the moon and started suddenly falling back to Earth.

The first time he met Chris Kraft, the godfather placed his hand on Mill's shoulder. Mill vowed to never wash the spot again. "I was honored and glad to be in the front room," he began. "I think management chose the best people based on their skill level and knowledge base, and I wish I had worked harder to be in the top. There was no discrimination or anything else. They chose the people that they thought were the best, and I certainly have no disagreement with any of the people they selected."

Except for maybe one or two, but that's another story.

After the IMU issue, problems got progressively worse. While Young and Duke were activating the LM *Orion*, a helium leak developed in the regulator of one of its two RCS systems and wound up being vented overboard. "We were scrambling to work that problem, because the mission rules said we had to have both systems of RCS to land," said John Wegener, who was on the control console at the time. An ullage volume was created by transferring propellant into the ascent tanks, and that provided a "blowdown capability" in which the trapped pressure forced enough gas into the faulty RCS system for it to be used as a backup. As it had happened on so many other occasions, the ground actually came up with the solution before the flight and had simulated it with a crew other than Young and Duke. "The procedure worked fine, so that was our excitement during that period of time," Wegener continued. "That's what we were fooling with."

Mattingly had his hands full, too, wondering what was wrong with the backup servo on the CSM *Casper*'s SPS engine. It developed a wicked shimmy every time he tried to operate it, and no matter what he tried, the wobble would not go away. Gerry Griffin had no choice. He waved off the landing for at least one revolution of the moon and possibly for good if the MOCR and its vast network of resources could not work things out.

Terry Watson was on the GNC console, the same Terry Watson who had taken up Milt Heflin's offer of powering down the *Apollo 10* Command Module on its recovery ship just three years earlier. Watson had grown up near his father's Baltimore machine shop, turning his model rockets on lathes there. His dad worked for the National Advisory Committee for Aeronautics (NACA), NASA's earliest predecessor. Watson was a prodigy and skipped his freshman year at Georgia Tech, where he majored in mechanical engineering. After making the move from Landing and Recovery, he got his feet wet in the SSR before settling into his slot as GNC. "I thought I belonged there," Watson said. "You're obviously a little nervous, but it didn't take very long to get over that."

Casper was on the far side of the moon when Mattingly first attempted to test the backup system, so Watson and fellow GNC Gary Coen had no way of knowing what was about to happen when Mattingly came hurtling back around with Young and Duke trailing not far behind in *Orion*. As soon as capcom Henry W. "Hank" Hartsfield reestablished contact, Mattingly told him about the backup servo failing to cooperate.

Watson remembered Coen taking a look at his data and figuring out, on the spot, that the Rate Feedback Sensor had failed. When Watson asked how Coen could be so sure, he just shrugged his shoulders. Watson, a mechanical engineer, trusted the electrical engineer's diagnosis. "I understood plumbing, and he understood electrical stuff," Watson said. "Turns out, he hit the nail right on the head. That was the problem."

That was causing the oscillation, but what could be done about it? Gerry Griffin had decisions to make at the flight director's console, and whether to continue with the landing was only one of them. If the SPS was not operable for a return to Earth, an *Apollo 13*–like lifeboat rescue with the LM might be necessary. Griffin and his team had five laps of the moon to come up with something, and as they did, *Orion* and *Casper* flew in close formation, ready to dock again. "We were close to aborting the landing, but finally got it done after waving off a couple of lunar revs," Griffin admitted. "As I went back over the transcripts I was reminded how much effort it took by the entire nationwide Apollo team to reach the decision to go ahead and land."

That nationwide team included the Rockwell plant in Downey, California, where sims were conducted with a high-fidelity mockup of the SPS engine. They determined that the backup servo would not, in fact, shake the engine to pieces if it was needed. "They came back with the statement that if you had to use that system, if the engine was thrusting, it would put enough load on the engine that the bell would not wiggle," Watson said.

"It was no problem to do a burn with that failed rate transducer. Rockwell felt that in the event we had to use it, it would be okay. So we pressed ahead with the mission." After a delay of three and a half hours, Griffin made his call.

The landing was on.

Two and a half hours later, Young and Duke settled into the Descartes Highlands. For twenty hours, fourteen minutes, and fourteen seconds spread over three EVAs and three days, the two astronauts worked, but not nearly as close to a frazzle as the crew that proceeded it. Their diet was filled with potassium-rich foods such as orange juice, and that led to a rather entertaining exchange concerning . . . well . . . farting. They were tired by the end of the third and final EVA, but not to the point Young could not put on one last show for the camera and capcom Tony England. He began to hop, flat-footed, from the surface.

We were going to do a bunch of exercises that we had made up as the lunar Olympics to show you what a guy could do on the moon with a backpack on.

A smile was almost evident in England's voice.

For a 380-pound guy, that's pretty good.

As Young moved to the back of the Rover and continued with one more jump, Duke was suddenly inspired to join him. He shot straight up, and for a split second, looked like he would keep right on going. His backpack throwing his balance off, Duke flailed his arms and legs in a desperate attempt to regain control.

Wow! That ain't any fun, is it?

Duke had already stumbled to the ground at least once during his time on the surface, nearly impaling himself on a core sample tube in the process. This time, he took an even harder backward fall.

Young scolded Duke, every bit the stern parent.

Charlie . . .

If telmu Jack Knight could have joined Young, he would have. "You remember Al Shepard's golf ball, right?" Knight said. "For some reason, the guys wanted to do something memorable."

Knight's fear was that the oxygen supply on Duke's backpack took the brunt of his fall, and it was pressured to 6,000 psi. In other words, Duke might have used a bomb as his cushion. Knight got on the loop to flight director Pete Frank.

Flight, I'd just as soon he didn't do that again.
Frank was in complete agreement.
Yeah. Me too.

When the *Apollo 17* crew of Gene Cernan, Jack Schmitt, and Ron Evans splashed down only a mile from its target point in the Pacific Ocean on 19 December 1972, exactly eleven years, six months, and twenty-five days had passed since the day President Kennedy told Congress that he believed the nation should chart a course to the moon.

The Apollo lunar missions were over, and those who had worked them in the MOCR were moving on to other things. Many went into management, others focused their attentions on Skylab, the Apollo-Soyuz Test Project, or even the Space Shuttle. Some were caught up in the dreaded "reductions in force," otherwise known as layoffs. The last three missions to the moon were the most productive three missions to the moon, but the team was breaking up.

Bill Stoval had been angry when he did not get assigned to the launch of *Apollo 13*, but he more than made up for it later by working each of the final three launches and lunar ascents and rendezvous of the series. It was a decent tradeoff, because to him, leaving the surface in the LM and coming back together with the CSM in lunar orbit was more "FIDO-ey" anyway. And then there was this. "The whole world thought just getting to the moon was a big deal. Well, I didn't," Stoval began. "I thought going to the moon and doing stuff was a big deal. There wasn't any doubt, to me, that we could go to the moon, land, and bounce around. To me, *Apollo 17* was ten times harder than *Apollo 11*. *Apollo 11* was just syrup and candy. It was balls to the wall in terms of history, but in terms of doing stuff while you're there and really pushing the envelope, they took very good care to make it very, very safe."

The applied science of the final lunar missions intrigued Stoval, and he had hoped to see the cast-off LM ascent stage crash into the moon's surface in view of the Rover's still-active television camera. "It went faster than a bullet. What the hell was I thinking?" Stoval asked, not expecting an answer. "We filled up the day. We did all those spacewalks with the light backpack. We had all this seismic stuff, the mass spectrometer stuff, jettison booms. Those were busy times. Apollo didn't end with *11*. To me, it started with *11*."

If there was a tragedy to be found in the end of Apollo's lunar landings, that was it. Just as the missions were beginning to hit their stride and fulfill the enormous potential of scientific return, they were stopped dead in their tracks. It is no stretch to imagine that if Apollo had continued on its course unabated, Mars might very well have been the next step. At the very worst, even with the moon landings at an end for the time being, it might take twenty years.

The country was in the last terrible stages of Vietnam, and with the OPEC oil embargo and Watergate just over the horizon, America's focus was elsewhere. "I can tell you that all of us thought that we'd probably be on Mars in twenty years from that time," said Gerry Griffin, the lead flight director on *Apollo 17*. "It just never happened. Frustrated? I think disappointment might be an ever better word. There was just something that was empty about it. I could see it coming. I was off doing other things, but I knew we were going to be stuck in low-Earth orbit for a long, long time."

Those who worked in the MOCR during Apollo continued to leave their marks on the human spaceflight community for years. Don Puddy, Phil Shaffer, Neil Hutchinson, and Chuck Lewis would eventually become full-fledged flight directors, while others like Tommy Holloway, Harold Draughon, Gary Coen, Jay Greene, Randy Stone, and Al Pennington would join them at the console during the Space Shuttle era. They were back in the third-floor control room, home again.

Hutchinson was the one man who could lay claim to having worked on each of the first three rows of the MOCR—serving as guidance in the Trench, GNC on the second row, and flight director on the third—and on each of the first three *floors* of the Mission Control Center, having started out as a supervisor in the RTCC. He never charted a course for the flight director's console, never so much as even thought about it. When Arnie Aldrich became deputy manager of the Skylab program, Hutchinson had his sights set on moving up from deputy to chief of the CSM Systems Branch.

Hutchinson, a native of Portland, Oregon, was named deputy of the CSM branch before he ever actually sat a second-row console, and that ruffled a few feathers here and there. He immediately dove into getting up to speed as a GNC. "Here's how you get to be a manager at NASA," he explained. "You can technically beat up everybody else around you. Sometimes, that makes the worst managers in the world, because guys that are really, really

22. While Gene Kranz (center) still sported his familiar crew cut, Gerry Griffin (right) had let his grow out a bit more by the time *Apollo 17* rolled around. Neither had anything on Neil Hutchinson (left), whose longer hair and mustache did not stop him from becoming a flight director. Courtesy NASA.

good engineers and really, really good technically sometimes can't do the people thing worth a damn."

But flight director? Never. "There was *no* goal, trust me," he continued. "For one thing, setting the goal to be that man is bullshit, because you'll never get there. Really only two people—Kraft and Kranz—decided you're fit for that duty. I'm probably not going to mention names, but there were several people who aspired mightily to carry that title and never made it."

For Hutchinson, the deciding factor was Kraft. From the time he arrived at NASA in 1962 until he left the agency in 1986, he rarely made a single move without first seeking Kraft's counsel. "I was privileged to be one of 'Chris's Boys,' and there were only about a dozen of us," Hutchinson said. With Aldrich on the move onward and upward, his underling desperately wanted the gig and, yes, went to Kraft about it.

I'm going to go be the CSM branch chief.

No, you're not. I want you to be a flight director.

Oh . . . but I can't do both of them.

Of course not, so you need to go be a flight director.

Only eight other men had ever been named to that most important of titles in the MOCR, but if that was what Kraft wanted him to do, that is what Neil Hutchinson was going to do. He wanted the chief's job, but Kraft insisted that it was not the right fit for him. Hutchinson, Shaffer (who was best man at Hutchinson's wedding), Lewis, and Puddy were going to be flight directors.

Hutchinson was also one of the first in the room whose hair was a little bit longer. His mane was nowhere near a regulation Gene Kranz crew cut. "I was always kind of my own guy," Hutchinson said with a laugh. "I probably had a broad Jerry Garcia tie while everybody else was wearing black stringer ties, and yeah, my hair was pretty long. I went to kind of a different drummer sometimes. I felt like I didn't really need to explain anything to anybody. I think some guys may not have thought that was very cool. It didn't bother me." It was good enough for his wife, and at the end of the day, that was all that mattered, right?

Damn straight, Hutchinson concluded. He would go on to lead the very first flight of the Space Shuttle, STS-1, in April 1981.

Chuck Lewis was also new to the flight director ranks. He worked his first mission as an assistant flight director under Pete Frank on *Apollo 9* back in 1969, and while he had not necessarily disagreed with the assignments of Frank and Milt Windler, he would admit that he was maybe a little surprised.

When his turn finally came on *Apollo 17*, he was ready, if not just a tiny bit frightened. Or maybe *a lot* frightened. "Initially, I was scared to death," Lewis admitted. "I mean, really. You think of the responsibility you've got, and thoughts went through my mind like, 'I hate to make a fool of myself, because the whole world's listening to the flight director loop. You wonder, 'Why did they pick me?' You've got a lot of expectations to live up to." He got over it quickly, knowing that he just had to be himself and that he had to try to do the best job he possibly could. That was how he had gotten to that point, so why bother changing?

After *Apollo 17*, Lewis led the American flight control team in the Soviet control center for the Apollo-Soyuz Test Project. He later worked in the training branch before returning as a Space Shuttle flight director, including a handful that were controlled from the room on the third floor. The last year or two at NASA, he was enduring severe bouts with cluster headaches. "I had health issues, frankly, and they were getting worse," Lewis

23. The *Apollo 17* Lunar Module *Challenger* lifts off of the lunar surface. It took three tries, but Ed Fendell finally got the perfect shot on the final departure from the moon. Courtesy NASA.

said. "I had several series of headaches, and they were really bad. I lost a lot of time. I didn't think I had any choice. I had to get out of it." Lewis retired in 1994, and it was five years before he had another episode.

Apollo 17 set marks for the longest stay on the lunar surface; the longest single EVA and the most total time outside; most distance driven by the Rover, not to mention the farthest away from the LM one had ever traveled; heaviest load of rock samples collected; first night launch; and Schmitt was the first professional geologist to land on the moon. The list of superlatives was a long one, and it all boiled down to the fact that the best really had come last. It was just about as trouble-free as a mission could get, and if the worst that could be said was that Cernan and Schmitt ripped the fender off the Rover during their first moonwalk, so be it.

At the INCO console on the left end of the third row, INCO Ed Fendell had perfected the art of following moonwalking astronauts with his television as they moved this way and that on the surface. He found that there was a trick—as soon as one began to move, he would zoom out to capture a wider view as well as the direction the astronaut was headed. The one shot that had always eluded him was to follow the LM ascent stage upward on its journey from the surface, as far as the camera's eye could see. On *Apollo 15*, there was a problem with the motor that panned the camera upward and the LM almost immediately shot out of the frame, and on *16*, the Rover was awkwardly parked and Fendell was able to capture only a few seconds of the lunar blastoff.

For *Apollo 17*, however, he nailed it. As strange as it might seem, Fendell did not follow the action through a viewfinder like an ordinary cameraman would on Earth. He had fellow INCO Harley Weyer work out the timing of his moves beforehand, came up with a script, and hoped for the best. "The command for that camera to start the move up was sent two seconds before liftoff," Fendell said. "The other commands were all sent from the script. I did not look at the TV picture, because if I had, I would've screwed up." Fendell was already known as Captain Video, but *Apollo 17* sealed his legacy once and for all. "I became well known all over the world, this, that," he said. "I won a German Emmy award, all kinds of shit."

The Command Module *America* splashed down in the Pacific Ocean at 1:24:59 p.m. in Houston. The Apollo moon missions were over. The great space race between the United States and Soviet Union was over, and America had scored a decisive victory. Glynn Lunney saw the Cold War as a forty-four-year contest, divided into quarters and beginning with the end of World War II in 1945 and ending with the 1989 fall of the Berlin Wall.

The Soviets got out to an early lead with the launch of *Sputnik* and then stretched it out with the first human in space, Yuri Gagarin. By halftime, however, the game was over. "In our theater of competition, the space theater, we were surprised and engaged at the beginning of the second quarter," Lunney said. "We had won the day and the enemy left the field of competition at halftime. It went on for a long time after that in other fields, but not in ours."

Third-floor comm loops fell silent, its console monitors darkened. It would be nearly a full decade before another crewed spaceflight was flown out of that room, as control for all three Skylab missions, the Apollo-Soyuz Test Project, and the first four Space Shuttle missions shifted to the one a floor down.

The third-floor MOCR had played a major role in the grandest adventure mankind had ever known, but in January 1986, it was to be part of NASA's greatest tragedy to that point.

11. The End of an Era

The roses came into the control room like clockwork, targeted to arrive on the day of landing for each of the 110 Space Shuttle flights that came after the *Challenger* accident.

They were a gift from Mark and Terry Shelton, and their daughter MacKenzie. A tradition that lasted nearly a quarter of a century was born on the spur of the moment, on 3 October 1988, the day STS-26 came back to Earth following a four-day mission. Words could not describe what a relief it was to be flying again after the staggering loss of the STS-51L crew a little more than thirty-two months earlier, and that first bouquet was a small token of appreciation from Mark and his family.

But could they even get to the right place? Shelton had no connection to mission control, other than having been a space buff since a 1960s visit to MSC during his childhood. "I didn't actually decide to do it until the day the STS-26 mission was to land, and I didn't know that I even could get it done in time," said Shelton, a Dallas resident. "I called information to find a florist near the space center, and then I asked the florist if they could deliver roses to mission control. At first, they said they couldn't do it, but then they said they would try. But I had no idea if they actually made it or not."

They did, and they were noticed. They caught the eye of Milt Heflin, who was by then a flight director, almost as soon as he walked into the room. They were so different, not necessarily out of the place, but just unexpected. He walked over, read the card, and wondered who the Sheltons might be. Almost as soon as *Discovery* landed, Heflin called the Sheltons and confirmed that, yes, the flowers had in fact arrived and how much the control team appreciated them.

From that point on, all the way through STS-135 in July 2011, the flowers became almost as much a part of the décor as the rows of consoles and large displays at the front of the room. The arrangements included one flower for each shuttle crew member, and once the Russian *Mir* and International Space Station were operational, more for each spacefarer already on orbit. A single white rose stood in memory of those who had lost their lives.

If for some reason they were delayed in getting there, the control teams— they were not a superstitious lot, were not supposed to be at any rate— sometimes got a little antsy. "The Sheltons have sort of become a part of our team in mission control," Heflin said. "I almost look at them as kind of a distant back room, just like the technical support rooms located around the control center. It gives me a very warm feeling."

Heflin was not the only one who was impressed by the gesture. When Gene Kranz retired from NASA in February 1994, Shelton called to see if he could purchase a ticket to the celebration that was being held in his honor. When he went to pick them up in Kranz's office, however, he was not allowed to pay for them. That was not the half of it. Kranz apparently heard his voice, and bellowed to his secretary.

Is that Shelton?!?

For the next few minutes, Shelton visited with Kranz. It was a nice moment between a man who had been a driving force in mission control for so long, and Shelton, who appreciated him for that very fact.

Kranz's retirement was just the latest in a long line of changes during the evolution of NASA in general, and mission control in particular. No longer were the rooms on the second and third floors of Building 30 known as MOCRs. During the Space Shuttle era, each became a Flight Control Room, FCR for short and pronounced "FICK-er." A decade earlier, there had been an even more significant name change. The sprawling complex upon which the Mission Control Center was situated was renamed the Lyndon B. Johnson Space Center on 19 February 1973, in honor of the former president who had helped pull the strings to land the center in his home state and who had passed away less than a month before.

The MOCR was now the FCR, and it was JSC and not MSC. Apollo was over, and it was the Space Shuttle's turn at bat. In a sense, the bouquets sent by the Sheltons flight after flight, year after year, represented a sort of comforting constant in a world that had changed drastically since *Challenger* went down.

Jay Greene was old school, of that there could be no doubt.

The New Yorker was part of the invasion of new flight controllers into Houston, arriving on campus in 1965 having absolutely no idea where he was going, who he was going to work for or even what he was going to be doing. He settled in as a FIDO, and was on console when *Eagle* landed on the moon.

Like so many others, he never planned to become a flight director. That changed one day in 1983 when George Abbey walked into his office. "Throughout my career, George has come in on many occasions and said, 'Guess what you're going to do,'" Greene said. "I don't know if I was fired during some of those or not. I don't think so. But he came in one day, and he said, 'We need some more flight directors, and I want you to do that.' That wasn't a request, and so I moved down."

As Emerald Flight—he wanted green, the reason being obvious—Greene considered himself somewhere between Cliff Charlesworth and Glynn Lunney, his best friend among the flight directors. Charlesworth, he said, would not try to do somebody's job for them. If he could not trust somebody to do their own work, they would not be on his team for long. And Lunney—Lunney could sometimes drive people crazy, his mind working so fast that he could almost churn out action items faster than they could absorb, much less answer. Greene could sometimes be abrupt, but that did not stop him from sitting his first shift as flight director during the launch of STS-6 on 4 April 1983.

It was *Challenger*'s first flight, and Greene would be in the exact same spot for its last.

STS-51L was the thirty-fourth crewed flight to be flown out of the control room on the third floor, and it had seen its share of near-misses—*Gemini 8* and *Apollo 13*, in particular. It had also been through the glorious triumphs of *Apollo 8*, *Apollo 11*, and so many others. A crew had never been lost in flight, and there was no reason to believe it might happen any time soon. Such a thing was recognized as a possibility, of course, and that was just one of the things that made what happened here seem so incredible. Against all odds, astronauts always came home. Always.

Then came the morning of 28 January 1986.

Richard O. "Dick" Covey was Jay Greene's capcom that day, and while Greene was working his seventh launch, Covey was on his first.

An astronaut since 1978, he had flown in space once before, as the pilot of STS-51I in the late summer of 1985, just a few months before. He was concentrating on learning the ropes as a capcom, but he could not help but look around the room, see the plaques of missions that had been controlled out of this very room, and marvel if only for a fleeting moment.

Wow. There's some serious shit that happened in this room.

Serving as capcom was, for Covey, a plumb role. If he could not be flying himself, being as close to operations as possible was the next best thing. Working the console was not a guaranteed springboard into another flight assignment, but it certainly did not hurt. He found Greene to be "very direct. He was very demanding of his team, but he was a consummate operator. He never lost sight of, 'Okay, this is what we've got to do to get things done right and safely.'"

As closely as he worked with Greene and the rest of the FCR, Covey was even closer to the crew of Francis R. "Dick" Scobee, Michael J. Smith, Ronald E. McNair, Ellison S. Onizuka, Judith A. "Judy" Resnik, Gregory B. Jarvis, and S. Christa McAuliffe. His was the voice the crew would hear during its ascent, and each needed to know exactly how the other was going to react on the way to orbit.

That was on a professional level, and he knew all but Jarvis and McAuliffe very well personally, too. Covey and his family were closest to Onizuka, and had been ever since the two of them started in the air force's test pilot school together in 1974. Onizuka and Covey were members of the same 1978 astronaut candidate class and were joined by Scobee, McNair, and Resnik. When Covey flew a chase plane for STS-3 in March 1982, McNair was in the backseat. He knew Smith's family well, too.

Even Greene had gotten to know each of his shuttle crews reasonably well. It was such a departure from the days of Apollo that Glynn Lunney once advised him that maybe he was getting a little *too* close. Greene wanted to see his friends fly, and he was as frustrated as anybody over two launch postponements caused by a delay in the landing of STS-61C due to bad weather at KSC. That flight eventually landed at Edwards Air Force Base in California in the early-morning darkness on 18 January. Those delays were followed by two more scrubs, the first of which took place early in the countdown on 25 January because of an unacceptable weather forecast throughout the launch window.

One domino, and then another and another, seemed to fall two days later. The countdown was stopped at T-minus nine minutes because a handle refused to budge from the hatch, and that was followed by a problem with a portable drill. An hour and twenty minutes later, winds at the nearby landing strip were deemed too brisk. The liftoff would take place the next day. "We scrubbed because we had a government-supplied handle that went on the hatch of the vehicle, and they couldn't get it off," Greene said. "Had they gotten the handle off, 51L might not have happened. Somebody else might have had it happen to them, but not those guys. We also scrubbed on a beautifully clear day, based on a bad weather forecast."

What happened the next day was forever seared into the consciousness of the '80s generation. Their grandparents had Pearl Harbor, their parents the JFK assassination and Vietnam, and their children 9/11. If *Apollo 8* and *Apollo 11* were mankind's first grand triumphs to be broadcast live around the world, the *Challenger* accident was the first overwhelming global tragedy to be captured in such fashion.

Temperatures dropped into the low twenties overnight at the Cape, and there had been one hourlong delay in tanking and another to allow for melting of ice that had accumulated on the launch pad. Nevertheless, launch day started out as so many others had in Houston. Covey went through comm checks with the crew, which seemed very positive, ready to go. Ground crews and the Launch Control Center were worried about monitoring the ice. "There was discussion—not a lot of discussion—about the icing on the pad and the cold temps," Greene noted. "The shift prior to mine had worked the problem, and they concluded that as far as the orbiter was concerned, we had no concerns about the weather."

There were catastrophic problems lurking in the cold O-ring seal of the Solid Rocket Booster (SRB) on the right side of the huge, orange External Tank. A split second after ignition of the SRBs, black puffs of smoke appeared near a lower field joint. Just after 10:38 a.m. in Houston, data processing system (DPS) engineer Andrew F. Algate—responsible for the shuttle's onboard computers—noted *Challenger*'s departure from the launch pad.

Liftoff confirmed.

Greene offered a crisp reply.

Liftoff.

Moments later, FIDO Brian D. Perry was on the loop to Greene. *Challenger* had automatically rolled upside down to get onto its correct heading to orbit.

Good roll, Flight.

Rog, good roll.

Booster Jerry L. Borrer was next, reporting another programmed procedure to bring the thrust percentage of the shuttle's three main engines down as it passed through maximum aerodynamic pressure. Again, Greene shot back a quick acknowledgment.

Throttle down to ninety-four.

Ninety-four.

Another exchange between Borrer, Greene, and Perry took place as the main engines throttled down still more.

Three at sixty-five.

Sixty-five, FIDO.

T-del confirms throttles.

"T-del" was FCR-speak for "throttle delta time," and what Perry was saying was that the continued decrease was right on the money. So far, so good.

Thank you.

Ten seconds later, a small flame became visible on the right SRB. A growing blowtorch was eating into the side of the External Tank. Still unaware of the crisis that was beginning to unfold, Borrer gave another update.

Throttle up, three at 104.

This time, Greene was on the horn to Covey.

Capcom, go at throttle up.

Less than a second later, Covey relayed the information to Scobee.

Challenger, *go at throttle up.*

The veteran astronaut came right back.

Roger, go at throttle up.

The exchange became a part of history, as sadly iconic as few other lines had ever been, because of what happened next. *Challenger* was engulfed in the eruption of the External Tank, and did not explode so much as it was broken apart by the cruel aerodynamic forces to which it was suddenly exposed. Covey's attention was fixed on the limited amount of data he had available on his console monitor, and it was only after he caught the reaction of fellow astronaut Frederick D. "Fred" Gregory sitting just to his right that he looked up. A video camera caught Covey's reaction as he spotted the bulbous cloud, and it was one of complete shock. "Fred was watching the video when the explosion happened, and he said something like, 'Oh, look!'" Covey remembered. "My response wasn't to the initial explosion. It was to what clearly was something I didn't understand, but wasn't good."

Covey attempted no more calls to *Challenger*. "My logic was I don't need to make a call unless I've got something to tell them," Covey said. "If they called me, we could respond. If they were doing something up there that they could do, and we weren't going to be able to tell them to do something different, I didn't want to sit there and say, '*Challenger*, what's going on? What are you doing?' while they're sitting there trying to fight a fire. If they were able to do anything, I wanted to provide help."

Greene did not glance at a monitor located on the other side of fellow flight director Alan L. "Lee" Briscoe, who was seated to his left, until he spotted Gregory and Covey. Briscoe was watching a couple of displays himself, and he saw the failure IDs start to flash up on the one monitoring *Challenger*'s three main engines. He had never seen such a thing before, and he remembered making a quick remark to Greene.

Something's wrong.

"I kept hoping and thinking that maybe the shuttle was going to come on out of that cloud," Briscoe said years later. Thirteen seconds passed before Greene made his first call, and it was to Perry.

FIDO, trajectories.

Go ahead.

Trajectory, FIDO.

Flight, FIDO. Filters got discreting sources. We're go.

Discreting sources meant that radar was tracking multiple objects, and the information was not faulty. It was actually picking up pieces of debris as they began their long descent into the Atlantic Ocean, just off the Florida coast. The terrible news kept coming. Ground controller (GC) Norman R. Talbott got on the loop to Greene.

Flight, GC. We've had negative contact, loss of downlink.

Okay, all operators. Watch your data carefully.

Perry seemed to be holding out hope that all this would work itself out, that Scobee and Smith would somehow bring *Challenger* back.

Flight, FIDO. Till we get stuff back, he's on his cue card for abort modes.

The FIDO was not alone in his brief moment of optimism. "We got the report that they were tracking multiple pieces, and kept on hoping that some part of the vehicle would come out and everything would have a happy ending, because it was supposed to and it didn't," Greene said. The feeling was not misguided, either. Nothing like this had ever happened before within these hallowed walls. Many a crew had been lost in training, but this was not just another sim. This was real time, the harshest reality imaginable. Public affairs officer Stephen A. Nesbitt continued his commentary throughout, his voice never once betraying the heart that was almost surely about to beat out of his chest. If the final "throttle up" exchange between Covey and Scobee were the tragedy's most-often repeated lines, Nesbitt's narrative was a close second.

Flight controllers here are looking very carefully at the situation. Obviously a major malfunction.

Twenty-nine seconds later, Perry relayed a report from the range safety officer that confirmed what was already painfully clear.

Flight, FIDO.

Go ahead.

RSO reports vehicle exploded.

There was a brief pause.

Copy.

A few seconds later, rather than asking for and receiving information, Greene gave his first order.

GC, all operators. Contingency procedures in effect.

After nearly four more minutes of working with Perry to hustle recovery forces to the area, Greene gave another command.

Okay, everybody. Stay off the telephones, make sure you maintain all your data. Start pulling it together.

Several more seconds passed, and Greene began polling his team to see if anybody had seen anything unusual on their screens. First was Borrer.

Did you see anything?

Nothing, sir. I looked, and all the turbine temps were perfect, right on the prediction. All the redlines are in good shape.

Keith A. Reiley, who was responsible for *Challenger*'s Remote Manipulator Unit, Mechanical and Upper Stage Systems, was next.

We looked good, Flight.

EECOM? EECOM, *Flight.*

R. John Rector was on duty.

Flight, EECOM. *We looked normal.*

DPS?

All our data's normal, Flight.

Prop?

Propulsion officer Anthony J. Ceccacci answered.

Everything looked good, Flight.

GNC?

That was Jeffrey W. Bantle's role that day.

Flight, the roll maneuver looked fine, what we saw of it. We were on our way decreasing roll rate as we lost data.

Copy.

The worst day any of them had ever experienced at NASA was just beginning. "We secured the room, nobody in or out," Greene recalled. "We secured the communications. We got everybody getting their data together and writing incident reports. We worked for a long time trying to get the search and rescue guys to enter the area." For an hour after the accident, rescue forces were concerned that debris was still falling and were hesitant to send choppers into the area. Greene was able to admit that it was understandable, but at the time, he added, "It was disconcerting, that we could have had guys out in the water and they didn't want to get close to them."

Jay Greene never worked another flight in the FCR, and Gene Kranz's string of consecutive shuttle missions being on duty there would last only one more—the Return to Flight mission of STS-26. The two of them had shared an incredible moment in time sixteen and a half years earlier, when *Apollo 11* landed. Now, right here in the very same spot, it was almost as if the developing tragedy was sucking the air out of the room.

Kranz, in the room as the director of the Mission Operations Directorate, caught an eerily familiar flicker out of the corner of his eye. It was the explosion on a monitor that was close by, and he had seen enough failed launches during the early days of the space program to know exactly what had just happened. The only difference was the most major one of them all—this time, there was a crew on board. Almost as if by reflex, Kranz reached for a handbook that contained a series of checklists for what to

24. Flight director Jay Greene dejectedly holds his head in his hand following the breakup of the Space Shuttle *Challenger* on 28 January 1986. The third-floor control room had seen NASA's greatest moments and, now, its darkest. Courtesy NASA.

do in the event of an accident. He told Briscoe to make sure he had those pages handy, to make sure of everything that had to be secured.

Video shot that day in the FCR captured the reactions of both Greene and Kranz, and it is very nearly as heartbreaking to watch as the accident itself. "I looked at Jay, and the look on his face, it was something that you see only a few times in your life," Kranz said in the History Channel documentary *Beyond the Moon: Failure Is Not an Option 2*. If that was the case for Greene, the same could have been said of Kranz. There is no way to fully describe their expressions—the mixtures of shock, sadness, disbelief, and yes, maybe even anger. It would be hard to say how long Greene remained on duty that day. "That's pretty much what we did," he concluded. "Released the operators, was very calm, cool, and collected. Went home and completely broke down. It was a rough day."

Arnie Aldrich had wanted to become a flight director himself, and felt pretty good about his chances right up to the point when Kranz told him that it was not going to happen. Instead, Kranz said, Aldrich should expect a call from Chris Kraft. One thing led to another, and all of a sudden, Aldrich found himself in management. By 1975 he was already working on the Space Shuttle, and in the aftermath of the *Challenger* accident, he was director of the Space Transportation System at NASA headquarters in Washington. Playing such a key role in getting the agency back on its feet was the highlight of his career. "We made over 500 changes to the Space Shuttle, between *Challenger* and the next flight," Aldrich said. "I led all of that work, and I was pretty proud of it."

The Space Shuttle's fifth flight, STS-5 in mid-November 1982, was the first to be flown out of the third-floor control room, and there were a lot of familiar names on the manning lists. Don Puddy, Neil Hutchinson, and Chuck Lewis were now flight directors. Jim I'Anson was on console in the FCR, as were men like Bill Moon, Larry Strimple, Al Pennington, Will Presley, Gary Coen, Ken Russell, Gary Renick, Joe DeAtkine, Charlie Dumis, and Bill Boone. Ed Fendell was back, too.

Gerry Griffin was still around, and in a big way. He had always been the sort in search of some new challenge to attack, and when Apollo ended, he was not interested in continuing to work in the MOCR during Skylab. He headed to NASA headquarters, where he helped keep the Space Shuttle efforts on track from 1973 to 1976. After that, it was on to deputy center director roles at both Dryden Flight Research Center in California, where he worked under *Apollo 15* commander Dave Scott, and KSC. Another stint in Washington led to the ultimate job—director of JSC, his home for so long as a GNC and flight director. Griffin was only the third person ever in that prestigious position, after Bob Gilruth and his mentor, Chris Kraft.

He did not know it at the time, but Griffin got broken out of the pack in Washington, where he saw a side of the agency he had never seen before. He also came to view JSC in a slightly different light. "It was just another center," said Griffin, the JSC director from August 1982 to January 1986, just before the *Challenger* accident. "It was very important and a big center, but there were other centers around the country that mattered. Some of them didn't like JSC, because JSC was kind of like the New York Yankees—they always won, they got the ink, they had the astronauts, they had mission control. All of the guys out there in the hinterland that are building the hardware and developing technology so that those guys can do that don't get all that coverage."

The smart money might have been on Glynn Lunney to replace Kraft, and that is what Griffin thought as well. "A lot of people were assuming, and so did I, that it would go to Glynn," Griffin continued. "He was kind of a Kraft protégé, much like I was, except maybe even closer. I think the agency knew we were coming into a tough time, and I think they were looking for somebody that had a little broader experience. I'm just guessing, but I think that's why it came to me." Make no mistake about it, there were times during his tenure as center director that Griffin looked around and wondered to himself.

Good God, now I'm the director of the Johnson Space Center? How did I get here?

Tommy Holloway was another of the old guard who made the jump from Apollo to the Space Shuttle, and he was now a flight director as well, just like Puddy, Hutchinson, and Lewis. It was not a job he went after with guns ablaze, and in fact, he at first had serious reservations about it. Holloway was not a man who liked change—at all. He had worked in the Flight Crew Operations Directorate for the first fifteen or so years of his career, and that was absorbed by the Flight Operations Directorate shortly after the end of the Apollo lunar flights. Holloway kept right on doing what he was doing, and he was fine with that.

Another flight director was needed as the shuttle program was getting ramped up. Holloway got the nod, not that he wanted it. He was a branch chief where he was, and most other flight directors had come out of the Flight Control Division. "I haven't talked about this with a lot of people, except my wife," Holloway said. "Most people would never understand it, but I didn't know whether I wanted to be a flight director or not. I really struggled with whether I should accept the position or not, primarily because it's change. I am a person that is slow to change." He took on the role of flight director, but started out slowly.

So began a career pathway that led to some lofty positions—chief of the Flight Director Office; director of the Shuttle-*Mir* effort with the Russians; and manager of both the Space Shuttle and International Space Station programs. "In retrospect, any rational person wouldn't have thought about that over ten microseconds," Holloway admitted. "I was at the right place at the right time. I would've missed all that if I hadn't come to my senses."

Along with the Apollo veterans who were still around, younger controllers were taking their places in the FCR as well. None were more eager than the women who were working in the control room. Anne L. Accola worked in MPAD during the Apollo era and trained at one point to become a flight controller, while Frances M. "Poppy" Northcutt and Parrish N. Hirasaki had worked in the SSRs. Northcutt was featured in an ad for her employer, and the headline read rather suggestively, "TRW's Poppy Northcutt keeps bringing astronauts home." A 28 April 1970 article in Fredericksburg, Virginia's *Free Lance-Star* about her contributions to the flight of *Apollo 13* ran a similar headline, except this one called her a "girl."

The first couple of paragraphs were a far cry from the politically correct climate of the next century. "A former beauty contestant whose name has been linked romantically with Astronaut John Swigert Jr., played a key role in bringing the *Apollo 13* crew home safely," wrote reporter Will McNutt. "Bachelor girl Poppy Northcutt, 26, a tall, winsome blonde mathematician, was the only female working inside the Mission Control Center during the *Apollo 13* emergency." The story went on to detail the fact that Northcutt had no plans for marriage, dished more on her supposed romance with Swigert—there was none, according to the writer—and how she was a "popular, fun-loving girl" who liked to "swim, dance, ski or sail. She used to wear glasses, but switched to contact lenses. She also bleaches her hair."

Whether on the second floor of the MCC or the third, women began appearing in NASA control rooms, front and center. There was Carolyn L. Huntoon, a medical experiments officer for *Skylab 4* who later became JSC's director; Sharon R. Tilton and Ellen L. Schulman, surgeons; Lizabeth H. "Betsy" Cheshire, computer command; Anngienetta R. "Angie" Johnson, payloads, the first female African American flight controller; Linda G. Horowitz, aerodynamics officer; and Jenny Howard, booster, to name but a few. The gender barrier had been broken down, and it had been broken down for good.

FAO Marianne J. Dyson eventually became an award-winning children's author and speaker, and also wrote the manuscript for a memoir titled *Fire in Mission Control: The Story of a Woman Flight Controller.* She had been keen on the space program since the first grade, when she and virtually every other person in the country watched in amazement as John Glenn became the first American to orbit the earth. The Canton, Ohio, native loved all things space even more than her other great passion—horses. She wrote a massive sixty-page paper titled "The Apollo Program" for an eighth-grade English class, and when her father brought home posters of Neil Armstrong and Buzz Aldrin, they shared space on her bedroom wall with one featuring Peter Tork of the Monkees. There were no female astronauts at the time, but when *Apollo 13* proved to the world that flight controllers could be heroes as well, that became her goal. "I loved how the men in mission control had used their knowledge of space and spacecraft to find a way to rescue the astronauts," Dyson wrote. "If women couldn't be astronauts, maybe I could be part of the team that solved problems for them?"

Hired as a programmer and analyst in the Flight Activities Branch, she started work at JSC in January 1979. John Wegener had worked the control console during Apollo, and when he took her on a tour of the room, it seemed much smaller than it had appeared on television. As they made their way up the rows, they eventually came to the FAO console. She had a question, even if she did not actually ask it of Wegener.

Would I really get the chance to sit here someday?

For her, there were no horror stories of sexual harassment as she started her journey with the agency. Only one man asked her out, but when she explained that she was already engaged and planning to get married in just a couple of months, he quickly gave up. She was eventually recruited to serve on the NASA speaker's bureau as "the substitute woman astronaut speaker"—if some group somewhere wanted a woman astronaut at its event and one was not available, Dyson got the nod.

That is not to say that it was always smooth sailing for Dyson or her fellow female FAOs, because it was not. When the lead positions for STS-5 through STS-8 showed up in her inbox, she did not like what she was seeing.

This can't be right.

Every female lead FAO had been removed from the schedule and replaced with a male counterpart. She and two other women issued an informal complaint of discrimination, because, as she wrote, "we owed it to the women coming after us to speak up, even though we were all nervous about what it might cost us personally." They met with their directorate chief, who promised to review the matter. After some frank discussions, Dyson concluded, "Finally came a sort of apology for the 'insensitive' way the reassignments had been handled. The three of us had obviously been caught by surprise, and without the benefit of discussions with our managers ahead of time,

25. Marianne Dyson was one of the first female flight controllers to work a console in the hallowed halls of mission control. Courtesy NASA.

we'd drawn conclusions based on incomplete information. In the future, care would be taken to inform employees privately if changes could impact the perceived standing of women in the organization. In summary, better communications would solve all our problems."

Michele Brekke became the first woman to be named as a flight director in 1985, but in the downtime after *Challenger*, she moved on to another position before STS-26 took NASA back to orbit. It would be another seven years before Linda Ham became the first of her gender to actually serve as a flight director, during STS-45 in the early spring of 1992.

Tommy Holloway had taken his turn at the FAO console on the third floor during a total of nine Apollo flights—including *Apollo 8*, *Apollo 9*, *Apollo 13*, and each of the six lunar landings. He spent many an hour in the room during simulations and flights, but while Holloway initially considered it just another control room, STS-5 was not just another flight. After just four tests, the Space Shuttle was for the first time officially considered fully operational and for the first time carried a crew of more than two people. On board were CDR Vance Brand, PLT Robert F. Overmyer, and mission specialists Joe Allen and William B. "Bill" Lenoir, and they deployed two commercial communications satellites during their five-day journey.

Those went according to plan, but the first EVA based from the Space Shuttle by Allen and Lenoir scheduled for the third day of the flight did not. First, Lenoir was dealing with space sickness, and what Holloway remembered most about the flight—more than any other issue faced by the FCR during the mission—were the briefings with the press about it. If they wanted to maintain a good relationship with the astronaut corps, the surgeons had learned a long time before not to show all their cards when it came to crew health. If that meant being a little cagey with the media about Lenoir's condition, that was the way it was going to be. "That's the most vivid thing I remember about the whole flight, the dialogue with the press," Holloway said. "One of those press guys accused us of lying to them, which irritated me." As lead flight director, the buck stopped with Holloway and he eventually put the issue to rest in what he called "plain Arkansas-ese."

Yes, Lenoir was not feeling well, but no, it would not impact the mission other than to delay the EVA by a day. That was before the suit issues cropped up. Allen's suit fan refused to work despite all kinds of attempted workarounds, and then Lenoir's suit would not fully regulate. The call was Holloway's, and he made it. "I canceled the EVA," he said. "Back in those days at least, the flight director had almost unilateral authority in making those kinds of decisions, although the program and mission operations management participated. But I canceled the EVA, and it was solely due to the problems with the suits."

At 8:50 p.m. in Houston on 13 November, a near disaster struck during the crew's sleep shift when a failure in an electrical cable on the first floor caused it to heat up and short out. Monitors turned to snow, and Dyson remembered lights in the room flickering off and the emergency lights coming on and casting an eerie glow. Flight director Gary Coen, she continued, put the room on lockdown.

An onboard computer alarm would have awakened the crew midway through its sleep period if the FCR team could not refresh *Columbia*'s state vector—the vehicle's true position and velocity at the time. Coen did not want to disturb the resting astronauts, but with no way to send commands to the spacecraft due to the power outage, it was impossible to clear the command. Robert E. "Bob" Castle, the sleep shift INCO, helped work on a code to pass along to a tracking station so that it could send up the workaround. What might happen if there was even a small typo in the code?

Within an hour and fifteen minutes, however, primary control was restored and Castle was able to in effect hit the snooze button. "I don't know if Gary would have actually done this, but we worked to give him the option," Castle said. "Folks worked feverishly and got the system back up in time for me to clear the SPC alarm without having to have the ground site do it."

Two of the best-known of the fourteen missions controlled out of the third-floor FCR before the *Challenger* accident were STS-7 in June 1983 and STS-41B in February 1984. Sally K. Ride was a member of STS-7's five-person crew, but while she was the first American woman in space, that was an issue for public affairs to sort out. The fact that a woman was on board the spacecraft was of little consequence to how the flight was actually monitored in the FCR. "Sally was a very capable individual," said Tommy Holloway, again serving as lead flight director on STS-7. "I think Bob Crippen (the flight's commander) treated her as she should've been, as just one of the crew members."

Although Bruce McCandless talked Neil Armstrong and Buzz Aldrin down *Eagle*'s ladder and across the lunar surface during the historic *Apollo 11* EVA, it was nearly fifteen more years before his own first spaceflight on STS-41B in February 1984. He made the most of his rookie trip to orbit and became the first astronaut to test the Manned Maneuvering Unit untethered backpack, followed soon by crewmate Robert L. "Bob" Stewart.

Hoot Gibson's series of photographs of McCandless's trek are among the most iconic of the Space Shuttle era, and the team behind the development of the MMU—NASA's Charles E. "Ed" Whitsett Jr. and Walter W. "Bill" Bollendonk of Martin Marietta—was awarded the National Aeronautics Association's prestigious Collier Trophy for 1984. Back in the third-floor FCR, EVA capcom Jerry L. Ross was watching it all very closely. As he began to power his way out of *Challenger*'s cargo bay, McCandless asked Ross to relay a message for him.

Jerry, pass to Ed Whitsett that we sure have a nice flying machine here.

Ross, who was still nearly two years away from the first of his record-setting seven Space Shuttle flights, was a junior member of the EVA team and had helped McCandless with the development of the MMU. They had flown to Denver together a few times to test the backpack in Martin Marietta's six degrees of freedom simulator, both in shirtsleeves and fully outfitted in spacesuits.

Yes, sir, Bruce. It looks like a real friendly machine, real solid, real stable, and it looks like you did a good job with all that engineering work over those years, as well as Ed and the rest of the crew.

Ross had been mesmerized by the MOCR as a young adult, when he was taking the very first steps that would eventually take him to orbit. He watched as much television coverage of the Apollo missions as he possibly could, up to and including static shots of the control room. He hoped to work anywhere within the space program and contribute in some small way. After being assigned to the Payloads Operation Division as a payload officer and flight controller in February 1979, he was named to the astronaut office in May of the following year.

Ross was on his way.

During one of his first flights as capcom, Ross pushed back from the console as the shuttle passed between tracking stations. That created a minutes-long loss of signal to and from the spacecraft, giving controllers a short break. A thought crossed Ross's mind as he looked around the room.

I always thought this would be a neat thing to do, and I was right.

McCandless was the acknowledged leader in the astronaut office during development of the MMU, that much was certain. "That was a big plum," Ross said. "I think it was one that was well deserved. Bruce was by far the most senior of the people that flew any of those missions. He'd been there since the Apollo era, and he had by far invested more time and effort in getting the hardware developed to where it was ready to go fly. I don't think there was a whole lot of doubt as to who was going to get the chance to go do that." Still, it was hard for Ross to remain on the ground and watch as both McCandless and Stewart took the MMU out for a spin during STS-41B. That was nothing against either of his fellow astronauts. "I would've traded places with everybody that flew," Ross quipped. "Any time the shuttle left the ground without me, I wasn't too happy about it."

The MMU flew just three times before *Challenger* fell so tragically back to Earth, and afterward, there were essentially no jobs left for it to do.

Robert M. "Rob" Kelso was as hooked on the space program as any kid ever had been and from about 1966 or so during the Gemini era, the native of the Houston-Galveston area in southeast Texas knew that it was what he wanted to do with his life.

He did reports on every space-related book he could get his hands on, and every chance he got, bugged his parents to bring him the quick fifteen minutes from their home over to MSC for tours. When a flight was over and it was time to debut its highlight film, Kelso was there. He bought mission slides from the gift shop. As a Boy Scout, he earned his Space Exploration merit badge. A senior manager at NASA sent Kelso and a couple of others who signed up for the program "jillions" of books and pictures and met with the small group every couple of weeks. On one behind-the-scenes tour, Kelso met none other than Jim Lovell and Jerry Carr and toured the vacuum chambers where the Apollo Command and Lunar Modules were tested.

With every step, he was falling more and more in love with the idea of working there. His senior year in high school, the center announced its junior co-op work study program, in which those who took part would go to school a semester and then work at MSC a semester. The only problem was that it was for minority candidates. He and his high school counselor came up with a solution. "It would never fly today, but I wanted this so bad, my counselor put on there, 'Rob has red hair, and that classifies him as a minority in some sense,'" Kelso remembered. That got Kelso's foot in the door, and he went to work in the Space Environment Simulation Laboratory.

Austin College in Sherman, Texas, did not have a co-op program, so one was invented for him. When he graduated, Kelso already had three and a half years of government service to his credit and a job offer to boot. He went to work for Maxime A. "Max" Faget, the legendary NASA spacecraft designer. In 1978 he got put on a recruiting list for the control room. He had dreamed of just such a job ever since watching from the viewing room and seeing controllers go about their business in the second-floor control room during Skylab. "I was just so fascinated," Kelso said. "I would spend hours in there, just watching. I thought it was one of the most beautiful things I had ever seen. It really did have this aura about it."

Faget let him off the hook, but with a caveat. He could go, but only after giving Faget a year's time on the job. After that, if Kelso still wanted to be a flight controller, he could go be a flight controller with no questions asked. "Max remembered that," Kelso said. "There was no contract. There was no memo or anything. It was a handshake, but that guy had such integrity. He said, 'I hate to see you go, but I know that's what you want to do.'"

Kelso worked his way into the SSR for the flight of STS-1, and he never looked back. The very next flight, he was training as the payloads officer in the front room, and on STS-3, the console was his during the entry shift under flight director Don Puddy. The more his career progressed, the happier and more satisfied he became. Reality was every bit as good as he had imagined working at JSC would be. The controllers who were mentoring the next generation of flight controllers early in the Space Shuttle era were the controllers who had worked the glory years of Apollo.

Kelso got one of his first big lessons when he first encountered Gene Kranz in the hallway on a Friday leading into a three-day weekend. The up-and-coming flight controller was both in awe and terrified.

This was, after all, Gene Kranz—tough guy of *Apollo 11* and *Apollo 13* fame, complete with his signature crew cut. Somehow, Kelso worked up the courage to speak.

Mr. Kranz, you got a big weekend planned?

Kranz shot a glance at Kelso.

Son, I'll start thinking about that at five o'clock this afternoon.

Listen close, and it is almost possible to still hear the air rushing out of the deflated Kelso. "I just stood there with my mouth open, just shrinking," Kelso remembered. "He got in the elevator, the door shut, and I just stood there. That was my first exposure to Gene."

Round One might have gone to Kranz, but Kelso got up off the canvas and dusted himself off. Working on Saturdays was not a problem, because that was when there was time to go through mail, write a few memos, and do some study. That was the way Chris Kraft and Kranz had done it, so that was the approach Rob Kelso was going to take as well.

He got to know Kranz better, too. Wednesday nights were the best, because that was when Kranz would sometimes take new controllers along with his family over to the local Knights of Columbus hall for a strip steak, baked potato, salad, tea, and a dessert, all for just a few bucks. "I think he figured that this way, us young engineers would get at least one good meal a week," Kelso said with a hearty laugh.

Better yet, Kranz would bring the party to his house, where he might share a story or two from his long and illustrious career. Kelso soaked in every word. "This went on for several years," he said. "Looking back on it, I realized what he was doing was not telling us just a bunch of good war stories, which is what they were. But it wasn't just to pass on stories. He was passing on values and heritage. He was passing on to us lessons learned. He was passing on culture to us that would serve us as we went into the shuttle program."

One day from out of the blue, Kelso was called to his boss's office. He wanted Kelso to work on a Department of Defense (DoD) payload, and there was no other way to put it. Kelso did not want to do it. The people who worked on those kinds of things always seemed to be behind closed doors, never to be seen again, out of sight and out of mind, it seemed, to management. They just disappeared. "To this day," Kelso concluded, "there's probably heel marks still on that floor where they drug me down the hallway to the DoD office."

Although Kelso took the job against his will, he was put in charge of reworking the operational issues of the Inertial Upper Stage (IUS) rocket used to deploy satellites. The planetary probes deployed by the shuttle used the IUS, and so did the Tracking and Data Relay Satellite (TDRS) and some of the DoD's payloads. He wound up behind those closed doors, responsible for the classified payload deployed during the January 1985 flight of STS-51C.

Virtually *everything* changed in the room due to what took place on orbit during STS-51C and the seven other DoD flights that were controlled from the third-floor FCR. After the *Challenger* accident, each of the room's six remaining flights was either wholly or partially classified. They were simulated and flown in what was known as "control mode"—basically anything that could be secured, was. The eyes of the world had once been on this very room, but that was no longer the case.

Holloway was lead flight director for the mission, and afterward was presented with a medal for his role. He got in line with a few others who were being honored, and the director of the Central Intelligence Agency hung the award around his neck. Holloway took a few more steps, at which point a military official promptly reclaimed the medal, put it back in its box, and then placed it in a safe. The recognition could not be recognized, because it too was classified.

Several years passed before he received a package at home. "I came home from work one day, and my wife said, 'What in the world is this?'" Holloway said. "This little box showed up. They didn't declassify what the flight was about, but they had declassified the fact that I got the medal. They had mailed it to me."

The journey of STS-27, another DoD operation, began at 8:30 a.m. in Houston on 2 December 1988. A little less than three full years had passed since the loss of *Challenger*, and while no one could possibly have known it at the time, an eerie link to NASA's second fatal crewed spaceflight was about to take place. As early as twenty-seven seconds into the flight, commander Hoot Gibson was noticing that he could see some sort of white material hitting the windows. At least one strike left a streak on the first window to the left of the commander's seat that was visible throughout the rest of the flight. Approximately eight-five seconds after leaving the pad, ablative material from the nose cap of the right SRB broke off and struck *Atlantis*. What Gibson and the rest of the crew, which also included pilot Guy S. Gardner and mission specialists Richard M. "Mike" Mullane, Jerry Ross, and William M. "Bill" Shepherd, could not yet see was the extensive damage done to the shuttle by the debris.

After checking launch footage and confirming that something had indeed struck the spacecraft after breaking free from the SRB, the FCR asked Mullane to use a video camera on the tip of *Atlantis*'s robotic arm to check the orbiter's belly. There were at least two dozen impact areas, and those were just the spots that Mullane and the rest of the crew could see on their onboard monitor. They could also look out the rear windows on the flight deck and clearly spot damage on the right Orbital Maneuvering System pod.

Houston, we're seeing a lot of damage. It looks as if one tile is completely missing.

Frank L. Culbertson, the capcom on duty, eventually told the crew not to worry about the strikes.

We've looked at the images and mechanical says it's not a problem. The damage isn't severe.

Gibson chimed in.

Houston, Mike is right. We're seeing a lot of damage.

Again, the capcom's response was basically the same.

Hoot, they've looked at it and they've determined that it's not any worse than what we've seen on other flights.

There would be plenty of speculation about what the ground knew, and when it knew what. There were no pictures or television being downlinked during the secretive mission, and encrypted video frames were transmitted at the rate of maybe one every three seconds or so. "I can remember at one time using the arm to look at whatever tile damage we could see on the vehicle," said Lee Briscoe, STS-27's Orbit 1 and reentry flight director. "It was so bad, you couldn't really see much of anything. I don't actually remember a whole great big lot of discussion during the flight that there was a lot of damage, how bad it was. If that had been something brought up as a terrible, terrible concern for entry, I would've known about it. I just don't know if everybody knew how bad the damage was during the flight or not."

The severity of the situation became all too clear as soon as *Atlantis* came to a stop at Edwards Air Force Base in California on 6 December. A total of 707 damage sites were found, of which 644 were on the lower surface and mostly on the right side. Nearly 300 of the strikes were more than an inch in size, and one complete tile on the forward right fuselage over an antenna cover was missing altogether. It was by far the most damage ever sustained by a vehicle that somehow managed to land safely.

A report released just two months later detailed the incident, and its eighth finding began innocently enough. "It is apparent that all shuttle elements have made great progress in eliminating debris sources as evidenced by comparing early and recent ascent photography," it read. Knowing what was to come on that January day in 2003, the very next sentence seemed nothing short of chilling. "There remains other areas for product improvements that could further reduce debris potential, particularly in the External Tank," the report continued, before adding in Finding 10, as if to spell it out, "It is the team's view that there is a general lack of awareness on the orbiter tile susceptibility to damage by debris." That particular finding concluded, "It is essential that all involved employees, both government and contractor, understand that loose objects or materials coming off the elements will cause tile damage at the speed encountered during ascent."

Still, the report recommended no delay whatsoever in flying STS-29, the next mission on the manifest. Fourteen years, one month, and eleven days after STS-27 landed, the flight of STS-107 left Earth. While *Atlantis* had avoided disaster following a debris strike all those years in the past, *Columbia* did not.

NASA kept right on flying and so did the DoD missions for the time being. Rob Kelso worked on interfacing the DoD payloads with the shuttle, flight rules, malfunction procedures, and so forth, all behind a closed door with a cipher lock to boot. There was a safe in the room, and if Kelso was going to work on any sort of classified material, he had to log in what time he opened the safe and what time he put it back. Making a quick trip out of the room meant putting it right back in the safe. If somebody came into the room, he either asked them to leave or covered up his work. Folders for carrying the documents featured a huge red "Classified" sticker. A Secured Telephone Unit (STU) was a classified phone with an encryption key that was used for hush-hush conversations.

It took some effort to even get into the third-floor FCR. Pre-approved clearance, special badging, pass codes—name it, and it was necessary to enter. Doors were locked well before simulations, and voice communications between the control room and the crew in the simulator were encrypted. Despite his initial reluctance, Kelso came to love every moment of his work on the DoD missions. "That was probably the best time in my whole career," said Kelso, who worked his first shift as a flight director during STS-33 in November 1989. "I loved those things. It just gave me a great pride in being an American, red, white, and blue, and knowing we were doing something very significant for the country."

There were times early in Kelso's career as a flight director when he got so nervous coming up on some big event—say launch or a satellite deployment—that he would excuse himself, head to the restroom, and maybe even throw up. Yet once he was back behind his console with his headset plugged in, it was if he was a part of the building. The jitters went away, and they went away instantly. "I was a nervous wreck, going to the potty, and all that before," Kelso admitted. "But once I walked in that door and I plugged into that console to take charge of the room and the mission, all that went away. You were now focused, locked in, and a part of this whole operation. You were part of that building, like you plugged in a toaster."

It is likely no one outside a very limited circle would ever know for sure just how significant the DoD flights were, and that was despite the fact that STS-33 astronaut John E. Blaha once told a crowd in Australia that the mission had ended the Cold War. Not only that, but Kelso has also hinted that STS-36 might have been *the* most important Space Shuttle mission ever flown. Only the first servicing mission to the flawed Hubble Space Telescope could possibly touch it, Kelso added.

Those kinds of statements were tantalizing and dramatic, but that was all, because both flights were DoD flights. On STS-36, for instance, Kelso estimated that there were fewer than ten people in all of NASA outside the crew who had full access to the mission. "You knew you did some incredibly important things, but you can't go tell anybody," Kelso said. "You can't go tell your family. You can't tell other managers."

A plaque he received during an anniversary get-together for STS-36 put it best, and gave him a sense of peace about his role in it all.

May you find silent satisfaction in that which is known only to an unheralded few.

The December 1992 flight of STS-53 was the final mission to be controlled out of the third-floor control room. After deploying its classified payload on the first day of the weeklong flight, the rest of the flight was unclassified. Intelligence satellites would be forevermore deployed by unmanned rockets, and the reason was economics—it was cheaper to risk blowing one up on the launch pad than to fly on the Space Shuttle.

Construction on a five-story extension to the Mission Control Center known as 30 South began earlier in 1992, and eventually it housed control rooms designated Red, White, and Blue. Kelso had the distinction of being the lead for the last flight out of the third-floor FCR, and he was also lead for STS-70 in July 1995, the first to be controlled from the new White FCR. Gone were the lighted console push buttons that Kelso could use to warm his fingers, replaced by newfangled touchscreen technology. Gone, too, was the old room's traditional tiered configuration. Each row of consoles was located on the same level, sometimes giving the room the appearance of a high-tech cubicle farm.

Kelso prided himself on being the first one in the control room for a shift, and he had a routine to get there. He would have himself a hearty breakfast, get mentally ready, and then walk over as if heading onto the playing field for some big game. He had an American flag present, always. He would have his flight data files in order, his displays and comm loops set up just so. He still came into the White FCR early, but it did not seem the same to be booting up a computer and placing his telemetry display windows where he wanted them.

Kelso missed his former haunt. "I loved the old FCRs—the old MOCRs—better," he said. "To me, I had a better sense of what was going on in that room. I just loved that room. There was better technology over in the new building, but it wasn't the same for me. There was that sense of history, almost like it was a cathedral or a religious feeling from being in that room."

Amen.

12. Legacy

Jerry Bostick was working late, as always.

When there was a flight to be flown or a sim to be simmed, the MOCR was almost always the best place to find Bostick or any of the others who showed that same kind of single-minded focus and dedication to their job. There was a television station over in Nassau Bay that carried a live television feed from the MOCR during flights, and one night, his son Michael spotted him. The young man promptly informed his mom Linda that there would be no need to fix Bostick a plate for dinner—he had seen his dad eating a hot dog at his console. It was not the first time, and it would not be the last, that Bostick had grabbed something quick to eat, nutritious or not, tasty or not, and gone right back to work in the Trench.

Bostick had a life before 20 July 1969, and he had another afterward. That was the way he gauged events for decades, even well into his seventies, by whether they took place before or after Neil and Buzz landed on the moon.

As proud as he was of his country for putting together such an ambitious program and seeing it through to fruition, as proud as he was of his and his friends' roles, he had all but missed the 1960s. Eight full years of his life had been dedicated to this vision, and it was, he said, to the detriment of his family. The hot dog incident was not an isolated one, and he had missed events bigger than just a meal. He was in the MOCR when Frank Borman, Jim Lovell, and Bill Anders read the Genesis story, and while it was one of the most memorable moments of his life, the fact remained that he was not with Linda, Michael, and daughter Kristi on Christmas Eve that year.

Apollo 11 represented a peak in both his career and his life. President Kennedy's deadline had been met with room to spare, the impossible achieved, but a troubling thought kept nagging at him. Jerry Bostick was barely a month past his thirtieth birthday, and now that he had reached the mountaintop, the only direction he could possibly go was downward. The questions piled up, one on top of another.

What is next? What do we do for an encore? What am I supposed to do with the rest of my life? Am I going to be content working here in the MOCR?

Work was not going to suffer, because Bostick could not begin to imagine giving it anything less than his very best. Still, his life was changing. He had sported a crew cut for as long as he could remember, but he began to let his hair grow long and even went so far as to give a mustache and beard a try. He wore "hippie" clothes—bell-bottom pants, paisley shirts, and wide, white belts. He got himself the 1968 Corvette he had always wanted, not that it worked all that well.

The biggest change was the most painful of all. In 1972 Bostick moved out of his house and into an apartment near the Houston space center. "It makes no sense now and it didn't help anything then," Bostick wrote in an unpublished manuscript. "Mike and Kristi visited me there, but I deeply missed being with them at home. The hardest part was spending Christmas alone. I didn't know what the answer was, but being separated from Linda and the kids wasn't it."

Terry Watson was at a similar professional crossroads. The Apollo-Soyuz Test Project was over, and NASA was not going to be flying for several more years. He did not particularly care for the weather in Houston, so he turned in his resignation. He traveled around the country, visiting family and friends and unwinding. "After working in mission control and after working the Apollo program, especially right out of college, it's a real hard act to follow," Watson admitted. "There were a number of years of soul searching of what do you do in life? What's meaningful?"

Watson helped a buddy in California with his automotive business. He went back to Texas for a bit, then hit the East Coast. He got the opportunity to take care of a sailboat in the Bahamas for a few months, sailing it down from Annapolis, Maryland, and back again. Freelance photography? He did that, too. He landed at the Jet Propulsion Laboratory in Pasadena, transferred to Goddard for a few months, went back to southern California, and eventually landed a job at TRW.

As it was for Jerry Bostick, *Apollo 11* was also a turning point for Bob Carlton. Up until then, it was nothing unusual, nothing out of the ordinary at all for him to be at the Mission Control Center as late as midnight or 1 a.m. He came home dog tired, got four or five hours of sleep, and then trudged back out the door to start the routine all over again.

He saw daughters Deborah, Pamela, and Mary Ellen for maybe thirty minutes over breakfast, and that was it. It was only after he gave up his spot at the control console after *Apollo 11* that Carlton's tensions eased. He fully understood and appreciated being able to play a part in one of the most stunning achievements his country ever accomplished, but it came with a price. "It robbed them of their father for several years," said Carlton, his voice somber. "If I had it to do over again, I'd never do it. The impact to my family, as far as I'm concerned, was just not worth it. My children lost their daddy for the key part of their life growing up." His wife, Bettye Jo, "hung in there" with him, and they remained married until her passing in 2004.

As difficult as it must have been for Carlton to think that he had not been a good father to his children, middle daughter Pamela Womack insisted that her childhood was not nearly as harsh as her father seemed to think it was. She was hurtling headlong into her teen years by the time the late 1960s rolled around, as self-absorbed as anybody might be during that sometimes turbulent phase in life.

Her dad was spending a lot of time at work, and there were times when it was difficult to dial down that intensity once he did make it back home. More than once, he startled his girls' friends when they called by snatching up the phone and barking, "Go!" He was, to put it lightly, tightly strung. Pamela came to understand that it was a phase just like her own adolescence, and it lasted only about three years as the march continued to Tranquility Base.

She was admittedly "clueless" about what Carlton was doing—lots of kids had fathers who were involved in the space program, and the astronauts were just guys that Carlton happened to talk about on a first-name basis. The flights were always on television, at least the early ones, so that was really no big deal, either.

Ho hum, another mission.

Pamela visited the National Air and Space Museum in her mid- to late twenties, and it was then that what Carlton had helped accomplish finally sank in. The sacrifice of the three years when her father was either gone from home, or cranky when he was there, turned out to be worth it. "During all the years before and after, he was a model and devoted dad who took us places and did things with us and generally put a lot of himself into maintaining a quality relationship," said Womack, a professor in the Lone Star College System in Texas. "I understood that it was just situational and was not emotionally scarred by it." Of course, Pamela added, she was her dad's favorite. But do not mention anything to her sisters, she cautioned, because Deborah and Mary Ellen were each under the "illusion" that *they* were his favorites.

Carlton and Merlin Merritt both exercised their faith in various ways during their post-NASA careers. Carlton researched and wrote an absolutely massive book of more than seven hundred pages titled *The Entire Endtime Sequence as Foretold by Jesus Christ*. Merritt, on the other hand, taught Christian education and math courses at Baptist University of the Americas in San Antonio for nearly a decade. He had seen several things take place during the flight of *Apollo 13* that he simply could not ascribe to coincidence. "There were things like a hurricane over the landing area that just miraculously moved out of the way, that even the weather people couldn't explain," Merritt said. "The ability for us to prolong the electrical power in the Lunar Module batteries and the oxygen supply was miraculous."

Some MOCR marriages crumbled, but plenty were able to withstand the rigors of NASA's heyday. Chris and Betty Anne Kraft; Glynn and Marilyn Lunney; Gene and Marta Kranz; Milt and Betty Windler; Gerry and Sandy Griffin; Arnie and Ellie Aldrich; John and Cheryl Aaron all stayed the course, and the list could go on. Rod Loe searched for just the right words to describe what it had meant to him to have had the support of wife Tina for more than half a century of marriage. She and the other MOCR wives were "a special brand of ladies" who held down the fort at home while their husbands were off doing the "man on the moon" thing.

It was a fact that had not been lost on MSC director Bob Gilruth, who sent out tokens of NASA's appreciation to several spouses a few weeks after the *Apollo 11* landing. Tina Loe received one of the packages. Its contents were framed and hung on the wall of their Houston-area home, where they remained for more than forty-five years. There was plenty of NASA "crap" on the walls of their game room, but this was something different, something special. Dated 14 August 1969, Gilruth's brief note was eloquent in its sincerity.

The successful landing of man on the moon and his safe return to Earth is truly one of the most historic accomplishments of this decade. I am sure you are justifiably proud of the part your husband played in this great national achievement. I am well aware of the personal contributions which the families of our team have made. With this in mind, I am enclosing a memento of the lunar landing which I wanted you to have. Please accept my thanks for the magnificent support that you, other wives, and families have given our Apollo program.

The letter was accompanied by a replica of the plaque that was attached to the front leg of *Eagle*'s descent stage, and read by Armstrong during the EVA.

Here men from the planet Earth first set foot upon the moon July 1969, A.D. We came in peace for all mankind.

Another note, this one addressed to Loe, meant every bit as much to the former EECOM. His son Greg wrote a brief article for JSC's *The Space Center Roundup* for *Apollo 11*'s twentieth anniversary, and not knowing if it would get printed or not, shared a copy with his father. Greg remembered the two of them spending time together, often at the Singin' Wheel, and learning for hours on end how to play shuffleboard with his dad's coworkers. He was one of them, Greg said, a member of the "Inner Circle."

That, though, was not the focus of the younger Loe's story. One day in May 1969, the two of them went in search of Mother's Day flowers for Tina. There was a florist near MSC, and as they approached the entrance, they met a gentleman who was coming out of the building. When Loe introduced his six-year-old son to the man, he shook hands with Greg and chatted for a few moments. When the man left, Loe knelt down next to his son and spoke.

Do you know who that is? That is Neil Armstrong. We're going to make him the first man on the moon.

Greg was forever changed. He had met many of his father's friends from work, and some of them had probably been astronauts. Armstrong was the first to register. "At that moment, I was no longer a six-year-old child," Greg wrote. "I was a six-year-old dreamer. No longer would I look into the sky and see only a sunny day or clouds and rain. From then on, I would look into the sky and see great men in great machines going where no one had gone before. Men doing things other men had never even tried." After the *Star Trek* reference, Greg continued, "But most of all, in the sky I saw the men who made it happen. The men who created the machines. The men who launched them. The men who put others up there and brought them back safely every time."

The very next line was the best one of all for Loe.

For the first time, I saw my father.

"Greg remembered all that, and put all this into a letter," said Loe, choking back the emotion. "He said, 'I knew right then what I wanted to do. I wanted to follow in their footsteps.' That meant a lot. That was a neat letter to get."

There is no way to fully describe how completely dreadful the 1974 made-for-television movie *Houston, We've Got a Problem* turned out to be.

The script was written by Dick Nelson, who also penned episodes of *Dynasty, CHiPs, Buck Rogers in the 25th Century, Barnaby Jones*, and *Murder, She Wrote*, and directed by Lawrence Doheny, who went on helm shows like *Magnum, P.I., Charlie's Angels, Baa Baa Black Sheep, The Rockford Files, Adam-12*, and *The Six Million Dollar Man*. The best that could be said about the movie was that it was apparently made with the full cooperation of NASA and Johnson Space Center. Scenes were filmed in the MCC hallways and control room and actual audio from the mission was used throughout, Tom Stafford had a line or two during a simulator scene, public affairs officer Robert T. White portrayed himself, and a handful of real-life controllers like Bob Heselmeyer were used as extras. That was where any semblance of realism began and ended. Stafford was lucky that only the top of his head was shown during his brief appearance, but stars Robert Culp, Gary Collins, and Sandra Dee were not as fortunate. Each stumbled through what surely was the low point of their respective careers.

This was the very worst soap opera imaginable. A FIDO tried to cope with his difficult, possibly unfaithful, and ultimately suicidal wife. She managed to make a miraculous recovery after swallowing a bottle of pills, was present in the viewing room for the landing, and afterward walked off arm in arm with her husband. The father of a Jewish EECOM passed away during the flight, and the son skipped the funeral despite his rabbi brother laying the mother of all guilt trips on him in the MCC lobby. Another controller missed a custody hearing, but only after berating his son on the phone for crying. Topping it all off was the underlying story of retro officer Steve Bell and his concerned spouse Lisa, portrayed by Culp and one-time real-life wife

Sheila Sullivan. Bell had a heart attack a year before *Apollo 13* and had to figure out a way to get through the stress of the flight without keeling over.

At one point, Lisa asked what was going to happen to the families of the crew and to her if the crew did not make it home alive. They were sitting on a couch in their den, comfy and cozy in their pajamas.

How about a punch in the mouth?

As opposed to a dead husband, I guess I'll take a punch in the mouth.

Moments later, more drama.

Babe, I'm gonna bring these guys home. I am. Because I'm the best retrofire officer that ever came down the damn street.

And then . . .

I can't cut my next physical, so this is the last go around for me. I'll ride it all the way down and I don't care what it costs. I don't care. That is not as selfish as it sounds.

As the mission neared its conclusion, Bell was in great distress as he read off his calculations for the reentry. With great dramatic flair—or not—the beleaguered retro gave coordinates for the splashdown, exited the MOCR, and suddenly collapsed to the floor in the hallway. The credits rolled with husband and wife holding hands in the hallway, not knowing if he would live or die.

Heselmeyer was one of those who volunteered as an extra, and he came away understandably disappointed by the experience. All the machinations that went into getting the film's light and sound just so impressed him not in the least. "It was a lot of sitting around and waiting, waiting, and waiting," Heselmeyer said. "Then you'd do your scene, and you'd sit around and wait some more. It was not my cup of tea. To this day, I view movies differently because of that experience."

It would not have taken much to improve on the flick—a cast of sock puppets, maybe—but for nearly twenty years, it appeared that *Houston, We've Got a Problem* would be it for Hollywood's interest in the flight. Thankfully, that was not the case. The documentary *Apollo 13: To the Edge and Back* debuted on WGBH public television in Boston on 20 July 1994, the twenty-fifth anniversary of the *Apollo 11* landing, and something even bigger was brewing on the opposite coast of the United States.

Michael Bostick, more than twenty years removed from spotting his dad eating a hot dog on television back in Houston, was by then a vice president at Imagine Entertainment. The space program was literally a part of his DNA, and when he heard that Jim Lovell and coauthor Jeffrey Kluger were in the early stages of putting a book together on the flight, it piqued his curiosity.

The book *Lost Moon* was not even a book yet, just a ten-page outline, but that did not stop Michael Bostick from bringing it to the attention of Imagine Entertainment cofounder Brian Grazer. Michael filled in the blanks for director Ron Howard, and the deal to obtain the movie rights was closed with a conference call that ended at about 1 a.m. in New York, where Howard was in the process of setting up production for his next movie, *The Paper*.

Jerry Bostick was at best skeptical. He thought of other space-themed projects like *Marooned* and cringed. When he went to see that one way back when, he had gotten up and left in the middle of it. The plain truth was that Bostick was unsure his own son, Howard, Grazer, or anybody else for that matter could pull it off. When Howard asked him why, Bostick pulled no punches.

I'm a space guy. I don't like space fiction. I'm just afraid that unless you're going to make a documentary, you're going to screw it up.

He came around, convinced by Howard that the movie was going to be both exciting and as accurate as possible. It did not hurt that the one-time child actor also thought that *Marooned* was a terrible movie, or that to make sure of the minutiae, Bostick, Gerry Griffin, and Dave Scott would be hired as technical consultants.

Just as it had for the television movie two decades before, NASA offered use of the actual MOCR for filming. To get the kind of shots he wanted to get, not to mention going to the expense of moving a film crew and equipment to Houston for a month or so, Howard and Grazer knew that it would be impossible to take the agency up on its offer. Instead, production designer Michael Corenblith built a nearly identical replica of the room on Stage 27 at Universal Studios. It was one of the largest stages in town, and had most recently been used during filming of *Jurassic Park*.

There were only a handful of minor differences between the Hollywood version and the real thing in Houston—each console now featured a reading light, to help with lighting for close-up shots; to save on weight, the viewing room had six windows instead of three larger ones; and the front left corner of the room came inward an extra inch because of a large overhead beam. Set decorator Merideth Boswell added small touches like duplicates of the Trench's matchbooks, razor-sharp pencils, ashtrays, and well-worn access badges. "It was overly accurate, I would say," Bostick began. "It was dimensionally accurate to within an inch. The carpet was an exact match, including coffee stains." Corenblith had gone so far as to ask Bostick if he had been present the day the viewing-room windows were installed, to see if there might be a way to duplicate its *exact* three-window setup.

One of the first assignments Howard gave Bostick and Griffin was to teach what he called "Flight Controller's School" that would last maybe three or four hours. Bostick dreaded the thought, far more than he ever had some tough simulation. Surely, the thirty-six members of the cast who were going to portray him and others in the MOCR were just a bunch of Hollywood prima donnas. They had their script, knew their lines, knew how to act, so what did they need him for?

Michael was there, and so were Howard and Jim Lovell. Instead of three or four hours, the session lasted for a day and a half and it stopped only when Howard insisted they had a movie to make. The questions of the actors were intelligent ones, too.

What's the difference between a guidance officer and a guidance, navigation, and control officer?

Could a flight controller possibly speak directly to the crew?

Who had the final say in the room?

During Apollo 13, *did the controllers ever go home or stay somewhere on campus at* MSC?

That was the question that tripped up Griffin.

"I lived just a mile or so out that way," he said, pointing to a corner of the set. He caught himself, and added, "Actually, I didn't. Out that way is Los Angeles. I lived in Houston. I'm going to have to keep reminding myself of that."

Hanks proved his keen interest over and over again. He teased Jerry Bostick about his accent, born from his upbringing in rural Mississippi.

Go, Flight, Bostick would say as he demonstrated conversations on the comm loop.

Go, Flight, Hanks would repeat, drawing it out almost like Forest Gump himself would have.

Once filming began on 15 August 1994, Hanks, Bill Paxton, and Kevin Bacon showed up on set to read their lines for the air-to-ground exchanges. Their own filming had not yet begun. For a scene in which controllers watched the television broadcast from space that immediately preceded the explosion of the oxygen tank, Hanks perched himself atop a nine-foot ladder in front of the screen to read his lines. Although Bostick had sweated bullets before meeting the Academy Award winner, he should not have worried. "I was amazed that all of these actors were so interested in what we had done, and thought it was so great," Bostick said. "Hanks is a space nut if you ever saw one. He engaged me in these space trivia contests, and finally I just quit, because he would always win. He could name the flight crew for every American and most of the Russian spaceflights, up through the first four shuttle flights, and he could tell you where he was when they launched."

Released on 30 June 1995, the movie *Apollo 13* was a smash hit. Earning more than $355 million worldwide, the blockbuster won Academy Awards in 1996 for Best Film Editing and Best Sound. Like few things ever before, the movie brought the work of mission control front and center into the public consciousness. It made stars of Gene Kranz, and to a somewhat lesser extent, Sy Liebergot. Kranz had been on duty as flight director when the accident took place, and that, along with his dynamic personality and signature crew cut, made him Howard's flight director throughout the movie.

As portrayed by actor Ed Harris, Kranz never slept, never ate, and worked almost every shift for the rest of the flight. Glynn Lunney was played by veteran character actor Marc McClure, who appeared in only a handful of scenes. Gerry Griffin and Milt Windler—the flight's other two "real-life" flight directors—were never mentioned. Howard's reasoning was simple. He told Griffin and Bostick that with a three-person crew in peril, their families, and a control room full of people, he simply could not have twenty main characters. That was good enough for Griffin and Bostick.

It was Jerry Bostick, in fact, who indirectly came up with the film's iconic "Failure is not an option" line. During pre-production, he sat down with screenwriters William Broyles Jr. and Al Reinert over lunch to discuss life in the MOCR. When one of them asked, as people almost always asked, if anyone in the room had ever panicked during the mission, Bostick never flinched.

That never happened. When bad things happened, we just as calmly as we could would lay out all of the options and failure was not one of them.

Bostick sensed that Broyles was distracted, bored, maybe, to be talking to a nerd from NASA. It must have been his poker face, because they knew almost immediately that Bostick had given them a gift, wrapping up in a nice, neat bow the MOCR's attitude from the start of the crisis to its conclusion. "It kind of sums up the collective effort of anonymous people, trying to solve problems and save other people," Broyles said in a 1999 interview. "To me this was kind of the core of how most of us would like to feel. We'd like to feel that our efforts would add up to something bigger than ourselves, that things we're doing every day might make a difference, that we're part of something that matters."

Ironically, Kranz did not meet Harris during production of the movie. The veteran actor instead went through the extended interviews that the former flight director did for the *To the Edge and Back* documentary to pick up on his mannerisms, and his efforts led to an Oscar nomination as Best Actor in a Supporting Role. After the movie's release, Jim Lovell wound up with more speaking engagements than he could possibly ever accommodate and he turned to Kranz for help. Both signed up with a speaking agency in Washington DC, and when Kranz penned his 2000 autobiography *Failure Is Not an Option*, that led to a pair of documentaries on the History Channel. "Frankly, it really never slowed down for the first three to four years," Kranz said. "Then, I started speaking to the military and about that time, my book comes out. That boosted it again. This thing has just been a series of events."

Liebergot was portrayed by Clint Howard, who appeared in many of his director brother's films. Since the movie's debut, Liebergot cowrote his own autobiography *Apollo EECOM: Journey of a Lifetime* and has done extensive speaking and autograph signings around the world. "I try not to get the big head over it," Liebergot said of his role in the MOCR. "I don't feel motivated to embellish my career. I've *never* embellished it, and I know people who have done exactly that. It's exciting enough. I don't need to be saying things that aren't true and end up with the disgust of my fellow teammates."

Four years after being retired from active service, the third-floor control room was once again modified. Only this time, its appearance was changed to resemble what it had looked like during the days of Apollo.

For the people who worked in the room, it was a chance to reconnect with their past. There were times when Gene Kranz walked in and could hear the sounds and the voices, Jay Greene's maybe, Dick Thorson's, or Steve Bales's pumped-up pronouncement during the hectic descent phase of *Apollo 11*.

Go!

The people who excelled in the room were people like Charley Parker, who were anxious to go to bed at night just so they could get up the next morning and go to work. "I'm very proud of the culture that we established in the room," Kranz said. "I'm proud of the people who grew to maturity in that room. I'm proud of the people who faced the risks associated with our business and were willing to stand up to it, to make the risk acceptable. I'm proud of the way we handed over to the next generation."

Ed Fendell could well understand the emotional reaction many have had to visiting the MOCR. It was the same overwhelming sense of history as when he visited the Reichstag in Berlin. Fendell, who is Jewish, cried when he visited the former home of the German parliament and site of Nazi propaganda and military events during World War II.

He walked outside to compose himself, and once he did, started walking again. Walking near the Berlin Wall, he encountered a graveyard for those who had been killed trying to cross over from East to West Germany during those terrible Cold War years. He cried again. Fendell found that same evocative spirit on Ellis Island, where he could point out the manifest, complete with signatures, from when his father's family came to the United States. In the main hall, he could sense the same kind of ghostly images from the past as Kranz did in the MOCR—every age, every country, every language, every kind of clothing.

It was from that kind of humble beginning that Fendell ventured forth into the MOCR. "I basically was a young man jerking around," he said in describing his Connecticut childhood. He worked in his father's "dinky" little corner grocery store. His father had been a bus driver and a trolley car driver prior to that, and they never had a lot of money. The Fendells always had a clean place to live and had enough food, but they were not driving a big car like the family down the street, either. He had no goals, and little to no interest in the classroom. Fendell was not even sure, given the amount of studying that he did, how he ever managed to get even an associate's degree in merchandising.

How he made it from that point to becoming an important part of the Apollo-era team is one of the MOCR's great stories. "Somehow, I'm in the middle of this fricking thing, this incredible, historic thing," Fendell said. "People know who I am. A lot of people, either then or later on, really respect me. To be one of those people is so lucky, so incredibly lucky, it's unbelievable that it's me."

With the passing of time came a bit of philosophical perspective and, yes, maybe even some wisdom. "We all thought we were so shit hot," Fendell said. "Later on, when I got older and got going, I realized that it wasn't that we were so shit hot. What it really was, was that we were led and mentored by such an incredible group of guys. It was leaders like Kraft, Kranz, Lunney, and others who made Apollo happen."

The Apollo astronauts, and the moonwalkers in particular, garnered the lion's share of fame, if not fortune. The majority of those who worked in the MOCR went on to live in relative anonymity, their exploits a thing of the past. And while John Aaron had been unsure if there was a story to be told about *Apollo 13*, it was Jerry Bostick's experience on that Hollywood movie set that convinced him that what he had helped accomplish really did matter after all. Bostick was amazed when autograph requests started showing up from all over the world, an average of maybe one or two a week. He can laugh about talking to young school groups, and having a little girl ask if *all* the astronauts and flight controllers were as old as he was. Thinking as quickly as he did in the Trench, Bostick grinned.

The ones who are still alive are.

Bostick stepped back in time on a movie set 1,450 miles from Houston, but better yet, he could do so in the real thing once it was restored to its late-1960s, early-'70s appearance. He walked into the room and was almost immediately in awe. Bostick would sit down on that familiar first row and think of things he had not thought of for half a century or so.

Did we really all work in here and do the things that we did?

Am I dreaming this?

John Aaron, Bostick concluded, put it best, as he so often did.

We gulped fine wine.

For the first time since the dawn of mankind, Glynn Lunney added, the moon had been entrusted in large part to the MOCR. That made the task in front of him all the more special. "To me, it was a somewhat sacred and noble enterprise," Lunney said. "I had the sense that we were doing something for the human species that had never, ever been done before. It was actually so big that people shied away from thinking about it. When President Kennedy said we were going to the moon, that was a big shock to everybody. My God, he must be crazy. Eight years later, we did it."

When he visited the room, Lunney had a sense of visiting a cathedral, a holy place where very special things had happened. It was a feeling Lunney's generation passed on to the flight controllers of the Space Shuttle era. None of them had more of a respect for the room, or for the people who had worked there, than Milt Heflin.

So many of the old guard had played a crucial role in his career, it was almost hard to keep track of them all. The Space Shuttle was designed to land like an airplane, so following the Apollo-Soyuz Test Project there was no need at NASA for ocean-based recovery forces. Where did that leave Heflin? Enter Rod Loe, who told the Oklahoman to come work for him and learn how to be a Space Shuttle flight controller. Bill Peters and Jack Knight took him under their wing, providing him with the guidance he needed to qualify as a backup flight controller for the shuttle's 1977 Approach and Landing Tests. Once on that team, it was flight director Don Puddy who built his confidence and moved him into a prime assignment for a portion of the tests.

By then, he *really* wanted to become a flight controller. He supported Bill Moon from the SSR back room for the first launch of the Space Shuttle, STS-1, on 12 April 1981. More than thirty years later, Heflin could still hear the whining sing-song sound of the strip-chart servos as they recorded the operation of the fuel cells and power systems. Heflin did a good job, and a couple of years later, Moon encouraged him in his efforts to become a flight director.

"You marketed not only your current but your previous work experience in recovery very well," Gene Kranz wrote in his critique of Heflin's flight director interview. "This is a very important part of your background that I think has contributed to your overall maturity as an operator and will

26. Just as so many of the Apollo-era legends had served as mentors to him, Milt Heflin played a vital role in the careers of flight directors he helped select. Shown here is the 2005 class that came under Heflin's tutelage. On the front row are Michael L. Sarafin, Holly E. Ridings, Ginger Kerrick, and Kwatsi L. Alibaruho, while Michael P. Moses, Brian T. Smith, Dana J. Weigel, Robert C. Dempsey, and Richard S. Jones make up the back row. Courtesy NASA.

provide you a good background as a FD." The coveted role was Heflin's, one of seven flight directors who were hired in 1983.

The going was not always smooth. After serving as flight director for four missions prior to the *Challenger* accident, boss Tommy Holloway had serious reservations about Heflin's ability to continue. Rather than cut him loose, the chief of the Flight Director Office told Heflin exactly what he needed to work on and outlined a plan that he had already set up to make sure those improvements happened. Heflin did not wash out, and was the Orbit 1 flight director for STS-53, the last flight flown out of the control room on the third floor. It was one of six missions Heflin worked in that grand space—two as an EECOM and another four as flight director.

In a very real and very significant way, it was people like Heflin who connected the past to the present, the third-floor MOCR to the future of human spaceflight. He stood on the shoulders of legendary flight control-lers to make it as a flight director himself, so much so that he became the head of the office. It was Heflin who hired Kwatsi L. Alibaruho, the first African American flight director, in a nine-member 2005 class that also included Michael P. "Mike" Moses, Brian T. Smith, Dana J. Weigel, Rob-ert C. "Bob" Dempsey, Richard S. Jones, Michael L. Sarafin, Holly E. Rid-ings, and Ginger Kerrick.

The torch Chris Kraft, Glynn Lunney, Gene Kranz, Gerry Griffin, and so many others passed to him was the same one he handed off to his class of flight directors. His predecessors took a dream, developed and nourished it, and the dream was safe with those new hires. There was no *Star Trek*–like way to instantaneously beam anybody anywhere, and until that kind of transport is developed, it would be up to people like Alibaruho to watch over the spacefarers who rode a controlled explosion into space and a fire-ball back to Earth. They would need a fire in their bellies, and the arro-gance that goes with being able to handle that kind of job.

Best of all, Heflin was close to all the unsung heroes, past and present. He was one of them. To him, it was a priceless gift.

Sources

Books

Berry, Charles A. "Perspectives on Apollo." In *Biomedical Results of Apollo*, edited by Richard S. Johnston, Lawrence F. Dietlein, and Charles A. Berry. NASA SP-368. http://history.nasa.gov/SP-368/s7ch2.htm.

Chaikin, Andrew. *A Man on the Moon: The Voyages of the Apollo Astronauts.* New York: Penguin, 1998.

Chaikin, Andrew, with Victoria Kohl. *Voices from the Moon.* New York: Viking Studio, 2009.

Collins, Michael. *Carrying the Fire.* North Salem NY: Adventure Library, 1998.

Dethloff, Henry C. *Suddenly, Tomorrow Came . . . A History of the Johnson Space Center.* NASA History Series, NASA SP-4307.

"Eugene F. Kranz (1933–)." In *"Before This Decade Is Out": Personal Reflections on the Apollo Program*, edited by Glen E. Swanson. NASA History Series, NASA SP-4223. http://history.nasa.gov/SP-4223/ch6.htm.

From the Trenches of Korea to the Trench in Mission Control: An Oral History of the Life and Times of John S. Llewellyn. Copyright 2012 by John S. Llewellyn.

From the Trench of Mission Control to the Craters of the Moon: Stories from the Men of Mission Control's Flight Dynamics Group: "The Trench." CreateSpace Independent Publishing Platform, 2011.

Grimwood, James M., Barton C. Hacker, and Peter J. Vorzimmer. *Project Gemini: A Chronology.* NASA History Series, NASA SP-4002.

Hacker, Barton C., and James M. Grimwood. *On the Shoulders of Titans: A History of Project Gemini.* NASA History Series, NASA SP-4203.

Kluger, Jeffrey. *The Apollo Adventure: The Making of the Apollo Space Program and the Movie "Apollo 13."* New York: Pocket Books, 1995.

Kraft, Christopher C. *Flight: My Life in Mission Control.* New York: Dutton, 2001.

Kranz, Eugene F. *Failure Is Not an Option.* New York: Simon & Schuster, 2000.

Liebergot, Seymour A., and David M. Harland. *Apollo EECOM: Journey of a Lifetime.* Burlington, Ontario, Canada: Apogee Books, 2006.

Lovell, James A., and Jeffrey Kluger. *Apollo 13*. New York: Houghton Mifflin, 2000.

Millbrooke, Ann. "'More Favored Than the Birds': The Manned Maneuvering Unit in Space." In *From Engineering Science to Big Science: The NACA and NASA Collier Trophy Research Project Winners*. NASA History Series, NASA SP-4219. http://history.nasa.gov/SP-4219/Chapter13.html.

Mullane, Richard M. *Riding Rockets: The Outrageous Tales of a Space Shuttle Astronaut*. New York: Scribner, 2006.

Orloff, Richard W. *Apollo by the Numbers: A Statistical Reference*. NASA History Series, NASA SP-2000-4029.

Ross, Jerry L., with John Norberg. *Spacewalker: My Journey in Space and Faith as NASA's Record-Setting Frequent Flyer*. West Lafayette IN: Purdue University Press, 2013.

Woods, W. David. *How Apollo Flew to the Moon*. New York: Springer-Praxis, 2011.

Wrone, David R. *The Zapruder Film: Reframing JFK's Assassination*. Lawrence: University Press of Kansas, 2003.

Periodicals and Online Articles

"*Apollo 10*: 'Son of a Bitch!'" Space Artifacts. http://www.spaceartifactsarchive .com/2013/10/apollo-10-son-of-a-bitch-.html.

"*Apollo 13*." http://apollo13.spacelog.org/.

Cass, Stephen. "*Apollo 13*, We Have a Solution." *IEEE Spectrum* I (April 2005). http:// spectrum.ieee.org/aerospace/space-flight/apollo-13-we-have-a-solution/4.

"Console Audio of *Apollo 11* Landing." NASA Office of Logic Design. http://www .klabs.org/history/apollo_11_alarms/console/.

"Dallas Family's Tradition Boosts NASA for 110 Flights, Says Thank You on Final Shuttle Flight." NASA, 9 July 2011. http://www.nasa.gov/mission_pages /shuttle/shuttlemissions/sts135/135_roses.html.

Dyson, Marianne J. "NASA's First Women Flight Controllers." Copyright 2012 by Marianne Dyson. Last updated 8 February 2014. http://marianne dyson.com/women.html.

"Experience the *Apollo 11* Lunar Landing." Thamtech LLC. www.firstmenonthemoon .com.

Eyles, Don. "Tales from the Lunar Module Guidance Computer." DonEyles.com. http://www.doneyles.com/LM/Tales.html.

Gainor, Christopher. "AVRO Employees and NASA; or, Canadians Putting America into Space." Avro-Arrow.org, 5 March 1996. http://www.avro-arrow .org/Arrow/employees.html.

"*Gemini 5*." Wikipedia. Last modified 2 January 2014. http://en.wikipedia.org /wiki/Gemini_5.

"*Gemini 9* Target B." NASA, National Space Science Data Center. http://nssdc
.gsfc.nasa.gov/nmc/spacecraftDisplay.do?id=1966-046A.

Harwood, William G. "The CBS News Space Reporter's Handbook STS-51L/107
Supplement: Remembering the Final Flights of *Challenger* and *Columbia*." http://www.cbsnews.com/network/news/space/SRH_Disasters.htm.

———. "Legendary Commander Tells Story of Shuttle's Close Call." CBS News
Space Place, used with permission by Spaceflight Now, 27 March 2009.
http://www.spaceflightnow.com/shuttle/sts119/090327sts27/.

Houston, We've Got a Problem. IMDB.com. http://www.imdb.com/title/tt0071630/.

Hutchinson, Lee. "Apollo Flight Controller 101: Every Console Explained." Ars
Techina.com, 31 October 2012. http://arstechnica.com/science/2012/10
/apollo-flight-controller-101-every-console-explained/.

Jones, Eric M. "The First Lunar Landing." *Apollo 11* Lunar Surface Journal, Apollo
Lunar Surface Journal. Copyright 1995. Last revised 25 February 2013.
http://www.hq.nasa.gov/alsj/a11/a11.landing.html.

———. "Post-Landing Fuel-Line Blockage." *Apollo 11* Lunar Surface Journal,
Apollo Lunar Surface Journal. Copyright 2003. Last revised 1 January
2008. http://history.nasa.gov/alsj/a11/a11iceclog.html.

Lindsay, Hamish. "*Apollo 13*: 'Houston, We've Had a Problem Here.'" Honeysuckle
Creek Track Station: 1967–1981. http://honeysucklecreek.net/msfn_missions
/Apollo_13_mission/hl_apollo13.html.

Lunney, Glynn S. "*Apollo XIII*." http://www.jsc.nasa.gov/history/oral_histories
/LunneyGS/Apollo13.pdf.

"May 18–26: Remembering *Apollo 10*." collectSPACE Messages, Mercury-Gemini-
Apollo. http://www.collectspace.com/ubb/Forum29/HTML/001015.html.

McNutt, Will. "Girl Helped Bring Astronauts Home." *Free Lance Star* (Fredericksburg VA), 28 April 1970. http://news.google.com/newspapers?%20
nid=1298&dat=19700428&id=2uEPAAAAIBAJ&sjid=YYoDAAAAIB
AJ&pg=7296,6562645.

"NASA: Excerpt from the 'Special Message to the Congress on Urgent National
Needs': President John F. Kennedy, Delivered in Person before a Joint
Session of Congress, May 25, 1961, Section IX: Space." NASA, 24 May
2004. http://www.nasa.gov/vision/space/features/jfk_speech_text.html
#.UtAEN7QSiN8.

O'Brien, Frank. "Lunar Orbit Rendezvous." Apollo Flight Journal. Last updated
1 January 2005. http://history.nasa.gov/afj/loressay.htm.

Ong, Elwin C. "Profile Apollo: Hugh Blair-Smith." NASA Office of Logic Design,
10 April 2005. http://klabs.org/history/bios/hugh_blair_smith/elwin
_mit_report.htm.

Saxon, Wolfgang. "Scott Simpkinson, 76, Engineer Who Worked on Space Program." *New York Times*, 15 August 1996. http://www.nytimes.com/1996/08/15 /us/scott-simpkinson-76-engineer-who-worked-on-space-program.html.

"STS-51L Mission Timeline." Wikipedia. Last modified 20 March 2014. http:// en.wikipedia.org/wiki/STS-51-L_Mission_timeline#Detailed_timeline _and_transcript.

Sublett, Jesse. "A League of Their Own." *Austin Chronicle*, 12 March 1999. http://www .austinchronicle.com/screens/1999-03-12/521565/.

"What Is 'Bigeminy' and How Is It Treated?" HealthCentral, Remedy Health Media. http://www.healthcentral.com/heart-disease/ask-doctor-44706-70.html.

Woods, David, and Frank O'Brien. "The Apollo 8 Flight Journal." Apollo Flight Journal, NASA History Division. http://history.nasa.gov/ap08fj/index.htm.

Interviews and Personal Communications

Aaron, John W. Email correspondence with Rick Houston, 8 October 2013.

———. Email correspondence with Rick Houston, 22 January 2014.

———. Email correspondence with Rick Houston, 30 January 2014.

———. Email correspondences with Rick Houston, 24 February 2014.

———. Email correspondence with Rick Houston, 25 February 2014.

———. Telephone interview with Rick Houston, 5 June 2013.

———. Telephone interview with Rick Houston, 13 June 2013.

Aldrich, Arnold. Telephone interview with Rick Houston, 7 June 2013.

Alexander, James David. Telephone interview with Rick Houston, 30 July 2013.

Arabian, Donald D. JSC Oral History interview with Kevin M. Rusnak, Cape Canaveral FL, 3 February 2000.

Bales, Stephen G. Email correspondence with Rick Houston, 10 January 2014.

———. Telephone interview with Rick Houston, 18 July 2013.

Boone, William J., III. Telephone interview with Rick Houston, 26 July 2013.

Bostick, Jerry C. Email correspondence with Rick Houston, 12 May 2013.

———. Email correspondence with Rick Houston, 15 September 2013.

———. Email correspondence with Rick Houston, 19 September 2013.

———. Email correspondence with Rick Houston, 16 October 2013.

———. Email correspondence with Rick Houston, 15 November 2013.

———. Email correspondence with Rick Houston, 2 March 2014.

———. Email correspondence with Rick Houston, 12 March 2014.

———. Telephone interview with Rick Houston, 26 April 2013.

———. Telephone interview with Rick Houston, 29 April 2013.

Briscoe, Alan L. Telephone interview with Rick Houston, 17 April 2014.

Brooks, Melvin F. JSC Oral History interview with Carol Butler, Glendale AZ, 25 March 2000.

Carlton, Robert L. Email correspondence with Rick Houston, 26 December 2013.

———. JSC Oral History interview with Kevin Rusnak, assisted by Sandra Johnson and Carol Butler, Houston, 10 April 2001.

———. Telephone interview with Rick Houston, 20 June 2013.

———. Telephone interview with Rick Houston, 22 July 2013.

Carr, Gerald P. Telephone interview with Rick Houston, 21 June 2013.

Castle, Robert E. Email correspondence with Rick Houston, 16 April 2014.

———. Telephone interview with Rick Houston, 18 April 2014.

Covey, Richard O. Telephone interview with Rick Houston, 4 December 2013.

DeAtkine, Joseph N. Telephone interview with Rick Houston, 30 August 2013.

Deiterich, Charles F. Email correspondence with Rick Houston, 9 October 2013.

———. Email correspondence with Rick Houston, 30 January 2014.

———. Telephone interview with Rick Houston, 24 June 2013.

Duke, Charles M., Jr. Telephone interview with Rick Houston, 17 July 2013.

Dyson, Marianne J. Email correspondence with Rick Houston, 17 April 2014.

Fendell, Edward I. JSC Oral History interview with Kevin Rusnak, Houston, 19 October 2000.

———. Telephone interview with Rick Houston, 15 July 2013.

Frank, M. P. JSC Oral History interview with Kevin M. Rusnak, Houston, 15 December 2000.

Garman, John R. Telephone interview with Rick Houston, 16 July 2013.

Gravett, William. Telephone interview with Rick Houston, 19 July 2013.

Greene, Jay H. JSC Oral History interview with Sandra Johnson, Houston, 10 November 2004.

———. JSC Oral History interview with Sandra Johnson, Houston, 8 December 2004.

Griffin, Gerald D. Email correspondence with Rick Houston, 14 July 2013.

———. Email correspondence with Rick Houston, 14 October 2013.

———. Email correspondence with Rick Houston, 13 November 2013.

———. Email correspondence with Rick Houston, 26 November 2013.

———. Email correspondence with Rick Houston, 8 March 2014.

———. Telephone interview with Rick Houston, 5 June 2013.

———. Telephone interview with Rick Houston, 11 June 2013.

Haise, Fred W., Jr. Telephone interview with Rick Houston, 31 October 2013.

Harlan, Charles S. Telephone interview with Rick Houston, 26 June 2013.

Heselmeyer, Robert H. Email correspondence with Rick Houston, 21 August 2013.

———. JSC Oral History interview with Sandra Johnson, Houston, 12 November 2004.

———. Telephone interview with Rick Houston, 5 August 2013.

Hirasaki, Parrish. Telephone interview with Rick Houston, 25 July 2013.

Hodge, John D. JSC Oral History interview with Rebecca Wright, Great Falls VA, 18 April 1999.

———. Telephone interview with Rick Houston, 2 July 2013.

Holloway, Tommy W. JSC Oral History interview with Rebecca Wright, Houston, 25 July 2002.

———. Telephone interview with Rick Houston, 23 January 2014.

———. Telephone interview with Rick Houston, 22 April 2014.

Hutchinson, Neil B. Telephone interview with Rick Houston, 17 June 2013.

Joki, James A. Telephone interview with Rick Houston, 14 September 2013.

Kelly, James J., Jr. Email correspondence with Rick Houston, 9 June 2013.

———. Email correspondences with Rick Houston, 12 June 2013.

———. Telephone interview with Rick Houston, 13 June 2013.

———. Telephone interview with Rick Houston, 6 March 2014.

Kelso, Robert M. Telephone interview with Rick Houston, 27 August 2013.

Knight, Jack. Email correspondence with Rick Houston, 29 July 2013.

———. Telephone interview with Rick Houston, 29 July 2013.

Kranz, Eugene F. Email correspondence with Rick Houston, 31 July 2013.

———. Email correspondence with Rick Houston, 29 May 2014.

———. JSC Oral History interview with Roy Neal, Houston, 19 March 1998.

———. JSC Oral History interview with Rebecca Wright, Houston, 8 January 1999.

———. Telephone interview with Rick Houston, 10 July 2013.

———. Telephone interview with Rick Houston, 31 July 2013.

Lewis, Charles R. Telephone interview with Rick Houston, 2 August 2013.

Liebergot, Seymour A. Skype interview with Rick Houston, 2 April 2013.

Loden, Harold A. Email correspondence with Rick Houston, 23 July 2013.

———. Email correspondence with Rick Houston, 22 August 2013.

———. Telephone interview with Rick Houston, 12 July 2013.

Loe, T. Rodney. Telephone interview with Rick Houston, 5 July 2013.

Lousma, Jack R. Email correspondence with Rick Houston, 10 October 2013.

———. Telephone interview with Rick Houston, 30 September 2013.

Lunney, Glynn S. Email correspondence with Rick Houston, 25 December 2013.

———. JSC Oral History interview with Carol Butler, Houston, 28 January 1999.

———. JSC Oral History interview with Carol Butler, Houston, 9 February 1999.

———. Telephone interview with Rick Houston, 16 April 2013.

———. Telephone interview with Rick Houston, 23 April 2013.

————. Telephone interview with Rick Houston, 1 May 2013.

Mattingly, Thomas Kenneth, II. Telephone interview with Rick Houston, 12 June 2013.

McCandless, Bruce, II. Email correspondence with Milt Heflin, 19 August 2013.

————. Email correspondence with Rick Houston, 28 August 2013.

————. Skype interview with Rick Houston, 22 August 2013.

Merritt, W. Merlin. Email correspondence with Rick Houston, 14 October 2013.

————. Telephone interview with Rick Houston, 20 August 2013.

Mill, Jerry W. Telephone interview with Rick Houston, 21 August 2013.

Miller, Harold G. Email correspondence with Rick Houston, 17 June 2013.

————. Telephone interview with Rick Houston, 10 July 2013.

Moon, William J. Telephone interview with Rick Houston, 15 August 2013.

Murray, Charles. Email correspondence with Rick Houston, 24 February 2014.

Parker, Charley B. Telephone interview with Rick Houston, 21 August 2013.

Pavelka, Edward L., Jr. JSC Oral History interview with Carol Butler, Houston, 26 April 2001.

Peters, William L. Email correspondence with Rick Houston, 16 September 2013.

————. Telephone interview with Rick Houston, 12 July 2013.

Reed, H. David. Email correspondence with Rick Houston, 9 May 2013.

————. Email correspondence with Rick Houston, 9 September 2013.

————. Email correspondence with Rick Houston, 24 October 2013.

————. Email correspondence with Rick Houston, 3 March 2014.

————. Skype interview with Rick Houston, 3 June 2013.

————. Skype interview with Rick Houston, 4 June 2013.

Renick, J. Gary. Telephone interview with Rick Houston, 2 August 2013.

Ross, Jerry L. Telephone interview with Rick Houston, 5 May 2014.

Scott, Craig. Email correspondence with Rick Houston, 29 December 2013.

Scott, Gary B. Telephone interview with Rick Houston, 10 December 2013.

Shaffer, Phillip C. JSC Oral History interview with Carol Butler, Houston, 25 January 2000.

Shelton, Mark, Terry Shelton, and MacKenzie Shelton. Letter correspondence with Milt Heflin, 1 June 1989.

Stachurski, Richard J. Telephone interview with Rick Houston, 13 December 2013.

Stoval, William M. Telephone interview with Rick Houston, 18 September 2013.

Van Rensselaer, Frank. Telephone interview with Rick Houston, 20 August 2013.

von Ehrenfried, Manfred H. Telephone interview with Rick Houston, 8 May 2013.

Watson, Raymond S., Jr. Telephone interview with Rick Houston, 10 December 2013.

Wegener, John A. Telephone interview with Rick Houston, 16 September 2013.

Windler, Milton W. Telephone interview with Rick Houston, 23 August 2013.

Womack, Pamela C. Email correspondence with Rick Houston, 28 March 2014.
———. Telephone interview with Rick Houston, 31 March 2014.
Young, Kenneth A. Email correspondence with Rick Houston, 11 November 2013.
———. JSC Oral History interview with Kevin M. Rusnak, Houston, 6 June 2001.
———. Telephone interview with Rick Houston, 18 June 2013.

Other Sources

Apollo 1. DVD. Spacecraft Films, Red Pepper Creative, 2007.
Apollo 9 Mission Report. NASA Manned Spacecraft Center Release MSC-PA-R-69-2, May 1969.
Apollo 9 Press Kit. NASA Release 69-29, Washington DC, 23 February 1969.
Apollo 10 Mission Report. NASA Manned Spacecraft Center Release MSC-00126, August 1969.
Apollo 11 Lunar Landing Mission Press Kit. NASA Release 69-83K, 6 July 1969. http://www.hq.nasa.gov/alsj/frame.html.
Apollo 12 Mission Report. NASA Manned Spacecraft Center Release MSC-01855, March 1970.
"*Apollo 13* Mission Timeline." Jerry C. Bostick Collection. Unpublished.
Apollo 13: The Real Story. DVD. Spacecraft Films, Red Pepper Creative, 2004.
Apollo 13: To the Edge and Back, a Thrilling Struggle against All Odds. DVD. WGBH Educational Foundation, 1994.
Apollo 14 Mission Report. NASA Manned Spacecraft Center Release MSC-04112, May 1971.
Apollo 15 Mission Report. NASA Manned Spacecraft Center Release MSC-05161, December 1971.
Apollo Mission Control Center: NPS Historic Furnishing Study and Visitor Services Recommendations. PowerPoint presentation.
Bennett, Floyd V. *Apollo Lunar Descent and Ascent Trajectories.* NASA Technical Memorandum NASA TM X-58040, March 1970. Presented at the AIAA Eighth Annual Aerospace Sciences Meeting, New York, New York, 19–21 January 1970.
Beyond The Moon: Failure Is Not an Option 2. DVD. History Channel, 2005.
Blair-Smith, Hugh. "System Integration Issues in *Apollo 11.*" Paper presented at Twenty-Ninth Digital Avionics Systems Conference, 3–7 October 2010.
Bostick, Jerry C. "NASA after *Apollo 11.*" Unpublished manuscript.
Dumis, Charles L. "The Debriefing." Unpublished poem.
Dyson, Marianne J. "Fire in Mission Control: The Story of a Woman Flight Controller." Unpublished manuscript.
Failure Is Not an Option. DVD. History Channel, 2003.

First Landing. iPad app. Spacecraft Apps, 2012.

Gemini 4 Flight Plan X.

Gemini 4 Press Kit. NASA Release 65-158, Washington DC, 21 May 1965.

Gemini 5 Press Kit. NASA Release 65-262, Washington DC, 12 August 1965.

"History of Flight Dynamics Officer Assignments by Mission and Phase." Unpublished paper.

"History of Guidance Officer Assignments by Mission." Unpublished paper.

"History of Retrofire Officer Assignments by Mission." Unpublished paper.

"Integrated Mission Control Center Will Be Nerve Center of Missions." 1964 NASA Public Affairs brochure.

Last Man on the Moon. Documentary film. Mark Stewart Productions/Stopwatch Productions, 2014.

Loden, Harold A. "*Apollo 10* LM Attitude Excursion." Unpublished paper, 23 July 2013.

Loe, Greg. "The Summer Day." Unpublished letter.

Loree, Ray. "MCC Development History." NASA, August 1990.

Miller, Harold G. "The Early Days of Simulation and Operations." Unpublished paper.

Narrative History of Apollo 13 Carbon Dioxide Absorber Modification.

"New Deputy Flight Directors Named." NASA Release 71-84, 23 November 1971.

"News Release." NASA Manned Spacecraft Center Release MSC 63-66, 27 March 1963.

"News Release." NASA Manned Spacecraft Center Release MSC 64-150, 4 September 1964.

"News Release." NASA Manned Spacecraft Center Release MSC 65-103, 9 November 1965.

"News Release." NASA Manned Spacecraft Center Release MSC 68-28, 3 April 1968.

"News Release." NASA Manned Spacecraft Center Release MSC 68-35, 14 May 1968.

Peters, William L. "My NASA Career." Unpublished paper.

"Philco to Develop Manned Flight Mission Control Center at Houston." NASA Headquarters News Release 63-14, 28 January 1963.

"Reorganization and Personnel Assignments of Flight Control Division." Manned Spacecraft Center Announcement 67-80, 9 June 1967.

Saturn V Launch Vehicle Flight Evaluation Report: AS-502 Apollo 6 Mission. George C. Marshall Space Flight Center Report MPR-SAT-FE-68-3, 25 June 1968.

STS-5 Space Shuttle Program Mission Report. NASA Lyndon B. Johnson Space Center Release JSC-18735, December 1982.

STS-27R OV-104 Orbiter TPS Damage Review Team Summary Report Volume One. NASA Report TM-100355, February 1989.

Young, Kenneth A. "The Trench." Unpublished poem.

———. "A Visit from St. Kranz." Unpublished poem.

Index

In the Outward Odyssey: A People's History of Spaceflight series

Into That Silent Sea: Trailblazers of the Space Era, 1961–1965
Francis French and Colin Burgess

In the Shadow of the Moon: A Challenging Journey to Tranquility, 1965–1969
Francis French and Colin Burgess

To a Distant Day: The Rocket Pioneers
Chris Gainor

Homesteading Space: The Skylab Story
David Hitt, Owen Garriott, and Joe Kerwin

Ambassadors from Earth: Pioneering Explorations with Unmanned Spacecraft
Footprints in the Dust: The Epic Voyages of Apollo, 1969–1975
Edited by Colin Burgess

Realizing Tomorrow: The Path to Private Spaceflight
Chris Dubbs and Emeline Paat-Dahlstrom

The X-15 Rocket Plane: Flying the First Wings into Space
Michelle Evans

Wheels Stop: The Tragedies and Triumphs of the Space Shuttle Program, 1986–2011
Rick Houston

Bold They Rise
David Hitt and Heather R. Smith

Go, Flight! The Unsung Heroes of Mission Control, 1965–1992
Rick Houston and Milt Heflin

Infinity Beckoned: Adventuring Through the Inner Solar System, 1969–1989
Jay Gallentine

To order or obtain more information on these or other University of Nebraska Press titles, visit www.nebraskapress.unl.edu.